THE HURRICANE JUMPERS

The Escape of HMS Calliope

By

GRAHAM HAGUE

The Hurricane Jumpers

Date of first UK publication May 2016.
Revised December 2020.

Published by Graham Hague

http://www.grahamhague.com/

ISBN-13: 978-1533146571
ISBN-10: 1533146578

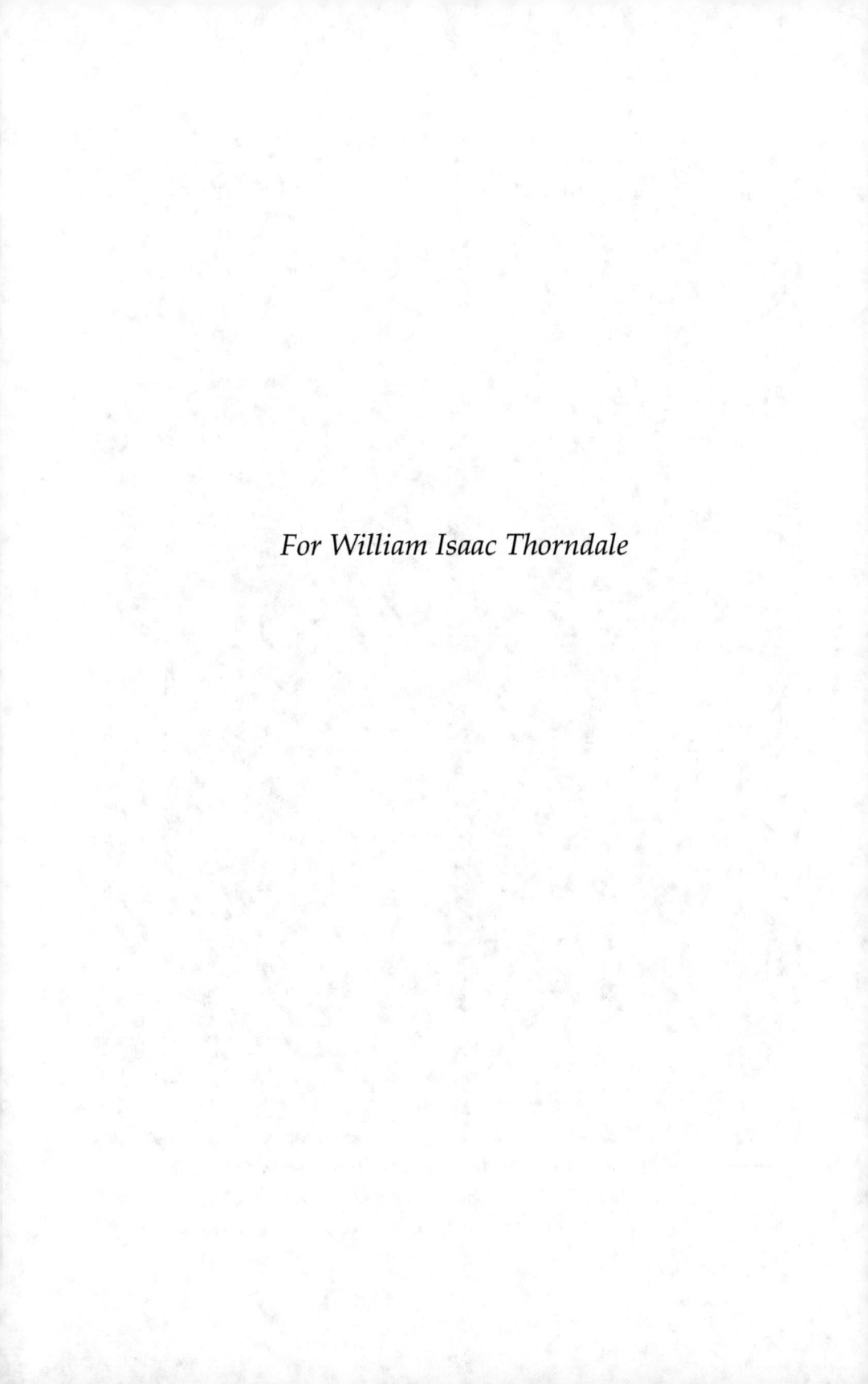

For William Isaac Thorndale

The Captain of HMS "*Calliope*", January 1887 to May 1890.

A painting of Henry Coey Kane in Captain's Uniform, circa 1891, artist unknown. Reproduced by kind permission of Castleknock College, Dublin, where the painting resides in the refectory.

Foreward by

CAPTAIN DAVID TALL, OBE RN

Graham Hague's painstakingly devoted, indeed reverent, research, has produced the most fascinating insight into the life and times of a young man from Surrey who saw active service across the world in the Royal Navy for some 14 years before continuing his service to the Crown as a Coastguard for a further 30 years, before his well - earned retirement back in Surrey.

Much of the book concerns the lead up to the escape of HMS CALLIOPE from the hurricane that swept through Samoa in March 1889, of which William Thorndale (WIT), the author's great grandfather, was one of the crew. All the other warships and merchantmen in Apia harbour, that fateful day, were either sunk or beached. Mr Hague captures the ferocity of the storm together with the fear and terror that must have prevailed throughout the storm, masterfully. He also captures the indomitable, visceral spirit, WIT and his shipmates displayed in ensuring their survival. The most telling phrase in the whole book for me, was that following a severe injury sustained in an accident at Simon's Town, South Africa en passage to Apia, WIT was given the option to convalesce either in hospital or onboard. He chose to rejoin his shipmates.

Although CALLIOPE and her crew, and particularly WIT, are the central characters of this fascinating book, I was moved by Mr Hague's generosity in including stories and pen pictures of some of the other ships and people present in Apia. Sailors, generally, are the same the world over. Brave, resolute, determined and fiercely loyal to their comrades-in-arms are but some of their virtues and characteristics which are captured wonderfully in many of the pen portraits included by the author.

It has been both a pleasure and a privilege to have been invited to write the foreword to this brilliant read.

I wish I had had the privilege of meeting WIT.

David Tall OBE RN (Served 1965 - 2001)
Captain RN
March, 2021

TABLE OF CONTENTS.

TABLE OF ILLUSTRATIONS.

INTRODUCTION

In March 1889, and virtually without warning, an awful hurricane struck the islands of Samoa. It created monstrous seas that few witnesses, well used to the ferocious types of storm that so often battered the islands, could ever recall experiencing before. On the principal island Upolu, seven warships of three different nations had gathered in tiny Apia Bay to glare at each other, and maybe to start World War One between them over ownership of the "Navigator Islands". They were congregated in a small bay surrounded by hard coral rock excepting one restricted way in and out. A bay that was also home to a large number of schooners, trading vessels and other such ships; a bay so crowded that manoeuvring in the port had been particularly difficult even in the few previous days of calm weather. And a hard coral reef that in a hurricane seven years earlier had claimed every ship in the bay and 20 or more human lives; coral that in the two most recent gales over just a few days, both as bad as the residents could remember, had even claimed three more unfortunate vessels. How would you feel about mooring your ship in such a port, in a season in which severe storms were guaranteed, and a hurricane more than possible?

The military men had little choice but to ignore the ominous signs, not being blessed with our hindsight or modern weather forecasting tools. The German Pacific Fleet was there to protect German Imperial interests - and perhaps to expand them; the American Pacific Fleet was there to protect American interests and curb the German; and naturally for those times, a British cruiser was also present doing the same thing for Queen Victoria's subjects. Germany was flexing her muscles in the area, and the American and British Vice-Consuls on the islands saw their own interests very much under threat. No-one would be the first to desert their post in that tense and unpleasant political climate, come what may.

But what did come was a disaster for virtually everyone, though as many have described it, it was also *"The Hurricane that Stopped a War"*. Two of the three ships from each modern, powerful sailing fleet were wrecked and lost; the other from each was beached severely damaged and virtually useless for any future naval service, at least until they could be repaired. Just a few of the small schooners of up to 100 or so tons were thrown severely damaged on the beach, whilst the majority, including the barques and traders of up to 500 tons or more, joined those other vessels nestling in the mud and rocky outcrops on the floor of the bay. One hundred and forty-four officers, sailing men and marines from the naval vessels lost their lives, as did three persons from the shore.

Have you seen television footage of a storm, such as Category 4 Severe Tropical Cyclone Katrina, when it hit New Orleans in 2008? The waves pounding the coast-line, wrecking pleasure boats and shore-front properties, and flooding the inland areas? Bending trees, ripping roofs, throwing debris like tissue paper and twigs? The hurricane at Samoa had no name, nor was it ever "rated" or "categorised". But the captain of the British ship, Henry Coey Kane, said the waves were so huge at Samoa that they engulfed his ship and ran "green" along its length, not even breaking. Look at the image of the ship on the front cover of this book, and imagine a wave top higher than the deck running the full length of the vessel. When they did break at her bows, the spray and spume reached the top mast. On occasion, HMS *Calliope* lay her full 250 foot length on the leading face of a wave! So just try imagining what it must have been like for the poor souls on the decks of any one of the ships. And then what it must have been like for those battened down below-decks in engine rooms and rudder flats from which there could be no hope of escape should the ship founder. Not that the deck crew would have much chance in the swirling, crashing whirlpools of water in a small bay where the currents threw everything all over the place and filled those waters with wreckage from river bridges, uprooted trees and the pitiful remains of those ships that were no longer afloat.

All the naval ships had two defences against stormy weather: heavy holding gear, and steam. But four anchors and chain gear, always considered by sailing men as one of the best protections from a storm, were dragging on all the ships, and the direction of that drag was straight for the solid, jagged, hellish dark rock of the coral reef – collision with that meant sinking against its edge and being broken up by the waves. And the steam power was effectively "only" around forty years old, and the various teething troubles with the equipment that utilised it were still not completely ironed out. Machinery of the time had been known to fail when subjected to prolonged heavy use, and in this storm, the use was almost "full steam" for twenty-four hours solid.

Today, the storm is remembered by just a few people around the globe. Natives on Samoa seem to know about it, and are justly proud of the heroic efforts of so many native ancestors and long gone Apia residents who for hours on end risked their lives trying to save drowning sailors, or get a line to a stranded ship. Deliberately entering the seething surf and crashing, thunderous breakers, trying to reach the hand of a man being dragged by the currents out to sea, swimming out to men who could not manage to swim inland, all of them being dragged anywhere the swirling waters wished. Again, think of the modern television images of hurricane-driven waves hitting a shoreline, and imagine deliberately entering the surf! It seems that it is mainly family members, descendants of natives and crews, with the history passed down from (in one case) father, grandfathers, great-grandfathers or uncles who have, or had, knowledge of the events of 1889 at Samoa. At the time, the escape of HMS *Calliope*, the only vessel to steam out of the port under her own efforts, was considered miraculous, unparalleled in naval history, and a wonderful demonstration of seamanship on the part of her captain, her officers, and her entire crew. One of the officers on the disabled American flagship USS *Trenton*, waiting for the destruction on the reef that was so cruelly beckoning to his own vessel, commented as *Calliope* headed for the open sea that he wouldn't give a penny for her chances, nor those on board, as even managing to get out of the cluttered bay and away from the ships and reef, the hurricane in the open sea was horrendous and survival chances were still very low. In his later memoirs, the American Admiral described *Calliope's* escape as *"...one of the grandest sights a seaman or anyone else ever saw"*.

You may wonder why I have taken a personal interest in this storm, compelling as it surely might be for any person simply interested in sailing ships of the nineteenth-century. Well, my great-grandfather, William Isaac Thorndale was a sailor on HMS *Calliope*, and endured, and fortunately survived, this ferocious storm and the terrifying Samoa Adventure of March 1889. And not only that, in the 1930s he wrote down his own memoirs, purely from memory, of his time as a boy, then a man, and finally joining HMS *Calliope* and so to be present at Samoa, representing in his own small way Her Majesty Queen Victoria's Royal Navy. He started the voyage that would include Samoa as "Leading Seaman" and was promoted to Petty Officer, "Captain of the Fore-Top" during the trip; an earlier injury on the voyage meaning it would turn out to be his last, most exciting and certainly most dangerous mission in a sailing ship.

I have tried to tell the human stories, as well as the one of "nature". So I describe my great-grandfather's early days, joining the navy as a boy, and progressing until he got home after Samoa. I also tell the story of HMS *Calliope,* and Samoa at the time. I have further tried to tell the stories of some of the others involved in the adventure, where I have been able to find a name with which to start my research. Naturally, being based in the UK and creating the manuscript as a hobby rather than with any expectation of making my fortune with it, I have researched in the UK mainly, and really only further afield by virtue of the internet, via which I have had contact with a few American sailor's families, and some German.

A few notes about the style herein: Where I reproduce statements, reports, and sections from my great-grandfather's memoirs for example, I have reproduced the style, names and grammar exactly as I found them. I use *"H.M.S."* if that was how the prefix was used in the quoted source, or *"HMS"* otherwise. These days, the use of the definite article *"the"* in front of a ship name (e.g. *"the Calliope"*) is deprecated, but seems to have been very prevalent in the nineteenth-century, so again it is retained in verbatim quotes here. Publications such as the *New York Times* even today seem happy to insert *"the"* in front of a ship name, so I guess I am being overly pedantic to omit it. So if a grammar error seems to appear in an italicised passage, it is in fact how the original source presented it. The German rank of *Lieutenant* was spelt exactly that way at the time, and not as *Leutnant*. I decided not to condescend to litter such apparent defects with *"(sic)"* to identify most of these situations, only resorting to its use where I think it absolutely necessary to aid understanding.

This book is the third revision, primarily to include data which have come to me since the previous issue, to continue to make improvements to the lay out, and to try and catch that last, elusive, error.

One final point: many of the images in this book are old (some c.1889), and the quality is not as good as I would like them to be. Some were old family photographs, copied and scanned which does not improve the sharpness of the image. But I rather include them than leave these images out. So please do not blame the printing process if you think a photograph reproduction herein to be a little grainy.

Graham Hague, Potton, March, 2020

Chapter 1: WIT.

"Ah my boy, a Sailor's life is lovely when you see him ashore in a neat blue suit and plenty of money but what of the dark stormy night at sea, a gale of wind, raining hard and the greater part of the watch trimming sail? Yes, a sailor's life is bold and free and as I put it [to] you, all you have to do is to sit down on the deck and let the winds blow you along with the lovely sunshine and starlight and balmy breezes of foreign climes…"

So spoke one of a group of retired Reigate seamen flourishing under the names of *Miles* Carpenter, *Budge* Worsfield and *Bundle* Farrington, to a 14 year-old William Isaac Thorndale on learning of his and a friend's determination to *go for sailors*, and demonstrating satire to be no modern invention. The boy didn't recall any more but the style suggests it to be something that a determined old salt could have kept up for some time. But whilst mischief might have provided the insincerity of the last part, that first sentence contained the real truth of the matter. A sailor in the nineteenth-century British Royal Navy was in for some unpleasant and dangerous work that a landlubber would not normally see and perhaps could hardly imagine.

In the days long before television or radio, encouraging old sailors to tell their sea tales was probably akin to watching an instalment of a television drama or adventure series today - entertainment for young men with little else to fill their spare time. Along with others of his generation, William had surely been enthralled by the vivid and exciting stories with which these *men-of-the-seas* had won their evening refreshment from the adults. But no more than does the remote reality of a soap opera today, the entertaining heroic deeds and dramatic events contained in the sailor's words were unlikely to beguile many of their listeners into an immediate and ardent desire to experience them for themselves.

For most sailors of the middle nineteenth-century, and possibly from time immemorial, a trip ashore during or at the end of a voyage would be accompanied by a few week's or more pay jingling in their pockets, a burning desire to make up for the lost time spent at sea, and more often than not an adoring host would be waiting at the foot of the gangway to help them do so. An uninitiated onlooker might find it difficult to imagine the danger and hardship by which those wages had been earned. And an impressionable orphaned lad, faced with a life of drudgery in a poor part of a major town and fully conscious of being a drain on the meagre resources of a kindly brother, could easily be mesmerised by the tales of those old salts: stories of desert islands with white sandy beaches and coconut laden palms; of wind and spray and a deep blue sea cut through by a sailing ship with all canvas crammed on; of painted natives and strange animals; of white-crystal icebergs and red-roaring volcanoes... and wish for the life himself in blissful ignorance of the accompanying risks and hardships.

WIT, as William Isaac Thorndale seems most widely to have been known by his peers during his long life, an acronym which will serve us well in this narrative and protect my two index fingers just a little, was born at Kingswood in the Parish of Reigate, Surrey, England on 17th July 1861, the fifth surviving and youngest child of a shepherd named William Thorndell and his wife Sarah, a domestic servant before her marriage. WIT was originally christened simply *Isaac*, and there is additional confusion over the spelling of the surname. The informant of the birth was his mother, who could neither read nor write, and the surname quoted in the register of births is clearly *Thorndell*. Whilst it seems quite possible that the registrar misheard the name, and Sarah would presumably have been unable to point out the error or help with the spelling, my research has led me to conclude that this particular spelling was accurate at the time. In fact, a strong Surrey accent may have made the name sound like *Thornd'l* leading to any number of interpretations for the registrar.

The best potential source of assistance, the 1861 census, was taken in April, aggravatingly for me just a few months before WIT's birth. But it does confirm a 43-year-old shepherd named William Thorndell as head of a household at No. 29 Cheaseleys Town, Kingswood comprising wife Sarah aged 38, daughters Lucy and Phoeby, son Michael and youngest daughter Eliza. Sarah's sister, Elizabeth, lived next door with her husband, Henry Etherington. Since William and Sarah's marriage certificate records the surname as *Thorndell*, and one of the witnesses as *Mary Thorndel*, it seems likely that any of these variations was used at one time or another until the proliferation of name recording by officialdom that we are subject to today finally regulated it. Whatever the original circumstances of the birth registration may have been, in the family he has always been known - and always knew himself - as *William Isaac Thorndale*.

Cheaseleys, in any spelling variation and whether as a street, or simply a part of Kingswood, appears to have long gone. The surname Cheaseley is a Reigate name, though I have not found any association with a family who might have been in a position to support poor houses in Lower Kingswood.

WIT's father William was born in 1818 in Abinger, Surrey, and had married Sarah in the village in 1845. WIT's grandfather was Aaron Thorndale and Aaron's mother was one Elizabeth Thorndale; taking his unmarried mother's surname suggests Aaron Thorndale to have been illegitimate, though usually the father's name is not then known. In this case, it is recorded as one Aaron Longhurst. The Longhursts were a powerful and influential family in the Ewhurst area of Surrey and can be traced back to 1515. I have tended to romanticise the notion that any blue blood in my veins comes from the dastardly seduction of an eighteenth-century innocent serving girl by the rackety young son of her influential employers, who would not consent to a marriage but who do seem to have acknowledged paternity. No-one is likely to be able to burst that particular bubble. There is, in fact, another similar bounder in my male ancestry, though not with any royal blood in *his* scurvy veins.

Before WIT was born, his father contracted a severe cold whilst tending the sheep belonging to his employer, a local farmer named Mr. Taylor. He lingered for a few weeks before finally succumbing to the fever, leaving his young family and WIT's mother to face an uncertain future; WIT was just 8 weeks old. These are WIT's memories of what he had been told about his father's death, but the certified cause of death was cancer, possibly aggravated by the fever on an already weakened constitution. Sarah put away her memories, her hopes and her dreams and devoted her life to raising her children as best she could, instilling honesty and morality as keystones of their lives, putting them all through school, and so nearly setting WIT, the last of her charges, at his own working life, when the cares and pain and sheer unrelenting labour that characterised the lower classes in Victorian England finally took the toll beyond that which the body could bear, and in 1873 she joined her husband in death at just 50 years of age. She had never re-married. As we have seen, at some time in her upbringing of WIT, probably very early on, she seems to have taken to calling him *William*, perhaps in deference to the dead husband I like to think she still loved, and the name stuck for the rest of his life. It also appears that at some time during her widow-hood, she moved to her husband's relatives in the Stepney and Chelsea areas of London, and it was in that latter registration district that she died.

Lower Kingswood today seems to me a somewhat depressing place, though I apologise to residents who may find it perfect for them and who might feel indignant at my comment. The village is not very neatly, but extremely effectively, sliced in two by the major dual carriageway from Reigate to London. I would not want to live on one side of the village and be desirous of crossing to the other. The *Wisdom of God* church is a Victorian brick monstrosity, the only saving grace a nice garden that surrounds it in place of the usual graveyard. Again, my view may be in a minority as its Byzantine style is architecturally almost unique in Western Europe, and is considered a must visit in those particular circles that like to visit churches. The door was locked when I encountered the building, so its interior may be more attractive than the outside was to my more traditional Christian eye.

WIT was always a small child, and seemed destined to be forever of slight frame and bearing, though photographs of him in his evening years show that the midriff spread we all fear would later be able to torment him just a little. His brother, living in Nutley Lane Reigate, took in the small orphaned youngster to bring up with his own. My research has narrowed down the brother to two possibles, both in fact brothers-in-law. Henry Baverstock, who had married WIT's eldest sister, named either Louisa or Lucy is perhaps the more likely. Neither the 1871 nor 1881 censuses show a family called Baverstock, Thorndale or Thorndell living in Nutley Lane, Reigate, so although it is quite possible that WIT went to live with his sister's husband and young family in that street in 1873, it is by no means certain. In the style of the day, I think WIT could well have referred to a sister's husband as a brother. Later in his life, WIT would christen a daughter with Baverstock as a middle name, which might have been in recognition of that past help. As for the other possibility, WIT's sister Phoebe Thorndale had married a Felix Walder and that family definitely resided in Nutley Lane, so he is another contender.

Whoever it was, the brother unhesitatingly took in WIT to feed, clothe and house alongside his own growing family, and made sure he completed two further years of the rudimentary schooling of the day, but was glad indeed when at 14 years old, the boy could at last start work and bring a much needed wage into the struggling Nutley Lane household.

WIT's first job was an appalling introduction to the misery and mind-numbing grind of Victorian England. Located some 3 miles to the west of Reigate were the chalk pits at Betchworth. The lad was woken at 4 a.m. in time to wash and dress and grab a hasty breakfast, then to set off to walk the country lanes and fields giving himself an hour and a half to be sure of not being late - and being turned back with no pay for the day. Although some major roads were macadamised by then, most minor roads would be little better than cart tracks, and before the advent of the automobile, those tracks were usually rutted, muddy and uneven. The A25 that now connects Reigate and Betchworth in a short, straight, direct route would have been most welcome to WIT! The country lanes he would have known are winding, and regularly change in elevation, and would have taken some considerable while and effort to negotiate each day.

Twelve solid, unremitting hours of hard graft followed, men filling small trucks and WIT leading the trace horses pulling them up the steeply angled track from the floor of the pit to the railway wagons at the top; lifting tons of chalk out of the earth, to return to the abyss and do it time and again. At 6 p.m. in the evening, he could make his weary way home - forget the ploughman and think of a small boy, reaching home in the darkening evenings at around 8 p.m. with just about sufficient strength to wash, eat a meal, undress and crawl onto his mattress. As winter drew ever closer and the utter cold added to the miseries, the boy knew he could bear the work no longer. After just 3 months of the toil, the fourteen-year-old was becoming an old and broken man.

WIT's chalk pits at Betchworth would become (marginally) famous in the television industry of the next century, providing a number of far-away planetary locations for the *Doctor Who* and *Blake's Seven* series of shows, for example. The local church provided the setting for the first of the group of nuptials depicted in the film *Four Weddings and a Funeral*.

WIT's brother, understanding the difficulties and already worried for the health of his small charge, on the face of it at least readily accepted the loss of the relatively good wage the boy brought home, 9 whole shillings a week, nowadays some 45 pence, and found him a new job for exactly half that wage at the firm of Messrs. T. S. Marriage and Co., Ironmongers, Metal Workers and Manufacturers, in Reigate's Bell Street; then, as now, the main shopping road in the town. WIT knew them as *"Marriage and Brooks"*. After a winter in the shop as a general dogsbody and with no prospects of improving his lot, WIT found his next position for himself, a notice for an *"Errand Boy"* in the window of the fishmongers just opposite attracted his attention, and the wage was precisely the same four shillings and sixpence per week, so he applied and was accepted. WIT most charmingly uses the phrase *"Errant Boy"* in his memoirs.

At last, WIT had found a good place to work. His master was Mr. Henry Ongley, a kind and warm-hearted man who in 1895 would become Reigate's 16th Mayor. The family treated their employees to a wholesome breakfast before the main work of the day started, supplemented by lunch and tea, and then allowed WIT to take home to his brother leftover unsold food which greatly helped him stretch the family's meagre budget as WIT found himself sharing the house with his brother's own growing young family. The shorter walk to work, the less physically demanding nature of the business, and the good and reliable meals all restored the young man to a strength that his slight frame would always obscure and belie. He was also fully conscious of the debt he owed his brother, and truly glad he was that he was now helping him so positively.

It is not to be supposed that WIT didn't regularly find himself in trouble, and the brother was by no means too diffident to deliver the punishment that would normally have been the prerogative of the dead shepherd. One incident to stick so clearly in WIT's mind that he repeated it as a seventy-year-old, was the time he and some friends were set upon by older boys from a neighbouring street, and were subjected to a pretty severe knocking about. WIT was ashamed to recount that his group took their revenge by pelting the house of the main perpetrators the next evening with a volley of stones which broke a large number of the back windows. Afterward, in cooler reflection, he acknowledged the injustice of inflicting retribution not on the lads but on their hard-up parents - something the *Boys of Nutley Lane* hadn't considered at the time. WIT usually preferred to fight his battles one-on-one, and generally did so; if found out in any of his *sports*, he would take his punishment in good part.

Work settled down to a reliable and comforting routine. The day started early, but WIT had never minded that. It was WIT who would take down the large rolling shutters from the front of the shop, stow them in their precisely made boxes and take them out the back. The shop was swept, and clean fresh sawdust obtained from the local mill was spread over the floor. Nothing much could be done then until the dust had settled, so breakfast was prepared in the back. The fish slabs were thoroughly washed down, cleaned and covered before breakfast was partaken, as it was important they be ready for the fish.

The fresh fish, in the days before widespread refrigeration, had to be fresh indeed. The various types of fish arrived in Reigate at the railway station, transported from the fish markets in London at which, very much earlier in the day, they had been divided up in their boxes of crushed ice. A cart waiting at the station brought the boxes to the back of the shop, where some were placed in dark, brick-lined cold vaults and outhouses, whilst a few after washing were displayed on their beds of ice for the casual trade. At last, the shop staff could partake of their breakfast. It was not yet 7 a.m.

I have tried to research the history of ice in the UK but though fascinating, it is a large subject all on its own. It seems the Romans and Persians had ice pits even before the birth of Christ, but the idea may have come to Britain sometime around the middle seventeenth-century. Many large houses built special shallow lakes that froze solid in winter, permitting ice to be cut into blocks and transferred to a specially built sunken cold house lined with straw, in which the ice remained solid throughout the year and was used by the household mainly for preservation. I have viewed such an eighteenth-century ice-house at Burghley House. Commercial enterprises were set up during the nineteenth-century but with only limited longevity. But I guess there was an ice manufactory somewhere in the area from which Mr. Ongley could purchase his material; I expect he too had cold houses in the gardens where he could store it.

The errand boys would then set off on their individual rounds to get orders. They would each of them have a specific route around the wealthier parts of Reigate, visiting particular houses to take orders for the day's requirements from the cook or servant told off to give them. WIT set off down Bell Street, into Cockshot (now Cockshot Hill), Woodhatch, Earlswood Common and Meadvale, just to the north of where now the Redhill and Reigate Golf Club shares a part of the rolling Surrey landscape with the local sewage works. A ball out-of-bounds there is likely lost forever. The return journey took him through Glover's Fields (that I have been unable to identify on the modern maps, so Glover's Road is probably how it is now known), and finally back to the shop to carefully transcribe the various orders from his own notebook to the shop's *Day Book*. There followed a period of feverish activity as the orders were read and made up, so that they could be delivered by those same errand boys repeating their journey, this time with a large and heavy basket on the handlebars of the bicycle.

The family took the time and trouble to show their boys how to gut and fillet fish, and to prepare the game that they also sold, so that in times of rush, the boys might help out wherever they could. WIT was keen to learn, and very happy in his work. There he might have stayed, perhaps eventually becoming a fishmonger or butcher himself, had he not had one of those foot-loose and fancy-free friends.

WIT himself acknowledges how the life of a boy can be so influenced by his friendship with another. This pal was called Charlie Jordan, and he obviously came from a very similar background to WIT. Just a few months older, his profession was *Hawk Boy*, which seems to be a lad who would keep a master plasterer continuously supplied with mortar. Charlie was permitted to read his master's old weekday newspapers during his free time. The momentous publication that was his favourite was called *Lloyds Newspaper* and each week the maritime news took the young man away from the boredom of his work to places around Britain and further afield. *Lloyds Newspaper* was a publication today named *Lloyds List* and which details ship movements around the world. It was published daily except Sundays, though there do appear to have been some Sunday Specials during the nineteenth-century. It is, of course, associated with the famous maritime insurers *Lloyds*, which in 1685 evolved from a coffee shop, the meeting place of sailors and owners who required news about shipping, run by its proprietor Edward Lloyd.

In what would turn out to be the significant issue, a bold advert had engaged Charlie's immediate interest:

"WANTED - Strong Healthy Boys for the Royal Navy - Great Prospects for Intelligent Boys - Apply for Full Particulars from Srgt. Skinner, Trafalgar Square, London."

I have not been able to trace the precise copy of the publication to verify the content of the advertisement, so have relied in my text on WIT's own memory of the wording. Lloyds Newspaper seems an appropriate place for such an advert, and it was something that would totally change Charlie and WIT's lives.

Charlie was immediately decided; one assumes his life as a Hawk Boy did not hold any equivalent *great prospects* that he could immediately recognise, and he carefully cut out the advert before the paper was finally used to light the fire in the drawing room or whatever, but like many youngsters, was not so keen to take up such a bold matter on his own. He approached WIT with the idea of applying, and showed him the scrap of paper.

WIT doesn't state whether he needed much persuading and it seems unlikely. Maybe he was happy to be led by his friend; maybe the stories of the many old sailors living in the town still echoed in his ears; or perhaps the romance just grabbed his mind. Whatever the reasoning, saying nothing to their respective families, the two boys applied jointly for the papers, and when they duly arrived at the house to which mail very rarely found its way, *the cat was truly out of the bag*.

At home, the news was greeted with shock and dismay. To join the navy was to be gone from family for many years at a time, and WIT was now contributing significantly to the family income. But WIT was adamant, deaf alike to tears, pleadings or threats, and showed an obstinate streak which my mother always believed had resurrected itself in me – I would *never* accept it to be true. It is unclear whether WIT would have taken any notice of the advertisement had he simply seen it for himself, rather than Charlie showing it to him, but having made up his mind that here was a chance to see a world that he had only been told about, and to experience those adventures of which he had only dreamed, there was no deflecting him from his purpose. The plan was pursued relentlessly, the advice *for* seized upon, and that *against* making no difference to the boys.

The papers were filled in and the truly important stuff could then begin. To open proceedings was a visit to a doctor for a fairly cursory health check. Next, the parent's, or in WIT's case, the guardian's signature of consent, something both boys had the greatest difficulty in obtaining. Finally, having cleared these hurdles, the kindly brother, resigned now to fate, took his young sibling to the local magistrate, Mr. Carruthers, in Reigate's Upper West Street, a Builder and Contractor, who asked a few questions of the brothers and finally, having satisfied himself on the determination, reliability and innate honesty of the boy, put his name at the bottom of the paper. The deed had been done.

A career in the navy for a young man then was by no means a trivial undertaking. Although Britain was officially at peace (this was the period of the *Pax Britannica*), there was always a skirmish somewhere in the world during that 100 years that demanded human intervention and often exacted a terrible price for it. For an ordinary seaman's family, it could mean a loss of contact with their relative for years at a time, with no telegram or letter to tell them what was happening to him. A ship setting out on a long voyage and not arriving often meant that knowledge of a loss could be anything up to a year out of date, and the risks did not only come from one of the Empire's many human enemies - the weather was perhaps the most fearsome opponent of those sailing men. Ignorance of the adventures the lads would soon be experiencing was probably as much a worry as the knowledge would have been. Having said all that, British newspapers were very quick to report on the exhaustive comings and goings of Queen Victoria's navy, and whilst details might be scarce about the ordinary seamen, as long as one knew the ship they were serving on, the newspapers would provide regular and accurate information about its movements and engagements; sometimes of course, a double edged sword.

Early in 1876, WIT and Charlie Jordan travelled to London by rail using the travel pass supplied to them for the purpose, and were thus treated to their first view of the capital, or the *Great City* as WIT referred to it, meticulously capitalised, in his memoirs. On he at least, it made a deep impression, though that modern icon of the city, the Tower Bridge, was at that time the subject of a newly opened competition, and not even a pencil line on Mr. Horace Jones' sketchpad. Arriving at the Admiralty Buildings near Trafalgar Square in the early evening of a bright spring day, WIT was treated to the first navy meal of his life, a basin of tea from which he and some thirty or so others all took a cupful, supplemented by a slice of bread each. Whilst meagre, it was nevertheless something of a novelty to be *provided* a meal.

When the simple repast was finished, permission was given for the entire group to go out and take a look around the area of Trafalgar Square, where in some 35 years time the imposing Admiralty Arch would funnel the city traffic towards Buckingham Palace and The Mall but which in WIT's time, and despite the absence of motorized vehicles, was a very busy junction, dangerous for an unwary pedestrian used only to rustic carts and plodding horses. The famous buildings and street names filled the young men with awe as at last they feasted their eyes on places they had only heard about, whose existence they had accepted in faith. Now, here they were in amazing reality. In particular, Sir Edwin Landseer's contribution of four massive bronze lions surrounding the fabulous celebration of Britain's greatest Naval Hero, Admiral Lord Nelson, had been unveiled in the square just a few years before the boy's visit, and was undoubtedly the prime target of their naval interest.

Reporting back to the sergeant by the allotted 9 p.m., the younger members of the potential intake were tired and ready for their bed, but any sleep was interrupted by the noisy return of the older men at their later time, and the strangeness of the surroundings made for a restless night all round.

Precisely at 6 a.m., both men and boys were unceremoniously roused from their slumbers. Having folded up the bedding and blankets as best they could, a cold bath completed the waking up process – this was WIT's description and probably meant a wash beside or under a shower. The breakfast, consisting this time of a basin of cocoa and the ubiquitous slice of bread, was very dry for the boys, but they were promised with a cheery smile that the next course would see them right. When it eventually came, they learned the first lesson of their navy lives: to be wary of what their more experienced shipmates would tell them. The *next course* was a trudge down the corridor for the medical examination.

Stripping down to nothing, the boys commenced all manner of sports designed to test out their fitness for naval service: leapfrog; running; jumping; and so on, each event followed by a visit to the doctor to be checked for pulse and breathing, heart and lung. Next, eyesight and hearing, and finally, in what seems to me to be the wrong order, verification of chest and height that the subject would pass muster. Here, WIT's slight frame seemed destined to exclude him: he states the requirement was for a boy aged 15½ to be a minimum 4ft 9½ inches in height, and WIT was just a half-inch under. The minimum chest size was 30 inches and as WIT managed to push his out to 32 inches, the doctor smiled at his worried face and passed him through. These dimensions are, as I say, WIT's own, and I suspect he may be slightly out with his memory. The *official* minimum requirement for entry of boys aged between 15 and 15½ into the Royal Navy was 4 ft 10½ inch height (without shoes) and 29 inch chest. It was dictated in *Admiralty Circular number 30, April 1873*: *"Examination of Second Class Boys on Entering the Navy"*. It is probable the seemingly strange order of test was deliberately chosen, in order to not exclude someone fit enough but not quite measuring up.

The long morning was getting cold for the boys, so they were pleased when they could at last dress and go off for their midday meal, or as WIT always termed it, their dinner. At last a proper meal, consisting of boiled beef, with potatoes boiled in their jackets (i.e. not peeled), including a significant portion of the field in which they had been nurtured. Hunger overcame the only slight reluctance instilled by the muddy brown water in which they bubbled, and a good meal was made, followed by Grace in thanksgiving.

The reader might soon suppose that this part of my tale, and therefore WIT's thoughts, to be somewhat preoccupied with food. I think the latter at least to be quite true, and WIT in his memoirs faithfully records his meals – it makes for an interesting social record today. I think it stems from those times when food was something to be really grateful for, and a regular supply of it was considered almost a miracle. To say grace and be truly thankful for a good meal was a real situation, rather than some trite religious recital. These days, if we're hungry, we can throw something in the microwave or order a pizza delivery – I do wonder what WIT would have made of that. In our modern western society, few people should go hungry under normal circumstances. In WIT's time, food was hopefully provided, though rarely in abundance, at very precise times of the day, and getting it was always an important event. Even unpalatable food was appreciated, and WIT records in his memoirs that throughout his naval career, he was very often hungry at sea. You will encounter some of WIT's (not so very) lip-smacking recipes later on in this narrative, and may even wish to try them out yourselves, if you are of a culinary frame of mind. Whilst I pride myself on being reasonably adventurous in my kitchen, I have no intention of doing so - one can take bonding *too* far.

The end of the afternoon saw the lads receive their final and most powerful introduction to the Royal Navy, in the form of one Sergeant Skinner, Recruiter. On his entering the room, there was no need for a call for silence, as here was a *manifestation*; fully rigged out to the amazed boy's eyes in a resplendent naval uniform they thought should really indicate an Admiral at least. It demanded complete attention. Facing his mute audience, the voice matched perfectly to the authority of the presence, and shuddered round the room:

> *"Boys Attention! All the boy's names which I call will march across to this side of the room."*

Not sure whether to be called meant acceptance or rejection, as their names were read out in turn, both Charlie and WIT moved over to the other side of the room where they waited in doubt until the sergeant put aside his note of paper, and regally addressed the remainder standing opposite:

> *"Well my boys, I am very sorry that you have not passed but better luck next time. All you want to bring you on is plenty of pudding and exercise and you will go through flying."*

WIT's relief at his success was then bolstered by the words of encouragement and advice given to the victorious, and such was his emotion that many of the actual words penetrated deep into his brain there to remain for the rest of his life:

> *"...keep yourself clean in body and mouth; obey all orders not at a walk but at the run; always be civil to your superiors; spring to attention when spoken to; never forget that you are from now onward one of those of Old England who has Volunteered to serve Her Majesty and Country in any Cause which you may be called upon..."*

The pride and happiness at his success filled the young man, which is not a thing to wonder at given that he was now making adult decisions and achieving adult success. He may just have realised that, now and for a while at least and maybe forever, the carefree fun of youth was over.

WIT and Charlie signed their names to the minimum ten year

service period (which would start from their attainment of age 18 years), and I have already pointed out that the register of his birth spells his name *Thorndell* but WIT, who was well able to read and write, seems to have accepted the recording of his name in the navy records as *Thorndale*. In all subsequent readings of the name from naval records, the middle initial *I* is read as *J*, a far more understandable error from a hand-written register. So Isaac Thorndell had become, by the age of 14½ years, William Isaac Thorndale, as he was to be known for the rest of his life. It is these changes and embellishments that make ancestry research challenging, rewarding and frustrating in equal measures!

Another rail trip the next day took WIT and Charlie to a 56-gun frigate under Captain Lang: HMS *Fisgard*. The spelling WIT used in his memoir was *Fisguard*, which would be sensible phonetically; my research suggests it was actually spelt *Fisgard* as reproduced here. It was one of the last Guard ships to be stationed in the Thames off Greenwich, and was one of the few ways at that time that boys could be inducted into naval service.

John Masefield had not yet been born when WIT and Charlie Jordan reached Greenwich and stared at the incredible piece of equipment that might have been the epitome of the poet's fabled *tall ship*. Getting close to a British man-of-war for the very first time was, for WIT, an experience he would remember to his old age with no less a passion than would one day be invoked by, to me anyway, Masefield's most famous phrase.

Fifty-seven years old when WIT and Charlie first gazed upon it, their first sight of the vessel was quite literally staggering; standing on the Greenwich hard beside the hull and looking up its sides to masts that seemed to stretch to the sky, so high they nearly fell over backwards as their eyes were drawn ever upwards. The thought of climbing that wooden mountain was horrifying and daunting. Ascending these devices was something that a country boy had maybe thought about, but he could never have imagined the awesome spectacle in its full dimension. The actual height of HMS *Fisgard*'s main mast was some 150 feet above the main deck – quite a considerable height in anyone's language. As the boys trooped up the gangplank to reach that main deck, they were told to salute the quarterdeck, a difficult thing for lads who had been taught neither how to salute nor where the quarterdeck was. They tried their best and were rewarded with amused faces from the older hands.

HMS *Fisgard* was, according to WIT, a 56-gun frigate, and commanded at the time by Captain Lang. My research tends to describe her as a *Leda* class, fifth-rate, 1,063-ton, 46-gun, three-mast frigate. The vessel was securely moored to a dock on the landward side of which lay a meticulously manicured lawn formally laid to paths and flower beds, and bordered by the imposing colonnaded buildings of The Royal Naval College, Greenwich with its towers and domes, created just three years earlier out of the Royal Hospital for Seamen. Today, the Royal Greenwich buildings are as grand as they ever were, indeed cleaner now and glow bright in the sunshine, and today share the wonderful location with the University of Greenwich, and the Trinity Laban Conservatoire of Music and Dance.

HMS Fisgard moored on the south side of the Thames at Greenwich, c 1875.

On a summer's day, walk around the University paths and listen to the hard-worked scales of violin or horn that emanate from an open upper floor window; watch strangely robed men hurrying here or there on unimaginable errands; then walk down to the river where the foreshore reluctantly yields an occasional find to the modern day mud-larks who waddle across it at low tide in a digitally beeping world of their own, walking where once the great hull of HMS *Fisgard* settled twice a day. If you do all that, visit the National Maritime Museum and the clipper *Cutty Sark* that lie close by. Whilst I was compiling this narrative, the vessel suffered the dreadful fire which looked so appalling on video, but which in fact, destroyed very little, as most of the ship had been removed and stored off-site. The refurbishment has created a wonderful historical object well worth including in a visit to the capital.

To further digress for a moment, the United Kingdom has a

number of "tall ships" that can fascinate the enthusiast making a visit, especially if like myself, they suggest how one's ancestor may have spent his working life. Obviously, HMS *Victory* at Portsmouth, with HMS *Warrior* nearby; HMS *Gannet* at Chatham Dockyard; and HMS *Trincomalee* in Hartlepool; and a few merchant vessels such as *Cutty Sark* at Greenwich and SS *Great Britain* at Bristol. And of course, I must not omit the fantastic museum of Henry VIII's *Mary Rose* in Portsmouth's Historic Dockyard.

The boys were told off for their messes, divisions within the crew which defined their allotted eating, sleeping and work groups, one of the older boys on the ship leading the new intake to the relevant areas on the vessel. Whilst there, a bugle sounded *Cooks* and the boys got their first lesson about orders. The call explained to them was for one boy to go to the galley and obtain a large kettle of boiling tea, whilst another went to the Steward to obtain the bread. In this context, a kettle is a large cauldron that has been set over a fire. Royal Navy warships of the time tended to have a brick-built range in their galley area to provide hot meals for the crew. Thus WIT's first meal aboard ship was dry bread softened by dunking in hot tea, unappetising certainly but as he recalled, very filling.

Once the meal was completed, the mess was rapidly cleaned up; the plates and cups washed up and put away; the deck swept and everything left spotless. Washing-up was a chore that was shared by boys in rotation, and was universally disliked. Mess decks were often cramped and crowded, and washing up at sea usually involved cleaning the utensils in a pail of cold sea-water, on a table at which an off-duty mess would be playing cards, mending clothes, or indulging in some other pastime; men who objected to being splashed with the water or being nudged out of the way. But since it had to be done, the grumbling was usually light-hearted.

Another bugle sounded, and this time the old hands tumbled out of the mess and ran to the ladders which led to the decks above, and the boys, realising they should follow though not understanding what was now in store for them, found that clambering up an almost vertical steep ladder whose steps overlapped each other was something else which required a certain amount of skill; all the boys eventually struggled onto the main deck with very sore shins. They stood as straight as they could for *Evening Quarters*, and watched the proceedings without comprehension.

Yet another bugle call, another unknown tune to the boys but one that galvanised the men instantly into a frenzy of action, and again the lads wondered what they should do but this time were told by an officer to stand still. Orders were shouted, unintelligible to the watchers but obviously understood by the men who proceeded to go aloft like monkeys in a tree. In awe, the lads watched the men climb the rigging disappearing at the top of each mast section, only to reappear and climb further and further up. Then to the intense surprise of the youngsters who had no experience at all of how a sailing ship was managed, the uppermost part of each mast came whistling down suspended from ropes, slowing only when it seemed it must smash into the deck, to be collected by other men at the bottom, detached from their hoists and stored neatly. Within seconds almost, the men had returned from their faraway treetops and lined up on the deck once more. The boys had, unknowingly at the time, witnessed an evolution that had involved sending down the royal yard, the highest spar on a mast to carry sail. Most were amazed at the precision, the co-ordination, and the efficiency of the work, and wondered whether they would ever be able to perform such work as well themselves.

The officer, having given the new boys an example of what they would need to learn, now marched them aft and showed them the quarter-deck, so that next time when boarding ship they could salute it properly. Here they were issued with some of their first navy equipment: clews, lashings and a hammock. They were then told to return to their mess and lash their hammocks ready for bed, each boy having been allocated a number to be matched with its position in the mess. The whole concept was a mystery to the lads, but some of the older boys kindly explained how to use the clews and lashings (thin lengths of rope) to attach their hammocks to the myriad of hooks screwed into the underside of the main beams running across the roof of the deck, each pair numbered in carefully stencilled white paint. Those same hands watching the new lads work were by now laying comfortably and nonchalantly in their own hammocks, lined with bedding which the boys were then told to return to the main deck to obtain. A horse-hair bed with a cover for it, and one blanket, a load which threatened to overwhelm the youngsters as they struggled to negotiate the gangways and ladders with it, was placed in the appropriate hammock, and now the old hand's evening entertainment was almost ready.

It may be noted that on smaller ships, the hammocks were usually berthed *athwartships* which means at right-angles to the fore-aft line of the vessel. On larger vessels, where better use of the available space dictated it, they were slung lengthwise along the axis of the ship. Most often, they were occupied by the different *watches* in sequence, so that for most of the time, an occupied hammock had an empty one either side of it, providing slightly more space to the seaman using it.

Before turning in, the boys were told they could go to the forecastle on the upper deck and enjoy the view of their first evening from the ship, and they found the vista quite breathtaking. Surprisingly perhaps, most boys had come from the country, but maybe those boys born beside the sea answered Neptune's calling in their father's or uncle's fishing boats or with local merchants, and saw no reason to commit themselves to years in a strictly regimented navy for very poor pay. The huge buildings of Greenwich, dwarfing anything WIT had seen in Reigate for size and style, stretched either way far along that side of the embankment that curved away on each end of the ship. The Naval Hospital and the Conservatories were pointed out by some of the old hands taking the opportunity for a final smoke before turning-in. On the far side of the river, factory buildings and warehouses were the distant objects. As the evening sky darkened and a spring chill from the river joined the lights twinkling on in the buildings, the boys were told to go below and reluctantly left the impressive sight behind. On the mess deck, they soon found themselves to be the amusement for the evening, and the old hands were ready to watch it. How to get into the hammock was the first problem, quickly followed by how to stay in it.

All the boys were of course much shorter than the men and older boys, and WIT in particular as we know was of no great stature, and it was a mighty difficult game for a sub-five-foot lad to get into a hammock slung three foot or so above the deck! Some managed to do so only by dislodging the bedding and had to try again, others whilst laughing at the antics of their mates had no better luck of their own. The difficulties were compounded by the fact that on a training ship, the hammocks were slung so closely together that there was little space between them once they were occupied. The normal allowance was 16 inches per hammock width; mark that out and see what I mean about a Victorian naval vessel being a very chummy place indeed!

This might be a good place to mention a publication which provides immense information for anyone wishing to understand just about any aspect of sailing ship seamanship, particularly in the Royal Navy. From how to make an anchor, to how to chase down and board another vessel. I have included it in the bibliography at element [39].

Eventually the old hands got bored with the fun, and as the men were looking forward to some sleep, a few wise words of advice were given and before long everyone was secure in their hammock. After such an exciting day, sleep came easily in a gently swinging hammock, hardly affected by the Thames lapping at the ship's side.

The singing of the birds which occupied the trees outside WIT's bedroom in the house in Nutley Lane gently permeated the dreamy sleep, but quickly became the shrill squawking of the Boatswain's Mate's pipe. Worse was to come, the raucous yells from the huge man as he walked up and down the centre line of the ship, tumbled the lads out of their hammocks faster than any douche of cold water might have done:

> "*Lash Up and Stow. Now come along here. Show a Leg. Now then my boys, out you come. No second sleep here.*"

In case there is anyone reading this book who is unaware of the origin of the phrase *Show a Leg*, here is the generally accepted explanation. In eighteenth- and early nineteenth-century sailing ships, women who were nominally wives but not always with that status supported by legality, were allowed aboard ships and could spend the nights with their partners, the main reason being to try and prevent desertion by the men, or at least, to remove one of the many causes of it. Men with nothing else to call home could, it seems, easily ignore the limited romanticism of fitting two persons into a hammock designed for one, take no notice of the very close proximity of a mass of other sailors doing much the same thing, and enjoy a night of intimacy with a loved one. In Napoleonic times, there might be upwards of 500 women availing themselves of the accommodation on a large warship. The early morning call for duty applied only to the seamen, so a shapely ankle displayed from out of the otherwise anonymously bulging hammock allowed its owner to remain undisturbed for a little while longer, and then all such females could arise together to perform their own ablutions in some degree of privacy. I imagine that if a sailor actually had the effrontery to wave *his* leg in response to the Boatswain's call, it was quite likely to be used as a handle to assist him out of the hammock. A variation on the original call was supposedly *Shake a leg or show a stocking*. It should also be noted that by WIT's time in the navy, females had long since been prevented from taking advantage of the cosy arrangement.

The boys quickly dressed, unhooked their hammocks, and began rolling them up before tying them in a bundle and stowing them out of the way. On some vessels, this was on the main deck under the bulwarks. The first full day aboard commenced, as always, with cleaning the decks. Shoes and stockings were left off, and everyone got down on hands and knees to scrub the main deck. Particular attention was paid to the corners and the edges under the rails: *Clean out the corners and the centre cleans itself* was one of many maxims WIT would become familiar with over the next few months. After a scrub and wash down, the majority of the water was wiped off with *squeegees*, broom handles with natural rubber heads, and the deck was left reasonably dry, but not well enough for a training ship.

Large cloths were brought out, and the deck fully dried off with them. In some ships, these were sometimes made of yarns and hemp from old rope and fashioned into a *skein;* with their user kneeling on the deck, they were swung around in great arcs to collect the water, keeping the swing low to avoid splashing any of the paint work around, to be then wrung out into a pail. It was a much easier method than simply dabbing up the water with the cloths.

The work before breakfast was not yet complete, as the bright metal work and brass fittings were thoroughly cleaned and polished, and all the ropes coiled afresh. Finally, the boys were told off for the mess deck, where they stripped to the waist for a cold wash before partaking of a thick slice of dry bread and a pint of hot cocoa.

After breakfast, the other decks, mess and gun, were cleaned and then the guns themselves were to receive the loving attention of the crew. WIT was fascinated by these weapons whose barrels and shape were not hugely different to the cannon that had demolished the French and Spanish Fleet off Cape Trafalgar some 70 years earlier. Though he had passed through the gun deck several times already, like most of the other boys, the protecting of toes and shins from the ladder's steps had precluded much looking around, and the murky darkness of the deck had hidden the black guns from close scrutiny. Now, with the gun ports open and light streaming in, the weapons, usually termed rifles, sat like monstrous queen ants, immobile and regal as their tiny acolytes fussed around them, menacing even in silence and torpor. Men and boys were allotted their own guns to clean, and it was instilled that pride must ensure that their rifle be the best polished, and have the cleanest and tidiest equipment, of any on the gun deck of the frigate.

WIT was issued his uniform such as it was, and with the others began to *learn the ropes* and all the other parts of a ship: the masts, the sails and the rules of conduct. WIT was told off for *Side Boy*, required to attend the deck gangway when any officer should be arriving or leaving the ship, a position he held for his entire time on HMS *Fisgard*. WIT suggests he was actually held back slightly by his height, being considered of insufficient stature to go on to sail training just yet. His extended time in *Fisgard* was spent learning the theory which would normally be given on the sail training ship, and in fact, as the young boy grew that last inch or two, the additional knowledge would soon stand him in good stead.

In September 1876, WIT and Charlie were sent to HMS *Implacable* under Captain Carr and stationed at Devonport on England's south coast and today the largest naval base in Western Europe, to commence their serious naval training. Rigging and sails and masts had all been theory so far, but now WIT was going to put his hands on these parts of the ship, and having had his additional training on *Fisgard* found himself being pushed ahead by the instructors.

To go aloft and furl or reef a sail was a major task for any sailor. There were no harnesses or safety lines; if you lost your grip it was probably the end of your career – and depending on height and luck, possibly your life. In 2009, archaeological excavations of the old cemetery at the Royal Navy's Haslar Hospital near Portsmouth disinterred one unfortunate individual from a slightly earlier period than WIT's, who had clearly suffered a fall from height; both arms and one leg were severely fractured, and his chin had hit the deck with such force that not only was the lower jawbone split in two at the point of his chin, both ends of the mandible had broken away and were floating in his cheeks. In the days before proper anaesthetics, one can only shudder at the pain the poor young man must have suffered, and wonder how he even managed to make it as far as the hospital.

Some crew on the American sailing ship Charles W Morgan, summer 2014.
[https://www.mysticseaport.org/voyage/mystic-seaport/crew-interviews/]

An engraved plate from "Nare's Seamanship 1862" [19] showing both the foremast and the mainmast with three groups of three shrouds; ratlines omitted.

The means provided for a sailor to climb the mast were the shrouds and ratlines. Refer to the images on pages 37 and 40. The shrouds are the group of usually four vertical ropes occasionally in paired groups, attached at the base to metal straps (called chain plates) at the bulwark, the side of the hull protruding above the main deck, and which ascend tapering inwards to almost a point at the junction of the lower mast with the top mast, called the cap. Across these shrouds are tied ratlines horizontally and spaced at between 15 and 16 inches on the leading shroud, which act as the steps of a rope ladder. Climbing these ladders, it was important to grip the shrouds with your hands and put your feet on the ratlines – grasping the ratlines to ascend was a fairly sure way of ensuring a rapid return to the deck. Interestingly, the modern service that uses ladders the most in their daily tasks (the fire service) don't seem to mind if the rungs or the side beams of the ladder are gripped. I guess the significant point is that on the ship, the rat-lines are thinner lengths of rope tied to the shrouds, which are therefore more likely to break or slip particularly when wet, so it is always better to be holding onto the much stronger shrouds *just in case*. In some vessels, the ratlines were strips of wood tied to the shrouds.

As the man reached the top of the shrouds, there were two choices to proceed onto the cap. The futtock shrouds were a much shorter set of lines extending out from the mast to the edge of the cap, and were the correct method of reaching the platform above, but required a sailor to be effectively suspended above a void, as the lines came back out from the mast. The other way was via the *lubber's hole* in the centre of the cap, a relatively easier and safer way of reaching this first objective.

If this was as far up as the sailor was going, he then had to fan out along the yard. There were two ropes provided for him to do this, one below the yard (to stand on) known as the *footrope*, and one above (to hold to). Both ropes passed through clews that kept them aligned to the yard. Having spread out along the yard, the men could drape themselves at around 45° with their upper stomachs against the spar or yard-arm and their feet pressing backwards on the footropes, and rely on gravity keeping them in place as they then used both hands to perform whatever duty was required, as can be seen in the image on page 36.

Even in the nineteenth-century, the Royal Navy felt it prudent to get the younger boys used to this procedure in some better degree of safety than at the yard itself some 50 feet above the deck. A *monkey topsail* was the solution, effectively a mast and a yard, with all the appropriate rigging, but of about 6 to 8 feet height on a large wooden base, fetched out of the ship and placed on the main deck. If a boy fell off the short spar protruding from that, he ended up with just a few bruises as an incentive to not do so again. An instructor standing on a crate beside him would be able to show him precisely where to stand, how to hold on, how to keep his balance whilst both hands were employed in work, how to release clews to set a sail and how to haul on the sheets to reef it.

My reading of WIT's memoirs has suggested a subtle sense of humour hidden deep within, and this may be illustrated by some comment he makes of this time in his training. His instruction regarding Knots and Splicing of Ropes, was:

> "...under the Instructor Beanny an old shell back of the Neptune Class for he had scales on his feet or something of the kind..."

I am not quite sure what he means, but assume it conceals some sort of sailor's joke. A *shellback* (one word) is the seaman's slang for a sailor who has already crossed the equator and undergone King Neptune's ceremonies, so with the comment about the feet, I guess WIT really means a highly experienced seaman. A later comment about another instructor, presumably less frivolous, was:

> "... I am pleased for to say that our Instructor's name was 'Webber' who in after years was one of the two Officers who were promoted to the rank of Lieutenant, the first in the Navy since Trafalgar days..."

The limited amount of research time I could allocate to each of these individuals has not managed to unequivocally identify precisely who they were and why WIT should have found Webber in particular to be so remarkable. I can only assume him to be one of the very few enlisted men of that time who crossed over to the officer line, and if that were so, he would be noteworthy indeed. My research is hampered by WIT recalling these names phonetically some 50 or more years after he heard them, so I cannot even be certain of the spelling, and I found over 250 sailors with the name *Webber* in Kew's National Archive's Seaman's Records.

Before long, WIT was considered sufficiently trained to go aloft, but was not permitted to reach the cap by the futtocks, being told to use the lubber's hole until such time as his instructor considered him capable of dispensing with it, and a proud moment it was for the boy when told he could use the men's way aloft; a little like one of today's new aeroplane pilots going solo I suppose, risky in a way but an important and necessary step along the chosen path. Refer to the sketch on page 40.

Christmas that year saw the first leave for WIT and Charlie Jordan in nine months, and a fine time was had at home among friends and family, who desperately wanted to know what the boys had been doing.

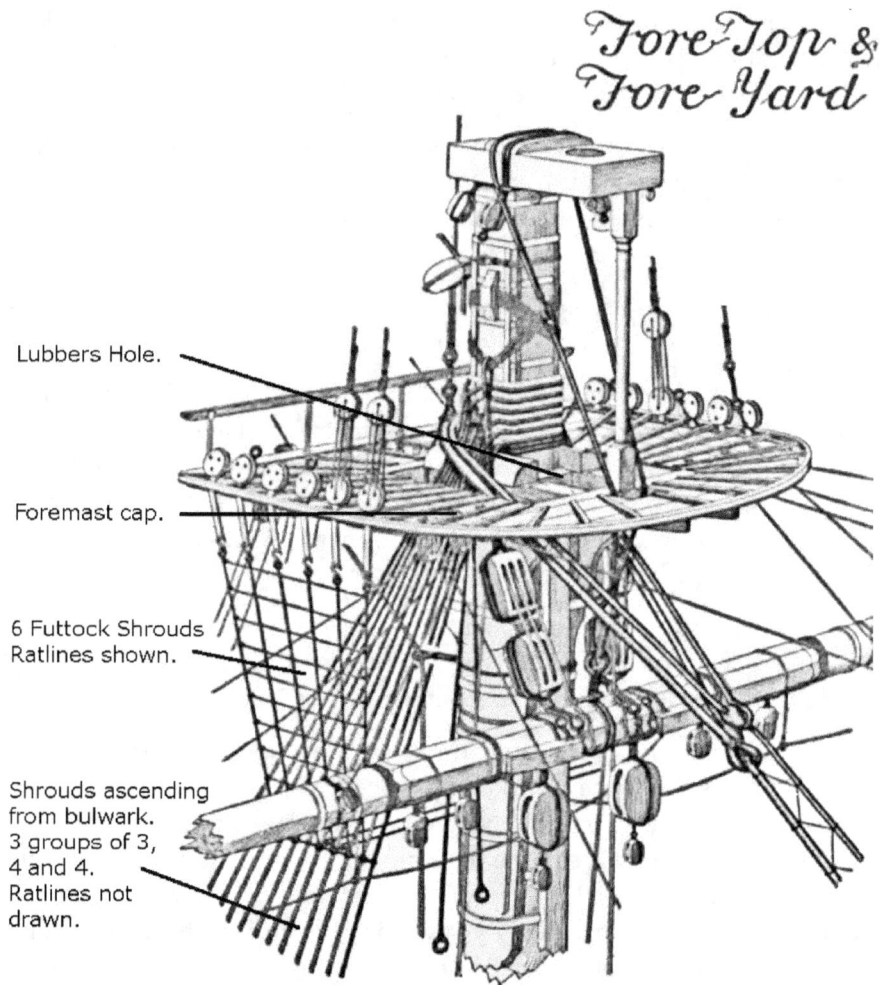

Fore Top & Fore Yard

Lubbers Hole.

Foremast cap.

6 Futtock Shrouds
Ratlines shown.

Shrouds ascending
from bulwark.
3 groups of 3,
4 and 4.
Ratlines not
drawn.

View of a typical mast top, showing the shrouds and futtocks.

Leave was soon over, and on their return the training doubled in intensity. Another of the many mottos forced into the boys was *Learn to Walk, then to Run, and after that FLY* and practice was definitely intended to make it come alive. After every pipe or bugle call was sounded, the last boy to take up his position was reminded of the maxim by (as WIT put it) the tickling of his buttocks with a cane. WIT's slight stature tended to leave him a little put upon, the bigger boys pushing him out of the way to ensure they weren't the ones to receive the *what-ho* from the instructor, and this same attitude affected his washing of his clothes.

The navy at the time was (and I presume still is!) superciliously concerned with the cleanliness of the boys and their clothes. Superficially, one might reason that since members of a ship's crew were likely to be confined for weeks or even months at sea, someone not very careful in his habits would soon cause friction amongst the other members of his mess. More likely at the time, however, it was to reduce the risks of disease or lice infestations, since I suspect the human aroma of a naval mess deck was never particularly fragrant. Twice weekly starting Monday morning, bright and early, was wash clothes time. One flannel, one shirt, one white frock, one jumper, one pair trousers and one pair of socks made up each boy's laundry pile (the men's was not much more), the other set of wearing-clothes, of course, being worn. Washing one's clothes utilised a large tub of cold sea-water placed on the main deck, whose high steep sides already made it difficult for the shorter boys to reach over and make a good job of washing. Again, the bigger boys usually felt little compunction against elbowing their way in to the circle surrounding the tub, the younger or smaller ones were often left to be the last in line and make the best of a somewhat less-than-pleasant bath of mucky water. It had a knock-on effect, since being the ones to pull the last few clothes out of the tub was followed by a frantic rush by their owners to the lines which had been lowered from the rigging to take them, the best and most likely drying-spot being the highest up the line, and obviously by now, already taken. There were no *clothes pegs* as we would recognise on a sailing ship, clothes were attached to the lines by tying them on with *cloth stops*, short lengths of twine or strips of cloth stitched to or passed through holes in the clothes for that very purpose, and far more reliable in the sort of stiff breeze likely to be encountered at sea. The last to tie on his clothes would often get the usual six with the cane.

Fortnightly, scrubbing the hammock was added to the chore, and there was a very jealously defended ritual order to that operation – the first to be washed would then find the sunniest place on the deck, and so stood the best chance of being dry for the coming night's sleep; needless to say, the stronger boys usually got the more comfortable repose at the end of that particular day.

This *pecking-order* mentality went further, including the meals. I have already described WIT's apparent obsessive compulsion to record his food, and the reasons for it. But a good story involves one of these meals and a bully getting his comeuppance, and I really cannot improve on WIT's own description of the event:

"I have said in the first part that I was very short, under 4 ft 10 in, so not

much to look at. So it seemed for when we went to any of our meals I knew my place was always at the end of the table, or on the Cable. Well this was on a Thursday, Roast Mutton, Potatoes and Plum Duff. Every day there is always a Officer and Petty Officer goes around to see everything is equally put out on the plates.

"This day, my dinner was a very small one so the Officer ordered my dinner to be changed for the Cater's who had a fine big plateful and when the dinners were changed the P.O. put his hand under the table and brought out a large lump of plum duff secured by a fork. Oh the surprise. All eyes was on our mess and a lot of alteration we made in quick time, for that was the biggest dinner I had received since I had arrived. That is to say, I had been cut short by the others, but after I got my own, you can just think the Dumb Motions that the Cater passed on to me, but I was blind to them and tucked in to the best dinner in the mess, for it was the best cut of meat, also the best potatoes and duff. I did enjoy it, but I expected I should have to suffer for it. So I should but for my chum coming forward and joy began to take the place of sorrow for after the Cater had struck at me and I dodge it, he was surprised to receive a smart tap and then he retired not to interfere with any of us again for he was soon removed from his position of a Cater of Mess and after that there was great changes in the smaller boy's food, for they got windy for they never knew how soon it would come their turn to be found out, for there was plenty of food if served out equally to all."

The early spring of 1877 saw training continue with a six week Gunnery Course and Field Exercise in HMS *Trudeyant,* an old hulk attached to the gunnery ship *Cambridge* at Davenport, after which WIT spent six weeks in the brig *Liberty* (Captain Connor) attached to HMS *Implacable*. It was in that brig that he went to sea, another of those first-time experiences he would never forget.

WIT had now been graded as a *First Class Boy,* which primarily defined his wages rather than anything else, so this might be a good point to mention the pay the boys received. Pay-time for all was Saturday morning, and in 1877 a *Second Class Boy* was provided with three old pennies, approximately 1 new penny in today's currency system. Admittedly, its buying power then was much greater, but it was hardly a fulsome reward for a week's labour. A first class boy, usually known by other boys as a *holy joe,* commanded double the wage, and that alone was a tremendous incentive for a boy to do well and attain that level as soon as he could. Unfortunately, the pleasure at standing at the pay table, cap smartly in hand, waiting to receive the remuneration, was regularly tempered by a penalty. *"Not entitled, broke a basin"* was one of a number of ways the paymaster might dash the hopes of a boy for yet another week, since the replacement of losses of things like that in the mess came out of the culprit's wages. WIT once spent three consecutive weeks in such a case, with not even a penny to buy a stamp for to write home.

One apparently fine summer's day, WIT and some 80 other boys trooped aboard HMS *Liberty* in Plymouth Sound, and were shown how to reef and furl the sail on the small boat. This time, it was to learn the way the *running* rigging handled, as they would be performing this work in reality. A number of older men were there to help out and ensure a disaster didn't occur. The trip out of the Sound down to the Eddystone Rock was the boy's first taste of the open sea, and quite an introduction it was; despite the sunshine, a heavy sea kept most of the lads at the side of the ship. After a week of *feeding the fish*, sea legs began to take over and most of the boys were eventually able to perform their duties. Teignmouth, Brixton and Torquay were all visited, but a sail along the Race at Portland Bill ensured the boys all got an idea of what they might one day have to face - even towards the end of his life, WIT still thought it one of the roughest seas he had endured anywhere in the world. The tidal race is due to the particular topography of the seabed just south of the Bill. An underwater shallow protrusion of land extending for some 1.3 miles (2 km) surrounded by the deeper water means the fierce current is rarely still, and has been recorded as running at 7 knots during a spring tide – very lively indeed. I guess the spirited introduction had been deliberately chosen for such a day as that, to wheedle out any who would obviously never make a sailor.

The ship returned past Portland to moor alongside HMS *Boscowain* in Weymouth Bay. One day, Portland would be the second deepest and one of the largest man-made harbours in the world but at the time was merely a series of breakwaters, started at the time of Trafalgar but only recently in WIT's time completed. It was during mining of the Portland marble to construct the breakwater that in 1805 a large flint nodule extracted from deep underground was cracked open supposedly to expose a live toad that had presumably existed inside it for many thousands of years – how's that for a digression? Modern science doubts the story!

1877 was also the year that saw the first signs of erosion to Smeaton's wonderful tower on the fearsome red granite of the Eddystone, and the commissioning of its modern replacement. I can heartily recommend Fred Majdalaney's book *"The Red Rocks of Eddystone"* to anyone interested in an incredible and agreeable true tale.

WIT seems to have enjoyed his training once his stomach had

become used to the sea, and especially his time as lookout. On a sailing ship, the lookout was placed on the topsail yard at sunrise, where he could see some 10 or 15 miles further than could the Officer of the Watch, Boatswain, Quartermaster and Signalman on the deck who kept their eyes open for more immediate dangers nearer the ship. At night, a watch was even more important and two lookouts posted in the prow of the ship one each side kept a close watch for red, green or white lights ahead that would indicate another vessel in close proximity, and their ears open to catch the warning sounds of a wave breaking on a reef.

WIT learnt more of the many things a sailor needed to know, among them swinging the lead: heaving the hand-lead-line forward allowing it to sink and checking the indicators tied to it to assess the depth. The lead-line was marked in a very specific way which needed to be learnt by heart so that it could be readily interpreted: a piece of leather at 2, 3 and 10 fathoms, the one at 2 made with 2 strips, the one at 3 with 3 strips and the one at 10 with a hole in it; white bunting at 5 and 15 fathoms; red at 7 and 17; blue at 13; and two knots at 20. Wax or tallow was packed into a recess on the end of the lead for the operator to see what it had picked up to ascertain the type of bottom - something which in uncharted waters could help the sailing master understand if there was a risk of shoals, for example. A 20 fathom *Hand-Lead-Line* weighed approximately 4 pounds.

The lead-lines just described were accurate for shallow lines; deep-sea lead lines could be up to 200 fathoms, 1200 feet or over 400 metres in length, nearly a quarter of a mile. Deep-sea lines required a number of sailors to operate them and the quartermaster was responsible for the calculation of depth indicated by them.

Sea time was soon over and it was back to HMS *Implacable* in Plymouth for more training. September 1877 was mostly damp and WIT learned invaluable advice about local weather and how it could be predicted. In this case forecasting did not involve a barometer or the inspection of a strip of seaweed, nor even a sniff of the air, but instead revolved around two stores ships that ferried materiel between the ports in the area. HMS *Fox* was a screw frigate *of the old class*, the 13th to carry the name and nearly 50 years old at the time, originally built as sail only but which had been converted to a screw-powered stores ship and used to support Colonel Markham's Polar Expedition of 1873 to 1875. HMS *Valois* was a paddle wheel steamer of almost indeterminate antiquity - I can find no record of the vessel so maybe WIT's memory is slightly at fault with the name.

It was a well-known "fact" in every port in the West Country, that if

Fox was coming in to Plymouth and it happened to be raining, it would not stop till she left the port. A similar but more localised rule applied to *Valois:* when she entered the port, one could expect either a full gale or torrential rain before she departed. Plymouth was already well renowned for weather prediction; even Captain Cook a hundred years earlier will have known the old saying that:

> *"The west wind always brings wet weather;*
> *The east wind wet and cold together;*
> *The south wind surely brings us rain;*
> *The north wind blows it back again."*

In apparent opposition to the experiences clearly suffered by the authors of these maxims, during the course of my work in the Defence business, I made a number of visits to Plymouth and very rarely found it wet. Of course, by my time, the old *Fox* and *Valois* would have been long forgotten ghosts.

In Britain, that damp September of 1877 was the harbinger of a bad autumn and winter, the weather for the rest of the year regularly teaching the boys the real meaning of going aloft in a gale to work a sail. It taxed the efforts of all on board, men and boys, and forged a strong team bond between them. Training was not relaxed just because of bad weather; rather it was vital that it took place when such dirty stuff could be expected. If one could manage a sail in a gale, to do so in milder conditions would be relatively easy.

The year 1878 arrived and proceeded with the boys becoming fully-fledged sailors well able to perform their tasks in whatever the channel could throw at them. They became confident, skilled exponents of a difficult and dangerous art. How dangerous it could be was brought home to them all by the loss of HMS *Eurydice* in a squall off the Isle of Wight, on 24th March of that year. The memories of the disaster deeply affected the sixteen-year-old WIT and stayed with him for his entire life, so are worthy of a few pages here.

The foundering of HMS *Eurydice* under Captain Hare off Dunnose Point to the south-east of the island was a national disaster of immense magnitude at the time as, indeed, it would be so today. The accident was made even more tragic by the fact that so many of the victims were very young seamen undergoing sail training. *Eurydice* was a wooden, fully-rigged, fast sailing ship of 921 tons, which had been built at Portsmouth Dockyard and launched in 1843 and later converted to a sail-training vessel, considered by many to be the smartest and quickest 26-gun frigate in naval service. She was 141 feet in length, 38 foot beam and just less than 9 feet depth of hold. On her outward voyage in November 1877, she had been joined at Madeira by HMS *Liberty*; I think it unlikely WIT was aboard *Liberty* at that time. On 6th March 1878, HMS *Eurydice* left Bermuda following a training cruise in the West Indies with her crew of about 310 augmented by some 50 invalids from hospitals being shipped home, and a number of other senior military personnel who had requested passage to England. Estimates suggest a total of about 368 souls were on board.

On the very last day of the voyage at about 3.30 p.m. she was within sight of her destination, her home port, Portsmouth. The newspapers reported the tragic events as follows, this article from *The Times* of 26th March 1878, 2 days after the event:

> *"The Eurydice ... was seen by the coastguard at Bonchurch at 3.30 on Sunday afternoon, bearing for Spithead under all plain sail, and with her port stunsails (an additional sail on an extra yard and boom at either side of a square sail, for use in light winds) set on the foretopmast and maintopmast, the object being clearly to arrive at the anchorage at Spithead before nightfall. There was an ominous stillness prevailing at this time. A heavy bank of clouds was coming down from the north-west, and the glass was falling rapidly. Such wind as there was came from the westward, and blew on the port quarter of the ship. The Isle of Wight is of peculiar formation on its southern fringe, having what may be considered as a double coast line extending from Blackgang Chine as far as Shanklin. The inner circle of the Downs reaches a height of 500 feet above the sea, and affords a deceptive shelter to ships well inshore. From the direction in which the Eurydice was steering she would be in comparatively smooth water, so sheltered would she be by the Downs, until she rounded Dunnose Head, where the disaster occurred. This circumstance will also serve to explain the fact that the Emma, schooner, which was near at the time, was not affected by the gale. At ten minutes to 4 the wind suddenly veered round from the west to the eastward, and a gale, accompanied by a blinding fall of snow, came rushing from the highlands down Luccombe Chine, striking the Eurydice just a little before the beam, driving her out of her course, which was heading to the north-east, and turning her bows to the east. This is what seems probable, though, from the manner in which the sea was concealed by the snow, nothing was seen of her at the supreme moment when she capsized to starboard. The air cleared as suddenly as it became overcast, the wind sinking away at the same time. As soon as anything could be seen, the masts and top-hamper of the ship were discerned above the water about 2¾ miles E.N.E. off Dunnose, a*

well-known and lofty landmark between Shanklin and Ventnor. The ship lies in 11 fathoms (66 feet) of water, and from her position she appears to have righted in going down."

The gale seems to have come from the higher island hills down the steep-sided Luccombe Chine river valley between Shanklin Old Village and Bonchurch, striking *Eurydice* utterly without warning and with only the black cloud as the sole sign of impending danger, and before any compensating adjustment to her sails could be made.

The small schooner *Emma*, Captain William Langworthy Jenkin, sailing a short distance behind HMS *Eurydice* as described having survived the same squall, picked up the only four or possibly six men from the frigid sea but unfortunately, all but two expired almost immediately. A report of the disaster lists the survivor's names as one Sydney Fletcher, Ordinary Seaman from Bristol, and one Benjamin Cuddiford, Able Seaman of Plymouth. In WIT's memoirs, he records the survivors as *"A.B.s Fletcher and Petteford"*, the phonetic similarity I think proving WIT's memoirs made some 50 years later came from memory and not a more modern reference work.

The court martial into the accident took place in August 1878 and decided that the vessel had foundered...

"...by the pressure of the wind upon her sails during a sudden and exceptionally dense snow storm, which overtook her when the approach was partially hidden by the proximity of the ship to high land and no blame can be attached to the captain, the officers and men of Eurydice...*"*

The accounts by her two survivors told of being over-whelmed with hardly any warning of capsize, and that the ship's rapid descent to the floor of the Solent had inexorably and inescapably sucked to their deaths those few who had managed to scramble off her decks. The dreadfully cold sea killed most of those in the water in just minutes.

Eurydice's hull was recovered, as well as the detached figurehead found by divers, with, so it is said, a telescope dramatically superincumbent across her breast, and towed back to Portsmouth, but was eventually broken up, not unnaturally being considered by most sailors as an extremely unlucky object, and it had suffered significant damage whilst submerged. To a four-year-old Winston Churchill when he stayed at nearby Ventnor on the Isle of Wight where he supposedly witnessed the disaster, the lurid tales of the divers seeing fish eating the young boy's bodies was apparently recounted sufficiently well to give him nightmares at a level he would later record in his own memoirs. Sir Arthur Conan

Doyle, at the time of the tragedy a resident of nearby Southsea from which town with Portsmouth most of the boys hailed, was motivated to pen a poem called *The Home-Coming of the Eurydice* which movingly concludes:

> *"A grey swirl of snow with the squall at the back of it,*
> *Heeling her, reeling her, beating her down!*
> *A gleam of her bends in the thick of the wrack of it,*
> *A flutter of white in the eddies of brown.*

> *"It broke in one moment of blizzard and blindness;*
> *The next, like a foul hat, it flapped on its way.*
> *But our ship and our boys! Gracious Lord, in your kindness,*
> *Give help to the mothers who need it to-day!*

> *"Give help to the women who wait by the water,*
> *Who stand on the Hard with their eyes past the Wight.*
> *Ah! whisper it gently, you sister and daughter,*
> *'Our boys are all gathered at home for tonight.'"*

On the West wall of the nave of St. Anne's Church, Portsmouth, to the north of the main entrance, a memorial records the names of 16 officers, 270 boys and men, 21 marines and 7 military passengers from the vessel. Other memorials in the church commemorate two of the Lieutenants lost, Stanley A. Burney and Francis H. Tabor. Sadly, the sister ship to *Eurydice*, HMS *Atalanta* (formerly HMS *Juno*), would disappear off Bermuda less than two years later with the loss of 390 lives.

The wraith of *Eurydice* is said to still sail the waters around the Wight, even a member of today's Royal Family is purported to have seen it! The tales began early, when it is recorded that Sir John MacNeill, partaking of afternoon lunch with the Bishop of Ripon in Windsor, suddenly exclaimed without warning: "*Good Heavens! Why don't they close the portholes and reef the sails?*", afterwards explaining to his startled friends that he had seen a most vivid vision of a ship in the Solent with all sail set and gun-ports open about to be hit by a monstrous black squall, exactly what was happening 70 miles away at that very moment. And in the 1930s in these waters, F. W. Lipscomb, the commander of a British submarine, was forced to take rapid evasive action to avoid a collision with an old-fashioned, three-masted sailing ship which had vanished when next he looked for it...

I have devoted a lot of space in this book to this subject because, as I have already noted, WIT was understandably most particularly affected by the tragedy. The boys who died were many of his age, on their first sailing voyage, as he was himself about to take. I don't suppose he will have been acquainted with any of them as many were young officer cadets undergoing the mandatory sail training of the time; he does not record personal acquaintance, but we all can surely understand his feelings. Following this tragedy, sail training for officer cadets in the Royal Navy was abandoned.

WIT's shore-based training was over, he would now hone his skills at sea. Soon after the *Eurydice* disaster, WIT was *told off* for his first sea-going sailing ship, HMS *Iron Duke*, Captain Cleaveland, bound for the China Station. This was the first HMS *Iron Duke*, a 10-gun, twin-screw armour-plated, central-battery ironclad battleship of the *Audacious* class of 6,000 tons and a complement of 450 men, as different from *Eurydice* as could be. She was originally to be called *Duke* but to distinguish her from wooden ships with the same popular name (mostly after *Wellington*) she was re-named *Iron Duke*. Launched at Pembroke in March 1870, she was commissioned in Devonport in April 1871. On 31st August, she became the Flagship of the Commander-in-Chief China and on her commissioning voyage became the first capital ship of any nation to use the newly opened Suez Canal. The current (2015) *Iron Duke*, the 3rd of that name, commissioned in 1993, cost some 670 times the £208,760 of the first.

HMS Iron Duke, c. 1871. (Public domain, a download from the American Naval History and Heritage Command).

WIT's great friend Charlie Jordan was told off for HMS *Danae* bound for the Cape of Good Hope, and these two boys, best mates since childhood and who had experienced together the joys and pain of naval training were parted, seemingly forever. Their naval careers would follow paths which appear never to have crossed. Whilst it was Charlie who had cajoled WIT into entering naval service with him, Charlie's time on HMS *Danae* was not exciting enough to exceed the attractions of Sydney Australia and the goldfields. As the Admiralty records so laconically put it, on the 7th January 1881, Charles Jordan joined a long list of British seaman to *Run*. The £3 reward offered for his return appears to have been claimed around May 1882 and Charlie spent some 42 days in gaol as part of his punishment. Despite this blot on his record, he then served on a number of ships but his service record ends with the information that he was invalided out of the service from HMS *Dasher* at Haslar Naval Hospital in Gosport, on the 7th March 1884.

Charlie's last vessel was the second HMS *Dasher*, launched at *Chatham* in 1837 as a two-gun paddle steamer. She was employed mostly in the coastguard at Weymouth, and with a crew of 12, plied her trade around the Solent, being broken up in 1885. Strangely for me at least, the last *Dasher*, a P2000 Archer class training craft, was constructed at a boatbuilding company (Watercraft at Shoreham by Sea) whose premises for many years comprised the view from my bedroom window, and I am quite sure I will have gazed upon the latest of these vessels during its construction.

I have found out no more about Charlie Jordan nor how he came by his injuries or illness or whatever it was, but despite his earlier fall from grace, I hope he did all right. The absence of any further comment by WIT may be due either to the disgrace associated with a deserter, or simply the lack of knowledge as to his adventures, although I suspect that as crews swapped between vessels, WIT would surely have asked after his old chum.

William Isaac Thorndale c. 1910 in Coastguard Uniform (author's collection). The medals (from left to right as viewed) are: "Alexandria, 11th July 1882, W.J. Thorndale, HMS Sultan"; "Long Service and Good Conduct, W.I. Thorndale, Boatman, HM, Coastguard" and "The 1882 Khedive Star".

Chapter 2: Early Naval Life & Action.

Although drills were forever being carried out to hone skills and test abilities, WIT's formal training was at an end, and he was now expected to be a fully contributing member of the crew, a *seaman* despite still being rated a boy. HMS *Iron Duke* was sailing away from Britain as part of Queen Victoria's Navy, to carry out duties that could include action at any time, and everyone on board was expected to share in the work, and the risks.

It might be imagined that his first trip away from England would be especially moving for the young man, but he does not record any major pangs in his memoirs; he seems to have been very resilient and open to change and new experiences and to have looked forward to whatever might come with an easy conscience and an enquiring mind. At every port he visited and when he was allowed to leave the ship, he took the opportunity to go ashore and walk for hours, seeing the sights in awe. His records of his excursions are testament to his wonder and interest, and would fill a book of their own. On one occasion, he records walking miles into the savannah of South Africa with a few mates, and meeting an English colonial planter, being supplied with oranges and other fruits in exchange for simply sharing his time to talk of the old country to the old man. The tale is quite warming and with others in his memoirs suggests that most colonials in the far-flung empire were not too proud to share their time and delicacies with lowly British tars carrying news of home.

WIT's record of the sea kit he took on board with him as he first set sail for a foreign station is worth recording:

"I will try to tell you the procedure when you are drafted to Sea. You have your kit made up to the full Sea Kit so you can dress in any rig that may be piped. This is a rough list of what your kit consist, do not think I am

going too far, but I am only trying to give you a true list of cloths in those days. 2 pairs Cloth Trousers, 2 Serge Frock, 2 Serge Jumpers, 2 White Frocks, 2 Uniform Jumpers, 3 Flannels, 2 Night Shirts, 2 Shirts with Collars, 2 Duck Jumpers, 3 pairs Duck Trousers, 2 pairs Socks, 1 pair Shoe, 1 Blanket, 1 Bed Hair, 2 Covers. (There was no Boots, Jersey or Monkey Jacket served out then, they came after)."

WIT's first naval service took him to China via the recently opened Suez Canal, then to Japan. During his passage through the Mediterranean, a visit to the shoemakers at Malta generated another note in WIT's memoirs that I think of interest:

"...then there was the Shoemakers with their purpose hide shoes which are very easy to wear, but the one fault was you could not get a good polish on them so that you could not wear them for Divisions, but they turned out alright for night watch when there was no Sail set..."

Presumably WIT means *porpoise*, but if so, I rather think the bit about the shine might have been his dry humour coming out again. He apparently did not want to trust them whilst aloft.

During his passage of the Suez Canal, WIT was daily experiencing new things. He recalls seeing a strange animal running along the side of the canal keeping pace with the ship, to which sailors would throw rotten meat or other spoiled food, and being told it was, in his spelling, a young *crocodial*. Apparently, the novelty was attractive to many sailors on the various ships plying the canal, and the beasts had become almost tame – well, at least, in terms of begging for anything to come their way, I don't suppose they would have objected to a bit of fresh meat should any have come within range.

The narrowness of the canal at that time (it was significantly widened on a number of later occasions as larger ships needed to use it) led to another surprising event. As *Iron Duke* proceeded, fitting its metal hull in the canal with barely a couple of feet either side, the mail steamer was seen to be approaching from the other direction, and that vessel always took precedence over any other, even a warship. So *Iron Duke* pulled into the next *station*, the passing place called by the French a *"gare"*, to allow the mail steamer to pass along unhindered. But *Iron Duke*'s crew rapidly unshipped and used the heavy hawser to tie the ship to the quay, something WIT thought to be unnecessary, unless a longish stay was intended. But the canal was so narrow the mail steamer was pushing up a head of water in front of it; the gare acted not only as a passing station but permitted the currents in the canal to dissipate safely. Any ship in the gare, even a big one like *Iron Duke*, was at risk from the swirling eddies and needed restraining; WIT likened the effect to being thrown upwards on a ship in a gale. The effect is no longer seen as the canal has been widened and deepened, and organisation of the passage of vessels improved by technology.

Transit of the canal was a wonder, but all on board, even the old hands, felt the passage through the Red Sea to be torture. Little wind, extreme heat, and the permanent film of perspiration on the skin made for an uncomfortable time all round. Meal times, however, were still a joy to WIT, and some more of his memories might now set the reader's taste buds jumping (my own stayed perfectly rigid):

> *"Now...I am going to give the Menu which was served in those days. Breakfast about 7.0 am (this is Sea routine), consist of 1 pint of Cocoa and biscuit, this is Daily. The biscuit in those days was not stowed in airtight Tins as now,* [WIT is writing in 1931] *But in Bread Bags stowed in the Bread Room, issued 4 times a week and placed in the Bread Barge so you could help yourself. I have seen it at times put on the Table in fair sized pieces, but it was not there very long before you could see it falling to pieces, so you had to put it in your Cocoa and try to get on with it or you would soon have nothing to eat. (I mention this only to point out the difference in the stowage then and I must state that this was not a thing that happened often, but it did so at times). The Dinners vary from day to day. I shall state the different day issue. Monday, Salt Pork, 1 pint Pea Soup. Tuesday Salt Beef and Plum Duff, this consist of Raisin, Salt Suet and flour. This had to made by the Cook's of the Mess. The Duff is either put into a cloth and boiled, or in a tin and baked as choice. Wednesday, Salt Pork and Pea Soup, Thursday, Boiled Australian Beef in tins and preserved Potatoes which are very nice. They fill you and make you think you are putting on flesh quickly, but that idea soon fades away, for you soon feel as if you want something to eat. So go on to Friday, Salt Pork and Pea Soup. Saturday, Salt Beef Plum Duff and on Sunday Salt Pork and Pea Soup. One day in it turn, you have Boiled Mutton in Tins and Rice, this is served in lieu of Boiled Beef, that is to make a change once in the week. You must know that I am giving you the Menu when there was no such things as a Ship's Canteen (many thanks have been offered to the Organisers of that Great blessing which came to all ships in after years). The first ship to have a canteen that I remember when in China was H.M.S. Shannon."*

The detailed way *Plum Duff* was made was entertaining, and I shall expand on WIT's rather brief recipe instructions. One would start by allocating approximately one pound of flour per man to be fed from the size of duff that could be made in the kettle; this would be about 12 pounds for most ships kettles. Obtain two pounds of raisins. The flour was then placed in the kettle, and the cook then required to stand about four feet from the kettle and to throw the raisins into it. Any raisins to fall outside the kettle could be eaten by the cooks without incurring any guilt or recriminations on their part. This tradition (a jealously guarded kitchen secret, I believe) will hardly have improved the aim a great deal. One pound of salt suet cut up into lumps, some salt, and half a gallon of water were then added to the mix, and the whole agitated sufficiently to disperse the ingredients fairly evenly (whilst continuing to eat those raisins still found lying on the floor). A large canvas bag was then filled with the dough, and the mass then boiled for a few hours until it formed a huge round ball of duff, sparingly dotted with some raisins on the outside to give the lie to the often-voiced accusation from the diners that none at all had found their way into the cauldron. Plum Duff was reputedly as heavy as lead, and not something to enjoy immediately prior to bathing.

If you wish to try the duff, you should precede it with *Mang*. Dead easy to make: procure a quantity of biscuit, pound to a powder, mix with pea-soup into a paste and eat it hot or cold. Or even better, *Hum Durgan*, made by frying small pieces of biscuit in fat until soft, served with copious amounts of salt and pepper. And to use up the very fine biscuit powder left when the biscuit bag had been emptied, the cook might make *Pow Sow*, by putting the dust in a kettle with some water until a soft paste results, mixed with flour, raisins and sugar before it is baked in a dish. The officers reputedly found this a very acceptable treat.

All these recipes are taken from *"The Cruise of HMS Calliope"* by Reverend Evans, privately published in 1892 and reprinted around 2010 [7]. I rather suspect that the allocation of one pound of flour per man made at the start of the plum duff recipe is slightly erroneous, and that the bake will have fed a large number of sailors.

At Aden, WIT was introduced to one of the new (to him) weaponry innovations of the time: a rocket. Whilst he seems to have been highly impressed with the device, his words about it do not fill me with awe, and his last sentence especially makes me thankful not to have been one of the unfortunates ordered to release the thing:

> *"We stayed here … carrying out drill and boat exercise, it was here that I first saw the Hailes War Rocket fired. It is a long Rocket, shaped after a shell with 3 grooves at the tail end and when fired the back flame passes along these grooves and so gives it Rotomotion, and forces it ahead at a*

great speed. It was used then for bush fighting and a very clever chap it often turned out for it turned and twisted about and you never knew if it would return to you for if it hit anything such as a tree or a bank it would turn in a second."

Hailes was WIT's spelling, I believe this name should read *Hale's* referring to the British inventor William Hale, born 1797. The possibility of the thing coming back at me is not something I'd consider at all clever.

The Englishman William Congreve had developed a rocket in the early 1800s that was really only a much larger version of today's firework: a tube of slow-burning gunpowder providing the motive force to a separate charge, with a stick for stability. They were supposedly used during the war of 1812 and again at Waterloo in 1815. At the battle of Fort McHenry in 1814, the American poet Francis Scott Key, temporarily detained on a British ship in the bay outside Baltimore whilst negotiating a countryman's release from captivity, is supposed to have watched the glow of Congreve rockets illuminating his country's *star spangled banner* in the fort and was so moved at its survival by the next dawn's early light, that he was driven to set his feelings down in words:

> *"And the rockets' red glare, the bombs bursting in air,*
> *Gave proof thro' the night that our flag was still there."*

…the third couplet from the first verse of *"The Star Spangled Banner"*, the song that in 1931 would become the US National Anthem.

The particular flag in question was a huge device, some 42 feet in length and 30 feet high, made by Mary Young Pickersgill from Baltimore and her daughter Caroline to the order of Major George Armistead at the quite staggering cost of more than 400 dollars. It now resides in the Smithsonian Institution's Museum of American History.

Hale's version of the Congreve, developed around 1844, used rotation to dispense with the stick, but otherwise they were very similar devices; they were used during the Crimea Wars of 1853-1856, and adopted (in a limited fashion) by both Union and Confederate forces for use during the American Civil War, especially by the Union during the siege of Petersburg in 1864-5, but with little real success that I have been able to uncover; rather, they gained a reputation of being particularly unreliable. During the explorer Samuel Baker's retreat from Masindi (Northern Uganda, previously Sudan), 14th to 24th June 1872, Hale's War Rockets were also used but were thought to be little better than the fireworks they were based on, having no explosive head. They were felt to be of limited use against a determined enemy, but could instil fear and disruption if they fell among mounted or native opponents. The Naval Brigades used them during the Zulu wars in early 1879, allegedly with significant success. The Navy most often used the rocket with a wooden plug instead of the explosive or incendiary head, relying more on its impetus as the destructive force. According to some sources, it was some 4 inches in diameter, slightly under 2 feet long and weighed 24 pounds with a claimed best range of 1 to 2 miles, though it is doubtful if it landed anywhere near where it had been aimed, especially at that distance. With no warhead, I even wonder what real damage it might have inflicted had its flight been true. In September 1883, local residents in the vicinity of Woolwich Arsenal in London were rather unnervingly showered with the things following an explosion at the nearby Rocket Establishment where they were made.

I think the reader might be quietly diverted by the way the Congreve rocket worked, and is possibly why the Navy chose to dispense with an explosive head on the Hale War Rocket. The charge of dynamite at the front end of the Congreve was fused separately to the gun-powder powered body, so after the battery crew had loaded the rocket into its tube, they were required to first light the fuse on the explosive head and only when that was burning brightly could they proceed to light the other fuse on the body to send the device on its way; one can readily imagine the feelings of all in the vicinity of the launcher should this second fuse go *phhutt*.

The rocket was not the only unusual sight for WIT, as soon out of Singapore HMS *Iron Duke* encountered a British ship, HMS *Thistle*, flying her homeward-bound pennant from the masthead:

> "...I wish to say that we met a Gunboat homeward bound after 5 years in China. What happened is still fresh in my mind. In those day we used to wear White Hats for hot weather and Black hats of the same pattern in Winter and wet weather, so to dispose of these things they piped all hands to muster with Black Hat, and when the Gunboat was a short distance from us, the order was given to man the rigging, and at the third Cheer, the Hat's was to be thrown overboard. It was a sight, only think of it, to see 800 hats thrown in the air at one time after our cheers. You could hear the return from the Thistle who's Ships Company consist of about 135 to 140 Officers and Men. I have often thought of this, I have never seen it since."

Along with WIT, I cannot imagine this to have been a regularly practised tradition! *Thistle's* log for Thursday 19th September 1878 simply records meeting *Iron Duke* at Aden. Why HMS *Thistle* might have merited such particular acknowledgement seems most likely to be because around

1875/6 the ship was involved in an incident at Perak on the western side of the Malay Peninsula. Warring between Malay and Chinese factions spilled over into British controlled territory, and the British Resident, Mr. J. W. W. Birch was assassinated in November 1875. The resulting punitive action by the British involved land forces under General Colbourn supported by the naval brigades from a number of vessels including HMS *Thistle*, whose crew distinguished themselves so well that no less than 75 of them received medals and commendations. Since Aden is nowhere near Singapore, I wonder if WIT may have mixed his ships up, and might well be thinking of another, or perhaps it was simply the location he was confused over. Nevertheless, the black hats being thrown into the air and settling on the sea is a fine reminiscence, even if it really indicates an eccentric Captain.

A sad footnote to this story. Commanding HMS *Thistle* at this time was Commander Francis Stirling R.N., who had received consistent praise for his actions in the Perak campaign. In the section on the loss of HMS *Eurydice* in March 1878 contained in chapter 1, I note that the sister ship to *Eurydice* was HMS *Atalanta*, lost with all hands off Bermuda, in 1880. *Atalanta's* captain at the time was Francis Stirling.

Christmas Day 1878 was not one spent in celebration, but rather holding onto anything securely fixed to the ship and hoping the gale would soon blow itself out. The extra special Christmas Day fare was enjoyed by only those most hardened of sailors, who found they had plenty to gorge themselves on as the majority declined the treat. A very poorly WIT was offered a Manila cigar by one of the other boys, and it being the only day of the year that boys were permitted to indulge in the habit, was persuaded to take a few puffs; it was, perhaps, the one thing to take his mind off his sea-sickness, and went a long way to ingraining in the lad a hatred of tobacco which would last his lifetime.

Soon after arrival in Hong Kong, WIT left the solid platform of 6,000 tons of HMS *Iron Duke* to join the 300 ton sailing ship HMS *Lapwing*, Captain Scott, but this was also temporary. Passage to Shanghai in China followed where he eventually joined up with his new ship, HMS *Charybdis* commanded by Captain Charles F. Hotham. This vessel was a 2,000-ton, 21 gun wooden screw corvette of pleasing lines. It was in this vessel that WIT turned 18 years of age, and was rated a man, and finally marked the start of his 10 years of service.

Charybdis was the third vessel to carry the name of the mythical female Greek water-spouting sea-monster that, accompanied by its sister *Scylla*, guarded a narrow rocky passage in Neptune's Aegean Sea, the siblings being the origin of the now less-well-used phrase of sometimes being caught "...*between Scylla and Charybdis...*" where we might today say *between a rock and a hard place*. Launched in 1859, *Charybdis* was loaned for part of her later life to Canada before being sold in 1884. The fifth and penultimate HMS *Charybdis*, a *Dido* class cruiser, was lost in the disastrous Operation Tunnel in the channel in October 1943.

HMS Charybdis undergoing refitting at Esquimalt, British Columbia, Canada in 1870(?). I am not perfectly certain that the date is correct. (Public domain).

The new rating was a very important milestone for the sailor. Not only did his wages increase dramatically (from around seven old pence per day for a first class boy to one shilling and one penny), but also he was allowed his rum ration, 1 gill of rum mixed with one-and-a-half gills of water per day. Men were allowed to smoke in the evening, but as you may have already anticipated, WIT declined this privilege. Another, more attractive advantage, was an improvement in leave. Boys were only permitted leave in certain ports, basically where they were less likely to be shanghaied or defrauded, or even worse, by the many rogues who frequented major ports of the day. Men were permitted more leave (when it was granted) in 4 rates, or classes, ranging from 1st Class Privilege (once or twice a week) down to 4th Class Habitual, once every 90 days or so. Loss of privilege due to breaking of leave or some other offence was therefore very much of a punishment.

I deliberately used the above phrase for abduction since Shanghai was at that time a port in which boys particularly were never permitted to enter alone; it was just not safe to do so, and even men usually didn't wander through it unaccompanied by a number of mates. The city name is the origin of the word although in truth, it seems to have been coined from the habit of abducting men to sail in ships heading *for* the port. In safe groups, sailors would walk through the English district, modelled as if it were straight out of a town lifted from the English countryside, then through other European Quarters, and finally the Chinese area in which the many dark and mysterious coffee shops and food houses held very little attraction even to an adventurous young man seeing them for the first time.

A strange sight to behold was the treatment of Chinese criminals under minor punishment, permitted to wander through the town unescorted but wearing a broad circular solid wooden disk, split in half but tightly buckled around their necks, so wide that their fully out-stretched finger tips could only just reach the edge and with the central hole a very snug fit around the throat. Not only was it tiresomely heavy, it made sleep very uncomfortable if not impossible. It was a crime for anyone to put food in their mouths; instead, anyone kind enough to wish to feed them (or more likely, who wanted a bit of sport) was required to place food on the edge of the board or even on the ground, and watch the prisoners wriggle and flip the board until with luck they could toss the morsel towards the centre of the board and catch it in their mouths - only then could they eat. The pastime was presumably less of a problem to habitual offenders, who had practised the art before, but punishment in nineteenth-century China was harsh, and perhaps hardened criminals found them-selves subject to a more unpleasant retribution. Be that as it may, I feel a return to such traditional punishment for minor offences could improve the behaviour of today's youngsters no end, and provide a similar level of free entertainment for their victims.

Charybdis sailed for Japan, and in Yokohama WIT saw his old ship HMS *Iron Duke* sail into the bay early one Sunday morning with Admiral Coote commanding the China fleet. The signal from the flag ship that an inspection would take place the next day, was followed by an order for the rig of the day, in this case: "*The Rig of the Day: White Hat, White Trousers and Check Shirt.*" Whether this was some kind of joke on the part of the Officer of Day wasn't clear, but it caused consternation in *Charybdis* since only the few men straight out from Britain still had this particular rig (known irreverently as the "*Zebra*" rig) in their kit. The Captain, having with mounting horror perused the signal with his First Lieutenant, hastened to the stores where the Steward assured him that somewhere in the hold would be some check shirts. At the same time, a frantic request went out to all the new men to share if they had a spare. The entire content of the hold was dragged out until, right at the back, the two bales of check shirts were eventually located. All the stores were then hastily dragged back as other men cleaned and polished the bright work before each being issued with a brand new check shirt for the inspection. Admiral Coote was, it seems, most surprised at the turn out which was, most probably, an inadvertent error in the order by his junior officer.

After a number of adventures in Russian waters, with trips back to Japan and China, *Charybdis* received orders to head for home, and returned to Singapore to await her relief, a new screw corvette on her first commission, HMS *Curacoa*, one of the early *Comus* class cruisers. After the orders were handed over, *Charybdis* set sail in April 1880 for the long voyage home to England, via the *Cape of Good Hope* and Simon's Town in South Africa. A few years later, WIT would make this voyage in the other direction in *Calliope*. It was on 16th October 1880 that WIT arrived back in Plymouth, England after his first voyage away from his country. HMS *Charybdis* was paid off on 9th November 1880 and the crew dispersed.

WIT returned from leave in January 1881 to walk straight into a strange dispute. His words describe it as:

> *"When I returned off my leave, and joined the Royal Naval Barracks at Sheerness under Captain McFarland. After joining the barrack, you passed the Doctor to certify you was in good health, then came the worst of all, for at that time, a great clothing dispute was in force, and everyone had to go through the Mill, P.O's as well as the A.B's. When you mustered your kit, the Ship's Police came and measuring your collars of Serge, Frock, Jumpers and other parts of your cloths, and if the collar was 1/2 inch longer than regulation, they would cut it with scissors, and not ask you, or give you a chance to alter it so you might make a neat job of it. If anyone made a complaint, they would get punished as it would be put down as a Disobeying Order's. So we had to stand by and see our cloths cut and spoilt that which we had taken so much pains to make ourselves. For we had to pay for everything in those days, and if you passed from one Port to another, you had to comply with Order of that Port."*

This dispute seems to have been a local one, since I have found nothing official about a crackdown being enforced from on-high. It does seem petty, and WIT's outrage at the damage caused to clothes he had made himself seems understandable. *"To go through the mill"* was an expression meaning to put up with some irksome imposition or task, and has dropped out of common use following the Second World War. At least the pain was not solely imposed on the seamen.

Work in the dockyards stopped when the *Great Blizzard* hit the country. The 18th January 1881 blizzard is on record as one of the worst ever experienced in the south-east of England. Trains were supposedly buried in upwards of 16 feet of snowdrift. The seas in the Channel and North Sea were amongst the most violent ever known, and shops and houses were flooded in many coastal communities. There was widespread destruction along the Kent coast in particular.

During his period at Sheerness, WIT worked on refitting the corvette *Champion* whose masts were found to be too lofty during trials in the Channel and which needed alteration, and Britain's first ever torpedo boat *TB1*, also known as HMS *Lightning*. This vessel was being fitted with a *"guide blade"* screw, basically a ducted propeller. WIT states it was originally made at Mr. Yarrow's yard, but I think this may have been a misunderstanding on his part. The records show it to have been built at Thorneycroft, Chiswick, Yard number 47 in 1876, though TB17 and TB18 had been built at Yarrow in 1878.

In March 1881, WIT was drafted to the Flagship of the Nore, HMS *Duncan*, a Wooden line of Battleship, Capt. Mustan, after Capt. De Arcy. HMS *Duncan* was, at the time WIT joined her, stationed at Sheerness as a harbour flagship and in 1882 became a barracks ship. He remained in her until she was paid off on the 31st December 1881, was given leave, and returned to Portsmouth and joined HMS *Duke of Wellington* (Captain Anningworth) waiting to proceed to the Gunnery School. Events intervened when, as WIT describes it, the Egyptian War came on and ships, and the men to operate them, were suddenly needed for action. WIT was drafted to HMS *Sultan*, Captain Walter Hunt Grubb, later Sir and someone we will meet again. After commissioning, fitting out, coaling and provisioning ship as quickly as possible, the vessel left for Plymouth. Arriving there, the ship was again coaled and left immediately for Gibraltar, there to coal again.

HMS *Sultan* was an Edward Reed-designed central-battery ironclad, launched from Chatham Dockyard in 1870, and originally named HMS *Triumph*. She was quite a size, 5,234 BM (Builders Measure) tonnage with a complement of 633 men. She had eight 10-inch and four 9-inch muzzle-loading rifles.

HMS *Sultan*'s arrival at Malta, where coal, provisions, ammunition and other stores were taken on board, was the first real opportunity to grant leave to the ship's company, but it was rudely interrupted. An urgent order was received to proceed with all speed to Alexandria and terminated the second watch leave early. At 4 a.m. the gun was fired and the Blue Peter hoisted to call all the men off leave, and just over 2 hours from the order being received, HMS *Sultan* was off to war.

HMS Sultan c.1875. (Public domain, a download from the American Naval History and Heritage Command).

The bombardment of Alexandria in 1882, its causes and repercussions, has been the subject of a number of books, and it would be wrong of me to try and reproduce the official data here in what would be a highly condensed précis. But WIT's memories of his experiences during that time do deserve to be recorded in full, and in his own words:

> *"…we arrived at Alexandria where we found the Mediterranean Fleet under Admiral Sir F Beauchamp Seymour.*
>
> *"The following ships were assembled, 'Alexandra', 4 guns, 25 Ton and Ten 18 Tons, 'Invincible', Fourteen Guns, 'Inflexible', four 81 ton guns in turrets, 'Temeraire', four 25 ton and four 18 ton guns, 'Sultan', Twelve guns, 'Superb', 16 guns, 'Monarch', six guns, 'Penelope' Eleven guns.*
>
> *"Those which I have mentioned were all classed First Class Battleships, all of which were some of the finest Battleships of that time. Also there was the following gunboats, 'Condor', 'Bittern', 'Cygnet', 'Beacon' and 'Decoy', each carrying four guns. I am only naming the big guns carried by Battleships, as it would take a long time to explain each class of gun carried by the different ships. All ships carried Machine Guns, Gardiner and Nordenfelt Guns.*

"Well, after joining the Fleet, Drills was carried out daily under the orders of the Admiral who would visit one of the ships when least expected and order a drill to be performed whilst he was on board, and it was never known to what ship he was to visit, so it kept us all in trim. (I am giving the account of the foregoing from memory as I never attempted to keep a log as it was not allowed in some ships, and so all I am stating is what I remember of the different things that occurred).

"Well, all things were not going very favourably on shore, and no settlement could be come to. From the ships anchored in the bay, you could see great preparation going on; but still we carried on with drills and other work until 10th July 1882. Then we knew something was on the move, for we all cleared ships for action, and making every preparation for splinters flying by making splinter nets. So the day passed and night came on, and in the evening the Boatswain's Mate Piped the word that every man was to make out his "Will", and place it in his Ditty Box. So ended the evening. 10.0 p.m. pipe down was the order so all hands went and turned in, except those on duty. Early morning, Hands was called, hammocks lashed up and stowed, then to Breakfast. Then the order to weigh anchor and this was done. Battle Line was formed and we steamed up towards Fort Pharao which is a Island. The Fleet turned and was proceeding back. (During all this time, the Ship's Companies had been at their Action Stations awaiting orders).

"When the Challenge gun fired, there was no waiting for the reply was a blaze of fire all along the fortified coast, and then the Bugle sounded Action. And action it was, every man doing his bit and the guns loaded and fired as quickly as possible. In those days, everything was done by hand, and it was nothing to see the men trying to lift the Projectile up before the Shell Whip could be hooked on; so the work went on. Shells exploding all around us and a good many hits were made, for we had 2 killed and several wounded by a shell which came in at the back of the Forecastle. There was several minor accidents during the day, I cannot explain all that took place on board for I was at my Gun in the Main Battery, one of the 18 ton guns carrying a shot 410 lbs.

"The fighting continued all day. We relieved Guns Crew after we anchored as we put a Kedge anchor out and swung broadside on so as to engage the Fort allotted our ship, the Lighthouse Fort, and we knew it was there for they gave us a warm time of it until last in the afternoon, when the wind from the sea helped us a lot, for when a broadside was fired the smoke blew toward the land and they could not see us so clearly. Now during all the day, we did not know what might happen to any of us for we were fighting in a new class of ship which had never been in action before. As it was the trial of the steel ship which superseded the Old Wooden Walls of the Crimea in 1854 & 5. So may think of our thoughts all that day through, to know if was to come out on top, which it proved for the future that ships of the class could hold its own against Forts.

"So our days fighting was done, for they all seemed to cease fire at one time, except an occasional round, and then you could hear the shot pass over or fall short in the water. The signal was made from the Flagship to cease fire, so anchor was weighed and we formed into line and proceed to the Anchorage, and anchored for the night.

"The following morning, the killed was taken out to sea and buried with the usual Naval Honours. On the return of the Funeral Parties to their respective ships, the Fleet weighed anchor and formed in line and proceeded along the coast, but no guns were fired, but on the approach of 'Inflexible' toward Fort Pharao she observed great movements going on, so she dropped one of her 100 ton gun shells on the Fort, and a great explosion took place and then everything was quiet. During this time, the gunboats were busy under the Forts, if small this class of ship done a lot of damage to the forts, and also to the people who manned the guns in the forts.

"I cannot say much about the other ships of the Fleet, as we had our own duties to perform, but I am sure that every one did their duty well, and also every ship done what was expected of them, no praise could be given to any one ship.

"So ended that part of the work, then came the Landing Parties from different ships who landed when great caution had to be taken in clearing the City of all the enemy, and a great task it was for they pillaged and fired the houses as they retired and it became more dangerous as we proceeded amongst the larger buildings for the high walls seemed to shake and look like falling at any moment, but we had to go on through it and pleased we were when we got into more open space, so we could see about. So we went on until the city had been combed out, and no enemy left in it to do any harm.

"The Naval Brigade had performed this work before the Military arrival, which was brought up as soon as possible and glad we were to turn over this work to them.

"We again returned to our ships and off we went to Abukia Bay where they had other strong Forts and everything was made ready for a combined attack by Land and Sea; our part was to attack by water, so *boats was manned and armed, and the guns was loaded and trained already for the attack. The boats was taken in tow by Steam Boats and all left for the attack at the same time Military made their forward attack. But the enemy did not wait, they took to the train which waiting for them and so ended Abukia Forts and all boats was recalled to their respective ships.*

"We stayed in Abukia Bay waiting orders, which was signals by searchlights made in the sky which could be plainly seen, the Orders came at last and we proceeded back to Alexandria, and found several ships of the Channel Fleet had arrived, and then everything was prepared for a Naval Brigade for to land and take over the outer places around the city which we occupied, and the Military was making their preparations for a Great forward march; during this the 1st Armoured Train was brought into being, mounting a 40 pounder in the truck prepared for it and it proved of great value, it was always on the move.

"It was not all honey for the Naval Brigade, as they were at the call of anyone, and it was hard work as we had our own work and was called on to help any other, the work sometimes taking hours and then we had to mount guard during the night, but it had to be done, so it was always 'Jack can do this' and 'Jack can do that'. Yes, and any other things which came along, but it was always done cheerfully and so was completed with a spirit of good cheer. During our time ashore, we had to sleep under the Canopy of Heaven, as we had no other means of cover, only our blankets.

"Well time went on, day by day, and weeks followed and during this time the forces were making their movements for the great attack which the People at Home knew more about than we did, for we got no news. We often made sallys, so as to keep the enemy on the move. And that is all we knew about the Great Battle of Telekaba and break up of Ariba Pasha Army.

"We went back to the ships, and then we left to recoup as there was a lot of men ill, so we had a trip around the Grecian Isles and went from place to place until the crew was brought back to health again."

To explain a little of WIT's memoir: his *Fort Pharao* is today, I am guessing, *Fort Pharos*. A sailor most often constructed his own *ditty box*, usually a wooden box with an opening lid, hinged at the rear, with a simple lock. In it he placed his most treasured possessions – which were admittedly probably few. Perhaps a simple likeness and a lock of his sweetheart's hair, his pay-book, a few clothes and things like that. Sailor's ditty boxes were highly personal, and a grievous crime it was to interfere with someone else's.

Admiral Seymour's report on the bombardment lists forts Ada and Pharos as returning fire at the off-shore squadron.

I think WIT's concern about ships taking on forts is that a fort is a formidable enemy for a ship to engage. Although stationary, so in most cases was the bombarding vessel, so there was little advantage there. A fort had a large stock of powder and shell, usually safely stowed out of harm's way; whilst a ship had limited stocks which were nevertheless a serious liability should they be hit. A fort could have several very large rifles, out-gunning any but the largest battleships, and had the ultimate advantage of not being liable to sink. Wooden hulled ships as used in the Crimean campaign would have been at much greater risk from forts, and indeed, there is a very tenuous connection that joins that war, and WIT's concerns, to Apia in Samoa. I'll digress to that later.

Where WIT refers to *Abukia Bay* I am again guessing that he means what is, now at least, *Aboukir Bay* and *Telekaba* as *Tel-el-Kebir*.

I think a very short précis of the background might help the reader understand all this, so here is a very brief piece of history about this interesting campaign, as it could be considered a precursor to the uprising in the *Soudan*, the siege of *Khartoum* and the death of Gordon. As I have already stated, if detailed information is required, there are many books about this campaign that will be better than anything of mine.

In the time of Lord Beaconsfield's administration, the unsettled conditions in Egypt had led to the establishment of a "Dual Control"; that is, France and Great Britain, without actually taking direct management of the government, exercised a joint form of control over the Khedive and his administration. In 1881, the anti-European party, headed by Arabi Pasha, succeeded in dominating the Egyptian Government. As a result, in 1882, a riot was fomented in Alexandria, in which a number of Europeans were murdered. It appeared to the Admiral of the British squadron lying at Alexandria, Sir Beauchamp Seymour, that Arabi was aiming at a military dictatorship. It seems probable the riot was an attempt to gauge the strength of British reaction. After sundry warnings to Arabi, Admiral Seymour decided to bombard the Pasha's fortifications on the 11th July; the French refused to support the British and had already withdrawn their fleet. Seymour carried out the operation by himself - it is this engagement described by WIT. A direct struggle between Arabi and the Egyptian army was now inevitable. The French once more declined to intervene; and a British expedition was dispatched under Sir Garnet Wolseley. Two months after the bombardment of Alexandria, Arabi was completely crushed at Tel-el-Kebir.

The British Government re-established an Egyptian Government acting under British *advice*, with the promise of prompt withdrawal of British control once the Egyptian Government was seen to be self supportable.

But events elsewhere interfered with these plans. South of Egypt, in the Soudan, a Mohammedan fanatic, the epithet given him by the British, calling himself *the Mahdi* (Muhammad Ahmad) set himself up as ruler. Egyptian troops sent to quell the uprising were destroyed in November of 1883. Rather than taking on another adversary in the region so soon, the British Government settled on a policy of withdrawal, and the task of withdrawing the British garrisons was entrusted to General Charles George Gordon. The Mahdi, however, was intent on confrontation, and Gordon found himself trapped in the siege of Khartoum. With initial ignorance by the British military of the seriousness of the situation, much precious time was lost before a magnificent effort under Sir Charles Wilson reached the city in January 1885; just two days after its fall and the dreadful massacre of the entire garrison, including Gordon himself.

This victory led Muhammad Ahmad to become the ruler of most parts of what is modern day Sudan, and established a religious state, the Mahdiyah, that was governed by Sharia, a harsh and unyielding enforcement of Islamic law. But he was not destined to enjoy his success for long, dying in June 1885 though the state he founded survives him still.

HMS *Sultan* returned to Gibraltar to join the Channel Fleet and set off into the Atlantic where a trial was performed that left WIT in awe for the rest of his life. After seeing how the steel ships had performed in battle under steam, it was now time to test them under sail alone. The entire fleet was made to join in a 12 hour race starting at 6 a.m. in which no steam was allowed, but every tiny handkerchief of sail was fair game. Plain sail, studding sail (extensions to the yards outboard of the ship) and even the sails on the cutters lashed to the deck were set to catch every ounce of wind possible. WIT records it as a magnificent sight, and I am sure it was, and one surely never to be seen again. It seems a shame the only non-sailors to enjoy it were flying fish and the skipping clouds. *Sultan* gradually drew ahead of the 10,600 ton monsters, the 5-masted *Minotour* and her sister ship *Agincourt*, and eventually won the day.

After further adventures that included towing a broken-down Dutch mail boat to St. Vincent, *Sultan* returned to Gibraltar where the ship's crew received their medals for the Egyptian campaign, the Egyptian Medal from Her Majesty's Government and the Khedive's Star from Khedive Tewfik Pasha.

A line drawing of one of HMS Sultan's large guns being run out during the bombardment of Alexandria. (Illustrated London News, No.2254 — Vol. LXXXI, Saturday, July 15, 1882, p.53).

In 1884, the fleet left for Bantry Bay in Ireland, before *Sultan* returned to Spithead on Saturday 4th August 1884 after 2½ years at sea. WIT seems to have been pleased to get back, as from a 50 year old memory he records the time as precisely 11.35 in the morning! I have no proof that by then they had already met, and that his enthusiasm was therefore romantic, but on 25th October 1884, WIT married Jane Dowling at St Peter's Church in the tiny parish of Portsea Island. I cannot believe WIT would wed precipitously, so I am sure that somehow he and Jane had already met and become engaged, and that it was indeed his forthcoming nuptials that had delighted WIT so much on reaching England.

Jane was the daughter of a Surrey family named Dowling that had deep roots in the area round WIT's home town of Reigate, so she might well have been a childhood acquaintance, or someone he had met whilst on leave. Her mother was Harriet nee Rapley; her father William was a shoe or boot-maker, and she was a general domestic servant, having been born 18th April 1858. Her brother Jesse was a gamekeeper at a big house near Guildford, and her niece, Eva Annie Dowling would become the mother of Great Britain's most celebrated brother and sister film producers of the twentieth-century: Sydney and Betty Box. Betty produced many films including the "*Doctor In ...*" series, and married Peter Rogers who produced all the "*Carry On...*" films, whilst Sydney, with his first wife Muriel, won the 1947 Oscar for Best Original Screenplay for "*The Seventh Veil*". My mother was immensely proud of her second cousins, and my siblings and I were always taken to Brighton to see a Betty or Sidney Box film as soon as it came down from its London showing.

WIT was now a Leading Seaman, well-trained and competent, and embarking on the trials and rewards provided by a married life. But his ability to handle the sails on a military ship had for a while been threatened by steam, and the ship on which he was to endure the most awful risks and excitement of his life must now enter the tale; the *other woman* feared by so many navy wives, his next ship: HMS *Calliope*.

Chapter 3: HMS *Calliope*.

CUR-LIE-OH-PEA ... is the nearest phonetic pronunciation I can get to the way the name has always been spoken within my family. The American version seems to harden the first syllable to *CAL* as in calorie rather than *CUR* as in curtain (or better, *CUH*), but whatever is your preference, please *do not* pronounce the name to rhyme with *Sally-Hope* unless you wish the spirits of a few hundred angry sailors to disturb your night's repose.

Classically, Calliope was the muse of eloquence and epic poetry, the fair-voiced sister and eldest daughter of Zeus and Mnemosyne - please feel free to choose your own pronunciation for that one. Καλλιοπε is the Greek rendition, literally meaning: *beautiful voice*. I have to say it seems to me a very fine name for a human female. Mechanically, it is a steam-powered, fairground organ popular in the States, and in nature *Selasphorus Calliope* is a tiny humming bird. The name has also been used, not surprisingly, for more than one musical group. All these associations of the name might conjure up visions of musical sounds and gentleness, of garden fêtes on a warm summer's day, of peace and harmony and sweetness, but this didn't prevent the British Royal Navy finding the name so attractive for their warships that it should be used a number of times.

Naval history claims the first HMS *Calliope* as a small *Cherokee* class brig also described as a *ten-gun sloop*, built by John Dudman and launched at Deptford in 1808. These Henry Peake designed vessels had two square-rigged masts, an enormous bow-sprit, and despite an initial nick-name of *coffin-brigs* as five of the class were lost between 1810 and 1813, they eventually worked well under sail. This *Calliope* served well against the French, in October 1810 capturing the 14-gun privateer *Comtesse d'Hambourg* after a protracted and thrilling North Sea chase and generally providing at least one of her commanders, Captain John M'Kerlie, with a good living. By August 1829, her leaking, fetid holds could be patched up no longer, and she was found to be so severely unseaworthy in nearly every respect, that there had been no alternative but to break her up.

HMS Chanticleer, a Cherokee class brig launched in July 1808 a few weeks after the first HMS Calliope. This is the closest image to that HMS Calliope I can find, and is a pencil and watercolour by Nicolas Cammillieri . The two ships will have been to all intents and purposes identical. (Public Domain).

The next *Calliope*, a 6th rate 26-gun *Andromache* class frigate of 709 tons, was built at Sheerness Dockyard and was launched in October 1837, crewed by 24 officers, 39 petty officers, 69 seamen, 33 first and second class boys, and 35 marines. She was a three-mast vessel, square rigged on all of them. The *rate* of a ship roughly defined the number of guns, and effectively indicated the size, a *first rate* being the most powerful. The definition was changed over the years and doesn't seem to have been applied rigidly in all cases. During the fifteenth-century there were only three divisions of ship: "*Great Ships*", "*Middling Ships*" and "*Small Ships*". James I changed the system to introduce four "rates", First, Second, etc. It was Charles I who introduced the two additional rates. Later came terms such as "*line-of-battle-ship*" and "*ship-of-the-line*".

On 29th January 1840, the second HMS *Calliope* was the first naval visitor to a small but thriving new colony set up on a spit of land in New Zealand and named by Captain William Hobson in honour of the first Sea Lord of the Admiralty at the time: Lord Auckland. In recognition of *Calliope*'s visit, a point in Auckland harbour was named after her. There is an enduring misconception that Auckland's Calliope Dock, in its time the largest dock in the southern hemisphere, was named for "our" *Calliope* which was the first to use it during a visit in April 1888. The fact that the Samoan HMS *Calliope* happened to be in the area and so could visit Auckland Harbour at the time of opening was coincidental, and not to invite her to be the first to use Calliope Dock during the grand opening would have been strange indeed. The dock (now *Devonport Dock*) was originally named after the point, and the point was named after that earlier *Calliope's* visit in 1840.

The only image of the second HMS Calliope I have been able to find. It is a watercolour by Francis Meynell R.N. executed at Garden Reach, Calcutta, 1841. HMS Calliope is being towed by a naval paddle wheel tugboat. (Public Domain).

This second *Calliope* was a well-travelled vessel and enjoyed, or endured, many adventures around the oceans of the world. One of her many logs record that one of her sailing masters, Captain Robert Knox, was always ready to bring out the lash in the times before corporal punishment of that type was stopped.

In the first half of 1840 her then captain, Thomas Herbert RN (later Rear-Admiral Sir Thomas Herbert, KCB, MP and eventually Third Lord of the Admiralty) whilst in South America, regained for the nation by purchasing for the not inconsiderable sum of 50 guineas, the "K2" chronometer, manufactured in 1772 by Mr. Larcum Kendall as a second official copy of Mr. Harrison's prize-winning "H4" - a cost of more than £5,000 in today's money. What a shame these august mechanics were not as inventive in their choice of chronometer names as was the Royal Navy for its ships.

K2 had been built for £200 as a much cheaper version of K1 (£500 in 1770, over £90,000 in today's value) but, whilst still good, was not as successful. In 1773, K2 went to Spitsbergen in HMS *Racehorse*, followed by a few other trips until ending up with Lieutenant Bligh for the 1787 expedition to Tahiti, fitted in HMS *Bounty* as part of the scientific aspect of her now infamous mission to take bread-fruit plants to the West Indies. The mutineers took K2 off the ship before they burned the vessel at Pitcairn Island. After a few adventures of its own, and some difficult times for the men through whose hands it passed, it now resides in the Royal Observatory's National Maritime Museum at Greenwich along with K1 (taken to the Pacific by Captain Cook in 1772 and 1776) and K3 (by Lt. Flinders to Australia in 1801). Before being bought by Herbert, its previous owner (whose family sold it on his death) was supposedly a muleteer named Castillo who had paid three doubloons for it in around 1830. I don't know what value that might represent today, but it doesn't sound much; it was a wonderful investment for his family at any rate.

The commander of the Far East Fleet in November 1841, James Bremner, arrived on HMS *Calliope* at what was to be named *Possession Point* on the coastline of Hong Kong Island, later ceded to Great Britain under the Treaty of Nanking in August 1842 and now returned to Chinese control. During a later voyage, the vessel took Governor Fitzroy along a river in Queensland, Australia in 1854 on a surveying trip; to celebrate this event the inhabitants of the nearby gold-mining settlement of *Nuggetty Gulley* changed the name of the local river to Calliope, and later the township itself was named Calliope after the river. It is today a thriving community justly proud of their heritage. Given the subject of this book, it seems almost disloyal to admit it, but I would love to live in a town called Nuggetty Gulley.

In 1849, the ship was back in England where a serious accident on board on the 8th February 1851 at Devonport resulted in the death of Surgeon's Assistant Mr. Nettleton, and serious injuries to the Captain, Sir Everard Home; also to the Quartermaster; to seamen Jenkins and Dominey and to Oxford a Marine. However, the injured men were all fit when she left on her next voyage and were present when the vessel was struck by lightning a few days before arriving in Sydney. Little damage to the vessel was caused. On 7th November 1853, Captain Sir J. Everard Home died on board after an illness, a great sadness to the officers and crew. On the 9th June 1855, she returned to Plymouth after her last voyage away from her homeland.

So after a long and distinguished career, this *Calliope* was broken up in November 1883, an act which ignominiously ended a life of stirring action that had degenerated from a warship of the greatest maritime power on Earth via a seaman's chapel at Plymouth to a prolonged sad existence as a mast-less, floating factory in a stinking river backwater near Devonport.

Coincident with the hardly noticed final death rattle of a once fine and proud warship, the last of a group of eleven "C" class corvette cruisers was on the stocks in the Portsmouth dockyard, and looking for a name to follow the sequence defined by *Comus, Carysfort, Champion, Cleopatra, Conquest, Curacoa, Constance, Canada, Cordelia* and *Calypso,* so the choice had perhaps been fairly easy to make. Another fair-voiced maiden would thus be sent into the world to speak the name of Victoria and her government wherever it needed to be heard.

The third HMS Calliope in Portsmouth Harbour c.1887 (Public domain, a download from the American Naval History and Heritage Command).

A corvette is often described as a frigate with a single gun deck, but to me at least, the phrasing is slightly ambiguous, since in the days of sail, a vessel with three masts all square rigged and a bowsprit such as *Calliope,* was officially termed a *"ship",* and such rigging was said to be a *"ship rig"*. It doesn't really matter for the purposes of this story, and the reader is urged to consult the reference books if he wishes any detailed explanation.

The longish gap between *Cordelia* (launched October 1881) and

Calypso (launched June 1883) has lead to *Calypso* being thought of as a new class leader, and *Calliope* being quoted as the second of the *Calypso* class. Fred T. Jane (of *"Jane's Fighting Ships"* fame), groups all eleven cruisers together as *Comus* class but today seems isolated in that view, and it is fair to say that *Comus* (launched 9 years earlier) and *Calypso* were dissimilar in many ways and were really a different class technically if not militarily. HMS *Calypso* was, outwardly at least, a larger version of HMS *Comus* but photographs of all the various vessels show them to be very difficult for an amateur such as myself to distinguish.

So a *Calliope* had carried Britain's flag along the marine highways and round the then often uncharted back-waters of her once extensive empire for many years before Sir Nathaniel Barnaby (1829-1915), the foremost British Naval architect of his time, had sat down at his desk in 1875 and sketched out his plans for a new design of lightly armoured cruiser; a screw corvette intended from the outset as a steam-powered, steel-hulled, long-range, manoeuvrable fighting ship - HMS *Comus*. Plans that, highly modified for each successive vessel as practice and changing theory refined the design and new naval requirements made further alterations to the principles, were finally drawn up and labelled for the fabrication of the last of the type, indeed the last British screw corvette to be built in the United Kingdom: HMS *Calliope*.

As stated, she had a "full ship rig" and was therefore classified as "ship-rigged": three square-rigged masts with which to augment her steam power, the fore- and main-masts each being furnished with 4 levels of sail: "coarse" or "main-sails" located on the lower yard of the lower mast; "top-sails" on the top-sail yard, and located on the topmast; "top-gallant" yards and sails and above them, "royal" yards and their sails, both located on the top-gallant mast. Note that some ships apparently had more levels of sail above the royals: in ascending order, the "sky-sails", "moonrakers"and even others rejoicing in various outlandish names such as "heaven poker", "angel poker, "cloud disturber", "Trust to God" and "angel whispers". *Calliope*'s designer restricted himself to the four levels of sail on the front two square-rigged masts, that classic style known as a "ship-rig".

Lyon and Winfield in reference [26] describe Calliope as "barque-rig" which is clearly incorrect: a "barque" had 3 masts with only the fore- and main-mast carrying square sails, the after-mast (mizzen) being rigged "fore-and-aft".

In case you are wondering about the names of the mast sections, when a sailing ship designer first put an additional sail above the "courses" - at the time, the single level of sail - he provided a second, smaller mast to take it, and naturally assumed that would be the limit, so called the additional mast and sail the "topmast" and "top-sail". However, as more sails were added above the top-sail, the Royal Navy, at least, did not want to change the names of sails that sailors had over many years become accustomed to, and just left the top-sail and topmast so named, despite it no longer being at the top of the complete mast.

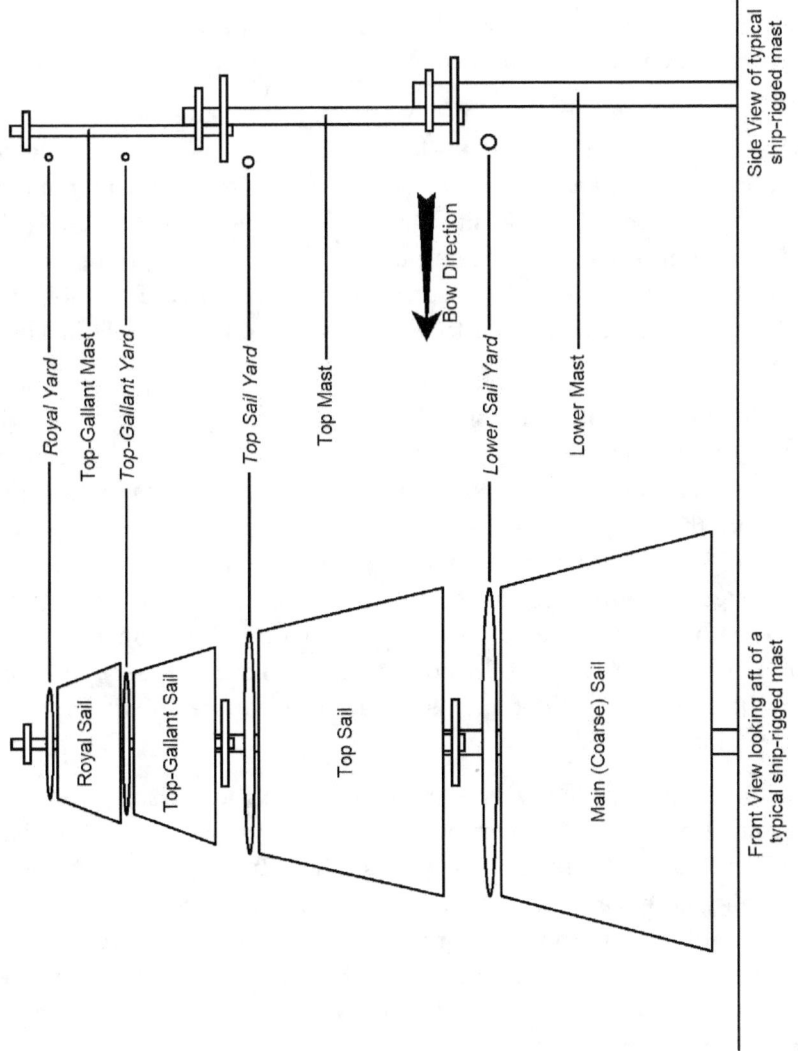

A highly stylised representation of a "ship rig" sail layout on the fore- and main- masts of a "ship-rigged" vessel.

Another complication arose when the topmast became so large (as the evolving manufacturing and rigging techniques permitted), the top-sail bent to it became too heavy to manage, and it then became necessary to split the top-sail into two levels of sail on that mast, which were then called the "lower-top sail" and "upper-top sail"!

Despite the fact that before even her keel had been laid, it had always been expected that she would sail many more miles than she would steam, Barnaby had never been beguiled into compromising her steam abilities in favour of the wind. After Samoa, nor would the designers of at least two other nations, and as we shall see later, *Calliope's* sailing distance expectations ended up rather unfulfilled.

The transverse hull frames were iron, but the hull itself was designed in steel, that is the skin plating, transverse bulkheads, longitudinal skeleton, and so on. The steel hull was encased either side in wood, and this form of composite structure was intended to utilise the strength of the iron whilst combining it with the fabricating techniques of the carpenter. Such *sandwich* type construction methods are the staple of modern aircraft and naval vessels today, effectively only the materials have changed.

The hull bottom was sheathed in a fouling resistant material intended to reduce the need for prolonged stays in dry dock to clean the hull. *Muntz Metal*, an alloy of 60% copper with 40% zinc was named after its inventor, the British businessman George F. Muntz and had been patented in 1832. The *teredo*, known as shipworm but technically a mollusc, was a damaging scourge to wooden vessels in tropical and Pacific waters, and the sheathing was aimed at reducing fouling and hull damage caused by it, thus extending the vessel's operational limits. Perversely, although the sheathing worked well, problems would be encountered with the bolts that attached it to the hull.

The bow, confidently jutting forward like the set and prominent chin of some powerful boxer, carried a large forged brass underwater ram, and the same material was used for her stern and body posts. In the event of it becoming necessary to put the ram to its deadly purpose, the bowsprit could be rapidly run-in to protect it from the destruction it would clearly otherwise risk. The bow led into graceful hull lines that were interrupted only by gun port sponsons, leading finally to the curved stern overhanging her single large screw.

The ram bow would become very popular in military ships of this time, but rather than as a weapon, the underwater protrusion deflected some of the water as the ship proceeded, and assisted the vessel to cleave through the seas, giving an hydrodynamic reduction and so slightly increasing the vessel's speed. It is not sure if this was a surprise to designers of the time, or if someone had deduced it would do so. Modern large tankers also employ a large bulbous underwater extension to the keel for the same reason.

Two relatively powerful engines drove this propeller, being supplied with steam from six boilers and furnaces. The engines were horizontal-compound, double-expansion, reciprocating units, and had a design power of 3,000 Indicated Horse Power, some 600 more than the other ships of her class. I should point out that Wikipedia quotes a single engine of four cylinders as do Lyon and Winfield [26], but Conway [20] and Swan [13} both suggest two engines "in tandem".

Before being vented through the smoke stack to assist the draught, or condensed to water to be used again, the exhausted steam from the high pressure cylinders was used as the driving force in a second set of low pressure cylinders of much larger diameter, thereby making the engine considerably more efficient and less costly in coal to run.

The phrase "compound-engine" when referring to a marine steam engine suggests that the steam is expanded in two cylinders, but in fact there may be more. The "double-expansion" identification is often used in place of "compound" and indicates that the steam is initially introduced into the "high-pressure" cylinder via the inlet valve, where it drives the piston downwards. After about a quarter of the piston travel, the inlet valve closes, the remainder of the movement of the piston being achieved by the still expanding steam, which therefore does the work required without further using the boiler's steam pressure, so being much more economic and efficient. At the end of the piston's travel, the exhaust valve opens and as the piston moves up the cylinder, the steam, still at some pressure, is passed to the next stage, the low-pressure cylinder, where the function is much the same. Because the pressure is lower, however, to extract the work requires a larger cylinder volume, usually obtained by increasing the diameter, or bore, of the cylinder rather than its stroke length. The system reduces the heat lost by the steam at each stage, simplifying the cooling requirements for the engine as a whole. Compound marine engines became virtually universal in steam ships after 1880. The definition "horizontal" indicates that the cylinder lies on its side, i.e. in a horizontal direction. "Reciprocating" simply means the piston moves side to side, driving a wheel via a crank to translate the motion from linear to rotational, needed to drive the propeller shaft of the vessel. In later vessels such as RMS *Titanic*, the pistons were aligned vertical; for many years the Royal Navy preferred the horizontal arrangement so that the machinery was kept below the vessel's water-line, where it was considered (originally at least) to be safer from damage in an engagement.

Barnaby and the shipbuilders were well aware that when it was required in a warship, the steam pressure must be reliable and the equipment which produced and made use of it highly capable. The order for the marine engines and boilers was placed with J. & G. Rennie & Sons, of Blackfriars and Greenwich, London, a well-established firm of engineers founded by the two sons of a very famous engineer, Sir James Rennie (1761-1821). This Scot, a man in the mould of Stevenson and Watt, had designed many high-profile engineering marvels, including the Southwark, Waterloo and London Bridges, although his equally competent sons, John and George, finally completed the latter. The most efficient version of marine screw design, the so-called *conoidal propeller*, had been patented by George (1791-1866) in around 1839/40, long before his firm manufactured *Calliope*'s engines, and still forms the basis of today's modern propeller designs. The boilers were steel comb chamfers, with end plates of iron, and were fitted in the hull with an anticipated eight-year life.

I haven't seen it myself, but I am advised there is a restored J & G Rennie compound steam-powered pumping engine in the Brunel Engine House at Rotherhithe. A number of Rennie products had been displayed in the 1876 South Kensington Museum exhibition. The company appear to have left London for Essex around 1915, where they became the Rennie-Forrest Shipbuilding Co. of Wivenhoe, near Colchester, but don't seem to be trading any more, or at least, not under that name. I found just one source that states the company was wound up in 1923.

Calliope was officially a 2,770-ton screw corvette, but she differed markedly from the earlier ships of the class and with *Calypso* (launched the previous year) benefited enormously in being the last, incorporating many hard-learned innovations, amendments and enhancements to the original concept. The immediate "C" class predecessor to these last two vessels, HMS *Cordelia*, had been launched more than 30 months earlier, and the sailing characteristics she had displayed were invaluable when *Calliope*'s plans were marked up for the builders. Ten feet longer than the original of the type and with nearly 400 tons more displacement, *Calliope* was some 235 feet (71 metres) in length between perpendiculars and 44 feet 6 inches (13.5 metres) in extreme breadth, with a mean draught of 18 feet 8 inches (5.7 metres).

At this point, it may be prudent to warn the reader that there is often a wide range of these data for ship dimensions, depending on where one obtains them. Whilst there are few *major* disparities between the sources of the data presented herein, where there are *minor* differences, it is difficult to know which version is definitive – if any is. Throughout this book, where I have described the physical details of a ship, it has been culled from a number of references as being, in my humble opinion, the most likely or a reasonable average. To be brutally frank, such pernickety worries about a few feet of length hardly seem to be important for this story, but this solution to the problem means that my data are not suitable for the reader to take as definitive references.

One of the historical criticisms of the Barnaby era of British Royal Navy shipbuilding was the perceived obstinate adherence to his own axiom that: *"The best defence is a powerful offence."* Although Barnaby always started off with the concept that his design was a fighting ship foremost, defence was by no means ignored in the "C" class corvettes, as implied by Barnaby's own description of them as *protected cruisers.* A steel shell-proof armoured deck one and a half inches thick (38 mm) covered the entire area over the engines, boilers and magazines, and was located some three and a half feet (1 metre) below the waterline. The usual description of a protected cruiser was that the armour was in deck form only, and did not include armoured sides, but in *Calliope's* case, additional armoured plating, nearly 1 inch thick (25 mm), sheathed the hull sides. Between the armoured and main decks, the exposed hull above the waterline was constructed of water-tight enclosed spaces, intended to limit any flooding caused by a shell penetrating the hull during battle.

Calliope's bunkers could hold 428 tons of coal with capacity for 100 tons more elsewhere, and ingeniously, this additional storage was in the sides of the hull; the *"coal armour"* in the side spaces being formed into two additional coal bunkers each side, one above the water-line and the other below, both providing additional resistance to shell penetration, and further restricting the flood damage if a shell should manage to pass through. The lower coal bunker could be emptied before the upper so preserving the more vulnerable above-water-line protection for as long as possible between re-coaling; torpedoes were at this time not the level of menace to warships they would very shortly become, and protection was thus always concentrated against an above-the-water-line threat from shell-fire.

Calliope was primarily a warship, and was therefore required to carry armament. In contrast to her *Comus* class predecessors, all of which had been armed with two 6-ton guns, and twelve 64-pounders all muzzle loaded, *Calliope* was provided with four 6 inch (5 ton) Mark IV breech-loaders on sponsons two on each side fore and aft; twelve 5 inch (38 hundred-weight) Mark II breech-loaders mounted on Vavasseur carriages six each side on the upper deck; four quick-firing four-barrel Nordenfelt guns and two two-barrel; and two five-barrel Gardner guns supplemented by two two-barrel.

The Nordenfelts were the primary defence against the recently developed and still not very effective torpedo threat. At this time and as had been the case for centuries before, a fighting ship in a one-on-one battle should fear nothing but another ship of equal or greater armament; to be concerned about bombs from above or torpedoes from under the surface of the sea on which she imperiously sailed were threats yet to make their presence really felt. Nevertheless, a further element in *Calliope*'s armament was a supply of six RL Mark V Whitehead torpedoes, which could be launched from two Torpedo Guns Mark VIa, discharged by powder and air impulse, a single tube located on each side of the ship. It seems few sea-going members of the Navy at that time regarded these devices as truly effective weapons. USS *Housatonic* was sunk in 1864 by a spar torpedo delivered by CSS *Hunley*, which failed to survive the mission, this being claimed as the first sinking of a warship by a submarine. Many claim the first sinking of a vessel by a self-acting and independent Whitehead torpedo to have been the 1891 destruction of the insurgent's flagship *Blanco Enchilada* by a torpedo from the Chilean cruiser *Almirante Lynch* during the Chilean Revolution of that year.

The breech loaders were a marked improvement over muzzle loaders, and it is strange for me to imagine that even in the 1870s Royal Navy ships were being designed to carry muzzle loading rifles that differed little from Nelson's time apart from the size and accuracy of the projectile fired by them. Though conceived many years before, problems with safely producing a breech-locking mechanism had significantly delayed the implementation of the more modern weapon.

The largest shell on board weighed some 100 pounds (45 kg), and required a 42-pound (19 kg) powder charge to launch it on its way. The six-Inch BL Mark I, a six inch Bore, Breech Loading rifle, had been first fitted to HMS *Rover* in around 1880; it had a length of 26.3 calibres, being a measure of the length of the barrel as a multiple of its bore, weighed 4 tons and discharged its 80 lb (36 kg) projectile with a muzzle velocity of about 1880 feet per second (570 metres per second). The much-improved Mark IV was introduced on a large number of ships a little later, including *Calypso* and *Calliope* during build and the last few of the *Comus* class vessels as retrofits. The Mark II fitted in HMS *Comus* had proved unsatisfactory and was replaced with the same muzzle loaders fitted in the rest of her class. The five-inch breech-loaders each weighed nigh on two tons, were 25 calibres in length, and fired a 50 lb (23 kg) projectile with a muzzle velocity of 1,750 feet per second (533 metres per second).

Calliope's launch at Portsmouth on 24th June 1884 was attended by many notable personages of the day. Most senior was Admiral Thomas E. Brandreth, Controller of the Navy and Third Lord of Admiralty; this position was one which underwent regular changes throughout the nineteenth-century as reforms to the Navy Boards were first implemented, then changed, removed, and reinstated. The *Controller* had only been reintroduced to the board as *Third Lord* in 1882, under Lord Northbrook's reforms. Also present was General, His Serene Highness, Prince Edward of Saxe-Weimar, KP, GCVO, PC (1823-1902), a British military officer of German ancestry. In 1897, he achieved the highest military rank in the British Army: Field Marshal, and who was attending a state visit to England at the time of the launch. Representing the Admiralty again was Admiral, Sir Godfrey Phipps Hornby, but this seems to be an error in the contemporary reports, and should really refer to Sir Geoffrey Thomas Phipps Hornby (1825-1895), Admiral of the Navy and Commander-in-Chief, whose wife Lady Phipps actually performed the naming ceremony. Lieutenant-General Sir George and Lady Willis along with Admiral, Sir Lewis Jones, Admiral Chads and many others, including Mr. W. Owen as chief constructor with R. Burnaby and C. J. Huddy as representatives of the dockyard, were also present. Men from the works were given time off to watch the ceremony, although as was traditional, only those who had actually worked on the vessel were given the rest of the afternoon as a holiday.

During the morning, the dockyard labourers began the effort of knocking out the stays retaining the blocks to the slipway so that the vessel would remain on the slipway held by the dog shores only, diagonal braces used immediately prior to launch. By 11 a.m. the Reverend J. Williams had completed the religious service reintroduced for Royal Navy launches by Her Royal Highness Princess Alexandra just a few years earlier, and all was now ready. The dockyard gates were opened to allow members of the general public access, and the slip was soon crowded with spectators. Once the hammers and battering rams had removed the last block, Lady Phipps gave the customary speech of naming and then operated an elaborate electrical switch to despatch the brightly beribboned bottle of wine to its traditional doom. Champagne was first used in 1891 when Queen Victoria named HMS *Royal Arthur* at its launch.

The final remaining dog shores that had been so rigid and well-made as to keep the ram in touch with the launching platform built around it throughout the festivities, were instantly let go by a linked mechanism, and within moments the ship commenced her stern-first slide into the water. The ceremony was performed without a hitch, and Lady Phipps took home with her a silver memento of the occasion: a miniature ship's wheel inside of which was fitted an aneroid barometer, designed by Barnaby himself. The choice of that instrument for the keepsake might be considered later as strangely appropriate.

　　　After her launch, more than two years of fitting out followed, part of which time was spent laid up in reserve. It was towards the end of her fitting out that the vessel's first captain would make his presence known on board. An Irishman, his appearance was almost archetypal of that race. A barrel chest, jet-black eyebrows and thick luxurious beard, made the appearance of a big man seem larger still. By now in his forties, he had served the Royal Navy for many years and had achieved consistent praise, and a thoroughly deserved high reputation for his seamanship and leadership qualities. He was also blunt and very much to the point with both superiors and subordinates.

A print of HMS Calliope as published in "Her Majesty's Navy" by Charles Rathbone Low in three volumes (1890). Many books were broken up and the prints sold separately, as with this one in the author's collection. Originally published in colour. Note the smokestack is in the lowered position.

Captain Kane began the formal commissioning of *Calliope* on 25th January 1887 with the ship somewhat unusually in dry dock, Portsmouth's South Locks. One of the many mechanical problems ship designers had to contend with at the time on what might be called a steam and sail hybrid ship, was what to do with the propeller and associated engine room equipment whilst the ship was under sail. The two most obvious difficulties making up the problem were the smokestack and the engine transmission gear.

The smokestack, nice and tall to produce a good draught in the furnaces, was located amidships, generally central and directly behind the fore coarse sail, in perfect position to interfere with the wind into it. The solution to that problem was to make the stack telescopic: the funnel could be raised when under steam to produce a good draught, and lowered when under sail to avoid spoiling the wind.

A solution to the propeller problem was more difficult to engineer, and was the reason for *Calliope's* extended stay in the dock. With the screw connected via a large shaft to massive machinery, then whilst under sail the sea passing over the propeller blades would be trying to turn all that weight and would be quite unable to do so; the effect would be similar to throwing out a sea anchor. The drag of the blades would so severely impair the movement that the ship's performance would be badly compromised under sail, and the greatest insult was that the more efficient in use the propeller happened to be, the more drag it would impart whilst stationary.

Early steam and sail hybrid ship designs embodied an ingenious solution, though difficult to manufacture and awkward to implement. The propeller itself could be lifted from the water into a recess under the stern, its shaft *"dog-legging"* at a knuckle joint similar to the type seen on motor cars today in order to permit suspension movement of driven wheels. Once out of the flow of water, the propeller obviously no longer offered the resistance to the vessel when being driven by sail alone, the embodiment was known as *"hoisting screws"*. Combined with lowering the funnel to assist the wind into the sails, these two apparently disassociated actions gave rise to one of the more intriguingly named drills common at the time: *"Up Funnel and Down Propeller"* and, of course, its vice versa. A couple of drawbacks were the possible comparative weakness of the knuckle joint in a heavy sea, and the need to orientate it prior to the lift.

Another option embodied in ships of the *Eclipse* class, for example, was to make the *blades* on the propeller shaft removable. A diver would need to go overboard and remove the blades from the hub or refit them to it; a somewhat impractical solution if there was any sort of sea running, or a naval action in the offing.

These two technical difficulties had been faced by steam sailing ship designers since inception of the screw as the propulsion method of choice to enhance sail, following a series of sea trials between HMS *Rattler* (screw) and HMS *Alecto* (paddle) in early April 1845 that had culminated in an entertaining tug-of-war between the similarly matched vessels won comprehensively by *Rattler*, which managed to tow *Alecto* at about 2½ knots via the stern-to-stern hawsers. At the time, the fact that *Rattler*'s engines were slightly more powerful than *Alecto*'s was somewhat conveniently forgotten, but the result was nevertheless correct.

All the ships at Samoa embodied a telescopic smokestack; in the case of the German vessel SMS *Olga*, both her twin funnels were so mechanised. To avoid the need to raise the propeller from the sea when sail was to be used, *Calliope's* twin-bladed screw embodied two design principles, one established, the second more recent. In common with many other vessels, the propeller could be uncoupled from the engine drive shaft and allowed to rotate freely as the ship sailed under canvas; this combined with a feathering arrangement on the blades of *Calliope's* screw was intended to greatly reduce the drag when the propeller was not being driven. The blades could be turned in line with the axis of the ship and so present their smallest aspect to the sea; it is a method still employed in propeller driven aircraft, and provided in the event of an engine failure for that same reason of reducing drag. On *Calliope*, the innovation was also intended to make the conversion time from sail to steam to be as short as possible, potentially very important in a warship, and it was this novel feathering mechanism which had broken down during the preceding trials.

Dockyard personnel worked hard on a resolution to the problem as the crew drew their stores for the final sail and steam commissioning trials that would be followed by the voyage to take *Calliope* to her China station. Sails were drawn and *bent* – that is laid on the deck, tied to lines and lifted to their yards, and attached to the yard jackstay and the running rigging, and when all was deemed correct, furled in accordance with navy practice.

Provisions were loaded, and coal taken on. The first of a number of batches of food taken onboard consisted of 843 pounds of fresh beef and 420 pounds of fresh vegetables.

Before long, the propeller problem had been resolved, though I have been unable to ascertain precisely how. The only rather enigmatic reference to it that I have been able to find, is in the ship's first log which, on the page recording *Calliope's* equipment, describes the propeller as a *"Griffiths, Originally Part-Feathering, Now Fixed."* To my mind, the implication is that the mechanism could not be made to work properly, and was ultimately dispensed with: the blades were originally feathering, but had been fixed into place during the commissioning trials. Gardiner in *"Conway's All The Worlds Fighting Ships"* describes all but *Carysfort* and *Constance* of the nine *Comus* class being fitted with *"hoisting screws"*, those other two being fitted with *"feathering screws"*. By the end of the 1870s, hoisting screws were rarely being implemented in new ships. Both *Calypso* and *Calliope* are recorded as being fitted with feathering screws which, at sailing speeds over 5 knots, were allowed to *"turn over"* - taken to mean the drive shaft was uncoupled from the engine so that the water current only tried to turn the propeller and its shaft. I have obtained copies of *Calliope*'s builder's plans held at the National Maritime Museum at Greenwich, but they don't furnish any clear data to help solve the mystery.

On the 27th January 1887, *Calliope* was floated out of the dock and taken to Spithead to adjust compasses. This involved placing the vessel in a precise location and then turning her to take sights and headings of a number of specific landmarks, whose true and undistorted compass bearing from the point was known. In this way, the deviation in the ship's compass caused by the close proximity of the iron works in her hull could be empirically allowed for, and the data were recorded on the first page of her first log. Later that same day, ammunition lighters came alongside and the warship loaded her powder and shell; something that for obvious safety reasons was never permitted within the inner confines of Portsmouth Harbour in proximity to other ships and the shore. By midnight, she was ready for sea.

The next day, the Portsmouth Commander-In-Chief Admiral Sir George Willes, KCB, inspected the ship exercised at general quarters, and pronounced himself satisfied. Dense fog on the 29th lifted slightly allowing the ship to weigh and proceed towards St. Helens, but the return of the bad weather forced *Calliope* to anchor just off the point. The crew were issued with their arms and accoutrements. The commissioning trials started properly on the following day, when the sea fog finally lifted at around 1 pm.

The first steam trial on 2nd February 1887 was terminated early when a heavy sea got up, but *Calliope* had attained 14 knots against the designed for 13 and three-quarters, which had proved encouraging to Kane. To the experienced crew, as fondly critical of a new ship as a grouchy but loving grandfather with a young child, she seemed a good boat, though inclined to be lively in a head sea, a characteristic which seems to have been typical of all the ships of the class. In fact, in any sort of head sea, the engines had trouble maintaining a reasonable headway. Sailors of that time were particularly superstitious beings. They might be critical of a new ship's handling, or be disturbed by capriciousness in her response to the sea, but they knew better than to openly insult the object that would be their home and their well-being for many years. No new ship could ever hope to be as stiff, or as easy to manage, as one of their previous postings, but this new ship was the one to coddle, and cajole, and bless. Almost as a reward for their efforts and forbearance, on the 3rd of that month her crew received their first issue at sea of soap and tobacco, later that evening trying out her electric searchlight for the first time.

After some further trials of sail and steam, *Calliope* returned to Spithead on the 6th and the dockyard spent over two weeks on the myriads of mostly trivial problems that such trials were intended to highlight. The 22nd was spent dressing the ship with flags and manning the masts in salute to Her Majesty Queen Victoria who had arrived in HM Yacht *Alberta* on her way to Windsor. Two days earlier, a royal salute had been fired in honour of Princess Louise of Wales, causing Master Gunner Charles Martin to begin the first of a series of records of munitions expenditure.

Often the first indication of the worth of a particular ship's design would be her handling under sail or the performance when driven by steam; when the completed ship lifted its anchor and first set its canvas or fired its furnaces. Victorian naval designers relied on experience and intuition and made their names in that way; computers that could model the characteristics of hull and sea were, of course, not even the stuff of dreams. Many British ship designs of the time, wonderful devices on paper, were converted into ships that were utter abominations, virtually useless in their function and often downright dangerous to the poor souls put aboard them. This was why few suddenly magnificent design innovations appeared *out-of-the-blue* as it were - such a ship's plans would need to be sold to those paying the bills before even a rivet was placed in the brazier, and money-men throughout the years and whatever country they hail from have always been a difficult bunch to persuade to take a chance. Most innovations were small changes and cautious experiments, and even then, could be disastrous. The first voyage of a new ship - even one developed from a long line of similar designs - was always an adventure.

Britain in the second half of the nineteenth-century seems often to be regarded by naval historians as lagging behind the more innovative designs of France and Italy. It is possible such a stand was deliberate, or at least, accidentally advantageous. Before the advent of the aeroplane,

Britain was fully conscious of its island status and that any attack would ultimately come from the sea, so successive British Governments deliberately built up a huge navy, supposedly equal to the size of the next two most important maritime nation's forces added together, and thus were always able to throw large numbers of ships at a problem. As a result, the Admiralty seemed content to let those smaller navies take the risks of trying out new ideas. Once an innovation was proven useful, British naval shipbuilding was very quick to then incorporate what it liked. The most dramatic demonstration of this was the conversion of HMS *Warrior* from wooden hull to ironclad, primarily the result of a scathing attack on the Admiralty by Prince Albert on his return from a Royal Inspection of the French Fleet at Cherbourg in 1858. As he sat at his desk to pen a missive criticising the government that would be considered politically unthinkable for a royal today, the French steam-powered-ironclad *Gloire* was already under construction, and represented a tremendous threat to British naval dominance; by the time it was launched in 1859, the Admiralty response to Albert had been to modify the plans for HMS *Warrior* to incorporate an iron hull and screw propulsion. In actual fact, the *Warrior* class of frigate had not originally been intended to provide direct competition to *Gloire*, it was Albert's intervention that forced the changes.

The closing sentences the Prince used in his letter to such good effect were:

> *"The war preparations of the French are immense, ours despicable. Our ministers use fine phrases but they do nothing. My blood boils within me!"*

Kane will have had as clear a demonstration of the dangers of new or risky designs, as one might ever wish *not* to see. As an officer on HMS *Lord Warden*, he will have awoken on 7th September 1871 during fleet manoeuvres in the Bay of Biscay to see the surface of the sea seething with the mass of bubbles marking the place where on her maiden voyage the 6,900 ton displacement HMS *Captain* had capsized and sunk, taking with her virtually her entire complement; a ship designed by the amateur Captain Coles which was so extraordinary even on paper that it had caused concerns to be raised by both the Admiralty engineers who reviewed the plans, and by Lairds who built her; concerns this time ignored but which, within a short time, had proved fatally real for hundreds of men, including Coles who was aboard at the time.

Ship's logs of the period held space for the first captain or the sailing master to record his views of her sailing characteristics. Robert Knox's comments regarding the second *Calliope* in 1854 were: *"The ship sails tolerably, and is weatherly in a breeze, but does not carry her sail well, being over-sparred."* In this case, *weatherly* means capable of sailing in one direction with the wind coming from the side of the vessel, with little drift to leeward. In real layman's terms that even I understand, it means being able to sail with the wind *slightly greater* than at a right angle to the direction of travel, with little drift in the direction of the wind. That practice is known as sailing *close-hauled,* and seems on the face of it impossible; it is somewhat complicated to explain how it can be achieved. Kane, however, clearly felt it unnecessary to record his views of his new ship's performance in her log. He may have done so in his *"Captain's Log"*, but that document appears to have been lost.

It was not solely the ship that was put through her paces. The crew were drilled in as many of the evolutions as could be found time for, both night and day: general quarters; fire stations; making and shortening sail; working the ship under canvas. It was vital the men knew how to handle this steam-powered ship under sail alone.

The 24th February was the next real full-speed steam trial, and here a niggling little problem was identified. After only a half-hour at full speed, the gland around the high-pressure piston rod showed signs of leakage, and the engine was stopped to allow re-packing. The piston rod had become quite hot by the friction, it being that which had alerted the engineers to the fault. The problem seemed to have been cured, and three further hours of trials, the last hour under forced draught, followed without mishap.

Just like a coal fire at home, forcing oxygen to the seat of the fire causes it to roar and blaze. If you are of sufficient age to have witnessed it, you will have seen father holding a sheet of newspaper across the top two-thirds of the open fire grate, partially blocking it and so causing the draught of a newly lit fire to pull in air only at the bottom where it is then directed straight to the flames. Normal, or induced, draught used the physics of the hot air rising in the funnel and exhaust equipment to pull in air for the furnaces via the ventilators on deck. Forced draught actually pushes air into the furnaces using mechanical devices. The more intense heat so generated can quickly get a hesitant fire going, and the dramatic increase in the heat output in a ship's furnaces can be used to increase boiler pressure and so improve the vessel's speed. The downside is that burning fuel under forced draught is inefficient and costly in fuel use, so using this technique was usually an emergency measure only, certainly so in a steam ship where coal stocks were always precious. The engine-room crew were able to use the large air intakes on deck to deliver air directly into the furnaces like a bellows, to provide the vessel's captain with extra power if for any reason it was needed.

The results of the trial were very encouraging indeed; under normal draught, the boilers had delivered 84 and a half pounds per square inch of steam pressure, the screw had turned at just under 80 revolutions per minute and the combined High- and Low-Indicated horsepower was almost 2,822. The ship had achieved 13 and two-thirds knots under these conditions. Under the forced draught, the improvement was considerable, the 85 and three-quarter pounds of steam in the boilers giving 86 and a half revolutions and just more than 3,848 total indicated horsepower, driving the ship at marginally over 14 and a half knots. I have taken these performance figures from *The Cruise of H.M.S. Calliope* by the Reverend A.C. Evans and augmented by the ship's log. The engine's design aim was 3,000 Indicated H.P. at normal draught.

A second trial on the 26th had achieved 13½ knots before again, the packing around the high-pressure piston rod failed. The next two days were spent with the engineers trying to resolve the problem with the gland, which was eventually corrected. Somewhat surprisingly, a further steam trial was deemed unnecessary, but this was almost certainly the result of the need for the ship to take up her station as soon as possible. It is doubtful whether the captain of a modern ship that did not have sail as a backup would have been so trusting, and Kane, whose subsequent actions proved him to be a cautious man when it was prudent to be so, must have been under strong pressure to accept the rectification as good without a practical demonstration of its worth. This acceptance probably caused him some misgivings later.

The engine's horsepower design aim (3,000 IHP) was quite a high figure for the time and a real challenge to the engineers, and under normal draught, the installed equipment achieved only marginally less than the requirement (2,822 IHP). Kane signed the documents to accept the vessel for and on behalf of their Lords of the Admiralty, and *Calliope* was formally passed over and added to the Royal Navy's list. The builders could now be paid their last instalment of the £120,100 that the vessel eventually cost.

At 5 pm on the chilly evening of 1st March 1887 and with the last of the 60 tons of coal taken on that day still being forced into the bunkers, *Calliope* left England on her maiden voyage for the China station, and her terrifying adventure in Samoa. But if the crew had thought the intensive trials were over, they were soon to reconsider. Captain Kane's intent was to use the outbound sailing time to mould his new ship and crew into the single entity that would be fully prepared to face any eventuality it might encounter as a British warship in foreign waters. The men were starting the voyage as a green crew in a shiny new ship, and by the time they reached China they must all be members of an experienced, confident and well-ordered team.

Chapter 4: Samoa.

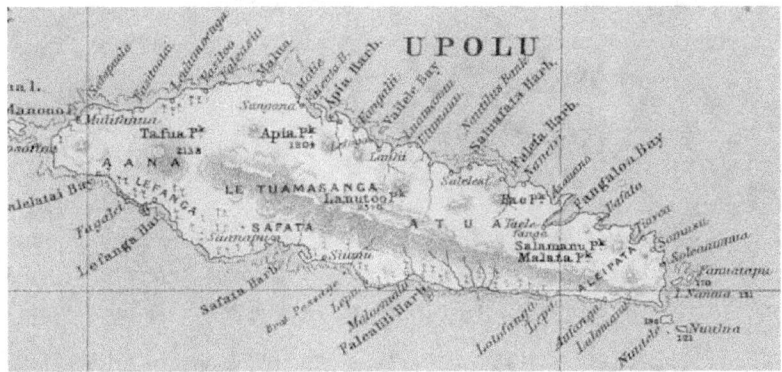

The island of Upolu, Samoa. Apia Harbour and Town are on the north coast. Apia Peak is shown nearby. Source: The image was scanned from a National Geographic map of 1885 in the author's collection.

To my admittedly simplistic mind, it was a telling indication of classic European arrogance that the older history books recorded the islands that today make up the chain named Samoa as having been *discovered* in 1722. For native Samoans, this flag-in-the-ground statement of when their history started must have been irksome and insulting, though modern comment seems to be more sympathetic.

The islands are of volcanic origin, created from an ocean floor vent gradually building up material to form an island that over the millenia is carried away by tectonic movement, so producing a chain of islands progressively getting geologically younger as they near the active region and surrounded by ocean of quite immense depth, anything upwards of 18,000 feet (5,500 metres). There is an active volcano on Savai'i at the western end of the group, though it has been quiet for most of the twentieth-century - not always a good sign, but there are no suggestions of an imminent re-awakening. The whole island of Upolu is considered in some sources as a massive volcanic shield, that fortunately has been dormant for many years. Upolu is the second in line of newness, and is slightly smaller than its younger neighbour, but is the most important economically and is the seat of governance of the group.

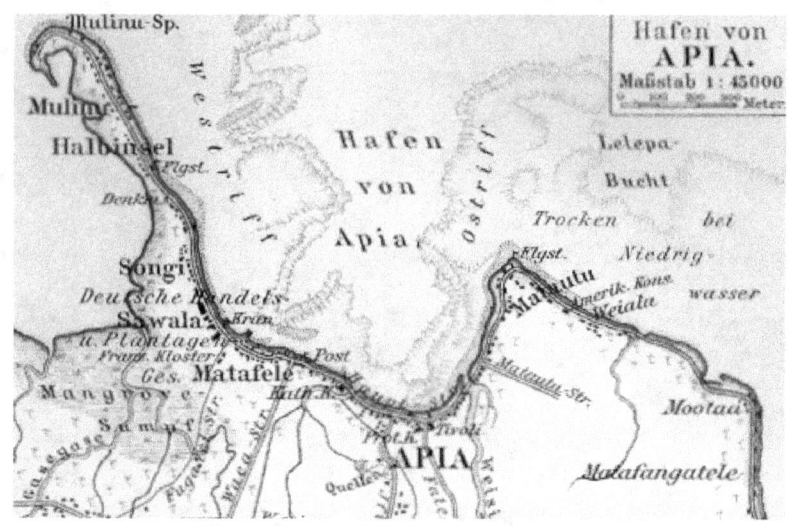

A German map of the "Port of Apia" dated circa 1885. The western and eastern coral reefs are shown, and demonstrate the reduced area available for vessels to moor. Compare it to the map on page 152 based on that produced by Captain Kane.

Located some 171°W of the Greenwich Meridian and 14°S of the equator (and so almost as close as one could get to being on the opposite side of the world to Britain), the islands enjoy a warm climate ranging from 32°C in December as generally the hottest month, to 24°C in August as generally the coolest. The wet season between November and April provides most of the nearly 6,000 millimetres (233 inches) of average annual rainfall, the majority of that staggering volume being concentrated in the interior. In comparison, the highest average annual rainfall in the United Kingdom is, at present anyway, *Crib Goch*, in Snowdonia, which has an average of 4,500 millimetres (176 inches) of rain per year over the recent past, but whilst this is excessive for the UK, it is significantly less than the average for Samoa. Some sources give *Sparkling Tarn* in the Lake District as the UK record holder.

Due to their method of formation, the islands are generally mountainous with narrow coastal fringes that attract the settlement of humans, and where habitation is easiest to build. The soil is rather poor in areas away from those fertile coastal regions.

As with any land mass or object within the top few metres of the tropical ocean, the islands are encrusted by the molluscs which have built up and fringed them with coral reef. This bordering coral reef is tenacious and hard, but is defeated by one natural substance: fresh water. Where rivers vent their outflows into the ocean, the surrounding coral reef is generally absent. The combination of a gap in the reef, and entry by river-way at least part way into the inland areas of the islands, mean that in such places, men can anchor their boats and settlements inevitably grow up around them. Apia, on the north facing coast of Upolu, was a native village which was created years before any European visitors came, so that Samoan natives could take advantage of the harbour produced by the fresh water outflow of two major rivers: the Vaisigano and the Mulivai. In the Samoan language, the term *vaitafe* means *river*, and *vai*: *fresh water*, so I believe it would be technically incorrect to call the Vaisigano, for example, the Vaisigano River. In reality, the harbour was really simply absent reef. The name Vaisigano seems to have undergone a number of spelling changes over the years; the one used here is the modern one.

Robert Louis Stevenson, writing of Samoa's chequered history just a few years after the storm, dismissively describes the harbour at Apia on Upolu as *"so-called"* and comments that it would hardly warrant a symbol as such on any chart of his native Scotland. In many ways, this misses the point – to Samoan natives in their canoes, it was a perfectly good harbour as such harbours go. Using the port as initially a whaling centre, then as a means of colonising and exploiting the islands, to bring in large loads of supplies and take out saleable produce, for Europeans to complain about its adequacy as a haven for their large trading vessels is not really fair.

For those larger ships seeking its protection, there were some things about Apia harbour that in particular made it a port to be wary of. Not only was it small and surrounded by hostile reef, excepting a single and restricted way in and out, it had some other vagaries which added to its risk: the river outflows which had sculpted it from the coral, especially when swelled by the voluminous tropical downpours of the rainy season, could produce powerful and unpredictable swirling currents in the bay that could scour away much of the silt in which anchors and chains made their best purchase; the waves marching in from the north were constrained by the reef and swelled in magnitude, becoming considerably more menacing in the centre of the bay such that their final, booming crash on the shore often made normal conversation in the port almost impossible; and those troublesome violent gales that inevitably swept the islands at some stage of the year occasionally did so with their powerful winds heading directly into the maw of the bay, making escape from it difficult and the coral reef the inevitable destination for a dragging ship.

The harbour had a long established bad reputation amongst

visiting sailor-men; after the storm to come in March of 1889, Captain Leary of USS *Adams* would tell the readers of the *Los Angeles Herald*:

> *"There is hardly any anchorage in Apia harbor, and it is a very difficult matter to keep a vessel off the shore in ordinary weather. The anchors keep dragging, and when I was there with my vessel I found it necessary to carry my anchors out every morning to keep the vessel from going ashore."*

There were natives living on Upolu long before the *civilised* world found them out. The anthropologists seem generally to concur that Polynesians from Asia or Hawaii initially settled the group of islands, and this idea does seem to be supported by the limited archaeological evidence that has been unearthed. The ancient human history might go back some 3,000 years or more. Whatever the academics might say, the native Samoans have their own views, and I see no reason to scorn them. To the Samoan, they have always lived on the lands. They originated on the islands and have always been there. The god Tagaloa created the world from a rock in the vast expanse of space, and from that also created the *"Sea"*, *"Land"*, *"Clouds"* and *"Humanity"*, followed by *"Spirit"*, *"Heart"*, *"Will"* and finally *"Thought"* before creating the human populations and islands which include Samoa, a name derived from the *"Sa"* (sacred) *"Moa"* (fowls) owned by Lu, the son of Tagaloa. Another explanation for the name is the phrase *"Sa ia Moa"*, Sacred to Moa, which was later truncated to the name we know today. There are a great many other definitions, all of which have equal measures of merit and implausibility. All this is a highly abbreviated and probably less than accurate account of the history as Samoan natives see it, and I hope I may be forgiven for glossing over what is interesting but supplementary to the main story, and a digression that even I can see would take up too much of this narrative.

That earliest recorded European visitor in 1722 was the Dutchman Jacob Roggeveen but he didn't land; his search for the *southern continent* and its hoped-for riches in gold plunder that had already led him to rediscover Easter Island in April of that year was to him a far more compelling aspiration, but one which he was destined never to realise.

In early May of 1768, the French explorer Louis-Antoine de Bougainville (1729-1811) on the 550 ton frigate *Boudeuse* during his epic round-the-world expedition, sailed through Samoa and initially named the group *Les Petites Cyclades*, before changing it to *Archipel des Navigateurs* - *"The Navigator Islands"* - supposedly in recognition and honour of the navigating abilities of those islanders he encountered in ocean going canoes with large sails, many miles from the islands. But still no booted

European foot had disturbed the golden Samoa sand.

In December 1787, a European finally landed on Samoa but rapidly came to regret his action, or at least, to mourn the outcome. The French explorer Jean-François de Galaup (1741-1788?), also known with the additional moniker "comte de La Pérouse" or "comte de Lapérouse", this second version being the construction of name that he appears to have taken up on entry to the French Navy, came ashore from his ship *La Boussole* on the north coast of Tutuila in what is now American Samoa. After initially enjoying a happy intercourse with the natives, whilst gathering fresh water a group of his men was attacked by the Samoans and Lapérouse lost twelve members from the expedition, most of them crew from his accompanying ship, the *Astrolabe,* in a skirmish which also accounted for some 30 to 40 natives. The French dead were ten irreplaceable crew members and two hugely important officers; one Jean-Honore-Robert de Paul de Lamanon, a celebrated French physicist, mineralogist and meteorologist; and the other Lapérouse's dearest friend and Captain of the *Astrolabe,* Paul-Antoine-Marie Fleuriot de Langle. French aristocrat parents of the time certainly knew how to name a son! When he eventually left the island having wrestled with and overcome a desire to exact terrible revenge on the entire population, Lapérouse named the anchorage where the fight occurred (now known as Aasu Bay) the *Baie des Assassins* - *"Massacre Bay"* - in bitter condemnation.

The details of the attack are discussed at length in Lapérouse's records, though the reasons for it are still elusive. Like all such things there are two sides to a tale. The Frenchman's own account seems to suggest the natives simply increased in number and attacked without obvious reason. It is a little tricky today understanding precisely what Lapérouse meant, as his original manuscripts are in late eighteenth-century French (not my strongest subject!) and English translations whilst readily available are supposedly open to a fair amount of question regarding the accuracy of their interpretation. For my research, I used the version published by the Hakluyt Society [22] in which Lapérouse devotes a number of pages to the subject from what is a very interesting and highly detailed account of his visit to the Navigator Islands.

In Lapérouse's version, de Langle had previously espied a pretty village with an apparently safe beach, and prevailed upon his commander to allow him to land there for water on the following day. In fact, circumstances conspired that on that day, the landing area was out of sight of the main ships, and a rocky outcrop meant the beach was not as safe as it had earlier appeared to be. As the landing party stood on the sand, the number of natives on shore suddenly increased and soon became threatening; some sailors thought a volley of musket shot to demonstrate their superior power might be in order, but events quickly overtook them. A stone from a native slingshot felled de Langle with a mortal blow, and was the signal for a volley of stones loosed with astonishing power and accuracy, quickly followed by a surge of natives armed with their fearsome clubs against the heavily outnumbered French. Ranged against the 60 or 70 Frenchmen, Lapérouse later determined the number of natives at some twelve hundred, though this will probably have included women and children.

A number of sailors, perhaps some 8 or 9, died very quickly, or having been felled and unable to reach a boat, were mercilessly despatched by the clubbing of the natives who overran them. Those who had struggled to the boats were able to kill a number of natives, but this seems to have been hardly noticed by the crowd to whom musket shots now had little alarming effect. Eventually, by abandoning two of the boats and throwing overboard all the water casks on the third vessel to lighten it, one boat finally managed to leave the bay, and fortunately the natives were busy with their plunder and murder so didn't attempt to follow.

It took an hour or more for the crowded boat to reach the main ships, but once the red flag tied to its mast was seen, the distress of its inhabitants was realised by the crew of *La Boussole*, and they were taken on board all of them injured to some extent or another. The shocking news they brought regarding those left behind could so easily have turned the situation to disaster. The crew of the *Astrolabe* in particular, highly close to their now dead captain and of course their shipmates, had to be restrained from emptying their weapons at those natives on the ship who, still in ignorance, even then pestered them to barter the doves or fruit they held in their hands.

The other view of the event, propounded by the missionary George Turner in his Samoan narrative *"A Hundred Years Ago and Long Before"*, was that a native visiting one of the ships and perhaps being tempted to pilfer some small trifle was roughly handled and eventually shot by musket, receiving a mortal wound from the ball. His friends took him back to shore where his death rattle set up such anger and hatred in their hearts, that the natives exacted what revenge they could on whosoever happened to be nearest.

Lapérouse left Samoa, continuing his voyage around the Pacific Islands and the West coast of Australia, before both ships and men disappeared sometime in 1788. The reader is advised that details about this voyage of discovery, and the expedition launched in 1791 by Rear-Admiral Bruni d'Entrecasteaux partly in hopes of rescue and partly to continue the expedition, bear hunting out as they provide fascinating tales of their own.

The Lapérouse expedition was one of high expectation, and whilst primarily French, was well-supported by British scientists and naval men. The ultimate fate of the expedition was unknown for many years, but modern evidence suggests the vessels eventually reached the island of Vanikoro (sometimes known as Vanikolo) located 118 km to the south-east of the main Santa Cruz group. The *Boussole* seems to have struck a reef, and many of its survivors were massacred by natives. The *Astrolabe* was also damaged by the reef, and most of the remaining voyagers used her timbers to build a small sailing craft, heading off for an unknown fate in that vast ocean. Those that remained ashore had all gone or perished before an expedition by the Irishman Captain Dillon reached the island in 1826 and enough evidence was found to explain the mystery as described above. It is fortunate that in March 1788 Lapérouse had despatched his records to Paris in a British ship from Botany Bay in Australia before his final voyage else a wonderful scientific record would have been lost forever.

A further fascinating suggestion is that whilst Captain Edward Edwards on HMS *Pandora* was searching the area for mutineers from HMS *Bounty*, he passed Vanikoro on 13th August 1791 and observed smoke signals rising from the island. Convinced that mutineers would not so advertise their presence, he ignored the signs and carried on without stopping. Almost certainly, the smoke was a distress signal from survivors of the Lapérouse expedition. Edwards has been characterised as "...*one of England's most "ruthless," "inhuman," "callous" and "incompetent" naval captains*...", he must have been a pretty unpleasant person to earn those labels!

The islands of Samoa before long came to the notice of a powerful and autocratic German trading company, Cesar Godeffroy and Sons, based in Hamburg. The coastal land was excellent for growing coconuts and kopra, and plantations were soon set up. Once again, the story is of European exploitation and duplicity. Natives were encouraged to *sell* their land rights for trinkets and pittances, a transaction of which they had no notion or experience. Plantations were set up, and soon conflict began. A native used to going into the bush and picking what he liked, often from a neighbour, felt able to do the same in the plantation, whose European *owners* were far less relaxed about the idea. Natives were prevented from moving into these areas, parts of their own island that had been their free home for centuries.

Very quickly, German commercial enterprises realised that management of the natives would be best achieved by manipulation of the leaders. The classic colonial methods: find someone who will accept foreign interference as long as he himself can make something out of it. In fact, the resulting unsettled and highly charged political situation in Samoa was the main reason for so many naval ship's captains to cram their vessels into a trap just waiting to be sprung, so must be touched upon in any recounting of the tale.

On encountering the word *"politics"* and its associations, my own eyes tend to glaze over; I've always dismissed politics as something that can only ever be of interest to the politician engaging in it, or to the media who seem to make such a big thing about reporting it. Whilst I know the decisions politicians make directly influence my life, I don't believe any opinion of mine carries the slightest weight with them except perhaps when it is time to mark my "X". I will freely admit that, unlike the founding fathers of America, I am not of the same mind as the famous orator and politician, Marcus Tullius Cicero, who in his writings *"De Re Publica"* referred to politics as:

> *"For there is really no other occupation in which human virtue approaches more closely the august function of the gods than that of founding new States or preserving those already in existence."*

I would say a true politician speaking of his own profession. But in fact, my research on this aspect of the story I found to be surprisingly refreshing, and I hope the result will engross rather than bore any reader who happens to share my more modern feelings.

If what I might term a *normal* person can be amused at the posturing self-importance, and disgusted by the self-aggrandisement, of politicians today, the antics engaged in by the various consuls in Samoa in 1888-9 are in many cases hilarious, tempered only by the sobering thought that – as always – it was the little man who paid the ultimate price exacted by political lunacy. Being the conduct of negotiations between persons, groups, or nations, surely diplomacy has as one of its intentions the means of preventing conflict or reducing the risk of such; it seemed in Samoa to be the anvil on which would be forged the sword *from* the ploughshare.

A full recounting of the politics that occupied the thoughts and exercised the wit of the people at Apia in 1888-9 might more resemble an improbable farce, and if it were not for real human beings losing their lives, we could easily laugh at it. To fully chronicle the intricate historic detail leading up to the political pressure-pot would take a book of its own, and has been nobly performed already by a few such as R.L. Stevenson [9], but whether the tales should be described as a reference to a series of historical events, or a book of comedy horror stories is, for me at least, difficult to decide. Restricting ourselves to the last few months before the storm gives a revealing and amusing insight into the various personalities and their interplay. As an outsider, I could find it easy to dismiss the diplomatic posturing as the stupid actions of children, pushing and shoving each other over a particular juicy iced bun at a party. It probably appeared so to natives watching at the time, and during my research, I lost count of the number of times I felt a gasp of bewilderment coming on.

Before describing the antics of the foreign Vice-Consuls in Apia, I should give a little background to the country in which they were operating.

Samoa's governance consisted of a number of chiefs, generally each town had its own chief, some more than one. These chiefs were not permitted to talk directly to the people, and used "*talking men*", Tulafale, as a means of communication. They were effectively ministers, or representatives, of the chief. These Tulafale were supposed to stay permanently with the chief carrying out his orders, and protecting him from any danger that might arise. The chief's wives had the same restrictions, and also used Tulafale, in this case, "*talking women*". The chief's wives Tulafale were the chief's Tulafale wives, and so on for the children.

The position of Tulafale was hereditary, and whilst a chief could appoint another chief, he could not appoint a Tulafale. The position has great power in Samoa. If, for some reason, a Tulafale was considered incompetent, the people of the town could expel him, and his position and wealth and possessions would pass to the next in line. When a chief or Tulafale died, his family decided on the next most suitable family member to take his place, but this might be only temporary, as a meeting of the people was convened to take place after the burial. After this meeting, at which the deceased family were excluded, a second meeting was held to include them, and the new Tulafale or chief finally elected.

When the incumbent King was near death, no-one was allowed to pass his house, not even a boat out at sea unless it was out of sight of land. Guards were posted to enforce the rule. On his death, his Tulafale would call together all the Tulafale of the islands, and announce the fact, and a piece of land about one acre was chosen. Young men with axes would chip a small piece off of every coconut tree on the piece of land, and no-one was permitted to touch the trees until after the King was buried. These trees were then fired, and people come from all the islands to view the King's remains.

For the first few hours after his death, no-one was allowed to see him except family, but then everyone would be expected to come to his house and pay their respects; any chief or Tulafale who had known of the death but had failed to visit would be punished by depriving them of their lands and title.

Every evening, a daughter of a chief along with her family would visit the house and sing songs praising the deceased to his family members. When they became tired, other families arrived to take over. In the morning, a breakfast was prepared from food brought by the people and consumed in a nearby house, as eating, drinking and smoking were not allowed in the house of the dead man.

After about a week, the people came to take a last look at their King. He was placed in his coffin: a canoe with a cover attached by cords at each end. The coffin was wrapped in mats before being placed in the grave which was also lined with mats. Women went to the sea shore and collected gravel which they spread over the coffin in its grave, followed by eating the food that had been prepared by the men. The women then prepared food for the men as the roles were reversed. The ceremony ended with collecting the leaves from the fired coconut trees, and extracting oil from the coconuts.

The election of King, or tafaifa, seems to have been by popular vote of the people, in which the *"names"* of five provinces of the island elected their favourite as candidates. In 1881, *Laupepa* held the names of three provinces: Malietoa, Natoaitele, and Tamasoalii; *Tamasese* held one: Tui'a Ana; and *Mata'afa* one also: Tui Atua. Thus it was that Laupepa was King. Those latter two provinces seem to have retained their name since the 1200s.

Since it was traditional that the King should hold all five names, or provinces, and since those of Tui'a Ana and Tui Atua always determined to elect their *own* chiefs as king, there was an immediate impasse. To make this all work, it was determined that Tamasese would spend two years as Vice-King followed by Mata'afa taking over that role.

Whilst to be nominated with names conferred power and prestige on the individual, it might be worth pointing out that to be King of Samoa at that time was not in reality as wonderful as it might seem to us plebeians today. The Hollywood idea of being chaired around the islands by dozens of beautiful scantily-clad young native girls seems attractive but was unlikely to be the normal method of transport for a nineteenth-century Samoan King, except perhaps at very special ceremonies. The King didn't issue many edicts or proclamations of his own and when he did, it seems he didn't really expect anyone to take much notice of them. The local town chiefs made the laws, and brought them to the king to be ratified; he had no power of veto.

War in Samoa was rarely far way under circumstances such as these, but seems to have been prosecuted in a way incomprehensible to us. If one had no wish to fight in a particular war involving one's province, one simply didn't do so. Simpler by far to killing each other was to destroy each other's fruit trees, which decimated the economy for years afterward. The practice of severing the heads of defeated enemies when outright conflict did erupt, a ritual which horrified the local missionaries, was found by the natives to be justified by a pedigree in the bibles clutched by those same pastors, when David slew Goliath and did the same thing. The missionary's response to the natives discovery is not recorded.

The Samoan King in late 1888 was still Laupepa, but effectively imprisoned by the Germans miles from his home and family. The usurper was Tamasese (in 1888, Tupua Tamasese Malietoa Titiamaea), meaning *"adopted child"*, a man who the Germans could control; and then there was Mata'afa Iosefo, also known as Tupua Malietoa To'oa Mata'afa Iosefo, who by opposing the Germans was allied to the American and British and therefore represented the exiled King. Mata'afa means *"strong eyes"* in Samoan. To the Europeans, conflict in the islands tended to have only one serious effect – an impact on the trading profits that was their real reason for being there. Economics was a far stronger and more powerful influence for peace than was humanitarianism. But because it was often necessary to protect one's interests from real and prospective threats, the various European consuls liked to back up their words with a military presence.

In the Pacific at that time, a few submarine telegraph cables ran up the western edge from Australia to China and Japan, but none crossed to the American continent, and most certainly none were even under consideration to run via Samoa. So at a time when it was impossible to obtain guidance on day-to-day concerns from one's leaders on the other side of the world, and with rapidly changing circumstances precluding the opportunity to wait the number of days often required for messages to reach a station containing those few cables to criss-cross the oceans, it came down to the individuals on the spot to make decisions based on their own perception of the current situation against their – often rather generalised – original orders.

This inevitably led to personalities, egos and simple likes and dislikes pervading the interaction between the politicians themselves and filtering down to the natives on Samoa. People empowered with the control of their nation's destiny in a tiny outpost on the other side of the world rather naturally assumed in their own eyes the importance of their nation itself. If a consul felt himself insulted, the insult was deemed to have been made collectively to his nation; to its people; to their leaders. It had to be answered immediately, dealt with, and disposed of. And, more often than not, the like must be given in reply. If a consul raised a proclamation that another didn't like, it spawned a counter-proclamation. The birth of one would create many others. For example, over just three days, the three consuls felt compelled to issue the following:

German Dr. Knappe's proclamation declaring Martial Law in Samoa:

> "PROCLAMATION. By order of the Imperial German Government I hereby proclaim the state of war for the Samoan Islands. Any assistance to the rebels will be punished by Martial Law, irrespective of any nationality. The introduction of contraband of war is prohibited. All vessels and boats are liable to be searched by German authorities. The Police of Apia henceforth will act under instructions from the Imperial German Government. The residents of Apia are requested to assist in keeping law and order. Apia, January 19, 1889. Dr. Knappe, Imperial German Consul."

British De Coetlogon's counter-proclamation on the following day read:

> "Notice to British subjects in Samoa. All British subjects in Samoa are hereby commanded to take notice that notwithstanding the proclamation of the Imperial German Consul in Samoa, dated the 19th inst., proclaiming martial law 'irrespective of nationality', they are subject solely and entirely to the jurisdiction of Her Majesty the Queen and to my authority as Her Majesty's Consul and Deputy Commissioner, and to that of His Excellency the High Commissioner of the Western Pacific and the other appointed servants of Her Majesty, and to Her Majesty's Orders in-Council. I enjoin all British subjects to observe strict neutrality, and by their conduct and action to maintain the dignity and honour of Great Britain. H. de Coetlogon;, H.M. Consul and Deputy Commissioner for Samoa. Apia, 20th January 1889."

Dr. Knappe wasted little time in issuing a counter-counter-proclamation:

> "A proclamation has been issued by Mr H. de Coetlogon, H.B. Majesty's Consul for Samoa, stating that the British subjects are solely and entirely

under the jurisdiction of Her Majesty the Queen, and under the authority of Her Majesty's Consul and Deputy-Commissioner, notwithstanding declaration of martial law in Samoan Islands by Imperial German Government. I herewith declare that all British subjects in Samoa are under martial law, and that they will be tried by martial law if they should interfere in any way with German authorities. (Signed) Fritze Corvette, Captain and Commandant I.M. Krz Adler. Apia, 20th January 1889."

And from de Coetlogon, the following day (and a little less belligerently):

"Notice to British subjects in Samoa. Having been officially informed by the Imperial German Consul that war has been declared by the Imperial German Government against the Samoan Islands, I strictly enjoin all masters and others in charge of British vessels in Samoan waters to submit themselves peacefully to all reasonable search for contraband of war. Apia, 21st January 1889. H. De Coetlogon, H. M. Consul and Deputy- Commissioner for Samoa."

Even the U.S. Vice-Consul had to get into the act on 22nd January:

"PROCLAMATION – To all citizens of the United States – Having been informed by the Imperial German Consul that Germany is at war with Mata'afa and his followers; I hereby notify you, that you are forbidden to take any part in the hostile operations on either side. So long as you remain non-combatants you are entitled to personal immunity and protection. Any offence committed against you or your property is an offence against the laws of war, and should be promptly reported to me, so that the offender or offenders may be brought to justice. W. Blacklock, U.S. Vice-Consul."

I am jumping ahead of time a bit here, as I have not yet properly introduced these consuls to the reader. I shall do so shortly.

To be fair, though it is a grudging concession on my part, the three main nation's consuls had each inherited a difficult situation from previous incumbents, and were stepping onto political standpoints that from the outset were entrenched, implacable and often to my eyes: stupid. To this sorry state of affairs, they also brought their own qualities, both good and bad in, it seems, equal measures. In many ways, their actions were a reflection of the way their nations might react, a war in miniature, coloured as they were by their national traits.

A detailed history of the politics is not the right content for this book, and therefore a series of (hopefully amusing) little snippets have been selected to illustrate the situation, little cut-scenes from the whole play. A reader interested in the full history of the politics could do little better than consult R.L. Stevenson's account [9] listed in the bibliography. As one might expect from the pen of so accomplished a storyteller, his book is interesting, amusing and makes for compelling reading to anyone seeking the history of the time. I have tried here simply to present the background to why so many ship captain's jammed their vessels into a tiny bay ignoring all their instincts urging them to get out.

Politically representing the German emperor in Samoa was Doctor Wilhelm Knappe, a man in his early thirties. He seems to me to have been a very poor diplomatist; in his view, the German position was right, there was no need to listen to a counter-position or argue against it, since no other position could have any relevance. This tunnel vision was not only limited to foreigners, he applied it equally to his military commander who tried to tread a wary path within the minefield of conflict. Kommander Fritze, the senior German Naval Officer at Apia, either did as he was told or Knappe would do it for him, and often the consul did indeed take the reins. The older, more experienced military man was frequently so concerned about Knappe's excesses that he would regularly write to Bismarck for explanation, or – more diplomatically – *confirmation* that the action taken by the consul had been legal. But such requests took time to answer, and in the meantime, the German community in Apia saw Knappe's stand as supportive, and that of Fritze as bordering on treasonable. In Germany then, Apia entertained a belligerent consul and a diplomatic military man.

Knappe had inherited a consul from his predecessor Becker (present in 1887) that was already at daggers drawn with the British Consul, one Colonel Henry de Coetlogon (present in 1888), a stupid situation brewed by the German when in fact, de Coetlogon and the British had been so fed up with the Samoa question that they would probably have allowed Knappe and Becker an almost free rein had they just left them out of it. Colonel Henry Watts Russell de Coetlogon to give him his full name, although the surname is spelt in some Foreign Office Records as Coertlogen; I have used what seems to be the most common as does RL Stevenson in *"A Footnote to History"*. Coetlogon was appointed Consul at Samoa in May 1888 replacing Mr. Wilfred Powell. The Coetlogon family name has Breton ancestry, from the Côtes-d'Armor department of Brittany in north-western France; the family had an ancestor who was Marshall of France in the seventeenth-century. The town today (2016) is a small village of some 230 population.

Though it would have been easier to make friends or at least be conciliatory, Becker preferred to antagonise, so Great Britain decided it would have to object and the stage was set for disagreement. In a childish and naïve frame of mind, Knappe was initially of the opinion that soothing the snooty British, mastering the native Samoan, and dealing gently but firmly with the upstart American, would occupy just the first few days of his tenure that would, thereafter, be a calm and successful sojourn and earn him the approbation of Chancellor Bismarck, perhaps even leading to better things in his career. It would take just those same few days to utterly destroy such foolish notions.

An example of differing cultures even amongst Europeans, which also serves quite nicely to introduce the reader to the level of farce pervading the entire scene, involved a local newspaper of the time, published by an amateur journalist, a British carpenter named Stephen J. Cusack: let's call this sketch *"The Affair of the English Printer"*.

The rather extravagantly named *"Samoa Times and South Sea Advertiser"* was, to most of its readers, an innocuous reporter of the rather silly facts it encountered; its author, hardly uncovering major scandal by dint of any dramatic investigative journalism, seemingly preferred simply to repeat (and, no doubt, embellish) the juicy gossip doing the rounds of the bars in Apia Town. Its motto was *"Sworn to no master, of no Sect am I"* which seems a good ideal when one has managed to work it out, and it had been founded in the middle of 1888.

To the majority of British and American readers, the Saturday weekly with its somewhat tongue-in-cheek condemnation of the more extreme stupidity of the diplomats was perfectly fair, the readership seeing no harm in someone subjecting a British or an American diplomat to ridicule and criticism. The German, of course, should not be ignored and was, admittedly, more worthy of notice, giving more scope for copy material. The publication's modern equivalent would be, I suppose, something like *Private Eye* in the United Kingdom, generating the same dichotomy of love and hate in its reception. In contrast to the *de rigueur* lampooning of officialdom, the *ST&SSA* (if I might so abbreviate it, despite the risk of it sounding like an American Wild West Railway Company) was apparently uncompromising in the respect it paid to private individuals and their privacy; many of today's newspapers could be improved by such deference. Most of its readership viewed it as a very mild publication, an amusement with which to while away a small part of the week. Cusack's interest seems to have been based in publishing first, journalism second, and like most of us with our human frailties, he probably enjoyed seeing the heat generated by his words, it being an added spur to continue heaping what coals he could.

But to the Germans, any criticism of their consul was an attack on them, their chancellor, and their nation; they seemed to have none of the political tolerance that their English-speaking opponents appeared to have been born with, and found it impossible to derive any delight from the articles which each week unaccountably amused the English and Americans. A few days after the *ST&SSA* published a particularly entertaining and, probably scurrilous anecdote concerning a German military resident named Brandeis for which Cusack actually received a fine, a group of German sailors took their leave ashore, and on landing at Apia began enquiring of the locals if they might be shown the *"English Printer"*; the man having been duly identified was subjected to some pretty rough handling which left him cut, bruised and dazed. Unfortunately for all concerned, except perhaps Mr. Cusack, the *wrong* English Printer had been pointed out: a recent arrival on Upolu only present by invitation of German industrialists desperate to counter the perceived amateur bias of Cusack with true journalistic professionalism, and maybe seeing in a Briton a way of avoiding those accusations of partiality that they were themselves flinging at Cusack. It would also mean they could deny Cusack German diplomatic printing income. The unfortunate Mr. *Jones* therefore received a thrashing for which he wasn't entitled and I'm quite sure had hardly expected as his welcome to Samoa. He and his erstwhile employers were among the few who failed to derive any amusement from the incident. A few months after the fracas, the new German Consul Knappe suppressed Cusack's four-page rag, an act that, far more than the indignity intended for its editor by German marines, set the fires of British diplomatic outrage blazing.

The *Samoa Times*, as it was unsurprisingly more commonly known, saw some hard times and eventually went out of business in 1896. Cusack had sold it in 1892 after ill health forced him to discontinue his editorship; there is no record of his life afterwards. Coincidentally, Her Majesty's Consul to Samoa between the years 1890 and 1897 happened to be Sir Thomas Berry Cusack-Smith, KCMG, 5th Baronet of Tuam, but does not appear to have been a relation.

As a demonstration that the *Samoa Times* left no-one out of its sphere of targets, even British, here is a letter published in the first issue edition dated 29th September 1888:

"How Certain Merchants in Apia Make Money – To the Editor of the Samoa Times – SIR,- Let them ask you to oblige them with loan of

English gold and let them have it at the rate of ten per cent; take their word that whenever you require English gold they will give it to you at the same rate; then allow about a year to pass when you will ask the merchants kindly to let you have part of your English gold, and with a smiling face accept of their reply that they have forgotten all about the transaction, and be told that no written agreement in regard to the returning of the English gold had been made. Be thrown out of their stores by two white and half a dozen brown Samoans and go home to consider that during the time that the English gold was handed over and now, a difference of exchange to tune of 20 per cent exists. If you desire to learn the names of the worthies you may apply to yours, &c., Otto Adam."

Perhaps Otto, presumably a German, was naïve to loan out his gold to English merchants without a written agreement, but I wonder if he ever got reimbursed, one rather thinks not.

The British Vice-Consul in 1888-9 was a Colonel of the old school. An Army officer and later career diplomat, de Coetlogon at all times behaved as he felt he should, and had an impeccable reputation for correctness. The de Coetlogons were really out of place at Apia, surely more suited to the costumed courts of Europe than a native Pacific island. But they both tried – in their various ways – to behave in a proper fashion, and both eventually left the island with a spotless reputation, despite some antagonism from the German Legation. An amusing letter from de Coetlogon in the Foreign Office files written following the storm records the damage caused to the building, all windows smashed, fence down and so on, but almost apologetically points out that the building had clearly not been properly maintained by its previous occupant, and that it would be grossly unfair to expect the current consul to pay for all the repairs himself. Whether de Coetlogon got away with this hope is not recorded.

Another of those farcical asides that litter this saga involved the de Coetlogons, and may be introduced as: *"The Affair of the British Hospital"*.

As the clashes between the rival Samoans started to generate wounded, the de Coetlogons set up a hospital in the grounds of the British Consulate. It would treat all wounded, whatever their allegiance. As well as being a true humanitarian gesture, it was also hoped, perhaps once more naively, that the proximity of the factions in distress might engender a spirit of peace between them.

To Knappe, the idea was appalling; he simply could not countenance natives loyal to Tamasese being indoctrinated by the British, so immediately set up his own hospital, segregated purely for those natives of the leader enjoying German support, who therefore promptly left the de Coetlogon's. The result was that instead of being a symbol of reconciliation between natives, the idea of a hospital became yet another barrier between them. Germans on their daily business, should it happen to take them past the British Consulate, were wont to shout to the de Coetlogons to let their charges die, presumably there were some similar comments passing in the other direction, and a good idea was turned bad. The de Coetlogon's hospital would see some worse idiocy before long.

The British therefore had a diplomatic consul, but the various incumbents of its military role displayed the sublime and ridiculous extremes of military diplomacy and consular arrogance. The British naval military representative changed regularly as the Royal Navy relieved its ships at Apia. Most were of a similar mind to Fritze, and perhaps it takes a military man, who presumably is in the best position to understand the dreadful reality and consequences of battle, to be the one prepared to make every possible effort to avoid it. A politician can easily take a noble stand, be it for the defence of his country or the preservation of an ideal, but is rarely called upon to stand in a muddy trench or behind a sand dune and fire a rifle at another human being to support that ideal – to face up to an enemy trying their best to kill him first. So it is easy for politicians to rattle their military sabres in a passion of bellicose indignation and outrage. I say most British Naval Captains at Apia shared Fritze's desire to avoid conflict – you'll soon meet the Briton who seems to have had as much idea of diplomacy as Vlad the Impaler might have had of social philanthropy.

The American Vice-Consul William Blacklock was, at the time of the storm, one of the most diplomatic persons Apia had ever seen, easily on a par with de Coetlogon. Diplomatic perhaps, but he was nevertheless firmly intransigent in his position with the Germans. He had led a very adventurous life before arriving at Apia. Originally a businessman, he had taken up a post as clerk from which position he had been elected to the consulship. The previous incumbent of the New World's post was one Leary, a man who was as belligerent in support of the American diplomatic position as Knappe was of the German. It had been left to Captain Mullan on USS *Nipsic* to be a conciliating militarist as was Fritze on SMS *Adler*: Mullan curbing Leary's avowed desire to sink every German ship and flatten every Tamasese village, just as Fritze tried to curb Knappe taking similar action against the Americans and their native allies. So both Germany and America had, for most of 1888, a belligerent consul and a diplomatic naval presence.

I think it only fair to record that the American Vice-Consul Leary, at least, had a wicked sense of humour that permits me to forgive him a little for being a politician. When observing from his veranda one evening an unintelligible exchange of rocket signals between, in his opinion, factions opposing the American supported chief, he found it great fun to send off a few randomly distributed rockets of his own, intended to confuse and confound the grand plans being laid – whether it worked is sadly not known, but I love the idea. Another fine jest was to play on the well-known tendency for correctness by German controlled institutions such as the Post Office. Leary would regularly write an innocuous letter to the native chief in opposition to the Germans, with the chief's name imposingly inscribed on the envelope, and deposit it at the German Post Office demanding its immediate delivery as diplomatic mail, to be viewed with horror by the staff who knew only too well that to try and do so would mean an ignoble end for the unfortunate individual chosen as postman. I suspect they all ended up in the nearest waste bin.

In the end, then, the melting pot brew made up of German, American and British individual personalities, national traits, and economic concerns was as potent as any kava made by a native for a drinking ceremony. Conflict was ever present on shore, but that it might eventually involve warships shelling each other was a step that inevitably seemed to be getting closer.

The 18th December 1888, saw Knappe finally commit himself to outright military action to support Tamasese, in *"The Affair of the German Bombardment"*. Having postured and threatened and imperiously told the Americans and British that Germany was the authoritative power in Samoa, Knappe appears to have suddenly started believing his own histrionic rhetoric and, perhaps inflamed by the hardly balanced wishes of local Germans, talked himself into a showdown without any form of diplomatic agreement or guidance from Bismarck in the Fatherland. Fritze was appalled, but had insufficient will to argue the diplomat down. Dr. Knappe would later pay dearly for his belligerence in Samoa.

Cutters from SMS *Eber* landed Marines from SMS *Olga* to confront Mata'afa at Fangallii a few miles along the coast from Apia, to teach him a lesson about respecting German property and military might. But, just as might be expected in the nature of the farce I am describing, it did not go well for the Germans, as later while entering Laulii Bay with Fritze on SMS *Adler*, Knappe was met by the unedifying sight of *Eber* carrying out 39 wounded blue-jackets. Worse intelligence was to come, both men horrified by the news that 2 officers (*Lieutenants zur See* Sieger and Spengler) and 15 men, no longer in need of medical care, had been left behind at Fangallii; in German eyes, they had been butchered and murdered rather than killed in a battle of their own initiation. Starting off a campaign for which he had no official backing with an utterly unforeseen and costly defeat would hardly help Knappe's position – as it was diplomatically tenuous at best. As he contemplated the response to the event that would be splashed across the newspapers at home, his dismay can be imagined.

Having approached the bay ready to dictate to what he expected to be a browbeaten, dejected and chastened Mata'afa, he abandoned all such *"peaceable"* intentions and decided that his first action must be to reverse the military position. Readying *Adler's* guns for retribution, to his further annoyance, Captain Mullan on USS *Nipsic* chose that moment to cross the bay in his cutter. Since no ship of any nation was allowed to wander freely around the islands without a ship of some other nation following and watching, Knappe, expecting to dismiss the American with what he had hoped was the capitulation of Mata'afa, was instead forced to endure a long and involved diplomatic protest from the American captain.

Unable to persuade the angry German not to impose some sort of punishment, Mullan did at least obtain grudging consent to allow the women and children safe passage, at the same time as an American Lieutenant was ashore and warning the village of what was to come, which was then almost immediately evacuated of *all* its occupants. When Knappe was finally able to give vent to his pent-up rage, he shelled a deserted village and destroyed little more than a few empty huts and an upstart British Union Flag that had no more right to be there than had any other foreign emblem.

The Associated Press correspondent at Apia, JP Dunning saw this outright action by Germany as a declaration of war on their part, and the catalyst for the increased attention given to the islands by the United States. Orders were given for USS *Trenton* and USS *Vandalia* to leave San Francisco, and proceed on the long journey to Samoa to support USS *Nipsic*. It also prompted Dunning being sent to Apia as Associated Press correspondent, in which position he would be in excellent case to monitor the subsequent dramatic events.

There can be no better demonstration of peevish foolery than what Stevenson describes as the *"The War of the Flags"*. It began when Knappe decreed the village of Laulii to be German, and out-of-bounds to Mata'afa due to the proximity of a German trader. An earlier ludicrous edict had barred Samoans from approaching German property in Apia despite British and American protests that such a regulation was unfair on the majority of natives of the islands. If a village adjoined a German plantation, the natives effectively could not enter their homes. So these two semi-allied nations, identifying parts of the village to be British or American (or at least, to have British or American interests) planted their respective flags in the appropriate area and declared Knappe's proclamation to be invalid in them. It would spawn confusion and silliness.

Oliver Warner in *"Great Seamen"* records that soon after the start of this madness, Captain Kane espied a conference being promoted aboard *Olga*, at which all the German captains – and Consul Knappe – were one-by-one, and in full view of the rest of Apia Harbour, rowed out to the vessel, setting in motion: *"The German Bombardment, Part 2"*. I have been unable to verify that it was Kane, indeed the timing means it was more probably Lieutenant Pelly on HMS *Lizard*, who, in a story that is hoped to be not apocryphal, rightly concluded that a war meeting was in progress, and had himself rowed over to the German warship to demand of a bemused and befuddled deck officer to be taken to join it.

On entering the room, and with the mute but telling evidence of hastily covered charts on the table, the British captain argued passionately against any rash action. In this he was probably tacitly (though unknowingly) in agreement with Fritze, but Knappe was in charge and haughtily demanded to be told who should think they might interfere in the legitimate actions of Germans in Samoa. Pelly replied darkly that such a belligerent attitude might be answered by deeds rather than words, and left the conference to its deliberations. The various visitors to *Olga* that morning had been carefully observed at a distance by an interested Mullan on *Nipsic* who had made the same deductions as Pelly.

Later that evening, *Adler* slipped out of the bay with no lights showing, and Pelly's fears were confirmed. Mullan too, was not deceived, and given the morning's very public events, how Fritze might have supposed the vessel could have disappeared from such a small anchorage unnoticed is difficult to understand; perhaps he realised, and relied on, the expectation that he couldn't. The other nations, believing a bombardment of a village to be the intent, followed closely, resolute on protecting their flags and whatever dusty patch of Samoan soil over which they impertinently fluttered. Pelly in HMS *Lizard*, and Mullan in USS *Nipsic*, chugged along behind Fritze in SMS *Adler*, the three ships vying with each other for the water and risking collision, as they each waited for the music to stop and the chance to grab their prize. The scenes evoked appear ludicrous, but were in fact deadly serious: no military Captain would tolerate any kind of foreign interference to his flag, and after a minor and ineffective sortie ashore by her marines, *Adler* eventually returned to Apia with Fritze in confusion about the legalities of the affair, despair at the stupidity of the game and perhaps relief at having in his eyes an acceptable excuse to have abandoned the plan, only to be unmercifully regaled for his supposed temerity by a livid Knappe.

Though initiated by his rivals to try and thwart Knappe's excesses, the idea of the flag staking out "ownership" appealed to the German and he soon planted his own in Mata'afa's camp, countered fairly quickly by more British and American in Tamasese's. The disease spread, and flags of the three nations appeared like weeds in a vegetable plot. The consuls must have soon been running short of the things. The native Samoans surely found the business tiresome and silly, if they could comprehend it at all.

It is now time to introduce the reader to the archetypal British Victorian Naval Captain, the individual as promised earlier who wore no diplomatic badges on his uniform and left any nonsense of that sort to other, lesser mortals. He was a captain in charge of a warship – and that was his position alone. HMS *Royalist* with one Captain George Weightman Hand in command entered the bay to relieve Captain Pelly in *Lizard*, and in this arrival, Great Britain brought to the plot a militarist with not a diplomatic fibre in his body, the direct opposite to Mullan and Fritze. His temperament would be demonstrated very quickly, in the affair of *"The British Hospital, Part 2"*.

Before Pelly could leave, he needed to recover the canvas awnings he had thoughtfully leant to the de Coetlogon's makeshift hospital. Fortunately, he had on board *Lizard* some canvas belonging to *Royalist* from an earlier visit, so used them to replace his own and thus was able to continue the protection against the sun they gave to the hospital's native inhabitants on the veranda. Pelly obviously assumed that Hand would continue the kindness.

He was quite wrong. On hearing of the arrangement, Hand immediately despatched a message to the consulate demanding the return of the equipment and declaring in a matter-of-fact way that he could *"… get rid of these n*****s…"* at the same time. Whether intended as such to the natives, the insult was felt personally by the de Coetlogons, who almost immediately were shown that Hand meant what he said, as he arrived with a boatload of seamen and began tearing down the protective awnings from over the heads of suffering natives, the numbers of which had only recently been swelled by more fighting.

The de Coetlogons were so dismayed by the business, they spent the rest of the evening ferrying the wounded inside the consulate; only too late did their shattered nerves recall an invitation to dine with Consul Knappe, and the letter of apology, appearing weak and contrived, was received only *after* Knappe had dressed and the table been laid. He never forgave the insult and forever after, the two men, previously on good terms even as they threatened each other with war and despite sharing a common shortage of health, were never again friends.

Hand was surely an intriguing character; I believe it would be unfair to judge him by today's politically correct standards, but that doesn't mean I would have liked him even then. He was born on 4th July 1841 and began his naval career as cadet on HMS *Impregnable* on the 25th January 1856; HMS *Royalist* was his first command as Captain, an appointment made on 11th July 1882. Seemingly blunt on a rare good day, universally rude on the others, thoroughly confident in the rightness of the British position whatever it may be (or perhaps he just didn't care about its correctness), and utterly contemptuous of everyone else and especially natives, whether those opposing him or those he was meant to be protecting. He quickly obtained a reputation for blatantly displaying his contempt for everyone and everything, without favour or bias, and regardless of political or national orientation. He must have been an absolute tartar on his ship, and no doubt his officers and men would have been in awe of him. I would bet money his orders never needed to be repeated, and were carried out promptly and without question.

Hand's character, already slightly tarnished by the hospital business, can be given a quite different slant by an event that occurred a few days before Christmas 1888. German marines from SMS *Eber* for some reason began firing at a native boat in the bay. The crowded port meant that there was always a risk that a bullet discharged in the location might find its way to somewhere it should not, and indeed, some of the more wayward ricochets whistled rather close to the head residing on Captain Hand's shoulders, as he was standing on the beach awaiting return to *Royalist*. It was a useless struggle on my part to avoid the temptation to call the affair the "*War of Hand's Ear*".

It makes a wonderful image, to picture Her Britannic Majesty's Captain George Weightman Hand R.N., standing on the shore, staring across the bay in rigid fury as the whine of German bullets passed around him. What we can surmise of his character suggests the idea of ducking, or taking shelter, would never have occurred to him. Once the rattle of shooting died down, he demanded to be rowed over to the culprit German vessel, which he boarded quite alone, and thereafter proceeded to berate everyone he met, no matter their position on the ship. Deck officer, steward emptying galley refuse over the side, they were all the same to him, and each received the full glory of a furious British Naval Captain's tongue, delivered in a rage which probably meant the words were unintelligible if not the sentiments which lay behind them. It took nearly an hour before he was persuaded to depart, still seething with fury and resentment. Stevenson describes his feelings as *"insatiable of apologies"*; a phrase that seems to cover it nicely. The captain of SMS *Eber* even felt obliged to make a personal visit of apology to Hand the next day, and later to send over the German officer who had apparently exceeded his order in authorising the shooting, to personally make *his* apologies. Captain Hand must have made quite an impression! There will be a little more about this incident later, as discussed in the British parliament.

It seems this was not, in fact, an isolated incident, a similar close call having been undergone by Lieutenant Pelly while in the port earlier on HMS *Lizard*.

It was Hand too, who resolved in his own forthright way, a thorny problem for Fritze, *"The Affair of the British Tourist"*. Consul Knappe, having declared martial law, apparently completely illegally and without authorisation from Germany, later effectively arrested the British merchant vessel *Richmond* that he accused of running contraband to Mata'afa. It would be fairest to acknowledge that he was probably correct in this charge, though the British saw it rather as legitimate support to Mata'afa which needed to be performed surreptitiously due only to Knappe's unfair proclamations making it an offence – a shaky position on which to stand. *Richmond's* crew and her very few fare-paying passengers were ordered to remain on board until the vessel had been searched by German Marines, generating protests and the inevitable counter-proclamations from de Coetlogon.

Knappe was therefore astounded to learn that the next day, a British tourist, one Mansfield Gallien, bored with this enforced prolongation of his stay in the islands, had decided to go ashore and seek a personal interview with Mata'afa to establish the Samoan side of the story – quite in defiant contravention of the German consul's blunt and unambiguous directive. Perhaps Gallien had read de Coetlogon's reply proclamation that German martial law could not apply to British subjects, more likely he was simply demonstrating the breathtaking contempt that Victorian Britons held for any *Johnny foreigner*. However imprudent the visit might have been in the political climate of the island, Gallien seems to have enjoyed it, and eventually returned to the *Richmond* satisfied with his day's excursion, taking the time on the way back to openly share the circumstances of his interesting trip with a number of Apia residents in the various taverns which were common in the town – taverns frequented by all the antagonistic nationalities and mostly owned by Germans. Hardly surprisingly, the tale of his trip ashore quickly got back to Knappe.

To a calm mind, the blatant openness of it all would hardly seem to have been the actions of a professional spy or smuggler, but during the night, Gallien was rudely awakened by marines from *Olga* under the orders of Knappe, dragged half naked off the British ship and taken to *Adler* for imprisonment, prior to being tried under court-martial for which he might, given Knappe's fury more at the impertinence than the real criminality, expect the death penalty.

Fritze, the diplomatist in uniform, was once again appalled at the actions of his consul and, believing such an arrest to have been utterly without legitimacy, immediately sent word to Bismarck: "*Is arrest of foreign citizens on foreign vessels legal?*" he asked, knowing full well what the answer would be.

Whether it might arrive in time to save Mr. Gallien was doubtful. It was Captain Hand, learning of the arrest and dismissive of de Coetlogon's diplomatic outrage and planned official protests, who solved the problem. He made a polite visit to his opposite number Fritze on SMS *Adler*, during which he partook of some tolerable wine with the German, before casually suggesting to his host whilst indicating Mr. Gallien whom he had requested to meet: "*I wish* you *would set that man ashore, to save* me *the trouble.*" The emphases on "you" and "me" being especially pertinent.

Perhaps this not very subtle threat was diplomacy of a sort. Fritze was more than prepared to comply, and though he again suffered badly from Knappe's invective when the release was made known, it is perhaps significant the consul made no effort to go and get the tourist again. The kidnapping, if I might call it that, even prompted questions in the House back in Britain when it became known. Hansard records further debate as follows, recorded in HC Deb 18th March 1889 volume 334 cc38-9:

> "*Dr. Cameron asked the First Lord of the Admiralty whether any report had yet been received at the Admiralty concerning the seizure of Mr. Gilan, a British subject, on board the British ship Richmond by an armed guard from the German warship Adler at Samoa?*"

> "*Lord G. Hamilton replied: A telegraphic report has been received from the Commander-in-Chief on the Australian Station from New Zealand,*"

dated February 19, to the effect that the Germans had proclaimed martial law at Samoa, and claimed the right of search over British ships, and that British subjects (no names given) had been removed from the British ship Richmond, by armed boats from the German ship Adler. They were subsequently released on the demand of the captain of the Royalist. A further telegram on February 21 states that the captain of the Calliope, which ship has replaced the Royalist, had informed the German authorities at Samoa that he could not acknowledge the establishment of martial law or the 39 jurisdiction or rights so claimed over British subjects or Courts. The claims so advanced were abandoned. No report has been received with reference to the statement quoted in the second part of the question. With regard to the latter part of the question, Captain Hand reports that a cutter belonging to the German ship Eber chased a boat containing unarmed natives, and fired upon them as they were escaping into the bush. Captain Hand, of the Royalist, was on the beach at the time, and hailed the German boat to call their attention to his being there, and to his being exposed to their fire. On his remonstrating with the captain of the Eber, that officer expressed his regret at the occurrence which had taken place contrary to the instructions he had given as to firing, and repeated the same to Captain Hand on the following day on board the Royalist. He further sent the officer who had committed the breach of orders to Captain Hand to apologize, and to explain that he had acted contrary to his instructions."

I assume the name "Gallien" to have been misspelt in the Hansard record. The owners of the *Richmond* later lodged a claim for damages against the German Government, the outcome of which is not known. Hand placed a detachment of British marines on board to prevent any repetition of the act.

The supposed interference to Knappe's ineffective assault on Fangallii mentioned earlier, by a naturalised American called John Klein, a war-correspondent representing the *New York World* and the *San Francisco Examiner*, caused gross indignation in many German hearts which rattles on even today, far more so than Mr. Gallien's ill-advised day-trip; we'll call this one *"The Affair of the German/British/American Traitor"*. The Teutonic-sounding name of the naturalized American (in reality born a British citizen) gave rise to possibly baseless accusations of Klein's actual participation in the affair in traitorous alliance with the native side, and he was forced to hide in the American consulate whilst the Germans demanded he be given up and tried for his life under court-martial; he was only saved by being spirited out of the islands under cover of night on the

American warship USS *Nipsic*, forfeiting all his possessions and (rather inconsequential) wealth in the process. In seems he had just happened to be present as the German landing boats had entered the coves, and had even hailed them asking for their intentions, a somewhat impetuous request which was answered by a fusillade of rifle fire. R.L. Stevenson does, however, seem to feel it likely the Samoans and Klein did indeed open fire first. Whichever it was, perhaps a righteous indignation along similar lines felt by Captain Hand may have been the catalyst for the embellishment of his subsequent participation in the affray, which quickly led to the preparation and refining of an excellent story, one which he hoped would guarantee its raconteur a good supply of evening refreshment for a few days at least. To his disappointment, the only ones to believe him were the Germans, and he paid dearly for his imprudence and the ornamentation of the story. He is still "credited" with leading the Samoan attack in some German web-sites today. It was reported in the Thames Star, 1st May 1889 that he had made an affidavit to Vice-Consul Blacklock, in which he refuted the German accusations levelled at him. The Washington State Department later conveyed this document to Berlin, but it clearly received short thrift.

All these anecdotes are at the same time amusing, petty, and deadly serious in their own way. The basic conclusion is that the diplomatists who saw themselves as representatives of their country, were implacable in their desire to protect their nation's people and interests, and were backed up by military might should an opponent decide to use theirs. They were, as already stated, arguing themselves into a war. And the war that was brewing might not have been limited to a simple fracas in some native islands on the other side of the world leaving the exchange in Europe to words only, but could easily have dragged the three nations into a First World War 25 years sooner than eventually happened.

Hidden under all this was Samoa, a beautiful island to a romantic eye. Hardly idyllic before the Europeans came, in the way local disputes were resolved by native killing native, but in that respect, no different to anywhere that humans existed then. Indeed, not much different to many areas of humanity today.

But just as then, there are still dangers today. On 29th September 2009, the Samoa and Tonga islands were subjected to a terrifying series of tsunami as a result of an offshore magnitude 8.1 earthquake centred in the ocean about midway between those islands, occurring on the outer rise of the Kermadec-Tonga Subduction Zone. It is perhaps the worst natural disaster to have hit the two groups of islands in recorded history; more than 189 persons were killed, mostly in Samoa, and most of them, children. The south and west coastlines of Upolu and the other islands in the chain seem to have been very badly hit.

In 1889, nature used a different weapon.

Chapter 5: Outward Bound.

On Tuesday, 1st March 1887 at 5.30 p.m., HMS *Calliope* left Plymouth Sound and the cold, dreary skies of Victorian England, pushing her way into the south-westerly swell which so regularly seems to cast up the channel from deep within the Atlantic. The winds were relatively quiet as the crew inwardly said their goodbyes to the coastline they would not see again for more than three years.

Kane was ready to stamp his authority on the ship and crew, no more clearly demonstrated than right at the start of the voyage. Just four days after sailing, it was discovered that the Shell Room lights had not been extinguished the previous day, when the magazines had been reported as "closed" by Master Gunner Martin after General Quarters. Martin had placed the keys to the room in the key box, the placement indicating that all was well and the magazines had been checked, yet clearly he had failed to do anything of the sort. Kane considered this action such a serious neglect of duty that a clear statement to that effect was ordered to be written into the ship's log, quite a public rebuke which would later be obvious to the Admiralty when the logs were subsequently read at the end of the voyage. It is perhaps significant that no further records of a similar nature were made. It should also be noted that Master Gunner Martin redeemed himself later in the voyage by taking charge of a hazardous attempt to disengage *Calliope* from an island schooner that had become entangled with the British ship in one of the major storms to precede the hurricane.

Despite the absence of further public chastisement, it is not to say there are not some other notes worthy of comment. The log was also used to record those items on the ship lost or damaged, along with a comment that the loss was either *"by accident"* or by *"carelessness"* or *"neglect"*, the latter two usually incurring for the culprit the loss of wages to pay for the item. The first man on the voyage to fall foul of this edict was Royal Marine

Artillery Gunner Albert Shearman who lost overboard the device known as (in the quaint services lingo of word reversal which existed long into the twentieth-century) a *"Rod, Cleaning, Nordenfelt, 1 inch"* for which he was charged half-cost. The log is littered with such losses, usually items from the guns and most frequently (for some probably sensible reason) gun-sight protective covers. It seems likely that the ship's store will have been provisioned with many spares for the deck equipment. Although discipline was an absolutely essential aspect of Kane's commissioning cruise, it was thankfully no longer enforced by such medieval means as employed by the previous *Calliope*'s Sailing Master, Robert Knox, who littered his log with records of lashings by the cat for various misdemeanours and crimes.

Though the experienced sailors took delight in detailing to the new boys the horrible storms which would be encountered in the fearsomely reputed Bay of Biscay, in fact the crossing was quiet and almost uneventful, the passage aided after a while by a stiff north-easterly breeze which bulged the ship's canvas and raucously blasted its moaning, sinusoidal song in the taught harp-strings of the rigging. The strong swell persisted for the entire crossing, testing and probing the handling characteristics of the new boat and the skills of her crew. The general pronouncement from the old hands was that she was a good sea-boat but confirmed their earlier observations that she inclined to be excessively lively in a head sea.

On the Friday following departure, the ship arrived at Funchal on the southern coast of Madeira Island, the so-called *"Pearl of the Atlantic"*, and replenished her coal stock in what is (by today) the 500 year-old capital. Not much fuel had been used so far, but no ship's master in that period would ever pass up the opportunity to fill his bunkers to the brim, and Kane was every bit as prudent in this respect as the best of them.

If you have access to Google Maps, enter the string: 32.65N, 16.9W to display the group. For many of the places I record WIT and *Calliope* visiting, I shall give a string in square brackets that, if entered in Google Maps search box (without the brackets), will take you to an airborne view of it, should you think it worth the effort.

Calliope was soon followed into the bay by HMS *Wye* returning to England from the Barbados, and the outgoing *Calliope*s shared the joy and pleasure the *Wye*s were surely feeling on the last leg of their journey home. The pleasure was tinged with the thought that though HMS *Wye* would be home in days, for the *Calliope*s it would be counted in years before they too saw friends and family again. At this encounter, an injured *Calliope* seaman was transferred to the home-going vessel for passage back to England. It is coincidental that when *Calliope* was in Portsmouth at the end of her voyage, the first ship to enter after her return happened to be HMS *Wye*.

Calliope proceeded some 500km to the north-east to St. Vincent on Portugal's stormy, wind-swept coastline in a very stiff breeze that forced the reduction of the canvas to a bare minimum, and the rocky Cape [37.02N, 8.99W] was reached on the 20th. The log does not record the reason for this somewhat backward step. Here, coal was again taken on, and a number of crew took the opportunity to go ashore and view the hill that was, at the time, supposed by many to represent the profile of no lesser a person than George Washington. I have been unable to find any independent description of this natural phenomenon that WIT describes, and I do not know if it exists today. WIT's view was simply that the hilly vista made for an unpleasant walk in the humid heat, and was unimpressed by nature's sculpting of the famous American President's face, but nibbling on grapes plucked from a roadside bush was a novelty he far more appreciated.

Sailing on the evening tide of the 22nd, *Calliope* arrived the next day at Porto Praya on St. Jago, one of the Cape Verde islands, in time for some important celebrations. The spelling is WIT's and probably phonetic rather than accurate for the time; today the port is known as Praia [14.91N, 23.502W].

On the 21st March 1887 had been born in Lisbon the son and heir to the Crown Prince of Portugal, named Luiz Filipe in the contemporary account, and the fêtes and parties on the island were still in full swing. The British officers and men thoroughly enjoyed the spectacle but for many their thoughts were on the trip to come, heading for the southern tip of South Africa nearly two months sailing time distant. Prince Luís Filipe, as his name is recorded today, would sadly never see his 21st birthday, being assassinated with his father King Carlos 1 by revolutionaries 2 years before the eventual overthrow of the Portuguese Royal Family.

On Thursday, 24th March at 8 a.m., *Calliope* weighed her anchors and in a confident force 3-4 wind set off for the run to the Cape of Good Hope. Over the next three months, *Calliope* was to run more than 7,000 miles under her canvas alone, nearly 2,000 under steam alone and some 1,200 under both. The sailing distance in this quarter-year would contribute three-quarters of the sail-only distance for the entire voyage.

It is worth recording at this point, that ship's captains not only had the need to ensure their crew could properly handle the vessel under sail, they were duty bound to avoid the unnecessary expenditure of coals. When steam first made its presence widely felt in naval ships, some interesting Admiralty Circulars governing its use were issued.

In 1856, circular number 263 made the position clear:

> *"Steam Power Not To Be Used But In Cases Of Necessity. Admiralty, August 26th, 1856. My Lords desire to call the attention of all Officers in command Her Majesty's Ships to Circular, No 177, as well as to the Orders which have been given from time to time respecting the expenditure of Coals, and to impress upon them the necessity that exists of working their ships without the aid of steam, when the duty required can and ought to be performed under sail alone - not only on the score of economy, but for the important purpose of ensuring the efficiency of screw ships as sailing ships. My Lords are therefore pleased to direct that in future the use of steam power shall not be resorted to when the service on which a vessel is employed can be satisfactorily performed without it; and that their Lordships may know whether this order has been duly observed, all Commanding Officers are, whenever steam is raised, to cause the same to be noted in the Log Book, together with their reasons for so doing, stating whether it be the emergency of the occasion, the necessity of performing the service with the utmost despatch, or other cause which, in their opinion, may justify their having recourse to steam power."*

A later circular that year (number 270) would require all such expenditures to be underlined in the log in red ink, and despite their age, both these instructions were still in force for *Calliope's* commissioning voyage. Even as late as 1860, the English Seamanship Manual continued to sum up other concerns quite candidly:

> *"Engines and machinery, liable to many accidents, may fail at any moment and there is no greater fallacy than to suppose that ships can be navigated on long voyages without masts and sails."*

It is, of course, grossly unfair with our benefit of hindsight to laugh at the Naval Secretary who penned those words. I think he must have been a staunch traditionalist, unimpressed by modern steam power.

Shortly into the commissioning trip, on the 27th March large patches of discoloured sea were observed, with no explanation being found among the old salts. A similar phenomenon would be encountered in the southern Indian Ocean a few months later.

Initially good speed was made, but gradually the winds lightened until, still some 250 miles north of the equator, they had fallen entirely, and a couple of her boilers were lit. On 31st March under steam and in longitude 26½°W, the line was crossed for the first of what would be many times on the voyage, just about mid-way between the Sierra Leone coastline of Africa 1,650 km to the north-east, and the Brazilian of South America some 1,200 km to the south-west.

Normally the catalyst for some rowdy initiation ceremonies aimed at those unfortunates for whom the event was their first transit from one hemisphere to the other, Kane decreed that neither King Neptune nor his voluptuous consort would appear on this occasion, considering the proceedings as demeaning and humiliating and out of place on a military vessel. In this, I think he was quite right. Eric Newby in his wonderfully illustrated book *"Learning The Ropes"*, describes his own crossing-the-line-ceremony some fifty years later in the windjammer *Moshulu* as *"… a pretty rough affair…"*; carefully chosen words which seem to me to disguise a disgusting situation bordering on sadistic brutality, in no way justified by it being a long-standing tradition. In 1776, HMS *Resolution*'s sailing master William Bligh, not known for being a particularly sympathetic man, whilst noting Captain Cook's permission for the duckings on the fateful third and final voyage of discovery to the Pacific commented on them as a *"vile practice."*

The next day, a wind got up and steam was taken off. The south-east trades blew for much of the month as *Calliope* headed for the coast of South America, turning east once she had passed Tristan da Cunha [37.11S, 12.29W] until about 30°S when they became once more light and variable. On the 5th April, *Calliope* exchanged colours with the French barque *Yvonne-Maire* of Nantes. By the end of April with *Calliope* in latitude 37°S, the Cape was still some 840 miles distant, but the winds again picked up and on the 5th May she entered Simon's Bay on South Africa's Western Cape to find Her Majesty's Ships *Raleigh*, *Flora* and *Wrangler* in the harbour. The bay lies on the western edge of the huge south facing *False Bay* dominated at its centre by the southern edges of Cape Town [34.18S, 18.44E].

There are a great many references to both Simons Town and Simonstown in the public domain, even amongst people living in the place and advertising holiday accommodation or whatever on the internet, but I believe the name should be apostrophised in the possessive form I have used in my text: *Simon's Town*. Residents please forgive me if I am wrong to use the same construction for the name of the bay.

During this long voyage, the crew had been drilled incessantly, daily exercises to hone their skills in handling their ship in dirty weather or fierce battle. To someone like myself, presented today with an image of a sailing ship festooned by a myriad of twisted and intertwined, tangled ropes, the operation to make a sailing ship actually work is a mystery, and following a great deal of painstaking research on the subject, most of it still is. I think the only real way to understand properly would be to serve in a tall ship on a long voyage. And in these days of advancing years and broadening beam, I would probably struggle to get up the gangplank let alone a mast. New boys entering the navy in WIT's day will, no doubt, have thought precisely the same thing about the masses of rope stretching to the heavens, but that is what training and experience is all about. No one can even tie their shoelace until someone shows them how.

Like many things, much of the complication the image of a sailing ship presents is down to repetition. If there are three masts, all square rigged like *Calliope's*, then most of the dazzling array of ropes can be ignored, since learning them on one mast, or even on one sail on that mast, learns much of the whole. Obviously, the reader does not need to know how to operate every line on a sailing ship to read this book, and if he or she is sufficiently interested in finding out more, then there are a mass of publications available which will do the job far better than could I. The Internet, too, can be a source of a wealth of data, but like anything which is only semi-controlled for content, you have no real way of knowing how true or accurate the information is.

Fortunately, by the time they reached the Cape the crew of HMS *Calliope* had become a skilled and integrated team of individuals who performed difficult and dangerous tasks with the confidence of knowledge and experience. To them the ropes were lines, and were not tangled or twisted at all, but carefully placed to be accessible when required for the task they serviced. The experienced sailors helped bring on the boys, reinforcing their training on how to go aloft, and what the ropes did. Their names had been learned, for example a *halyard* was used to "*haul a yard*" up to its seating by men on the deck using blocks-and-tackles and pulleys, and a few years later, by powered winches. Not all names were so obvious. Each operation with a sail, to furl it or set it, used some of these many ropes in combination, and before long a seaman could be woken from a deep slumber and perform a drill within moments without thinking about the things he had to do.

During the course of researching this book, and the necessity of at least attempting to understand some of the aspects of handling a tall ship, I have come to respect the designers of these vessels as very clever persons indeed. If you think about it, they will have designed an almost self-contained machine, which could not only perform incredible voyages in rough weather, but be repaired for nearly all damage without recourse to boat-yards or maintenance docks. Vessels carried spares for each mast and yard arm, and at a pinch, the carpenters could take a suitable tree trunk from ashore and fashion a temporary new mast complete from it. The crew of a sailing ship could replace these structures using just ropes and their own efforts. They could run an anchor out abeam of the ship and another the other side, and tip her far over to get at the hull. The ways to perform these functions, and so many others, will have been learnt by the crew over the years, and a good and knowledgeable sailing master and boatswain were vital to the efficient operation of a sailing ship.

South Africa, and the Simon's Town area, was a fine place to spend some leave time. The British had first begun using it as a naval base in 1814, and that function for the South African navy remains to this day in some form or another.

Unquestionably, it has no historical place in this book but I must again digress many years forward, to a wonderful tale about a Great Dane hound that, in 1940, was making a nuisance of itself riding on the local trains in Simon's Town. He was well known to, and a great favourite of, the visiting sailors, many inebriated examples of whom he had led back to their barracks in Simon's Town (whether or not they happened to be quartered there). He seemed only to recognise the distinctive uniform of British sailors, leaving other nationalities well alone.

He was not so popular with the train authorities when he regularly took it into his head to drape his not inconsiderable form over a couple of seats for a ride between the local stations, though even when a conductor managed to force him off at one of the intermediate stops, he seemed always to know where he was and simply waited for the next train to arrive and take him wherever he had originally wanted to go, usually to one of his many *lady-friends* spread around the area. He obviously thoroughly enjoyed to travel in this way, but faced an uncertain future from the threats of the local authorities until someone decided to enrol him in the British Royal Navy, and a request to that effect was somehow approved. This would guarantee him, as it did all RN volunteers during the war years, a free pass for the trains. The story goes that, with a sailor speaking on his behalf, he was enrolled as "*Just Nuisance*" (from: Surname? *Nuisance*; First name? *Just Nuisance*), with the rank of Ordinary Seaman (later promoted to Able) the first and (so far!) only dog to hold any rank in the Senior Service. His trade was described as "*Bone-crusher*" and his religious denomination: "*Scrounger*". Later on, it was whilst indulging in what was patently his most favourite activity, riding on a fast moving vehicle (in this case, a truck), that he was badly injured when making an impatient leap before waiting for it to stop; the ensuing health problems eventually leading to his enforced demise on his 7th birthday: 1st April 1944. I know, I know, but despite the date, the story does seem to be true. A statue in his honour adorns Jubilee Square in Simon's Town, and there are today annual parades at which his many supposed descendants are welcome guests at a look-alike competition! A book was written soon after his death, whose proceeds went to the war effort, and others have since followed, the author has a copy of a more recent publication, *"Just Nuisance A.B."* by Terence Sisson, ISBN 094998938X and has often shared the delightful story with friends. Search the internet for *"Nuisance, Simon's Town"* if you don't believe me.

Sailors who had visited the area before, such as WIT when homeward bound from China seven years previously on *Charybdis*, organised parties ashore to see the sights. But it was during this latest visit whilst on a work duty on the inauspicious Friday 13th May 1887 that WIT would suffer a serious accident that would ultimately end his sea-going career, in a similar (though not as permanent) manner later experienced by *Nuisance*. Bringing back the last load of ammunition from the stores wisely located some two miles out of town, the cart took charge and as WIT attempted to jump clear; he was tangled in the drag rope and dragged some yards before the other sailors managed to bring the horse under control. He regained consciousness in the naval hospital in Simon's Town, being heavily bandaged around the chest. A number of ribs on the right side had been broken, though fortunately the lung had not been pierced, and many of his chest and arm muscles on the right side had been torn.

I can bond somewhat with WIT here. Following a recent car crash and the failure of my car's air-bags to deploy, I know just what it is like to suffer a fractured sternum and ribs!

After 2 days of painful immobility, WIT was visited by Kane himself, who asked the sailor if he should prefer to remain in hospital until discharge, then to try and catch up with his ship as other naval vessels arrived and went on, or to go on with *Calliope* and complete his recovery on the cruiser: WIT immediately and unhesitatingly elected to stay with his vessel and ship-mates. Kane, apparently touched by the loyalty shown and understanding that the sailor would be in far more discomfort on the bouncing ship than in the hospital cot, arranged on the Sunday before departure for a number of burly seamen to arrive at the hospital, and to carefully carry their injured shipmate (accompanied by two other invalids from the hospital) in ceremonious procession through the town, still in his bed, down to the dock to be taken by the skiff back to his ship. That same Sunday, Admiral Walter Hunt Grubbe, Commander-in-Chief Cape Town visited the ship, and pronounced that he was well satisfied. WIT had earlier in that decade served on HMS *Sultan* when she was commanded by the then Captain Walter Hunt Grubbe. The next morning's tide took *Calliope* out of the bay and on her long cruise through the southern oceans for New Anjer (now Anyer) and Singapore.

During the passage, *Calliope* ranged well to the south, touching almost 43° southern latitude at one point; in calm winds and seas, the journey was slow but as pleasant as it ever could be on a working naval vessel. During the early morning of 28th May with *Calliope* in 42°48'S and 52°E, as the still hidden sun warmed the eastern sky with a pinkish glow, the air temperature suddenly chilled by some 10°F and minutes later, one of the pair of look outs on the top-sail yard shouted "*Iceberg, Port Bow!*" But this was no perilous *Titanic* situation, and the huge and magnificent block of ice passed safely down the port side of the vessel that shivered in its shadow. All who were able came out on deck to witness the incredible and somehow horrifying spectacle. WIT's mates came into the hospital bay and lifted his cot so he too could view the thing through the porthole. The sun's rays low above the north-eastern horizon pierced the many facets of the iceberg like a renaissance chandelier, and a glorious technicolour display of light bathed *Calliope's* decks and crew. For it to have been so memorable to all who saw it, I guess it must have been truly large.

Calliope called at the lifeboat station on St Paul's Island [38.72S, 77.53E], a tiny speck of rock located on the junction of the underwater Mid-Indian and South-East-Indian ridges. With Ile Amsterdam, the only land in thousands of square miles of ocean almost equidistant from Africa, India and Australia, the station was provided with tinned stores and a lifeboat. Shipwrecked sailors who were fortunate enough to reach the island could be sure of food, shelter, and a six-monthly (or so) call by warships plying the seas around the area. The island gives the appearance of a right-angled triangle with the square sides to west and south of about 4 km with the hypotenuse bulging around the flooded crater that so clearly advertises its volcanic origin. *Calliope's* visit during which she fired signal guns and sailed once completely round the island was met only by the cry of sea-birds and the boom from the waves crashing against the rocky coast. With no returned signals from the station, or signs of a boat trying to leave the bay, it was assumed the station was unoccupied and the cruise continued, the course shaped for Batavia and the Sunda Straits.

Two years after *Calliope's* visit, a gentleman named Charles

Lightoller spent 8 days on the island after the barque *Holt Hill* ran aground on it. This man was later second officer on RMS *Titanic*, and survived that 1912 disaster as well.

It is interesting to note that this diversion is recorded in WIT's memoirs, but I could find no mention of it in the ship's log, which one would have expected. However, a plot I made of *Calliope's* daily position from her log clearly shows she deliberately called there. Today, I can find no mention of a lifeboat station ever being on the island.

On 21st June in 16°S and 107°E, another natural phenomenon was encountered which enthralled all present - a milky sea, similar to that experienced soon after the start of the voyage. As dusk approached, the sea ahead was observed to be white and frothy, which showed up clearly in the darkening evening and gave the appearance of a snow-covered scene. To WIT, the most likely explanation was a disturbance of the sea-bed, but Chaplain Evans preferred to ascribe the phenomenon to "...*the presence in the water of myriads of luminous 'infusoria'...*" a collective term for minute aquatic creatures and algae. The weird and ghostly effect, in the distance like low-lying mist in a graveyard whilst close by the boat just like milk, persisted all night, until the dawn's sun dispersed or obscured it.

Today, the effect, which can even be observed from satellites orbiting the earth, is attributed to bacteria such as *vibreo harvey* and is well-documented, with the concentration of such events being in the area where *Calliope* was that day. So Chaplain Evans was, I guess, pretty accurate with his interpretation.

The masses of cape pigeon and albatross which now accompanied the ship shared the landfall with Christmas Island [10.49S, 105.65E] during the afternoon of 25th June about as far distant from Christmas in time as one could get, some 220 miles south of Java Head. The tiny island was covered in lime trees and coconut palms, visible from the mast head from perhaps 30 miles distance in clear weather. Two days later, with the entrance to the Sunda Straits in view, *Calliope* anchored off the town of New Anjer [6.06S, 105.92E]. Six years earlier, in late August 1883, the nearby huge volcano of Krakatoa had blasted itself into dust and ash, the debris and the resulting *tsunami* destroyed many of the coastal villages surrounding the Straits, including the town that had once been known simply as Anjer lying some 36 miles to the east; the new version had grown up from its ruins. It is now named Anyer and seems to be mainly industrial.

The stay was short, and on the 28th, an early morning start was made, passing out of the Sunda Straits proceeding slowly, stopping for soundings every hour or so before continuing, and eventually arriving at Singapore [1.25N, 103.9E] by the Banka Strait soon after noon on the 2nd July. By now the equator had been crossed for the second time in the voyage, but only by 85 miles and the place was as hot as one might expect with it being so close. Once again, the stay would be brief. Orders awaited *Calliope* on HMS *Orion* in the port to proceed at once to Hong Kong at best economical speed (some 10 knots) to join the fleet. The ship immediately tied up to the Tanjong Pagar wharf and coaling was started without delay, continuing long into the night. By daylight the next day, *Calliope* was on her way yet again. Fortunately for compliance with her orders, the weather was on her side and a fast and easy passage was made, the ship arriving in Hong Kong on 9th July dropping her anchor in the bay at ten o'clock in the morning [22.30N, 114.2E].

Hong Kong was, for much of the nineteenth and twentieth centuries, a British dependency, ceded to Great Britain in 1841 (Kowloon in 1860) as a result of the first Opium War between Britain and the Qing Dynasty, something to which the previous HMS *Calliope* had made a significant contribution. In 1898 came the agreement that the 99-year tenure of this and additional territory would end in 1997, when the ownership of the colony would revert to China. Without Hong Kong's fabulous harbour as a base for its China Squadron, Great Britain's influence in the Far East during that period would have been significantly more difficult to secure. The harbour was so good and so well located, that in 1888 shipping to the extent of some six and a half million tons used the port, a quite staggering amount for the time. It might also be interesting to note that it was Britain's distasteful intention to maintain an opium trade with China that on 7th January 1841 had led to an assault on some Chinese forts protecting the Canton estuary at Chuenpi and Tai Kok Tau on Hong Kong Island. The land-based military attack was supported by a Royal Navy squadron that engaged a large fleet of war junks, whose leader was sunk by a rocket from the previous HMS *Calliope*; the incident was followed just eleven days later by the cession of Hong Kong to the British. Whilst there are many hysterical claims made by activists about the Opium Trade with China that taint the topic with paranoia, it is difficult to see any redeeming features in the British position, which seems to be much the same as that taken by Columbian Drug Lords today – destroying lives simply to make profit.

I must also partially close the loop made in chapter 2 regarding the Crimea War, and the relative effectiveness of wooden hulled ships engaged in the bombardment of forts. In June 1859, as part of the second Opium War between Britain and China and a few years after the end of the Crimea War, some British wooden-hulled gunboats built for and used in the Crimea were being employed in the bombardment of China's Taku Forts, necessary before the combined British and French fleet could proceed to their destination: Peking (now Beijing). During the bombardment, the nine British gunboats of four guns apiece and two of six guns were getting a severe mauling, and at one point, an American vessel, a chartered steamer the *Toey Wan* not actually engaged in the conflict, entered the fray to tow damaged British and French vessels clear of the fort's unexpectedly heavy and accurate armament, thereby violating American neutrality. The American vessel was commanded by Josiah Tattnall, a veteran of the *War of 1812* conflict with Britain, who defended the actions that saved many of his former enemies lives by declaring that *"Blood is thicker than water"* and is now credited with being the first American known to have used that phrase. Some say the origin of the idiom is the Walter Scott novel "*Guy Mannering*" published in 1815, but many variations of it seem to have been in use for centuries before. The loop will only be fully closed when *Calliope* meets an American Admiral at Samoa.

In Hong Kong, the China squadron was absent, the Admiral being on a visit to Japanese waters at the time. *Calliope* was coaled and re-provisioned, and Captain Kane, taking a critical look at his ship as he returned in his pinnace from the port, decided that before he should meet his Commanding Officer, the ship needed sprucing up. Kane resolved to repaint *Calliope* to remedy the weathering affects of the long outward voyage. The vessel still retained her white-hulled home-waters scheme, but by now it was seriously streaked and discoloured by mottled rust and grime from the lashing of the waves and spray.

Today we joke (with some reason) that sailors with little to do are, as a last resort for a harassed officer, ordered to paint ship. *"If it moves: salute it; if it doesn't: paint it…"* is the axiom that applies to all the services. My own work in the modern defence business world has regularly brought me into direct contact with the consequences of this notion which seems as true a word as ever spoken. My old employer manufactures *radomes*, highly specialised composite structures that encase a sensitive radar set, usually used on board a warship for controlling missile systems. The radar performance is always impaired to some degree by these covers, but they are a necessary evil to provide environmental protection to the electronics, and one of the most disruptive of the materials from which they are fabricated is the paint; as a result, we were obliged to apply a carefully controlled paint formulation to a very precise thickness and (negligible) tolerance, so that the resultant degradation to radar performance is always repeatable and can thus be allowed for in the antenna design. It gives the paint sprayers who need to apply it, and the inspectors who verify it, considerable grief to get right. We often got these things back from the services for repair, objects on which we had lavished hours of sweat and, yes blood, and you can probably guess where this particular digression is heading. The large naval domes will have suffered such diverse mishaps as a heavy hailstorm in the South China seas (and I mean *heavy*, no-one in the open could surely have survived it, the weather-facing half was peppered with deep dents), to being clipped by the rotor blades of a helicopter on landing or take off. The repair invariably involves removing from the surface the external composite layers and paint coating prior to their replacement, and it is marvellous indeed to behold the edge of a chip of paint, mute witness to the repeated and liberal application of many repaints of red or yellow undercoat and warship grey – a technicolour *Dream-coat* if ever there was one and a situation which left us astonished that the radar's electromagnetic radiation could ever struggle through it on its outward journey, let alone do it again after being reflected back by a target.

Naturally, *Calliope's* Petty Officers had no need to be warned to leave such a structure alone, but whether they had already hit on the painting exercise as a useful punishment or time-filler is not clear. But in any port in these faraway places at the time of which we should really be concerned, an enterprising businessman could always make a little money, and keeping British warships spick-and-span was one such opportunity not left neglected. A Chinese entrepreneur was contracted to come and paint the ship's hull. On the appointed day, a horde of Chinese labourers arrived, armed with wooden planks, coils of rope and pots of paint. Swarming over the ship they let ropes down the side between pairs of which were suspended the planks, and over they went with their materials in a highly co-ordinated and effective manoeuvre. The first group were quickly chipping at any loose flakes of paint from the wooden outer hull and dabbing on primer, and before long the next group went over and proceeded from prow to stern each side, liberally daubing on the white paint using cloths. More Chinese followed them, this time brushing the previously applied paint with large brushes in sweeping criss-cross tracks as confidently and artistically as any modern window cleaner squeegees off his suds. After these came yet another group with smaller brushes still, and then finally the real artisans, the experts with their camel hair brushes, who applied the finishing touches to the paint-work so well that not a

ripple nor a run could be found to mar its sheen. WIT describes the end
result as so good that one could see one's face in the finish coat as well as if
it were a mirror. And the work was completed in just a couple of days, so
well organised was the operation. I would love to know how much the
entire business cost, but it doesn't seem to have been recorded.

Hong Kong had made an incredible impression on WIT when he
had first called in 1879, and things were no different this time. Entrance to
the massive harbour was always difficult due to the swarms of Chinese
junks and sampans, quite literally hundreds of which seemed to vie with
each other to get their tradesmen and wares on board each new arrival in
the port. Tailors; Shoemakers; Washerwomen; Photographers; Cabinet,
Clock and Watch makers; Jewellers with Chain Rings of all kinds and
descriptions; and the food: Fried Eggs; Boiled Eggs; Hams; Bacon; Bread
and Butter. For the sailors, the latter was the usual target; after weeks of
hard tack and dry biscuit, soft new bread was a wonderful delicacy. The
boats that brought all these traders to festoon the upper deck with all types
of desirable merchandise were clustered around the ship making a mat of
the shallow things spreading around her like an enormous water lily on a
great pond.

Just over a week after her arrival in Hong Kong, the now smart-
looking *Calliope* weighed anchor early in the morning of Sunday 17th July
1887 to join up with the fleet in Japan, passing out of Hong Kong harbour
along the Lymoon Pass under gentle steam. The passage was good, and
soon *Calliope* was entering the port of Nagasaki on the south-west coast of
the island now known as Kyushu, where again the fleet was found to be
absent. Kyushu (sometimes Kiushui) literally means *nine provinces* though
they were abolished in 1871. The entrance, on the glorious evening of 21st
July was truly magnificent, and the setting sun showed off this most
beautiful place to perfection. To the tranquil scene *Calliope* contributed the
shattering noise and smoke of a 21-gun salute to the Japanese flag,
followed by thirteen to an American Admiral also happening to be in the
bay. The wooded hills surrounding the bay like a gigantic green bowl
focussed the sound back into the town, and the overall effect was
tremendous.

Nagasaki [32.74N, 129.864E] was at that time one of the most
beautiful places on earth, according to a number of accounts not the least
of which is WIT's. He speaks of a *"Splendid Glen"*, with mountains behind
and the bowl of hills lined with trees all round. On his first visit in 1879,
WIT noted the limited shipbuilding going on in the port, and the small
number of ships in the Japanese Navy at that time. I am sure that when he

put his memories of the place down on paper in 1932, he could never have imagined the dreadful devastation that, at the end of the Second World War, would visit one of his best-loved places.

At the time of this visit, Nagasaki was a very important port for Britain and the west, being one of only a few to be permitted to trade with the old and new world powers. First opened to Portuguese traders in 1571 by the lord of the area, Omura Sumitada, it was a tiny village almost cut-off from the rest of Kyushu by the volcanic mountains which surround it, but which then proceeded to expand rapidly into a major town. The foreign influence inevitably brought Christianity to the area, ruthlessly suppressed by Japan's rulers. In 1639, the failure to eradicate the religion led to, or at least was a contributory factor in, a policy of isolation against non-Japanese contacts being imposed on all Japanese ports except Nagasaki, only broken by Commodore Perry in 1853.

Calliope coaled and set off in search of her Admiral once again, leaving Nagasaki on the 23rd July. This time her destination was Hakodate on the island of Yezo, now known as Hokkaido, *"North Sea Circuit"*, and the most northerly large island of the group making up Japan [41.78N, 140.714E]. The morning arrival on 27th July yet again found the fleet somewhere else, but it was expected back in a few days. On the 30th, *Calliope* was eventually united with her squadron, and after the fleet of ships sailed majestically into the port, she took up her place in the mooring line as dictated by the seniority of her captain.

Hakodate was another port that WIT knew well. Always a man who was interested in the places he encountered, here are his views from his previous visit:

> *"Here, leave was given and I went on shore, but I cannot say that I enjoyed it, for it was wet and we could not get our walks, so we had a look around the town. We paid a Visit as far as the Gates of the Sun Temple, and that was as far as we could get, for they would not let us in, as there was some Festival on at the time, so we returned to the Town and paid Visit to the Theatre. After getting our ticket, we had to take off our shoes and put on Straw Sandals, and then we were all marched in and mats placed for us to sit on. Here we had a very nice time, although we did not understand it, we could follow it for it was very exciting for there was love and Duels in it, as at home. We had Tea brought us after a time, and we enjoyed it very much."*

From long before the time of WIT's visit, Hakodate had a great number of temples, and when the port was opened to foreign vessels, a few were used as temporary residences, primarily by British, American and Russian diplomats and residents. A great fire in 1879 destroyed many, some of which were re-built in different locations. The name Hakodate appears to derive from *"box mansion"* and stems from the house surrounded by a barricade built by Masamichi Kono in about 1454 that from a distance apparently resembled a box. Hakodate has also been known as *"Teramachi"*, the Town of Temples.

The China station fleet now comprised, in addition to *Calliope*, the flagship HMS *Audacious* with Admiral, Sir Vesey Hamilton, KCB, with HM Ships: *Leander; Constance; Heroine; Swift; Linnet; Merlin; Wanderer;* and *Alacrity*. Later to join was a sister ship to *Calliope*: HMS *Cordelia*.

Cordelia seems to have re-commissioned on the same day as *Calliope's* original commissioning: 25th January 1887. She, however, had made her way to the China station by way of the Suez Canal, which took some 3,000 miles and a number of weeks off the length of her journey.

On the 1st August, *Calliope* weighed anchor to carry out firing trials at sea, but bad weather cut the exercise short, and the following day, the entire fleet left for Oterranai (I think this is now known as Otaru-kō) [43.20N, 141.18E] leaving only *Leander* to wait for the mail boat to reach Hakodate. The fleet arrived at their destination just after midnight on the 4th, and were joined a few days later by *Leander* with bulging mail sacks, a welcome contact with home for the men so many thousands of miles and many years away from family and friends.

The fleet sailed on the 10th, once again *Leander* drawing the short straw, this time to wait for HMS *Satellite* that was to join the squadron. The beginning of this leg of the cruise was not pleasant, a thick sea fog meaning the ships proceeded slowly in the unfamiliar waters, and 12 ship's fog horns blared their monotonic sounds through day and night, adding to the tension felt by the sailors who now couldn't see each other's ships nor the land which surrounded them. Late in the evening of the 12th August, the fleet reached Amur Bay, four miles off Vladivostok but due to the fog the limit of the safe passage, and there they waited for an improvement in the weather.

The next day, HMS *Linnet* eased her way through the passage and into Vladivostok Bay [43.08N, 131.76E] to seek permission for the fleet to enter. At this time, Tsar Alexander III's navy was becoming as concerned for security as the communists would be for most of the next century, and permission was refused. In keeping with a strict guidance laid down by authorities in the Russian capital St. Petersburg, at any one time only two

warships of any foreign nation were permitted to enter Vladivostok, then
the main naval headquarters of the Russian Eastern Navy. *Linnet* returned
to the fleet, and in company with *Calliope* re-entered the port on the 14th to
take on provisions for the fleet.

Security worked both ways, and particularly on *Calliope*, her new
breech loading guns must be protected from prying eyes, and the guns
were covered by tarpaulin. It was a wise precaution, as a courtesy visit was
soon made by a group of inquisitive and friendly Russian Officers, though
their hospitality did not extend as far as a return invitation to the *Calliopes*.
In response to polite enquiry, the excuse given by the British Officers for
keeping the guns covered was that the provisioning that was going on
would generate dust which must be kept out of the mechanisms; true
enough in itself, but the Russians seemed genuinely amused by the refusal
to display them and were by no means offended as they will probably have
guessed the real reason.

Calliope's log records that two Russian ironclads and three
corvettes were present in the port. One of the big ships was the *Dmitri
Domskoi* (later a Russian nuclear submarine), whilst one of the corvettes
was the *Rynda*. This latter ship, with a hand-picked top-class crew, was
taking Grand Duke Michaelovitch (Michael Alexandrovich) on a round-
world courtesy cruise, whose next objectives were Japan and then
Australia where *Calliope* would meet her again.

Negotiations for provisions took some time, but early on the 19th
August, bales of hay were brought out to *Calliope* and stowed on that spare
area of the deck between the boats. If the men wondered if this was to be
their provisions, they were wrong; it was food for the livestock, as a series
of boats arriving laden with live bullocks proved. Hoisting the beasts from
the small lighters to the deck of the warship was fraught with mischief, a
canvas sling being passed around the underside of the animal and slung
from the lower yard arm, the animal was then lifted high above the rest of
the herd waiting nervously in the array of boats before being swung over
the deck and down onto it. Once freed from its cradle, the ox was led along
the deck where it was tethered in its allotted space on the starboard side
whilst the next was loaded. So it went on, some little trouble being had in
persuading the first intended for the port side to leave its mates on the
other.

Without a butcher on board, the ship's Cooper, David Mahoney
(also known as O'Mahoney), acted as Herdsman, whilst sailors who had
some farming experience before joining the navy acted as Cattlemen, and
eventually the entire load of bullocks was tied in place on the main deck,

which even now had that distinctive appearance and aroma of a farmyard. Keeping a large fleet of ships supplied with fresh produce was always a problem, and it had been some while since the men had tasted fresh meat, but the state of the deck was soon to become one any Royal Navy officer would have nightmares over.

The cattle, once fed with hay and watered, seemed content with their lot, most lying down in their stall as *Calliope* proceeded to weigh anchor at midday, to join the main fleet which had set off previously for Wrangel Bay. I should point out that most of the place names I quote here are from WIT's memoirs and many don't seem to exist today; this is one of them. Wrangel Island is way up to the north some 4,000 miles from Vladivostok, so I do not believe that was the destination on this trip.

During the afternoon of that 19th August and with the ship in approximately 43°N and 132°E, the crew were treated to the spectacle of a solar eclipse, total just a few hundred miles away. The sun's disk was almost entirely covered, and the twilight associated with this astronomical event confused the birds in the vicinity who proceeded to congregate prior to bedding down for the night they thought was coming. The point where the greatest totality of this eclipse would be found was 50°36'N and 111°56'E at a local time of 12.52 p.m. It seems that this eclipse, which was attended by masses of scientific expeditions and experiments placed along the extensive track over the earth's surface, was mostly a cloudy washout for the land based observers, and it is likely the *Calliope*s got one of the best views of the event to be had.

Later that evening, *Calliope* caught up with the fleet and late the next day, she anchored off St. Vladimir Bay [43.92N, 135.5E], today a large, east-facing bay some 273 sailing miles from Vladivostok. Fortunately for the animals on the deck, the passage had been generally smooth. On the 21st came the entertaining task of transferring the bullocks from *Calliope* to the other members of the fleet. It seemed at first that the animals, having been subjected to the indignity once, were more philosophical about being lifted high into the air for a second time, but since the boats waiting for them were this time too small to take them, they were lowered into the water beside and attached using ropes around their horns. The boats then rowed back to their respective ships with a bullock swimming on each side, unconventional maybe but effective. The recipient vessels, however, did have some amusing problems passing the slings under the animals with them mostly submerged and thrashing their legs around, in order to get them onto their own deck. By the next day, of course, most of the animals would have already gone to a better place, which from the sailor's point of view, was the ship's range.

And now, at last, *Calliope* could discharge to the Admiral's flagship some other, not so very welcome, cargo: many tons of *"Patent Fuel"* that had been brought out from England for trials. It had been stored in the large Coffer Dam tanks under the mess deck, and its strong odour had been more than noticeable for the entire voyage, seeming to taint even the food with an unpleasant tang. The material was a mixture of coals that had been formed into briquettes or blocks, a composition fuel manufactured from coal fines with the addition of a pitch binding agent, probably what the crew could smell. The amount of patent fuel produced was, therefore, slightly higher than the actual amount of coal consumed in the transformation process. This fuel took its name from the fact that it was under patent at the time. *Calliope* kept a small amount back for use in subsequent trials by her crew.

In St. Vladimir Bay, the fleet now indulged in some extensive training, which included landing parties from one ship being repelled by others, and firing trials involving much of the various ship's armament. Eventually the fleet weighed and arrived at Goshkevitz Bay at noon on the 29th. I haven't been able to identify that place on today's maps, but it could be somewhere on the north Pacific coast of what is now North Korea. There is a Russian bay called Bukhta Gorshkova at [42.67N 131.23E] which may be the place. The entrance was at that time an unsurveyed channel, and Hamilton was cautious in his approach, setting his ships in-line with those steamers carrying the shallowest draft in front. The bay was found to provide an excellent anchorage, sheltered and deep, and would be used by others more readily thereafter, which makes me think it would have become well used and is probably now known by a different name. A couple of days later, the fleet left for Corea, now Korea. On the 2nd September, the fleet sought shelter from the edges of a typhoon, laying-to under sail, before entering Port Lazaref the next day and anchoring off the town of Gensan [39.2N, 127.45E].

Rumours that in 1885 Russia had signed an agreement with the King Of Korea to use Port Lazaref (also Lazareff) as an all-year naval port led the British, extremely concerned at the power of the huge country, to land on the island of Komundo (which they re-named Port Hamilton [34.05N 127.3E]) a few miles off the southern tip of what is now South Korea; the intention being to prevent its possible annexation as well. Once the rumours were found to be groundless, the British left the area in 1887. The town of Gensan has been given many names in its history: Port Lazareva or Port Lazareff in Russia; Genzan or Gensan in Japan; and

Yonghunghang or Yuan shan in China, before ending up with Wŏnsan and previously Wŏnsanjin as part of North Korea today.

Trials in running "Whitehead" torpedoes went well, and on the 12th the fleet sailed for Fusan, now Busan [35.09N 129.09E], arriving on the 14th September 1887.

A little of the history of the torpedo might be of interest. The term "torpedo" was first used for a form of floating mine, dropped into the water in the way of the intended target, or within a current which might be expected to bring it close to an enemy shipping lane. The British Royal Navy, along with other maritime powers, experimented with what was called a spar torpedo: an electronically detonated charge (by lanyard) placed at the end of a long spar, perhaps up to 40 feet long, which ran say ten feet underwater from the attacking vessel. To bring it into contact with the target therefore needed a very close approach and the defenders usually had something to say to – or rather, fire at – the attacker to deter him from doing so, and the potency of the weapon was therefore highly questionable. Of course, should it be possible to achieve such proximity between target and weapon, the results of a heavy explosion 10 feet below the water-line would be deadly to the recipient; CSS *Albemarle* was apparently sunk during the American Civil War by such a weapon in 1864 and USS *Housatonic* by a spar torpedo carried on the submarine CSS *Hunley*, though neither seem to have been recorded as a torpedo sinking in the way we would understand it today. Ships at that time, if they had side armour at all, were not very well protected from underwater attack. However, the threat was real enough to generate considerable interest in effective counter-measures.

The idea of a torpedo along the lines we recognise today had a number of problems to be overcome before it could be realised. The weapon would need to be powered, be accurate, and run along its track submerged at a maintained depth. These were the problems that were successfully addressed by the British inventor, Robert Whitehead (1823-1905).

Born in Bolton, England, the son of a *"cotton-bleacher"*, Whitehead had been well educated and served an Engineering apprenticeship at nearby Manchester Mechanics Institute. Whitehead moved to France, then to Milan where he started his first business, and eventually to Austria to work for that nation's government. The Austrian Empire Navy, after 1867 the Austro-Hungarian Navy, operated in the Mediterranean for a number of years, but after the end of the First World War, Austria no longer had any coastline and the service disbanded. Commissioned to come up with an improved torpedo design, Whitehead, ably supported by his son (also Robert), developed a floating torpedo which lacked versatility and reliability, but eventually in the early 1870s had refined his invention into a workable self-driven weapon, powered by a compressed air engine in the tail and carrying an explosive charge of some 18 pounds (8 kilos) of dynamite in the nose, and with a clever device which allowed the torpedo to maintain a pre-set depth for a range of some 700 yards (640 metres). It was only really let down by a hardly tolerable accuracy, and yes, I agree, no matter how "*good*" a weapon might appear to be, if it's one failing is that it doesn't hit what it is aimed at, it is really no more than useless. But it was a step along the way. Eventually, the length of a Whitehead had reached some eleven feet with a diameter of between 14 and 18 inches (350 to 450 mm) to deliver a charge of slightly more than 100 pounds (45 kilograms) of explosive, and the accuracy – or rather, the ability of the thing to run in a straight line in the direction it was launched – was vastly improved.

Calliope's time in the China squadron was going well, and the crew were finding themselves a useful and important part of the group, when Admiral Sir R. V. Hamilton received orders to despatch a powerful cruiser to Sydney for temporary service on the Australia station. The choice in all considerations could only be *Calliope*, and the semaphore from the flagship flashed the surprise signal for Kane to begin preparations for the long voyage. On the 15th September, Admiral Hamilton inspected the ship and complimented the officers and men on their contribution to his fleet. He was so impressed, he felt obliged to write to their Lordships expressing his satisfaction with Captain and crew. *Calliope* was permitted to stay for the fleet regatta on Saturday the 17th, followed on the 19th by exciting races between the rowing and sailboats from the ships. On the 20th, *Calliope* joined the fleet in steam tactics for most of the day until at 10.30 p.m. and with Hamilton's squadron returning to Fusan, she pointed her bow south to leave them behind for a new adventure.

The next day, the weather conditions were just about right for *Calliope* to carry out a twelve-hour steam trial, especially as she was now unhindered by the need to maintain fleet position. The trial was to use a mixture of Welsh coal and Patent Fuel to fire her boilers. Under the normal draught of 16 feet forward and 20 feet aft achieving 25 and 26 inches of vacuum respectively, the steam in the boilers was 78.3 pounds per square inch, driving the screw at 75.8 revolutions, and achieving 23.4 psi mean pressure in the high pressure cylinder, and 9.7 psi mean in the low. With an indicated horse power from the high being 898.5 and from the low 1120.2, giving a total of 2,018.7, her engines drove the ship against a 2 knot headwind on a smooth sea at 12.7 knots. I have not tried to convert these units from the imperial system quoted in the log, since I feel the relevance would be limited and the layout awkward. The results of the trial, whilst reinforcing *Calliope*'s known steaming characteristics, don't seem to have improved them to any noticeable extent, and patent fuel hardly seems to have set the naval world on fire at that stage of its development! In January 1911, Captain Scott reported favourably on the fuel made in the Crown Patent Fuel Works that he had taken with him on one of his last Antarctic expeditions, so perhaps the process had been improved in the interim.

The day of this trial to evaluate the worth of patent fuel was the last good weather day until Hong Kong was reached on the 26th September, the heavy seas persisting until *Calliope* entered the sheltered bay. A week or so of provisioning and coaling was supplemented by a visit to the dry dock in Kowloon to repair a Kingston Valve.

On the 7th October, *Calliope* left Hong Kong with orders to deviate from the normal course for Australia, and to pass through the Palawan Channel to look out for HMS *Wasp*, a fortnight overdue on her passage from Singapore, with 73 officers and men on board, somewhere off the Philippines. She had left Singapore on 10th September for the voyage to Shanghai via Hong Kong. A painstaking search started on the 10th, stopping at every likely-looking piece of driftwood, or land on which sailors might have been marooned, but each hope ended in depressing disappointment. *Calliope* steered along the north, west and south sides of Scarborough Shoal [15.13N, 117.75E] from between 1 and 3 miles out, from which distance men at the mast-heads were able to clearly see the edge of the reef, but no signs of wreckage nor shadow of a hull on the sea bed were visible. The shoal lies some 350 miles north of Palawan, an island forming part of the Philippines.

Searches of this sort were usually attended by all of a ship's crew whether on duty or off, as sailors on one ship always felt a natural brotherly concern for those on another, knowing full well that circumstances might one day mean their own survival depended on a sharp look out being kept by someone else. With nothing found at Scarborough Shoal, Calliope headed south to Palawan but again without success, and although hope was ever present that the *Wasp* crew had been picked up by some other ship, everyone felt sadness when after 3 days of intensive searching, the hunt was abandoned and on the 13th, *Calliope* headed south-east to intercept the regular steamer track from China to Sydney. In fact, all attempts by the Royal Navy to unravel the mysterious disappearance of HMS *Wasp*, launched only the previous year, were unsuccessful, and 73 more naval men were presumed to have suffered the same sad fate as 52 from her predecessor when their ship of that same name had been lost off the coast of Ireland just three years earlier. The name has not been used since.

On the 18th, in 126°E longitude, *Calliope* crossed the line for the third time, and on the 28th entered the Torres Strait [10.51S 142.07E], passed Cape York and anchored off one of the three small islets known then as Cairncross Island [11.25S, 142.92E], and where in the distance lay the appropriately named *Pudding-Pan Hill*, marking the spot where nearby in 1848 the famous Australian explorer E.B. Kennedy had unfortunately met his destiny at the hands of local aborigine cooks. Now the passage had to be made with care, the Great Barrier Reef lay close to, just waiting for any ship imprudent enough to try and avoid its clutches by navigation alone. Movement was made during the day only and under steam, with observers present all the time to watch for signs of reef or dangerous shoals, and the ship anchoring each night until on the 2nd November, Cooktown [15.45S, 145.32E] was reached and the passage became slightly safer. On the 6th, the reef was finally cleared but just a couple of days of good sailing followed before a strong southerly gale, known in the parts as a *"Southerly Buster"*, forced the ship to lay to and wait for it to pass, her bunkers by now being so depleted that coal expenditure to maintain passage was unjustified.

After 3 days, the storm passed and the cruise was resumed, only for another gale on the 12th to force a further 2-day delay. Eventually, the weather relented and *Calliope* entered Sydney North Head on the calm and sunny morning of the 15th November 1887. Kane moored her to a buoy in Farm Cove [33.86S, 151.22E] next to HMS *Diamond*, whose own crew immediately demonstrated the camaraderie of shipmates who knew what a long voyage without fresh provisions meant, by the despatch of a boat laden with fruit, bread and meat for the *Calliopes*, a very welcome kindness. Today, the magnificent Sydney Opera House rises majestically over the cove's western promontory, and the beautiful Royal Botanic Gardens provide a peaceful haven to the south.

One of the first tasks to be arranged was to repaint the ship black as befit those on the Australian station. Her home waters white hull and black funnel were changed to black hull and orange funnel, though the operation was performed slower and not quite as well as by the Chinese in Hong Kong those few months earlier. The Governor, Lord Carrington, accompanied by Sir Henry Parkes, visited the ship and expressed a warm welcome, as any new arrival with news of home, however much out-of-date, was always well received. The ship was coaled and re-stocked, and on the 27th November, Rear-Admiral Henry Fairfax, Commander-in-Chief of the Australian Squadron, arrived in HMS *Nelson* from Melbourne and Kane was able to report to his new Commanding Officer.

Fairfax had replaced Rear-Admiral George Tryon, a man we will meet later in the *Calliope* crew stories in Chapter 10.

It was here that *Calliope* suffered one of a number of recorded desertions on the voyage, Arthur Lee, a 19 year-old from Southgate, Middlesex, described as being 5′ 3″, with blue eyes, red hair and fair complexion. It was reported within a week that he had returned to his ship, but it wouldn't be his only such enterprise: when he disappeared for a second time in August 1888, there is no record of him changing his mind, either by himself or by being apprehended. The vessel suffered some 12 desertions whilst based in Sydney, Australia alone. This sounds excessive, and by today's standards, obviously is, but by the standards of the day it seems pretty average. The previous *Calliope* during her visit to China and Australia in the 1840s and 50s also experienced a number of desertions recorded in the log, and when recaptured, these men were subjected to 42 lashes. Those men who *"left the ship while on duty"* in our *Calliope*'s commissioning voyage did not have their names recorded in the log, and would not have received corporal punishment on their return. It is possible to glean some names from various diverse records, and we find the usual reward for anyone apprehending or giving information leading to the arrest of a deserter within 2 years was £3, sometimes supplemented by other rewards of up to £5.

On 13th December, the squadron left Farm Cove for New Zealand, and *Calliope* followed 3 days later, arriving at Russell [35.262S 174.11E], in the Bay of Islands, on Christmas Eve. Despite the imminent festival, later that same day coal was taken on at Opua a little to the south in the bay, and a mad rush it was for the crew to clean up the decks and walkways, and to festoon the messes with the traditional bunting. Within a short while, a one-day voyage meant the fleet arrived in Auckland [36.84S 174.7E] in the early evening of the last day of 1887, *Calliope* in company with the flagship *Nelson*, and *Diamond, Opal, Rapid* and *Swinger*.

In March, a visit that included New Zealand's Port Chalmers (near Dunedin) [45.81S, 170.63E] was the occasion for an invitation for the people of the port to come aboard the ship. A steamer brought the first load of men, women and children but before the second group could board *Calliope*, a heavy sea and gale sprang up from nowhere and the second batch was forced to return to shore. The visitors already on the ship could not be got off, and spent the day being entertained by the crew, the officers gave tea to the ladies and the crew provided mess deck fare to the men and children. The rough seas and wind continued till late in the evening, until eventually the prolonged stay was able to be broken and the steamer arrived to take the guests off. Lights were set up to aid the transfer, and eventually the party was leaving, singing songs and cheering the wonderful hospitality of *Calliope's* crew.

HMS Calliope is the first ship to enter "Calliope Dock" in Auckland, New Zealand on 16th February 1888. In the right background is HMS Diamond which entered the dock behind Calliope. (Author's collection.)

It was on the 9th May 1888 that *Calliope's* anchors first dug themselves into the silt-layered floor of Apia Harbour on the island of Upolu, Samoa [13.83S, 171.762W]. The event was the passage of the Governor of Fiji, Sir John Bates Thurston, KCMG, for a visit to the consul to discuss the difficult position that seemed to be brewing. *Calliope* found the American USS *Mohican* and the German SMS *Adler* in the bay. The stay was brief; lasting just 4 days, but the sour political situation between the German and American factions was unmistakeable.

On the first day of September and in readiness for the flagship HMS *Nelson's* return to England, Admiral Fairfax transferred his flag to the newly arrived HMS *Orlando*. Since *Orlando* needed some refit work after her long voyage, on the 4th, Fairfax temporarily hoisted his flag on *Calliope* and the fleet embarked on a long tour of the South Sea Islands, including Tonga and a visit with the island's King George, and later the port of Pango Pango [14.274S, 170.69W] on the south coast of the Samoan Island of Tutuila. Entering this wonderful natural harbour on what is now American Samoa on the 30th, the news of fighting and a deteriorating political situation on Upolu forced Fairfax to leave the next day, and on the 2nd October, *Calliope* again entered Apia's bay, this time in company with HMS *Lizard*, to find SMS *Adler* facing off against the American USS *Adams*. The politics now seriously worried the British Consul, Colonel de Coetlogon, and he requested Fairfax provide a semi-permanent Royal Navy presence to show that British interests would always be protected. Fairfax had anticipated the request and secure in the knowledge that in Captain Pelly, he would be leaving British interests well looked after, on the 10th *Calliope* and the Admiral left HMS *Lizard* behind at Apia. At this time, the German Vice-Consul was Herr Becker; Knappe was present to hand over. Similarly, Blacklock and Leary were representing the United States.

Whilst *Calliope* was at Apia at this time, the beautiful little schooner *Nyanza*, 218 tons, Captain James Cumming Dewar, arrived as part of her celebrated round the world cruise, having left Plymouth, England on the 21st July 1887. The story of this vessel and her voyage makes fascinating reading and was published in a book written by her owner, with the rather expansive title: *"The Voyage of the Nyanza R.N.Y.C.: being a record of a three years' cruise in a schooner yacht in the Atlantic and Pacific, and her subsequent shipwreck."*, Edinburgh and London, William Blackwood and Sons: 1892. Good condition original copies are hard to find, though.

An incident with the Australian schooner *Helena* of Maryborough, Queensland on the 23rd off Pentecost Island, New Hebrides (now Vanuatu) [15.67S, 168.28E] provided some unexpected excitement. Requesting medical assistance from *Calliope*, the state of the ship seemed to show the vessel had been involved in the illegal labour trade, though in this case the natives appeared to have come out on top, as the ship had been peppered with gunfire and two of her crew seriously injured. It is sobering to imagine that, no matter how one dresses up the practice with different names, the slave trade was still operating at that time. Even worse, it still does, of course, in one form or another. The injured were taken on board *Calliope* to be given passage to Australia for treatment, but the next day, the French frigate *Fabert* arrived. Although suspicion was high, the joint commission immediately set up to investigate the activities of the *Helena* found insufficient evidence to charge the captain, and on the 24th *Calliope* left for Noumea. Robert Heath, mate of the *Helena*, died of his wounds a day before arrival and was later buried in the island's cemetery.

On the 4th November, *Calliope* again entered Sydney harbour, and Admiral Fairfax returned his flag to *Orlando*. The rest of that year of 1888 was spent in trials and a short time in the dry dock on Cockatoo Island [33.849S 151.174E] to fix some defective bolts attaching the wooden sheathing to the iron hull, and the bolts holding the metal sheathing to the wooden hull. Adjacent to this dock was a cemetery of ship's pets, including one from HMS *Lizard* which had relieved *Calliope*, whose epitaph perhaps deserves to be recorded:

> "*In memory of Bill the Goat; HMS Lizard.*
> *Here lays the remains of Bill the goat;*
> *who had no rum to oil his throat;*
> *he joined the teetotallers for a change;*
> *and died that night on the ship's cook's range.*"

On 27th December, *Calliope* sailed for Auckland arriving on the 4th January 1889 to join *Orlando, Opal, Rapid* and *Lizard*, the latter having been relieved in Apia by HMS *Royalist*. *Lizard* brought news that the situation in Samoa had deteriorated far worse than when Fairfax had last been there in September, reinforced the next day by schooners bringing lurid reports of the fighting between natives and German marines. The fleet sailed on the 12th for Wellington [41.27S 174.85E] and here, Fairfax gave Kane his orders to return to Apia and relieve *Royalist*, the order taking to the islands a powerful ship and the latest weaponry in support of British interests. The next few days were spent in feverish activity, provisioning the ship and pressing every lump of best quality anthracite coal from the Westport colliery into every available space for it.

On the 18th, three midshipmen, Boyle, Richmond and Lindsay, were discharged to *Orlando* and Kane received four replacements to continue their training: Sidney R. Drury Lowe, Hugh Fitzroy Hopkinson, John Collings Taswell Glossop and Cecil Henry Fox. We'll meet these and their other midshipman mates already on *Calliope* again later.

On the 21st January 1889, Admiral Fairfax boarded the ship to wish her *bon voyage* with the knowledge it was quite possible that she might well soon need to use her military strength; he will have little thought her steaming capabilities would be her greatest asset, especially as the same tide on which she would sail brought with it SMS *Eber*, laden with wounded German marines in mute and depressing demonstration that diplomacy in Apia seemed quickly to be running out of options.

Also aboard *Calliope* at the time was a former Royal Navy officer, currently a Major in the 4th Kings Own Regiment: Major R.H. McCarthy; present as a guest of Captain Kane. McCarthy decided to remain with the vessel to share with his host the adventure in Samoa to come, obviously not expecting it to provide him with such a dramatic experience as awaited them all!

A fast passage took *Calliope* to Apia for the third and fateful time.

Chapter 6: Apia Bay, the Crowded Port.

Calliope's arrival in Apia bay on a bright and calm Saturday at the beginning of February 1889 was very welcome to the British consul, de Coetlogon. Dealing with the abrupt and belligerent Captain Hand on HMS *Royalist* had tired and depressed him, hopefully Captain Kane whom he had met before would bring some much needed common sense and courtesy to the post. In this new vessel, he was certainly bringing the most powerful ship of any which had so far congregated in the bay, both in terms of her engines and her armament. Before even the mud had settled around the British ship's anchors 9 fathoms below the surface of Apia Harbour, the consul had made his complimentary visit to Kane during which the serious diplomatic position was explained, and had received the requisite seven-gun salute on leaving.

As well as HMS *Royalist* (WIT in his memoirs thought it was HMS *Rapid*), Kane found the *Kaiserliche Marine* (German Imperial Navy) vessels SMS *Adler* and SMS *Olga* already moored in the bay. SMS ("Seiner Majestät Schiff") is the German equivalent of "HMS" and "USS", though the prefix was not commonly used by the Kriegsmarine at the time. The former was the German flagship, but though pretty she was an outmoded man of war. She was a 1,024 ton class one barquentine-rigged *Kanonenboot* (gunboat), of a composite iron and wooden hull built at Kiel dockyard Kaiserliche Werft, launched in November 1883 and carrying the senior German Naval Officer, Kommander Fritze. Her captain was Kapitänlieutenant (Captain Lieutenant) von Arend. *Adler* was commissioned in May 1885 and served overseas for her entire career. She was the only vessel of her type. Her 950 horsepower engines could propel the vessel at just over 11 knots in an obliging sea. Armed with one 150 mm (six inch) gun, plus five 125 mm (five inch) and five 37 mm revolving cannon and crewed by some 127 officers and men, she was 61.4 metres long, 8.8 metres in breadth and 4 metres depth of keel.

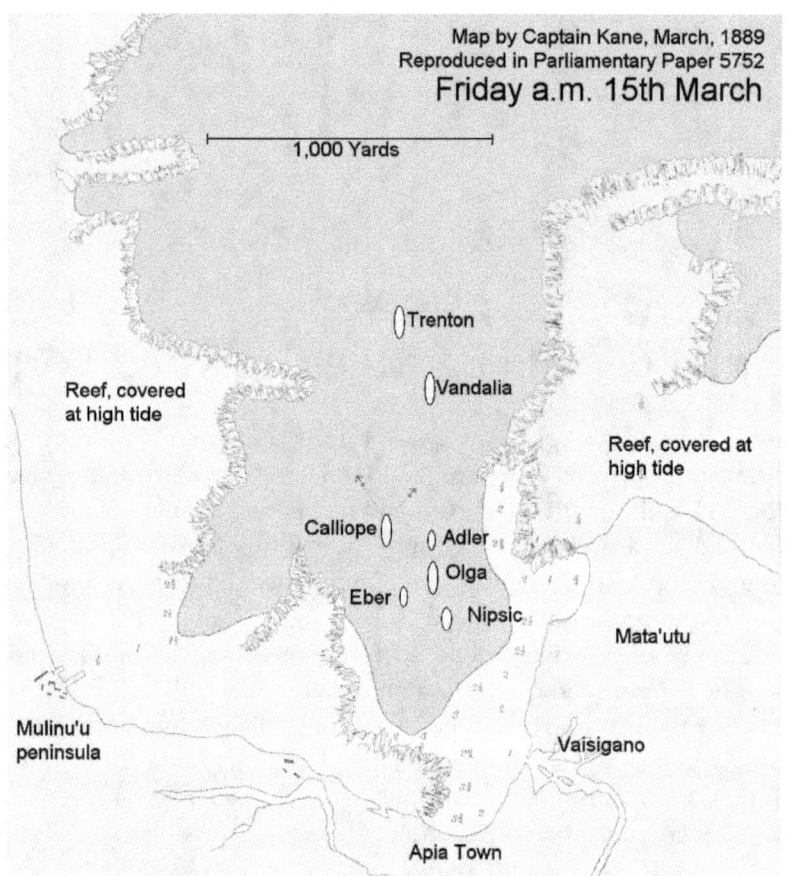

Apia Bay showing the approximate positions of the various warships on the morning of Friday, 15th March 1889. The layout of the reef, and the positions of the vessels, are taken from the chart produced by Captain Kane in his report, as reproduced in Parliamentary Paper 5752.

Images of the three American vessels and the three German at Apia are reproduced on the following pages. Not being able to find a photograph of SMS *Adler*, I have used a photograph of SMS *Möwe*, a sister ship to *Adler* and virtually identical, though of slightly less tonnage. And I should here point out that the details of the German and American warships present at Apia in March 1889 have been taken in the most part from the 1979 publication "*Conway's All The Worlds Fighting Ships 1860-1905*" [20], supplemented by some German and American web-sites on the internet.

Adams class steam sloop which may be USS Nipsic. (Public domain, a download from the American Naval History and Heritage Command).

USS Trenton c.1886. (Public domain, a download from the American Naval History and Heritage Command).

USS Vandalia, c.1888. (Public domain, a download from the American Naval History and Heritage Command).

SMS Olga, after conversion to a Training Ship, so c. 1892. Note that her masts appear no longer to carry sail yards. (Public domain, a download from the American Naval History and Heritage Command).

His Imperial German Majesty's *Kreuzerkorvetten* (Cruiser Corvette) *Olga* was, by contrast to *Adler*, a more powerful and important man of war, the best of the German Fleet by a long way. It was a strange quirk of seniority that meant Kommander Fritze was on the smaller *Adler*. *Olga* had sister ships SMS *Carola*, SMS *Marie* and SMS *Sophie*. A 2,387-ton *Carola* class, iron flush-deck ship-rigged corvette, she was built at Stettin, Germany by AG Vulcan builders. Commissioned in September 1881, she served overseas during the rest of the decade. She had the graceful hull-lines of a clipper, a swan-neck prow being her a most artistic line, and was distinguished by having two funnels with which to vent her furnaces. A single shaft, horizontal compound engine gave 2,200 IHP and a top speed of around 13.5 knots on a good day.

SMS Möwe at Sydney, c.1890. Sister ship to SMS Adler and virtually identical.
(By Australian National Maritime Museum on The Commons -
https://www.flickr.com/photos/anmm_thecommons/8260621678/, No restrictions,
https://commons.wikimedia.org/w/index.php?curid=42171921)

In 1884 the "West African Cruiser Squadron" was formed comprising the vessels SMS *Bismarck* , SMS *Möwe*, (sister ship to SMS *Adler*) SMS *Gneisenau*, SMS *Olga*, and SMS *Ariadne*. Rear Admiral Knorr became the head of the West African cruiser squadron in the flagship SMS *Bismarck*.

SMS *Olga* spent some considerable time in the squadron, and was engaged in *"The Yos Rebellion"* in Cameroon in 1884 (with SMS *Bismarck*), before being despatched to Samoa in 1888 under the command of Korvettenkapitän (Corvette-Captain) Freiherr von Erhardt (some references spell this Ehrhardt). She was armed with ten 150 mm, two rapid fire 87 mm and six 37 mm revolving cannon (some sources state twelve of the latter).

Later that same evening of 2nd February, the American naval representative arrived at Apia, USS *Nipsic*. Considerably smaller than *Olga*, she was a strange sort of ship with a chequered history and manned by a crew with a very colourful reputation. A 1,375-ton *Enterprise* class wooden screw sloop, she was rebuilt at the Washington Navy Yard, D.C. from 1874 and launched 1878, and the last significant ship to be constructed at that facility. She was originally the Civil War *Kansas* class barque-rigged gunboat *Nipsic* launched in 1863 of 836 tons, but in reality, she was a completely new ship apart from sections of the keel, with a displacement more than half again that of the original vessel. Length, 185 feet; beam, 35 feet; draught 14 feet 3 inches; her eight cylindrical boilers feeding a single shaft, horizontal compound return connecting rod engine which made her an 800 Indicated Horse Power vessel with a maximum of 10 knots, relatively slow by the standards pertaining at Samoa in 1889. She had a coal capacity of some 130 to 150 tons and a crew of somewhere between 178 and 193. This new *Nipsic* had been commissioned in October 1879 and served for several months in the West Indies. In March 1880, she crossed the Atlantic to join the European Squadron. *Nipsic* was transferred to the South Atlantic Squadron in mid-1883 and remained on that station until March 1886 when she joined the Pacific fleet. Whichever way you looked at it, USS *Nipsic* was getting old and had always been slow.

To crown all, she was crewed by men who had won for themselves, apparently quite deservedly and almost proudly, the Pacific Ocean's worst reputation as drunken, disorderly and obnoxious examples of a profession that rarely drew to it the exalted scions of society in the first place. She had been haunted by desertions and insubordination during her entire time in the Pacific. To own that reputation, at that time and in such a vast theatre as the Pacific, was no mean feat.

Her captain of some two years was Captain Dennis Walbach Mullan, USN, born in Maryland, probably in the early 1840s. Later on in that month of February (25th) he wrote a letter to his brother in Los Angeles and included the ominous sentences:

> "We are now in the midst of the hurricane season, and until April 15th we may look for heavy weather. The harbor is small with reefs outside and inside, making bad holding ground. There is no coal here and nothing to eat. Everything is very dear." Reproduced from the *Los Angeles Herald*, Volume 31, Number 178, 31st March 1889.

On the same day as *Calliope's* arrival, Kane despatched Lieutenant Marchant, R.M.L.I., eight marines and a signalman for guard duties in Apia.

On Sunday, 3rd February 1889, the day after *Calliope's* arrival, Kane discharged forty-two year old Chief ERA (Engine Room Artificer) James Richards accompanied by an AB seaman and a blacksmith to HMS *Royalist* for transport back to Sydney. Richards had been taken ill shortly after the ship left New Zealand and his condition had been deteriorating steadily in *Calliope's* sickbay. Unfortunately, he died a few days after *Royalist* departed Tonga for the run to Auckland and later in the evening of that same

Wednesday 13th February his body was committed to the deep, unknown to the *Calliopes*, her first death of the voyage.

So here too we should bid goodbye to the overbearing but colourful Captain Hand. Returning HMS *Royalist* to England in late 1889, he continued his service on HM Ships *Shannon* and *Aurora*, retiring from the Navy on 27th June 1894 attaining Rear-Admiral rank in 1897, but sadly dying in early 1914 an inmate of Holloway Sanatorium in the village of Virginia Water, in Surrey, England. His wife, Mrs. Annie Hand, had been permitted to draw his naval pension under section 335 of the Lunacy Act (1890), a sad end for such a character whatever one might think of him in today's climate of political correctness.

On the 4th February *Calliope* weighed anchor and Kane proceeded to re-moor the vessel under steam in a more convenient and suitable position in the bay. Diving parties were told off for training purposes, their practical learning involved commissioning the moorings and clearing the buoy ropes. Later that day, the German consul Doctor Knappe made his courtesy visit to the ship, and was saluted with seven guns on leaving.

The following few days saw bright blue skies, summery clouds, and a calm breeze, or as the log quaintly records it: *"light airs"*. On the ship, the spell of good weather was seized as the opportunity to take down the upper yards, unbend (i.e. remove from the jackstay) the upper sails and gaff sails, and do some of the mending, cleaning, and various regular maintenance work which is ever the lot of a sailing man. The masts were re-assembled, and the sails loosed for the day to hang limp in the hot static air so as to dry and prevent mildew or rot. On the 8th, the Royal Yards were taken down and the sails reefed. Drills proceeded as normal every day: pistol, cutlass, boarding parties, exercising all the paraphernalia of a military ship. Older seaman went to their seamanship classes, boys to signals and their own more basic seamanship. The crew were permitted to bathe every day, but shore leave was restricted to officers as a result of the antagonism between the German and American sailors; fisticuffs was regular and often violent between the men and Kane had no intention of allowing British sailors to be drawn into such affairs.

Late on the 9th February, Apia decided to show its new guest just what it could do as the end of the stormy season approached. At 2 a.m. on the 10th in a rapidly freshening force 2 gusting uncomfortably frequently to 8, the schooner *Matautu* was seen to be dragging in front of *Calliope*, and soon a collision had carried away *Calliope*'s port whisker on the jib boom. At 5.45 a.m. the officer of the watch ordered the topgallant masts to be brought down, and the fires in three boilers lit; the preliminary to the use of steam. At 8.30 a.m. in the dull dawn, Kane despatched a boat to take a party of seaman onto the errant schooner for them to try and pull it free from *Calliope*. The schooner's own crew had earlier wisely vacated the ship for the shore taverns when the gale had first announced its arrival.

It perhaps speaks volumes for the boredom that the enforced lack of shore leave for the British had instilled, that there had been plenty of volunteers to man the boat in the rough waters. Master Gunner Charles Martin was in charge of the party, and his crew succeeded in boarding the schooner and taking it away from *Calliope*'s bows, until despite their efforts, heavy seas from the north bolstered by the strengthening wind from the north-east finally pushed the little merchant vessel onto the reef. One *Calliope* sailor, Ordinary Seaman George Munden, went overboard, and was saved by a mate, Albert Smith, though not without considerable difficulty. The schooner was left to her fate on the reef, and *Calliope*'s boat crew were brought back wet and exhausted and the impromptu bathers with their feet badly cut by the coral but otherwise none the worse for the adventure. It was a warning, a small snarl and a snap from the mongrel, telling the human to watch out. Around 11 p.m. that evening some hatch covers and other deck gear on the British ship were carried away by the force 8 gusts, and by midnight the steam in the three boilers was ready in case needed by the engines.

During the 11th February, the gale increased in fury and at 2.45 a.m. a fourth boiler was lit. Steam was used to help hold position and ease the strain on the cables and it was a tense situation all that day. The crew told off for the afternoon machine gun drill and the torpedo and signals classes, all felt the weary effect of a gale blustering to force 8 and a heavy northerly swell, but were not permitted to escape their incessant training even for that. Late that day, it was felt wise to place an anchor watch, but *Calliope*'s huge anchors and heavy chain did their job admirably. The steam probably had not been necessary as it happened, but it had certainly been prudent to get it ready, and anyway, it would be needed on the morrow whatever the weather.

On the 12th the gale was clearly abating, but in a force 2 wind with force 6 gusts, *Calliope* weighed anchor and steamed out of port for the quarterly firing trials as proscribed by Admiralty Regulations – a waning storm however lively not permitted to break that rule. Performing the trials during the early afternoon whilst moored some three miles to the north of Apia bay in much improved weather, she was always well in sight of land and returned to re-moor in the bay at around 4 p.m. Some commentators, including Taprell Dorling, seem to have interpreted this event as *Calliope* prudently leaving the bay during a storm only to return and find it to have been unnecessary; the unconcerned survival of those who remained and some thought of British embarrassment being cited as one of the reasons Kane would stay in the blow to come, but clearly this was not the case.

The 13th saw the gale stubbornly hang on for as long as it could, forcing *Calliope* to re-moor under steam, before the dropping wind encouraged her engineers to allow the fires to go out at 11 p.m. During that evening the third German man of war, the fine-looking SMS *Eber*, had arrived in the bay.

SMS Eber c. 1888. [By Unknown author - Marine-Rundschau 1903. Berlin: Ernst Siegfried Mittler und Sohn., Public Domain, https://commons.wikimedia.org/w/index.php?curid=9016761].

Launched 15th September 1887, SMS *Eber* was a 723-ton barque-rigged iron-hulled *Kanonenboot* (gunboat), built at Kaiserliche Kraft Kiel, Germany. She was 51 metres long, 8 metres breadth and 3.8 metres depth of keel. She carried approximately 82 officers and crew and was armed with three 105 mm and four 37 mm revolving cannon. She was the newest and smallest of all the military ships eventually to moor in the bay, and powered by her 760 horsepower single-shaft compound engine, was capable of 11 knots. The very few images of her which exist in the public record show a pretty vessel but one in which the heavy and inefficient engine seemed just a little out of place and slightly impractical. Gardiner in *"Conway's Fighting Ships"* describes her as fitted with an underwater ram, but the image of the pitiful remaining wreckage after the hurricane does not support that view, presuming Admiral Kimberley's identification to be correct. Following her commissioning she was sent to the Pacific for active service, commanded by a vibrant and enthusiastic young man who seemed as if he might have a glorious future in the German Navy. Kapitänlieutenant (Captain Lieutenant) Eugen Wallis had commanded the vessel for as long as she had been involved in a number of the skirmishes in Samoa in the few months of conflict between Germany and the Samoan natives, having joined the ship in November 1888; she seems to have been the vessel of choice for operations among the inlets and shallow bays of the reef encircled island – as such her small size and draught made her ideal.

On the 14th, the rising barometer and dropping winds served only to demonstrate the capriciousness of Apia weather, as the gale suddenly increased in force again. Soon, a more powerful storm was battering the inhabitants than any they had so far experienced. The stormy season at Samoa was living up to its reputation of going out more with a bang than a whimper. Touching force 9 (a "strong gale" in the definition of the time under which it was recommended that a ship could just be able to carry close-hauled Close-reefs and Courses), fires were lit in three of Calliope's boilers at 9 a.m. followed by a fourth at 10.45 a.m. The sheet anchor was let go to help steady the vessel in the winds now blowing hard from the north-north-east and the heavy swell approaching the bay from the north, fast becoming a feature of these storms.

Shortly after 11 a.m., the American trading barquentine USS Constitution became the latest in the long line of victims of the bay, when the winds and seas pushed her against the reef and she began to break up, still half loaded. By good seamanship and piloting skill, a boat from Nipsic had succeeded in getting the crew off the vessel without loss of life. On that same day another small schooner, Tamasese, joined Constitution and Matautu at the bottom of Apia harbour, which must surely have been a veritable primeval forest of the rotting timber skeletons of countless earlier victims. In just five days, three vessels had succumbed to gale and reef, though thankfully with no loss of life.

The continuing swell and rising wind decided Kane during the afternoon to order the Lower Yards and Top Masts to be brought down, always the response to expectations of severe weather. Overnight the storm did its worst and began to abate at last. The wind veered to the north-north-west and dropped rapidly, the clouds in the overcast sky beginning to break up and the hazy blue starting to show through by morning. The swell was still strong, and the sheet anchor that had fouled the starboard hawser was weighed, untangled, and let go again during the early hours of the 15th. By 8 a.m., the weather had so much improved that the Lower Yards and Top Masts were put back up, and the sheet anchor weighed again, this time to be stowed. The starboard cable was also weighed and the ship steamed to clear the port cable of its kinks. Late in the afternoon, *Calliope* re-moored in eight fathoms and her fires were banked at midnight.

It is possible that this storm, also one of those mentioned by the Apia inhabitants as being among the worse the residents had seen, was the one in which the German gunboat *Eber* just touched the reef with her propeller. It was a close call, but the escape had nevertheless left the ship with damage that was extremely important and will have been appreciated as such by her officers. This gale also caused widespread damage on the neighbouring island of Savai'i.

On the 16th, *Eber* went out of the bay at 8.45 a.m., and at 11.30 a.m. *Calliope* allowed her fires to go out, the weather seeming settled at least for the time being. During the early afternoon, *Eber* returned to the bay and re-moored. This will most likely have been a short test of her steam gear to assess the problems with the screw.

The nicked and bent blades on the propeller might seem on the face of it to be a trivial problem, but if not repaired quickly, posed a dangerous threat. An out-of-balance propeller imparts excessive cyclic loads throughout the entire transmission gear and the engine, and can rapidly overheat bearings and shafts even unto failure. SMS *Eber* might well need her damaged screw to stay off the reef, but to use it risked total engine failure and the prudent thing to have done was to have left the bay immediately and to head to Sydney under sail for repair. One can only assume that Wallis made the request to Fritze but permission was refused out of a perceived military need. Certainly SMS *Eber* was the most useful of the German ships when engaged in operations against the natives, so Fritze would have been reluctant to lose the advantage she gave him.

The pattern in the weather was now exactly as before: after the storm came a few days of bright skies and calm winds. On the 18th, *Calliope's* sails were again loosed for the day to dry and re-furled late in the afternoon. The deck crew once again embarked on all the drills and care work required to maintain the sails, rigging and yards in first class order.

On the 22nd February, Kane dressed the ship with the American Ensign at *Calliope's* main mast for the day, but I have been unable to unearth the precise reason for this courtesy with any confidence. There are a few not really plausible candidates for the anniversary in American eyes: in 1821, the $5 million purchase of eastern Florida from Spain; or the 11th anniversary of the opening of the first "5 and 10 cent store" by Mr. Frank W. Woolworth in New York; or perhaps it may even have been the first anniversary of the American demonstration of an ancient Scottish "*game*" in which a Mr. John Reid of that country attempted to use a thin, knobbly stick to smack a small ball around a field until it eventually dropped into a hole in the ground. Less frivolously, on that very 22nd February 1889 were the states of the Dakotas, Montana and Washington admitted to the union, but this is as unlikely to have been the event being commemorated, as were any of the others I have listed. I have little doubt that any patriotic American accidentally picking up this book will scorn my ignorance when they come to this page. To them, the most likely reason for Kane's marking of the day would be that it was the anniversary of the birth of George Washington (in 1732), though it surprises me that a British ship's captain would so mark it in the late nineteenth-century.

During the afternoon of the 23rd, *Eber* departed once more, some three hours after the arrival of the USS *Vandalia* direct from San Francisco. Named after a city in Illinois on the Kaskaskia River and launched in October 1874, *Vandalia* was a 2,033-ton *Galena* class wooden screw sloop, though slightly bigger than *Galena*, built at the Boston Navy Yard, Charlestown Massachusetts and commissioned on 10th January 1876. Some sources describe her as *Swatara* class. She seems to have been around 216 feet long, 39 feet beam, 17 feet 3 inches draught and ship-rigged. She was rated a twelve-knot ship from her 1,150 indicated horsepower engine. Armed with eight guns, she was crewed by between 212 and 230 men. She had eight cylindrical boilers driving a single shaft, horizontal compound return connecting rod engine, and bunkers of 160 to 185 tons capacity. From December 1877 until March 1878, she had transported the former United States President Ulysses S. Grant on a tour of the Mediterranean Sea and its historic ports. *Vandalia* was assigned to the North Atlantic Squadron from 1879 until 1884, operating from the Grand Banks fishing grounds to the Caribbean. She decommissioned for overhaul in October 1884.

There are two variations in the pronunciation for this name, VAN-DAY-LEE-UH or VAN-DER-LEE-UH, the former seeming most popular today, and presumably how the town is known.

Vandalia re-commissioned in February 1886, and in August of that year left the east coast of America for the long voyage around South America to join the Pacific Station. She served as the Navy's Pacific flagship during much of the next two years, and enjoyed a major and expensive refit at the Mare Island Naval Yard until despatched to Samoa under the command of Captain Schoonmaker, USN. He became Commanding Officer of USS *Vandalia* in 1888.

Along with *Vandalia* came the next stormy instalment in the weather, a similar introduction to Samoa for the American crew as had been received by *Calliope* a few weeks earlier. The day after *Vandalia*'s arrival, the wind freshened as ever from the east and north of east, but this storm was not equal to the previous one, and the ships in the bay managed to ride it out without mishap.

The threat was sufficient to cause Kane to call again for the top gallant masts to be brought down, but the boilers which had already been lit to provide distilled water were considered enough prudence should steam be required for the engines, and by the morning of the 26th, even these fires were allowed to go out. The fresh and blustery conditions continued for a day or two more, again the seeming reluctance of the weather to fully abate, until the first of March dawned with calm winds, a blue sky visible between broken fluffy clouds, and the only use for the coal was once more for obtaining non-salt water for consumption by both the crew and the boilers. *Eber* had arrived back in the bay on the 27th February, and the hurricane season was now close to it's end, expected anytime between the mid-points of March and April.

But the pattern the seamen had become familiar with had still not yet ended, as after the same few days of calm weather, the winds again freshened and rapidly so, the 7th March beginning as calm but ending with a force 4 gusting to 8 out of the north-west, accompanied by cloudy, overcast skies, passing showers and very squally. At 4 p.m. on that day, *Calliope*'s topgallant masts were once more brought down, and the Lower Yards and Top Masts struck again. The standard engine room response to these storms was again initiated, three boilers being lit. On the 8th, the winds got stronger gusting between 6 and 8, and the rain and squalls more powerful and frequent. A heavy swell from the north again accompanied the weather, but the winds began to die down during the evening and at 10 p.m. the fires were allowed to go out.

The calm seas of the 9th and the 1-2 force wind signified the storm was passed, and though the previous ones had seemed to make a re-appearance within a day or two, this time the weather stayed calm. The Lower Yards and Top Masts were put back up at 6 a.m. and the crews continued their daily routine of drills, classes and routine maintenance of the ship.

At 8 a.m. on the 11th March, USS *Trenton* arrived at Apia, and Kane saluted the huge vessel with 13 guns in deference to the Admiral's flag flying from her mast, the salute being returned by the American. Later that day, *Calliope*'s crew was employed in storing provisions bought ashore that morning, and with an inspection of the food store which resulted in some

54 lbs of contaminated mutton and 198 lbs of beef being thrown overboard for the delectation of the marine inhabitants of Apia Bay who were far less delicate in their tastes.

Launched in January 1876, USS *Trenton* was a 3,900 ton steam frigate, some references suggest of the *Contoocook* class but in fact, much bigger than that vessel, she had been built at the New York Navy Yard and commissioned in February 1877; she was now the flagship of Rear-Admiral Lewis Ashfield Kimberly, USN (1830-1902), Commanding the U.S. Naval Force on the Pacific Station. She was by far the largest vessel to stake out a position in the bay in support of colonial sabre-rattling, but found *Vandalia* occupying a berth right at the mouth of the inner basin, so was forced to moor well out from Apia. Have a look at the "before the storm" map of Apia Bay on page 152 to view the approximate positions of the main warships in the bay.

Trenton had the distinction of being the largest warship begun for the US Navy in the years between the Civil War and the beginning of "*New Navy*" steel ship construction in 1882-3, though she suffered from a well-known defect in design in which heavy seas regularly allowed water to menace the boilers via the hawse pipes, located on the lower deck. Unlike many such supposedly *well-known features* only documented after the event, this was a real and widely recognised problem with the ship, and would undoubtedly contribute to her sufferings to come.

Her length was 253 feet, beam 48 feet and draught 20 feet 7 inches, her coal bunkers could hold 337 tons, and she was ship-rigged. Her eight cylindrical boilers supplied steam to a single-shaft compound return connecting-rod engine to give her a reputedly good turn of speed, one which surprised the British in the Red Sea one time as being between 14 and 16 knots, but which was officially 12.6 from the USN records which stated her indicated horsepower as 2,414. She was armed with eleven guns on her upper deck, 2 each side, 2 forward facing and 1 rearward on the poop. Her most powerful armament was the eight large guns, 8-inch rifled muzzle-loaders, four placed each side on the gun deck. These had originally been smoothbore, 11-inch guns. Twenty-four furnaces fed those eight boilers arranged four in line on each side in an engine room 94 feet long containing equipment which alone weighed nearly 800 tons. She was fitted with a very large underwater ram at the bow, its point some eight feet forward of her almost vertically straight stem and some nine feet below the water-line. She was the first American vessel to have electric lighting installed (in 1883) at a cost of some $5,500.

Trenton's captain was Norman von Heidreich Farquhar, born in

Pottsville, Pennsylvania, on 11th April 1840, and who commanded the steam frigate from May 1887.

On the 12th March, Kane entertained the American Admiral on board *Calliope* and so the beginnings of a brief but close and dramatic acquaintance were sown.

Lewis Ashfield Kimberly was born in Troy, New York on 2nd April 1830 and attained the rank of Rear-Admiral in July 1887 a few months after he took command of the Pacific Station. As a demonstration to Kimberly of Knappe's feelings about the political situation, the German failed to call upon the Admiral on his arrival, but waited till the next day; Kimberly was not unaware of the deliberate slight.

With the latest arrivals, the bay was host to eleven or so merchantmen and schooners, and many small island traders, plus the seven large warships; the port was crowded indeed.

The traditional Apia welcome for a new ship and her crew was not to be denied USS *Trenton*. A gloomy and threatening Wednesday 13th March was followed by heavy rain on the Thursday morning, and the wind again began to freshen, but in a departure from all the previous storms, this time from the south, beginning at force 1 to 2 in the morning prompting the top gallant masts on *Calliope* to be sent down again, and quickly becoming 1 to 4 during the afternoon. The squalls were, however, few and far between, and in Kane's opinion, he felt there to be no real wind at all. As the day progressed and the weather signs seemed to confirm bad weather of some sort was coming, and mindful that two of the last few storms in Apia that season had been as bad as most of the locals could remember, Kane was not the only captain to go ashore and enquire of the local experts what the consensus might be. Here he was reassured: the fall in pressure would be for rain only despite the current flurries, the wind would soon drop and the ships were quite safe. The barometer had begun another of its roller-coaster falls and the sky had been overcast all day, with squally showers and occasional heavy rain.

Apart from the wind direction, the signs were a photocopy of the previous storms, and in contrast to the shore experts, the various navigating officers on the ships could only read them one way – another storm was coming, possibly another big one.

In this case, though, it was to be incredibly bigger than those previous monsters, and *Trenton's* stormy welcome would befit her large size and consequence, a salute from nature that all present could well have declined.

Chapter 7: The Storm.

Before I (finally!) introduce those fateful two days to the reader, it is perhaps prudent to state the sources of my data. There were many accounts written at the time of the storm, and many more have followed since. The contemporary accounts are broadly similar, but differ in some of the detail. This is partly because the various viewpoints were subtly different. For example, although Admiral Kimberly and Captain Kane experienced the same weather conditions, Kane was mostly concerned about *Calliope* dragging onto the reef, or collisions with nearby ships, whilst Kimberly will have been very concerned at the volume of water *Trenton* was shipping affecting her boilers. So I have attempted to distil the various stories into just one, which is, therefore, my own. To any student of the storm reading this narrative, the original sources should be consulted first. So here is a list of those stories that I have, so far, uncovered. Two have the merit for me of never having been published before, which gives a little freshness to my interpretation. I have deliberately ignored the majority of the newspaper reports of the time, or rather, soon after the storm. They were rarely written by an eye witness, and often based on garbled tales repeated by more than one person, and I am afraid that some journalists of the time were not averse to filling in any gaps with their own, sometimes sensationalist ideas. The story made headlines in Britain, America, Germany, Samoa, Australia, New Zealand and maybe even further afield, and those few I have read are not always accurate, when compared to the early accounts.

Again, later accounts will have been based, as is mine, on contemporary stories, or so I should hope, so would probably only be repetitive in their detail. I hope my approach to telling this tale sees favour with the reader. I have reproduced a couple of the reports in full, as they contribute important data about the people who were present, and to document the players, major and minor, has been an important intention of my manuscript throughout.

1. Admiral Kimberly's initial report to the Secretary of the Navy, dated 19th March 1889, and which contains the details of the storm, plus an initial list of the casualties suffered by the Americans. Kimberly clearly intended the document to reach the United States by means of being carried by an American officer despatched on a small repaired schooner in order to intercept the mail ship from San Francisco to Auckland at Tutuila, and from Auckland to Washington via cable. It is reproduced in Admiral Kimberly's memoirs, which can be freely downloaded from the American Naval History and Heritage Command web-site [10]. I have a copy of a 1965 reprint of Kimberly's memoirs, which includes his many reports.

2. Captain Kane's initial report to Admiral Fairfax dated 20th March 1889. It was referenced "No. 19." in Kane's series of reports about the situation at Samoa, and was despatched via that same small schooner on the day of writing. It requested the Auckland postmaster to send a cable to Admiral Fairfax in Sydney containing the contents of the report, and to send another cable to the Admiralty in London. This report was reproduced in Parliamentary Paper 5756 [4].

3. Captain Kane's highly detailed and comprehensive description of the storm and *Calliope*'s escape. It is dated 24th March, so was written during *Calliope*'s return to Sydney after the storm. It runs to several pages of detail, and forms the mainstay of Parliamentary Paper 5756, and was given the reference "No. 21".

4. Captain Kane's report of the consequences of the storm. This is another very detailed report to Admiral Fairfax of the aftermath of the storm, again written during *Calliope's* return voyage to Sydney, and finished on the day of her arrival (4th April 1889). It chronicles Kane's visits to both Admiral Kimberly and Kommander Fritze. It has been given the reference "No. 26". Because it deals with people, I have included an extract from this report in my text. It too is included in Parliamentary Paper 5756.

5. Admiral Kimberly's letter to Captain Kane, apparently undated, but probably written soon after Kane's visit to the Admiral detailed in the previous listed report, so around 19th March 1889. Kane was certainly in possession of the letter when he left Apia on the 21st. I have included it in my text as it is nice history, and reinforces the depth of friendship between these two nation's representatives, in what some have described as the first joint military expedition between Great Britain and the United States.

6. Midshipman H.L.A. Hood account, reproduced in *"The First Commission of HMS Calliope"* by Captain E.W. Swan, published in 1939 [13].

This book also includes an account by Midshipman S.W. Nicholson, both of which provide useful data.

7. An account by the Associated Press correspondent J.P. Dunning who was resident in Apia at the time. Because he was actually an eye-witness, I believe his account, of which I have a copy, is genuine material, and the only one I have located made by someone on shore at the time. It is very comprehensive and runs to a number of pages. The story was published in "*St. Nicholas, an Illustrated Magazine for Young Folk*", reference [8]. Dunning compiled a massive article that was sent by a later mail, which was used in the *New York Times* and *San Francisco Chronicle* articles in the issues dated 14th April 1889.

8. A letter from Navigating Lieutenant Henry Pearson to J. O. Burgess, written at the Union Club, Sydney on 9th April 1889, and as far as I know, unpublished [32]. This letter gives an insight into the discussions in the wheelhouse as *Calliope's* attempt to escape from Apia was planned and executed. Pearson is also the only other witness, along with my great-grandfather, who states that *Calliope* passed *Trenton's* port side in the escape, so I am confident to use their view in my text.

9. "*SMS Eber, Report to the Right Honourable Imperial Kommander Fritze*", by Lieutenant Gaedeke dated 20th March 1889 [29]. This report, obviously in German, was downloadable as a PDF from the internet, but the page carrying it now seems to be closed, so I have been unable to determine its history. It is the only German eye-witness report I have. I would have liked to record it in full, but I have not been able to clarify any copyright issues, especially given that I did not perform the translation myself. I guess the original will be stored in a German archive somewhere, presuming it survived the Second World War which seems probable for it to have found its way onto the internet.

10. A slightly more general description of the events by Chaplain, the Reverend Arthur Cornwallis Evans, in his book "*The Cruise of HMS Calliope*". [7]

11. HMS *Calliope's* Ship's Logs, which are kept at London's National Archives in Kew as ADM53/12898 through ADM53/12901 [3]. From these I gleaned much interesting data, including a full list of the equipment destroyed by the storm, and the various barometer readings at the time before the barometer was disturbed by the weather.

12. The author's great-grandfather's memoirs, written in 1932, and unpublished, which have formed the backbone to the "personal" side of this manuscript. [30]

I have liberally illustrated my text in this chapter with verbatim accounts made by some of the people *who were there*. I make no apology for this, it seems to me that to try and précis their accounts would simply be an impertinence, as in truth, who could tell the story better?

So, to the first day of the storm.

Friday 15th March 1889 dawned blustery, dull and overcast over Samoa, but before long, the early morning gloom had been cleared by a searing tropical sun that once again turned the bay into the customary oven. The barometer on *Calliope* at 4.0 a.m. that morning continued the downward trend, another low of 29.39 inches in a falling pattern that was seemingly gentle but worryingly insistent, giving considerable concern to the navigating officer on the British vessel; most probably to the officers on all the vessels. The sky was soon a bright clear blue and the early morning temperature oppressive even for Apia, but the normally choppy waters of the bay were unusually smooth and oily. Though I don't suppose they could put their fears into words, it will have seemed to the experienced sailors that something unpleasant was in the air; all those who later wrote about it fancied the morning oppression to be a premonition.

The squally wind blowing off the land was freshening with gusts between force 1 and 3. Navigating Officer Henry Pearson had the previous day given Captain Kane his opinion that a serious blow was coming, and even at that stage, he warned of the possibility of a hurricane. The response was dismissive from the normally cautious Irishman; the 1883 hurricane on which many of the current fears were based, whilst denuding the bay of every ship which had sought its dangerous protection and costing a score or so of lives in the process, had found as prey only a parcel of *windjammers*: vessels unprotected by heavy holding gear, and lacking the modern shield to stormy weather: steam power. To Kane, the situation now was quite different to that of six years earlier, and beguiled also by land-based promises that there was no real wind coming, he was content to wait and see. The barometer was already significantly lower than the lowest value recorded those few years earlier (29.45 inches), but Kane was still not expecting a severe storm this time.

On *Calliope* that morning, the blustery winds were, as always, not permitted to halt the incessant round of drills and evolutions. The early watch had risen on the British vessel as usual for ablutions, scrub decks, stow hammocks and, at last, breakfast. A pleasant sight for the crew during that morning break was the loading of 212 pounds of beef and 333 pounds of fresh bread.

As on all mornings, the first real order was given to *"Clean Guns"*. *Calliope* was a warship first and foremost, and she had to be able to defend herself, or protect British interests, at any moment. Good maintenance of her armament therefore was crucial, and this included the small arms. This action was completed by 8.30 a.m. at which time the smaller guns were stowed and the larger covered over.

Once all was tidied away, the order was to *"Light Pipes"* so that those sailors who partook of the weed could avail themselves of the opportunity to have a smoke and enjoy a cup of steaming coffee brought up from the mess deck whilst the air was still reasonably cool, though as already observed, on that morning it was by now already uncomfortably hot. The weather signs were certainly ominous, and the crew could hardly have failed to notice that three of *Calliope's* boilers had been lit earlier that morning; they will have been instinctively aware that this would not have been done for the sole purpose of distilling water. The wind gusts had reached an alarming force 7 but still only intermittently and briefly.

At 8.50 a.m. came the orders to *"Out Pipes"* and *"Clear Decks"*, and at 9.10 a.m. was *"Divisions and Prayers"*, the crew being dismissed after the 20 minute service. Next came the first of the day's evolutions, that ceaseless performing of drills to make the crew so efficient that when an action was needed to be carried out for real under battle or storm conditions, it could be completed almost without thinking.

That morning, the drill call was *"Fall In for Station to Clear Ship for Action"* being the preliminary to a rather suitable evolution to be well versed in, given the very real and seemingly unstoppable drift to war that was happening in the islands. It would involve sending down to the deck the spars (also known as yards) from the fore- and main-masts. The entire deck crew were carefully and exhaustively trained in their duties for this drill. To open proceedings, sailors ascended their allotted masts and detached the spars from their housings, and lowered them to the deck. Ropes were *"snaked"*, that is coiled into those perfectly symmetrical spirals, and safely stowed away.

The bugler, Royal Marine Light Infantry Private John W. Carroll, then sounded off the next call *"Exercise Action"* and the drill was underway in earnest. Guns were made ready, and men took up their stations behind them. The Gunnery Officer of the day issued his orders to *"Train the Broadside on the Quarter"* or some other direction within the 80° scan angle of the main armament, and the crews carried them out. Seamen whose action stations were not to man the massive rifles were drilled in *"Repel Boarders"* using a boarding pike, a weapon not unlike a lance and especially potent at a ship's side, or with cutlass, sword and pistol. There was even a *"Tomahawk Party"*. The Marines of the Royal Light Infantry placed collision mats in areas designated by officers as having been the subject of a ram or torpedo attack, in order to lessen the potential influx of water should that actually happen. The off duty stokers metaphorically changed their hats to become the *"Fire Brigade"*; ready to put out fires wherever they may start. The surgeon had his *"Ambulance Party"* comprising mainly the ward stewards and cooks. Everyone had a part to play in this action.

This drill continued for quite a while, with *Calliope* under the noses of her potential allies, and her equally potential opponents. If only the former, it would have been a matter of simple pride for the crew to perform the chosen evolution in good style, efficiently and quickly. But surrounding the British ship and just a little further away than *Calliope's* length lay German warships: SMS *Adler* and SMS *Olga* to starboard, with SMS *Eber* astern, and there is little doubt that a good display of *"Action Stations"* might be a powerful psychological weapon against the Germans. If Kane decided to berate his opponents in the future as had been done in the past by Captains Pelly and Hand, it would do no harm if the Kriegsmarine officers had seen with their own eyes the evidence that they were dealing with the commander of a well-trained and efficient crew manning a powerful and modern warship. Further to starboard and slightly behind *Calliope, Eber* and *Olga* lay USS *Nipsic*, and her officers too would be professionally interested in the performance of the British crew.

At 10 a.m. Midshipman Hood recorded the barometer as 29.28 inches, the lowest even the oldest inhabitant of Samoa could ever recall. The warning signs were there.

At 11 a.m., the order was given to *"Secure from Action Stations"*, and to *"Clear Lower Deck and Secure"*. Guns were once again returned to their stowage positions and the various sick, fire brigade, and boarding parties stowed their gear and disbanded, the men returning to their normal duties. The next order was *"Square Yards and Haul Taut Ropes"*. The yards were re-assembled to the masts and *"squared off"*, a process in which the boatswain Mr. William Marshfield would take himself off in one of the launches, positioning himself directly ahead or on the quarter of the ship, and by use of appropriately coloured signal flags, indicate to the deck crew which yards were slightly out-of-alignment. White was the signal for the foremast, red the mainmast and blue the mizzen. Using the right hand signified yards to starboard, the left hand yards to port. Held at 45° below horizontal indicated the lower yards, horizontal the top-sail yards, at

45°above the horizontal it referred to the top-gallant yards, and for the royal yards, the flag was held directly above the head. Despite the inclement weather, it was a matter of honour for the ship to have her yards properly squared-off and ropes tight and the boatswain would not return to the ship until he was completely satisfied, no matter how long it might take. If you should ever be shown a picture of an unidentified sailing ship with her yards askew, you can be pretty certain she was not Royal Navy.

For the cooks and stewards, the next order, *"Sound Off Cooks"* at 11.45 a.m. signified they should begin to prepare the midday meal. At around this time, some naval prudence regarding the weather seems at last to have made its appearance in the bay. On *Calliope*, Pearson recorded a new barometer reading of 29.20 inches, a low figure few on the ship had ever seen it reach before, and an alarming drop in such a short time. As certain as they could be that a heavy blow was coming and that the shore-captains were wrong, the Navigating Officers on all the ships must have urged their Captains that some preparations should be made on the warships. The crews of the American and German ships that earlier had been regarding the British drill with a detached professional interest (or more likely: boredom), were suddenly themselves a bustle of activity. For the *Calliope*s the explanation was quick to come, as the order to *"Belay Cooks"* sounded, followed by *"Clear Lower Deck, Everyone Aft"*.

The entire company as could be spared assembled to hear Kane describe the weather predictions from the barometer, which by noon had fallen to that 29.20 inches and was clearly not finished yet. Kane repeated the Apia residents' views that the fall in pressure – the old salts already instinctively aware of it – was for rain only. Some of those older more experienced sailors probably snorted a little at that, quietly, of course. At this time of the day the wind was still from the land to the south-east, force 1 with not very cooling gusts to force 3, occasionally a little stronger, those earlier stronger blows seeming to have eased away. However, as Kane said, just in case another gale came up like the earlier ones and in view of the continuing fall in the barometer, the precaution was to be taken in *Calliope*, as had already started in the other vessels, to strike her top masts and lower yards; clear preparation for bad weather. This was considered by most sailors to be one of the heaviest evolutions to be performed on a sailing ship.

Each of the two larger masts on the three-mast *Calliope*, the fore- and the main-masts, were made in sections, and the evolution was to detach the top-gallant and royal yards from the highest mast section (top-gallant mast) and lower them and the top-gallant mast to the deck, and to lower the top-sail mast (the middle section) and house it against the lower-mast (lowest section) whilst retaining the top-sail yard should sail be needed to be set. The intention was to reduce the sail area to a more manageable amount (i.e. use the top-sail instead of the course) and to make it more accessible being lowered down from its normal position. Kimberly saw this evolution as "...*getting the top hampers down...*", and all the naval ships in Apia would perform the same evolution that morning. There were many other reasons for lowering the top hampers if a storm was approaching, just as preparing for a gale involved the entire ship's company in much unseen work below decks: storing fragile items, putting things in their storm cases, and so on.

To quote verbatim from the section how..."*To Manage in A Storm*" in reference [39]:

> "*If the gale increases, the topmasts should be timely struck, but the fore yard seldom, if ever, should be lowered down, that, in case of parting* [the anchors], *the foresail may be always ready. At these times, let there be more people on deck than the usual anchor-watch, that no accident may happen from inattention.*"

The highly stylised image on page 175 may help in understanding the procedure. In the right-hand part of the picture, the top-gallant mast, with its royal and top-gallant yards, has been completely detached and stowed on the deck, whilst the top-mast with its top-sail yard has been lowered. The lower yard has been detached, and is shown stowed athwartships (side to side) on top of the bulwarks, just in front of the main mast.

The drill started almost immediately, as at 11.55 a.m. the Boatswain's Mate Thomas Saunders sounded "*Strike Lower Yard and Topmast*". A quarter of an hour later, this difficult, heavy and awkward evolution was complete. This was what the two years of training since the commissioning voyage had started was for, and its efficient completion was something in which the officers and crew of *Calliope* could take just pride. Since German and American crews had already started the evolution, it was *jingoistically* important that the *Calliopes* performed it impeccably and rapidly. The lower-most yard on each of the fore and main masts was detached from the caps (where it is anchored against the mast) and lowered to the deck, lashed tightly to the lower mast and the nettings at the side of the ship, to protrude outboard like the unmanned oars of a long-gone Roman galley. Finally, the topmast was slid down against the lower mast and housed, that is, secured together. The topgallant masts had been removed and lowered to the deck earlier the previous morning.

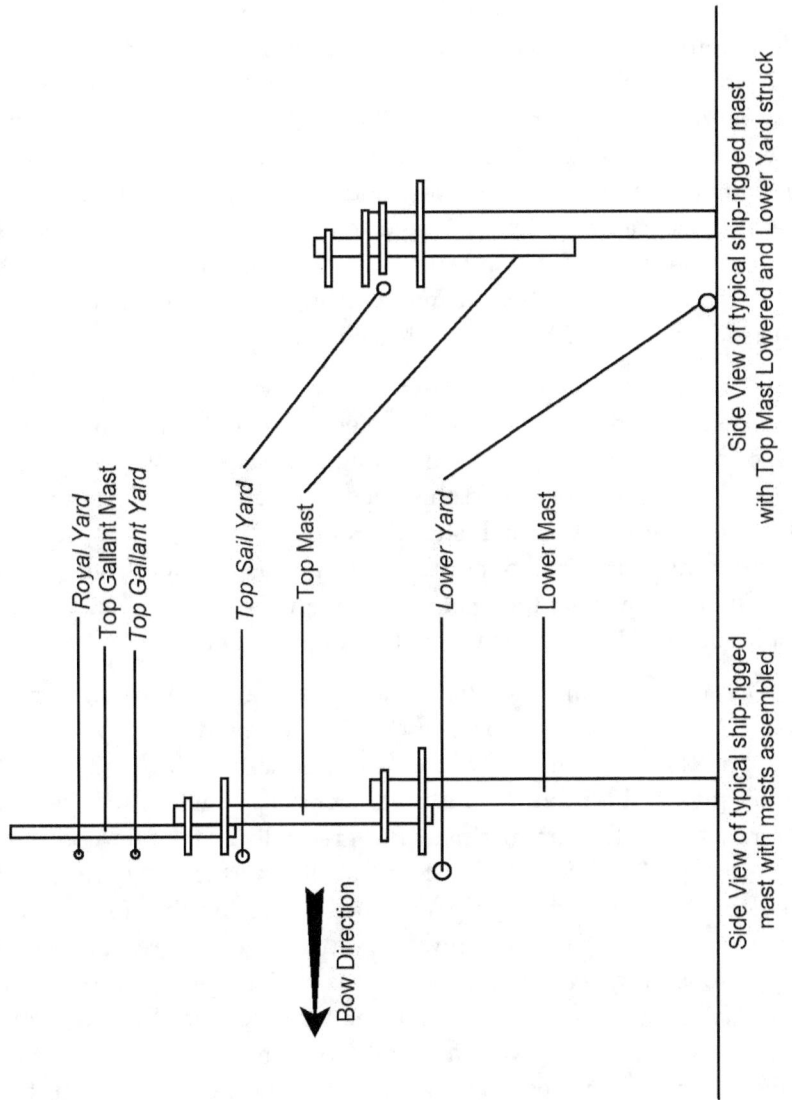

Stylised view of a ship-rigged mast, assembled and with top-mast housed.

Now, it was a matter of waiting to see what the weather might bring. During the afternoon, the wind ceased much of its repeated gusting and maintained in general force 1, only occasionally blustering to 3, with the direction variable. It was the classic calm before the storm, and few of the experienced men on board the ships in the bay were fooled by it.

At 2 p.m., the barometer stood at 29.11 inches, which seems to have been its lowest ebb. To be brutally honest, this was the time any sensible captain should have upped his anchors, abandoned the port, and taken his vessel out to sea to weather the unseen but surely approaching storm unhampered by the surrounding uncompromising reef or those other ships in close proximity. Whatever might be the shore experts previous opinion, the information now strongly suggested that a severe storm was approaching. In the days before satellite weather forecasting, experience in all aspects of seamanship and the sea was a vital part of ship management; the captain's invariable custom of an early morning perusal of the waves, sniff of the air and glance to the heavens a real part of his captaincy, rather than an affected mannerism. Gut instinct was not to be sneered at when reported by an experienced seaman.

Calliope's stokers brought the fires forward, and under low revolutions of the screw, the officers steamed her round her anchor to clear the hawse and remove the kinks that might weaken it should a heavy strain be applied. No sooner had this been done and the ship re-moored, than the wind started stiffening, shifting rapidly so that it now blew into the bay from the north. The opportunity for an easy escape from the trap was now flying away from them all with the sand bouncing along the Apia seafront road; yet still no-one made that first move out to sea.

The rest of that Friday afternoon saw a rapid change in the weather that astonished all those present. The normally choppy waters of the bay had been surprisingly and exceptionally calm and smooth, apparently giving the proof to the predictions of no wind, or that what wind there was would soon dissipate. But gradually as the afternoon wore on, that wind got ever fresher bolstered by the northerly gusts, and the skies darkened inexorably in preparation of delivering that forecast rain. Off-duty German and American crews on shore leave were recalled to their ships by the booming of a cannon and signals on the rigging. The off-watch *Adler* and *Eber* crews grudgingly left the bars in which they had been doing one of the few things that were available to them: getting drunk. Many found the return to their vessels in the increasingly choppy seas a difficult and uncomfortable experience, the latest arrivals in fact finding themselves close to not being able to get on board at all.

The waves very quickly became larger still, due to some combination of wind, barometric pressure and coastal topography. By 4 p.m. the wind was force 4 to 6 from the north, and the barometer had risen slightly from the low it had touched. At 6 p.m., it was blowing from north-east of north and had dropped a little, with the barometer climbing to 29.27, but any hope that might have given was false and cruel. The hurricane was simply drawing breath for the onslaught.

The sky had turned purple during that afternoon and filled with dark heavy clouds, and then the rain pounded down. To those of us unused to the heavy downpours of the tropics, it is difficult to adequately understand the torrential deluge that assaulted the bay and its occupants, flattening the heads of the waves, running like rivers over the decks of the ships and pouring out of the scuppers. For Samoa, well used to waterfalls of rain, the downfall this time was quite as bad as anything that had been seen before. And the wind was still freshening.

Darkness came early to the bay that afternoon. In those latitudes and at that time, it was expected around 5 p.m. but it was already dark by 4 p.m. The full moon due in the next day or two would be of no help with clouds as heavy as had brought the rain. Before long the ships could not see the reef, and soon even each other's storm lanterns were becoming difficult to observe, and any thought now of leaving the bay would have to wait for the light of morning. Most of the ships at Apia had no modern powerful searchlights of their own, though *Trenton* did have the distinction of having become the first warship in the American Navy to be fitted with electric light and *Calliope* too could run some electric lights, but the reef was too close and dangerous, and the bay too encumbered, for anyone to risk trying to leave with it so poorly illuminated. All of the officers of each nationality would soon be brought to realise that the opportunity to safely escape had now slipped through their fingers.

Much speculation was later made of the reasons why so many experienced captains ignored the weather signs, and elected to stay in such an obvious and historically proven dangerous trap as Apia. The military situation was undoubtedly the major factor, as no-one would have wished to be the first to effectively abandon their post. Kane had the least military compulsion to stay, so I guess for him it was simple pride; being so far in, the British ship would have needed to thread its way past other vessels on her way to sea, and he may have thought this would have given out an unwonted sense of excessive wariness. He was also quite convinced of his secure position. Even had Kane left, I rather think the American and German ships would have stayed to spite each other.

Of them all, it was probably Admiral Kimberly, as the most senior naval officer of any nation present, who should have led the way, but just consider. He had sped across the Pacific with the shouts of an incensed Congress waving a burned and shredded *Stars and Stripes* as proof of German warlike intentions in Samoa, and carrying in his guns and magazines the fledgling nation's will to show the old Imperialists that the New World of a recently and now truly United States of America could no longer be dictated to. He had been in such haste, that imprudently he had omitted to re-coal at Hawaii on his way to Samoa, and both USS *Trenton* and USS *Vandalia* were seriously short of fuel. A tender was on its way, but would not arrive at Apia for a couple of weeks yet. To use the little coal he had to escape Apia unnecessarily and risk leaving himself compromised if he should later need to engage in hostilities, was apparently a decision he felt he could not take, and was cited by most American commentators who later picked the effects of the storm to pieces in their many articles about it; Kimberly repeats that reason in his memoirs [10]. They also took the opportunity to bemoan the lack of re-coaling facilities at Pango Pango in nearby American Samoa, a perfectly justifiable criticism of the administration of that time, since both Britain and Germany had re-coaling facilities in Apia.

The wish to conserve his coal hardly works, though, unless Kimberly really thought he could weather the storm in the bay with his holding gear doing most of the work, which it seems he did. No captain puts his ship at risk just to save fuel. No, lack of coal was surely part of his thinking, but national pride and military need must also have contributed. And this was probably the German position, too. Their vessels had plenty of fuel stocks, to go with a lot of nationalistic fervour. Most people would agree, I think, that as well as duty, sheer bloody stubbornness to not be the first one to abandon the position for any reason, was why all the militarists stayed in what must have been seen to be increasing danger. But we are using hindsight; had they known then what was coming, of course they would all have left, whatever doing so did to their coal stocks.

The flag had been planted in the Samoan village Matafangatele, by one Captain Hamilton. I have been unable to find out anything about this man or his time on Samoa. I would guess him to have been an officer on an American vessel visiting the islands, possibly USS *Adams*, or he might have been an Apia resident. The flag had been damaged during shelling by SMS *Olga* in December 1888.

It appears that on the day the hurricane hit Samoa, news arrived in Honolulu that USS *Nipsic* and SMS *Adler* had commenced hostilities, with the American ship having been sunk in the exchange of shells. The source seems to have been a *"vicious, lying, telegram"* according to the Samoa Times, taken from the *Schlesische Zeitung*, a Breslau paper. Though obviously untruthful, the rumours led to fisticuffs becoming prevalent between Americans and Germans in the streets of Honolulu.

During that evening of the 15th March, the wind freshened inexorably from the north or slightly east of north so that, combined with the waves growing in stature in front of the men's eyes, nature seemed to be trying it's hardest to push the ships against the reef. At 7 p.m. the wind was a sustained force 7 from the north-east, three hours later it was force 8 and the heavy swell had set firmly from the north directly into the bay.

The staggering rainfall brought another terrifying dimension to the scene. The deposition on the land was every bit as fierce as that in the bay, and the masses of cascading water simply ran off the basalt land and charged into the rivers, turning them from meandering docile streams into fearsome weapons of destruction. Virtually all the bridges across the two major rivers that emptied into the bay, the Vaisigano and the Mulivai, were soon washed away. The normal outpourings from these streams increased ten and then one hundred fold. This water rushed into the bay, smashing into the oncoming waves and turning the surface of the harbour into a seething mass of unpredictable currents and whirlpools. No pilot could have anticipated how a ship would react to such a vigorous stirring. It had an equally dangerous, and subtly invisible, effect: that of scouring the basin of the bay clear of every grain of sand and stick of weed. And an anchor makes considerably better purchase in mud or silt than it does on a bare, rocky floor, although anchors found little to grab to on the floor of Apia Bay even in the best of times. These capricious currents made the ships behave unpredictably, reduced the efficiency of their anchors, and brought with them debris from bridges and trees inland that had the impetus of battering rams. The wind and waves tried to push the ships back against the reef and those oncoming forces from the land. Nature had combined her weapons in opposition to man. And she was increasing the power of her armament with every minute that passed.

On shore, many residents had groped their way in the darkness from their homes, to squint their eyes in a desperate attempt to survey the scene in their harbour, sleep being impossible in the howling gale and crashing of roofs. The tide in Apia was fast approaching the town; the front street was reportedly awash a hundred feet above the usual high water mark. These residents were well aware that a dreadful disaster was unfolding.

Night on a vessel in such a storm encloses the crew like a wet blanket, coldly insulating them from the normal reality of the world around them, heightening the unknown dangers, hiding the vessel from her fellows behind a mantle of loneliness and apprehension. The few remaining senses, aware of only the movement, the cold and the noise, are enhanced in proportion to the loss of the others, and above them all, or the sum of them all, was fear.

The wind was so powerful it shrieked in the lines and spars, almost deafening those on deck and making conversation a painful act of shouting into one another's ear. The astonishingly heavy rain was mixed with a cloud of sea-spray smashed up by the plunging bows that, could it have been visible to an onlooker, shrouded each entire ship like a burst steam pipe in a confined engine-room. By common assent of the land observers when later they came to talk about it, the waves were the largest they had any of them seen: some land based elders asserted that although the wind had not quite been the worst they had experienced, the seas had been by far the most dramatic the islands could have ever known - it was the accompaniment of these enormous waves which took this storm out of the *ordinary* and placed it above all others.

Hyperbole about weather must surely match that used by fisherman of their lost catches, or young men of their beer capacity, but it seems that since the various accounts are in so much agreement, the waves in this case must indeed have been monstrous. Kane asserts they ran green over the ship, even breaking on occasion higher than the topmast. Kane suggests that the ship was regularly *stood on end*, meaning she lay her full 250 foot length along the leading face of a wave. Kimberly too, regarded the incredible seas as his worst ever, and he was further out in the bay where the narrowing reefs and shelving floor of the inner portion had not yet elevated the wave height as much as it would closer in. Every human involved in the scene, and later writing about it, identifies the staggering weight of the seas as the most noteworthy element, dwarfing even the hurricane force winds and the hammering bullets of rain for comment.

Close your eyes. Imagine yourself cocooned by a pitch-black stormy night, sitting on a cold steel and wooden crate, lurching on a turbulent sea which lifts and bucks on huge waves crashing themselves over your little world; waves which roll you to and fro and toss you from side to side without pattern or predictability, and battered also by a howling gale and swirling, erratic currents. You are not still for a moment for your mind to make sense of this world. You can hardly hear anything, as the screaming wind fills the air with a deafening bedlam; you can hardly see anything with the salt spray stinging your eyes, mixing with the tears torn from them by the gale. Your brain struggles to make sense of the crazily tilting world you are in, and your most powerful senses are blotted out and useless to you. Hammering rain and steaming spray assault you like the jets from some enormous shower unit, stinging exposed flesh like thousands of native poison darts.

Have you ever sat at home at night as a gale thrashed around you? Creaking the roof, flinging the trees outside every which way around, so that you wonder if at any moment your house would be devastated by the elements? I well remember the October 1987 storm that hit southern and central England, and there was no doubt that it made me very apprehensive while it lasted. Samoa in 1889 was much worse, and these men were not on stable land but grasping hold to a capricious ship on the violently flexing seas, either exposed to the elements outside or locked down inside.

Consider also that somewhere close behind in the direction you fear you are being pushed looms a hidden mass of jagged rock and coral, sharpened stakes like the spears of some long-departed Roman cohort arising from the depths of hell, waiting to pierce and smash your world to pieces and drag you down with it, unseen and more threatening by its very invisibility. At every second, you might feel the crashing, jarring impact. You imagine it in the dark: are you getting closer, or are you still safely away from it? There is no way of knowing if the reef is 6 or 60 feet away, no way of knowing if your anchors are holding, or dragging.

Somewhere near to you, hidden in their own little world of darkness, are many other similar crates, some bigger, some smaller but each with their own occupants, each flying about on the waters and each seemingly ready to stove in your sides or cut your precious cables, your lifelines which so precariously tether you in position. Friend or enemy before the storm, now everyone is both at the same time – sharing this life-or-death struggle against a more powerful common enemy with you, but at the same time posing yet another danger to be avoided if possible, another hazard to watch out for.

For those on deck, desperately holding on to lines and fittings, exposed to the elements and lashed by wind, rain and spray, the twin evils of whirlpools and waves beckon, waiting to pull you into a drowning death or to smash your body to pieces against the rocks. And then imagine being *inside* that crate, battened down below hatches and stairways and decks, knowing that had the vessel foundered you would not have even the slightest chance of escape, not knowing if even now, it *was* foundering. Waiting to be turned upside down as the water rushes in, hoping for truth in the old sailor's self-comforting maxim that a drowning death is quick and painless. Boatswain Marshfield described being gripped by a wire and rope hawser around his ankle, and being *"shuttle-cocked"* here and there, battered and bruised. He only got clear by cutting the rope with an axe - he was lucky.

And imagine yourself enduring this spinning, cart-wheeling, sense-obliterating world for hour upon hour where every minute must have seemed endless.

The dangers facing the ships were legion. As each huge wave approached, the dead weight of the ship and the harp-taught anchor cables would tend to smash the bow of the vessel deep into its face, and the effort to lift the hundreds of tons of cold and heaving sea-water on the deck would leave the ship struggling to raise her prow and the wave would pass along, as Kane said, often running green along her length without even breaking. The ship would lift herself up to ride the long front face of the bigger waves and the straining engines would need to push her against the combined forces of gravity, sea power, and wind. As she crested the wave, the unsupported bow would then crash down into the following trough, and the see-saw action would lift the stern and its thundering propeller momentarily clear of the water – the loss of the resistance would cause the propeller to suddenly race ahead, and risk thrashing the machinery to bits before the governor could catch it, before once more becoming enveloped by water. And this was the most serious time of all: suddenly immersing an air-spinning massive propeller into the water would send an immense shock through the drive system and the biggest risk was the shearing of a blade. Should that disaster happen, the out-of-balance propeller would instantly wreck the engine that was so vital to life. Every wave encountered risked such a catastrophe. Every crash of the bow reminded the sailors that within a few seconds they may lose their propeller, followed shortly thereafter by their lives.

Steaming up to the anchors was another dreadful risk. If one was too close to the anchor and the chain was loose, it provided a reduced restraint, and the ship could be tossed sideways risking turning its head away from the seas; if close with a tight chain, the lifting wave of such height as faced these ships risked tightening the cable and the ship might then lift the anchor from its precarious purchase on the harbour floor - and it would undoubtedly be deposited some way aft from where it had lifted. The waves tried to smash the puny rudders from their stern-posts, and in most vessels, the off-duty watch took it in turns to hang for dear life on chains called relieving tackles, desperately trying to prevent the breaking of the convoluted linkage from wheel house to rudder. At times, 14 or more men were needed to hold the rudder safe. In reality, all night, there was no off-duty watch on any of the vessels.

Deep within the bowels of the ship, the roof level some three feet below the calm weather water-line, lay the engine room of *Calliope*, her heart. The engineers in that cavern knew two things: the ship's survival depended on the engines; and that should they fail, the only possible but hopelessly slim chance of survival would be afforded the deck crew above, and not themselves. The below decks personnel would simply have no chance of life. Under these conditions, everyone in the engine-room performed an amazing job. They could only allow themselves to think of their engines.

The forced draught applied to the boiler furnaces created starving monsters insatiable for their black, heavy, dusty food. Roaring with a noise that down below drowned out even the shrieks from the gale, the fires demanded shovel loads of coal almost non-stop, for hours on end, and the stokers, forming a sort of never-ending *chain-gang*, had to deliver it to the maws of the open furnace doors. And not just throw the coal in anyhow, each shovelful had to be expertly distributed across the embers, so that it might burn evenly and at its most productive. If piled in one place, some of the coal would not burn immediately, and efficiency would be slightly, but perhaps, for the safety of the ship, significantly impaired. And they had to do this in a confined environment, sweating as hot as the furnaces themselves, the pipes and even the air in the room itself seemingly running red hot; a world that pitched and rolled and yawed and did its best to throw them on the floor, or the wall, against a ladder or deck coaming, or a steam pipe tens of degrees hotter than boiling water.

The stokers only knew the next wave was coming when it arrived, and the body load they had placed on the one leg had to be immediately transferred to the other. Men took it in turns to work like they had never worked before till almost they could stand up no longer, to then be relieved by their fellows of the other watch; so that, exhausted, they could now stand behind them, leaning on railings, or walls, or even each other, their aching backs grabbing the small chance of rest that the other's work afforded them. And they did this turn and turn about for hour upon dreadful, mind-numbing, life-threatening, interminable hour.

Above all this in that steamy hellish engine room, it was that risk of smashing the propeller to pieces or breaking the shaft, which demanded the close attention of one man, who for more than 12 hours non-stop, and without relief, performed a simple to describe yet vital task. Staff-Engineer Bourke could not persuade the experienced Engineer Milton to pass the job to anyone else in case an error was made. Milton had done it before, but never in seas so ferocious, nor for such a sustained period of time. Unable to see the seas outside, and with the engine-room dancing around him, any attempt to estimate the attitude of the ship, and the position of its propeller, was impossible. But Milton had a simple device which told him what the ship was doing, and his eyes hardly left it for all that period of time: a spirit level.

Aligned with the axis of the ship, in the Engine Room it was the only reliable gauge of the ship climbing a wave or teetering on its crest. Milton watched the level as it told him the ship was climbing up the front of the next large wave and his hand on the steam valve kept it open: driving the ship at its maximum capability up and against this most awesome force trying to smash it backwards against the reef. But then, his eyes saw in the bouncing air bubble of the gauge – perhaps combined with the instinctive seaman's feel for it – that the ship had reached the crest and just before the screw reared out of the surf and raced itself to destruction, he snapped the valve closed, and the shaft suddenly free from the water spun by its own momentum only, not speeding up. Next the bubble moved aft and the bow tilted downwards and he waited those immeasurable fractions of a second before flinging the valve open, instinctively timing it so that as the milling screw buried itself in the water, the steam reached the cylinders and the previously set pressure was applied once more, so preventing the screw either from slowing down or from running faster than the captain's current order. He managed the shaft by this extraordinary method for some 14 or 15 hours non-stop, so that the true shaft speed hardly varied, whether it be pushing tons of water or the almost nothingness of spray and air.

Imagine if you can just how critical his timing was. Had he shut the steam valve too soon, whilst the screw was still in the water and with the ship still climbing the wave, the transmission gear would slow very rapidly due to the load of the water the propeller was trying to move, and the whole shaft and engine would slow with it. After cresting the wave, precious seconds would then be wasted on the wave back slope with the shaft in the water trying to bring the revolutions back up to maximum. Too many such miscalculations and the ship would be on the reef. If he shut it too late, the shaft would speed up in the air and the load on re-entering the water would be higher, the risk to the equipment the greater. It was an extraordinary effort by this man that afterward earned him, quite rightly, especial praise from Kane and the Admiralty. Even so, there were many occasions when a particularly deep trough or long wavelength would catch him out, and allow the propeller to clear and race even with the ship horizontal, and then the entire crew prayed for the strength of the machinery when it once again hit the sea and rattled and shook the length of the ship in doing so.

On deck, the sail men had their own problems, even though the ship had no sail set, not even storm sails. The gale driven torrent of rain and sea smashed everything breakable, and strewed the deck with dangerous debris. Whipping rope lines, spinning, splintered matchwood that had once been the jolly boat that had won so many races for *Calliope's* boat crew in calmer ports; it all impeded the work of the deck personnel and the visibility of the captain and his officers, so had to be removed.

Although a similar thing was happening on all the ships, perhaps the most extreme case of deck damage occurred on USS *Nipsic*. She had been in collision with SMS *Olga*, a crashing, jarring, explosion of force that had severely damaged the German ship and smashed off her bowsprit, and that had severed the American's smokestack, not a simple task for a dockyard to have achieved. The huge tube of sheet steel, its jagged torn edges like the polished blades on a Celtic Briton's chariot wheel, rolled along the bouncing deck of the ship as a lethal and devastating thing alive, flinging as it did so the ends of its broken wire stays like the lashing cat-o-nine-tails of an earlier age of sail. It had fallen in between the wheelhouse and the main mast, and seemed intent on destroying those parts of the ship which now confined it: as the vessel ploughed into a wave the stack was flung forwards into the back of the wheelhouse, then the climb up the wave catapulted it backwards into the mast. Everything on the deck between was soon smashed or driven overboard. The smokestack would have to follow soon, or it alone could lead to the ship's destruction. Men would need to get to it, secure lines to it, and somehow heave it over the side.

Whilst plans were being prepared, fate and wave current turned the smokestack aligned with the axis of the ship, and now its roll was side to side, constrained by the gunwales. It was now or never, and by a supreme effort the crew were able, assisted by a fortuitous roll of the ship, to push the thing over the side and into the bay without going with it themselves. The truncated stack emitted smoke and cinders from the raging furnaces blinding and scorching the faces of the officers in their path.

Large ships, close together, are an amazing sight, but when those ships are plunging and rearing, suddenly and unpredictably being thrown sideways by strange and powerful underwater currents, when the anchor chains are taught and groaning with strain, and when a hard and unyielding coral reef sits close behind waiting for a victim, such proximity must be terrifying and collisions between the ships were inevitable. The fury of the gale and the smashing, battering, force of the sea were by no means constant in their threat. A ship, her engines straining hard and thrashing her propeller through the silt laden muddy water might suddenly find the wind drop just a fraction, and the big waves provide a slight respite, and suddenly she was forging ahead, effectively out of control. Anything in her path was in danger and with the bay as crowded as it was, it was unlikely the rudder could be thrown over in time, every time, in precisely the correct way, to avoid whatever lay there. Impossible to prevent smashing into some other ship on which her crew were looking forwards at the weather they were about to face: deck crew and the officers looked forward at the seas, behind at the reef, and sideways at other vessels; for hours on end. The commanding officers tried to juggle their ship's position to avoid all the obstacles threatening its safety; it was impossible.

On *Calliope*, though such extremes as removing a smoke stack were not necessary, a great deal of similarly dangerous work was required. Men needed to move around the decks even in so dreadful a storm, and much rigging was cut away when it trailed itself around the deck. Boats, smashed to splinters by the waves, tended to clear themselves but the shattered planking made lethal weapons, spears thrown with phenomenal power by the ogres of nature.

During the early hours of Saturday 16th March, vessels in the bay began to lose the battle, amazing it was they had lasted so long. The German schooner of 462 tons (some sources state 660 tons) *Peter Godeffroy* collided with the 800 ton Danish iron barque *Santiago*, and both vanished in the seething mass of water. The German ship was owned by Mr. August Bolten, of Hamburg; she had been built of iron in 1869, but the shipping company of Peter Godeffroy was forced into bankruptcy in the year 1879. Presumably, its assets, including the ship, had been sold off at that time, and unusually the vessel had retained it's original name.

Other small schooners were being swamped and disappeared throughout the night, with no-one to record their demise. At 2 a.m. *Calliope*'s officers ordered her fourth boiler to be lit, and at 5 a.m. Midshipman Hood described the wind, somewhat nonchalantly in my opinion, as "*...blowing a perfect hurricane...*" Around 6 a.m., the military might, supposedly protected by modern steam and heavy holding gear, finally found that protection inadequate, and the pretty little SMS *Eber* was the first naval vessel to succumb to the unnamed hurricane.

The very few survivors of her crew told the tale. The fear of the damaged propeller injuring the engine meant it was used only in short bursts when considered absolutely necessary and this care seemed to be carrying the day. But nature would not be baulked, and a parting anchor cable trailed back along the ship's keel and fouled the screw, performing the same coup-de-grace that a failed bearing would have done. One of the few survivors, Lieutenant Friedrich Gaedeke, would later report that the first ensuing collision with the reef had irreparably damaged the rudder making it useless, and that at that time, and despite the fouled propeller, the engine was still running at "full steam" which managed to bring the ship about 20 meters off the reef. Right after that first strike the commander gave the order to haul in the chain, but while the crew were still freeing the winch the ship was thrown against the reef for the second time, at the stern and then with the whole port-side aft. Bringing her off was no longer possible and the engine was stopped. There were no further orders from the bridge. The ship rolled 30 degrees to port and 45 degrees to starboard, then about 45 degrees to port and 90 degrees to starboard, then again 45 degrees back to port. Finally, SMS *Eber* capsized to starboard against the reef. The crashing, tearing and ripping of timbers were probably heard on other nearby ships even over the cacophony of the wind, and the listeners will have known precisely what the sounds meant.

Hundreds of natives and Apia residents were witnesses to the terrible event, though in the semi-darkness they will have been unable to see very clearly what had happened. A cry of horror issued from many lips as they realised the ship had perished. All rushed to the water's edge, and some Samoan natives even entered the heaving water to try and help anyone who might have escaped the wreck.

Lieutenant Gaedeke, a young man with a handsome, boyish face, was standing on the bridge, and when the vessel overturned was holding on to a speaking tube, but let go as he was dragged deeper under water. A large wave swept him over the settling ship and onto the reef, where he was knocked insensible for a period. He remembered seeing the sinking keel of SMS *Eber* as he passed over it.

On recovering his senses, he made for the shore by part clambering and part swimming over the reef; four others were also able to reach solid land under their feet. Boatswain's Mate Eilart was thrown unconscious onto the beach, but in spite of all his efforts, Gaedeke could not bring him back to life. During the night, five other men of *Eber*'s crew dragged themselves to the shore with the help of Samoan natives, so that a total of 10 members of the crew of 83 who were on board were saved. Many of those inside the vessel were crushed in the impact, rather than drowned by the water. The 73 who perished are commemorated by a German memorial in Apia. Lieutenant Fillette, marine officer on USS *Nipsic* and on shore duty at the time, took Gaedeke under his care for the rest of the night.

It is reported in one reference source that a small number of *Eber's* crew were ashore on guard duty at the time of the hurricane, and so fortunately also survived the incident: one petty officer, three stokers, and one seaman, all unnamed.

J.P. Dunning, the AP correspondent we have met before, had left his house for the bay, and had taken shelter from the terrible rain and wind near the only light he could see, at the American Consulate. As dawn broke, he wandered down to the shore, and the sight of the ships dancing on the waves confirmed, should he have needed it, that the storm was something terrible. He met a group of natives; talking with them revealed that they too knew just how much danger the ships were in. Fear shone in the men's faces, and everyone had to shout to make each other heard over the roar of the wind.

Kane saw the putrid dawn bring light to the place where *Eber* had once been, but despite her absence, his concerns over her fate must wait till later – the living always come first, and anyway, he knew she hadn't left the bay by her own efforts, and therefore now never would. Pearson, wearing his waterproof over his pyjamas, begged his captain not to let go the sheet anchor unless he was steaming hard ahead, but Kane decided the risk was necessary as *Calliope* was now within 20 yards of the reef astern. The remaining two boilers were lit. However, Pearson's concerns were immediately realised, as Kane had to slip the anchor very soon after, there being no room to veer the cables and it (the anchor) was too close to the reef and preventing manoeuvring.

All the other schooners or barques that had added to the congestion in the crowded bay had gone or been cast ashore: *Lily*, pilot schooner; *Detran*; *Agar* (or *Agur*) barquentine 299 tons; *Mukonono* (or *Nukonono*), ketch; *Polo (or Upolu)*, schooner 68 tons; *Vaitele* (or *Viutele* or *Vaitelle*), cutter 16 tons; *Fituau*, cutter 19 tons; *Tafau*, schooner and *Vitumapa* (or *Utumapu*), schooner 12 tons plus the other smaller craft whose names were not worth the effort of the local journalists even trying to guess the correct spelling for the subsequent publications listing their destruction. A dreadfully crowded port was now almost empty, though the poor visibility would not have allowed Kane to know much about it.

The *Lily's* tale was most distressing, and we are lucky to have an account of it. Bizarrely, perhaps madly, her owner Mr. Douglas and his friend Mr. Anthony Ormsby, a trader with the British firm of McArthur's, had stayed on board the previous evening with the Hawaiian mate, who also acted as cook and steward. All through the night, their combined desperate efforts to keep the little schooner pointing at the wind had been successful. But nearby, USS *Nipsic* was in trouble and was being dragged sideways, at least as far as her captain Mullan could tell, and she needed to steam back into her reasonably good position to avoid yet more collisions with *Olga*. As *Nipsic* responded to her thrown rudder, she manoeuvred under no better than limited control, and she cut across the bows of the *Lily* to run her down, the large naval vessel's prow turning the little schooner to splinters. Both the cook and Ormsby were immediately thrown overboard by the crash, and were swept by the vicious currents alongside *Olga*, *Calliope* and *Vandalia* whose crews in turn when they caught sight of the men threw lines to the unfortunates in unsuccessful desperation. The currents took both of the *Lily's* crew out of the bay and left them to drown in the heaving seas. Douglas, hanging on for a while to some wreckage, was then pulled by that same current towards a similar death, this time far enough away to be unseen in the night, when suddenly he was forced against the bows of SMS *Olga*. Bouncing along the side of the German ship, no purchase could he keep until by good fortune, he was able, with what little strength he had left, to grab a line torn from the rigging hanging over the side at the stern of the ship. No-one on *Olga* knew of his presence, until by his own amazing efforts, he climbed the line defeating wind and wave efforts to drag him from it, and heaved himself over the side of the vessel, to collapse senseless and utterly exhausted on the sodden deck. After recovering, he would help guide *Olga* to her salvation and so would be able to tell his story after the storm had ended. Pearson describes Mr. Douglas as the *"English Pilot"* and the *Lily* being his Pilot Boat, so maybe he had stayed aboard in a desperate attempt to save his little ship, and perhaps his living.

At 8 a.m. that morning, Fritze on *Adler* also saw he had lost his *Eber*, and he knew too that his own vessel must be doomed. Her bowsprit was gone and her spars were damaged. Every wave dragged her ever closer to *Calliope* and the reef, her engines were simply not man enough to force through the wind and wave, and her holding gear was finding inadequate purchase. At one point, Pearson noted that one minute earlier, she had been as far away from the reef as was *Calliope*, the next her stern had touched it.

Fritze could see it was only a matter of time before he was thrown hard against the reef to suffer the same destruction as had clearly befallen *Eber*. He might have seemed to have no option but to just wait for death, but the German considered one amazing possibility. Let the largest of the waves throw his ship, not *against* the reef, but on *top* of it. Here we see an amazing decision being made. Surely, the seaman in him will have hoped that every wave was the last big one and that the storm would soon begin to ease, and let him survive. Common sense may whisper that this was not going to happen for hours yet, time he didn't have, but the gamble he was considering was another of those *all-or-nothing* things. If he was wrong, his memory would be stained with the dishonour of a crazy mistake that would seem to have cost the lives of his entire crew.

To explain what he was contemplating, the reader needs to realise the harbour was like a semicircular recess in the coastline, but that much of its apparent area was reef that was exposed at low tide and only covered by a few feet of water at high. This reef was somewhat flat-topped and, except at the river's mouths, extended out from the high water coast line all around the bay, and the ships had naturally anchored just outside it. What Fritze was thinking of doing was to allow his ship to be swept up and onto the flat top; in doing so, *Adler* might just avoid being smashed against the reef's vertical edge.

He and his officers watched the seas like never before, no longer hoping for small waves but now looking for that big one, big enough maybe to lift more than 1,000 tons of wood, steel, and humanity over the edge of the reef and onto the shelf, as dramatic a beaching as any captain anywhere could have contemplated. In the short distance his eyes could penetrate, he would have seconds to decide if a particular candidate was monster enough for his needs. If he chose incorrectly, the mistake would be fatal for all.

Some brave members of the crew were told to get ready to slip the anchors. They must have known they were not going to force their way out, that it was only the anchors that were keeping them out of the water, so they must have wondered at their captain's intentions. But they went to the chains, deluged by waves and spray, and turned to the wheelhouse to wait for the signal.

Fritze watched and waited, every wave not man enough was still able to further imperil the gunboat, until there, rearing up in front, was another monster. It was now or never, as this wave was either salvation or destruction. Hope was now crystallised into that brief few seconds as it approached. At the moment he somehow gauged to be right, the signal was given. What depth of hidden seamanship did he use to choose that particular moment? It could hardly have been any previous experience of what he was now trying to do. The crew in the bows, perhaps glimpsing over their shoulders the wave looming over them that whatever happened next was surely their own death warrant, knocked the pins out of the shackles. The chain rapidly disappeared as the wind alone forced the ship backwards, and deep within her, that same signal had stopped the engine. The wind pushed and the wave front lifted and the reef behind disappeared under the stern of the vessel. A shuddering crash bore witness to her propeller, rudder and stern post being ripped off by the coral and seemed to show the gamble had failed, yet even then she was indeed sliding over the reef. The monstrous wave pushed her a hundred yards over the reef before spending its energy in amongst the coral heads and gullies. The wave forced her sideways, and she fell over onto her port side, her back broken, her hull now defending the crew inside from the force of the hurricane, her prow pointing out to the sea she would never again sail on.

Inside the ship, all was bedlam. Canted over 90° on her side, many sailors had been injured, including Fritze. Even properly stowed items had crashed loose. Those on deck when the wave had hit were now gone, and a total of 20 crew would not see another day. But the amazing plan had worked; the majority of her crew were still alive. To say they were safe, however, would be an exaggeration. Every wave now pounded itself deafeningly against the hull, ripping off the copper sheathing, springing planks, rocking the vessel backwards and forwards and grinding her port side against the reef that now supported her with the gnashing sound of some hungry giant. There was still no hope of them getting ashore until the storm abated, and that seemed to be never. Over the next few hours, many crew were knocked senseless, recovered, and were again thrown into temporary, maybe blissful, oblivion by yet another wave. During the morning, numerous attempts to reach the vessel with a line were made by citizens and natives, but to no avail, despite it being but a few hundred yards from the safety of the beach. Some German sailors left the ship and struggled ashore with the help of those same natives they had been fighting only a few weeks before. Most sailors did the uncomfortable though sensible thing, and stayed with the wreck.

Kane was now clear of *Adler*'s dangerous presence ahead of him, but to starboard lay *Olga*, and she alone could easily spell destruction to them both. As *Adler* rose onto the reef, *Calliope*'s port cable carried away by the same wave, which actually helped the ship keep off the right edge of the reef. In the distance was gradually appearing the vessel that only the previous day had been as far away as the mouth of the bay: *Vandalia*. As Kane tried to put his rudder over to veer to port away from *Olga* each time she sallied towards him, he could see *Vandalia* ahead and fine off that port bow getting closer every minute. Even *Calliope*'s massive anchors and chains had dragged on the clean rocky floor of the bay and the vessel now found itself in a small angle of reef, closest on the stern port quarter and veering away both behind and to starboard: he had to ease, even back, her screw when *Vandalia* suddenly dragged even closer and lurched across his bow, and just a few feet behind the stern was the reef. Somehow, *Calliope*'s engines pulled her clear again, but *Vandalia* wasn't finished, and again came swinging across *Calliope*'s bow.

Kane saw Captain Schoonmaker on USS *Vandalia* and gave him a wave, turning to Pearson to say "*Ease the engines, we won't run him down; give him another chance.*" Unfortunately, it was not possible to carry this out as *Calliope* slipped even closer to the reef, and Pearson was forced to ring again for full ahead.

This time there was no escape, it was down to fate, which fortunately relented for a brief moment. The wave under *Vandalia* lifted her stern whilst *Calliope's* bow was still buried in its front, and as the ships swung together *Calliope* rose under the American: the bowsprit took the combined load of the dropping *Vandalia* and the rising *Calliope* and seemed to force the British ship's bow deep under the waves. Eventually, they disengaged, and the sudden release of load flung *Calliope's* bowsprit up and high out of its seating. It had been close, though some on both vessels thought that had not *Calliope* been jammed against *Vandalia*, that particular big wave might have been the one to throw the cruiser against the reef. It was equally fortunate for *Vandalia* that with *Calliope's* prow held under the hull of the vessel, the British ship's underwater ram didn't immediately hole the American, or destroy her propeller. An underwater ram made *Calliope* (with *Trenton*) an even greater menace to her nearby fellows than they were to her – should *Calliope* drive her prow into one of the others, it would be an immediate mortal wound as, of course, in time of conflict it was meant to be. Even so, *Vandalia* suffered severe damage at her stern from this collision.

Calliope's jib boom wreckage came back towards the foremast, threatening the yards that were lashed to it and even putting the mast itself at risk. Not long after, in a lull, *Calliope* raced forward, *Olga* tracked sideways and smashed her own already damaged bows into *Calliope*'s starboard side and splintered the British vessel's fore main-yard, which sprang its lashings and began to fling itself to and fro in the waves and pitching movement of the vessel. It was fortunate indeed the German vessel had no ram – *Olga*'s "swan neck" prow, whilst elegant, was not in the latest style of warship design and did no underwater damage, though before she sidled away from the British ship, *Olga* smashed boats and davits all down the starboard side of *Calliope*'s hull. Kane's damaged fore main-yard, earlier lowered to deck level and lashed to the fore-mast, was now risking disaster to itself, the fore-mast, and the men who courageously battled to secure it, as eventually they were able, all the time subjected to the onslaught of the waves. First Lieutenant Robert Kyle McAlpine was supported in the task by blue-jackets including gunner's mate William Elgie, and both men received bruises to their entire body and severe contusions to their faces, including the loss of some teeth, before the spar was finally brought under control. Elgie's facial injuries were the result of a severe slap in the face from a rope lashed by the seas breaking over him in the bow; McAlpine's from a flailing block or spar.

Lieutenant Arthur William Carter, the Kentish son of a parish priest, volunteered to watch the cables, a vitally important task which necessitated him placing himself in the utmost danger in the prow of the ship. He would watch how the cable slackened on the wave lee side as the ship steamed up towards the anchors, ready to call by hand signal for a reduction in speed in case a mild-spell in the storm might allow *Calliope* to over-run them, and watch as they tightened on the wave face in case he could tell if the anchors might be dragging. He stayed at this arduous task, despite nearly being carried away when *Calliope*'s bowsprit was destroyed in the incident just described, and spending much of the time deluged by the crashing water, until all the cables had been slipped as the ship began her escape.

At this point, Pearson and McAlpine were desperately trying to persuade Captain Kane that the only chance of survival for *Calliope* was to force her way out, saying: *"We must slip in another minute or she (Vandalia) will be on top of us and bear us down on to the reef and we shall not be able to get out between her and the Olga."* A desperate gamble was her only hope, but the only one left to play.

It should be noted, surprisingly perhaps, that during this stage of the storm, *Calliope*'s engines were rarely at full steam pressure, or the telegraph at *"Full Steam Ahead"*. It was vital just to hold station and not overrun the anchors, even though they were gradually slipping back towards the reef. The engines were throttled back when a lull in the wind and waves made *Calliope* suddenly surge ahead and threaten the vessels in front, and powered up again as soon as possible or necessary to avoid losing the headway which had been gained so arduously. Engines were throttled back when the stern was lifted out of the sea to try and reduce the impact on the propeller blades when they re-entered the water, and throttled up again as soon as they did. The seamanship needed to achieve this handling was supreme and incessant.

USS *Nipsic*, as we have seen, had managed to jettison the severed smokestack and had retaken her place in the centre of the bay but the loss of anchors meant she could no longer maintain that berth. Captain Mullan therefore decided to attempt to beach his vessel on the partially protected eastern shore of the harbour. He rather dubiously supplemented his few remaining coal stocks with pork fat from the ships rations and when full power was obtained, he slipped his anchors and turned across the waves heading for the sandy beach on his starboard side. The journey was very dangerous as the ship had to run alongside the treacherous reef and cross-wise to the waves. The desperate plan was ultimately successful, but the problems for the crew were still perilous. The ship was driven high on the beach yet the 30 or 40 yards from her starboard side to safety were virtually unnavigable. The waves were so enormous as to make any attempt to get a line to shore doomed to failure, initial efforts to do so by swimming soon left the seaman who tried it drowning in the centre of the Bay; a boat was lowered and immediately smashed against the side of the ship and all the men on board followed their fellow. It was reported that a few men, one of them Lieutenant R.G. Davenport, did manage to struggle ashore, though the Lieutenant would later be heavily criticised for his actions. A second boat was lowered, containing the ship's surgeon, Dr. E.Z. Derr and some other men, which capsized in the surf. Fortunately, they were close enough to the beach that Samoan natives, waist deep in seething water at one moment and lifted high off their feet the next, were able to bring them ashore, where they were taken to the American Consulate to recover.

Eventually, a seaman climbed along *Nipsic's* bow sprit with a rope tied around his waist and dropped into the surf where Samoan natives helped to drag him ashore. This rope was the means by which all *Nipsic's* crew eventually left their ship. On shore, Apia chiefs Seumanu Tafa and Salu Anae directed native rescue efforts. *Nipsic* crew-members were on the deck awaiting their turn to escape, being deluged with water and spray as the waves seemed to be imminently in danger of destroying the vessel from under their feet. Residents and natives held tight to the line and eased themselves into the water to help the escaping sailors by each passing them along it. It was very dangerous work, and at one point, a large wave dislodged J.P. Dunning from his precarious hold, and swept him towards the bay. Only the tremendous efforts of a couple of natives caught hold of him in time, and they pulled him back; otherwise, at least one account of the storm would never have been subsequently written.

The engine room crew of USS *Nipsic* in their haste to leave left the engine running and the screw turning which continued to thrash itself into a convoluted shape on the reef and beach. The only crew to lose their lives were the seven who failed to get the rope ashore during those initial, desperate attempts. Captain Mullan, who could not swim, was helped into an empty water cask, which was somehow attached to the line and the Captain pulled down it; Lieutenant John A. Shearman helped and seems to have been the last man to leave USS *Nipsic* to the mercy of the waves.

Nipsic was initially beached side on to the bay. Little did her crew realise it at the time, but this would later help some *Vandalia* crew get to *Nipsic* when washed from their own ship. Before the storm eventually abated, she was dragged around 90° with her bow on the beach and her stern facing the waves, as shown in the photograph on page 237.

During the morning, as Kane had watched *Nipsic* disappear hopefully to beach, and *Adler* so dramatically be thrown onto the reef beside him, some of his concerns disappeared along with those threats. But *Olga* was close, and *Vandalia*, at midday on the previous day well clear of *Calliope*, had by now dragged right in front of the British cruiser, and the storm was still increasing in fury.

The ships had anchors out, which made their close proximity far more terrifying: the anchors might not be holding, indeed they weren't, but along with the engines they were contributing in the fight against the gale, and to lose one would be serious indeed. Whilst a cable in tension might hold the strain of thousands of tons of ship, they can so easily be cut by another vessel driving on to them. Since most of the warships had dragged a considerable distance, the anchors had pulled in towards the axis of the ship and most cables stretched out fine off the bows rather than sideways, a slight twist of fortune in favour of the ships.

Kane was, of course, resident in the exposed wheel-house, giving his continuous orders direct to the helmsmen who guided sailors deep in the hull to pull on the rudder's relieving tackle when they found the rudder chains moving. Years later, Boatswain Marshfield could still recall the sight of his captain on the bridge, clad in his oilskins and clinging to anything robust that he could:

> "He was there at the beginning, he was there through it all, he was there at the very end. The seas smashed and smothered the cruiser. When the fog of the spume had vanished, when the solid green water had roared back into the sea from which it had been torn, he was there, soaking, battered, wearied, but undaunted still."

But Kane had to know how close he was to the reef, and could not see anything of it from his vantage point almost central in the ship. Now it was daylight, he needed a runner to go to the stern, estimate the gap, bring him back the information and then do it again and again. He turned to a 15 year-old midshipman named Cecil Henry Fox.

On loan from the squadron's flagship HMS *Orlando*, Fox was tasked by his captain to leave the frugal shelter of the wheelhouse, and make his way aft over a lurching, gyrating deck regularly awash with cold green seas, until he reached the stern. There, a terrifying sight would present itself. At one moment a towering cliff of satanic black coral reared twenty feet or more above his head with cascades of water streaming off its ragged face, flashing and sparkling in the grey half-daylight and whipped to a foaming cream by the gale, and in the next a wave had lifted *Calliope*'s stern above the level of the rock and the rollers crashed and exploded around him obscuring the reef and the rest of the bay in the wind-blown spray and rain. Throughout this awesome spectacle, he must forget his fears and try to approximate how close that jagged dark rock might be, to then make his way back to his captain with his estimate, on whose accuracy Kane needed to rely heavily to make his decisions: was *Calliope* dragging closer or holding station? Fox started to perform this duty in the early gloom of dawn, and continued into the morning of the 16th. He would later recall a difficult question he argued over with himself: whether to wear deck shoes or go barefoot. Were the vessel to founder, and Fox was probably one of the best positioned to consider the possibility, the shoes would be a handicap in trying to swim, but without them, the coral would cut his feet to pieces, should he actually be able to reach the reef. Shoes won whilst in the bay, and were to be taken off once the open sea was reached - if indeed it ever would be.

Kane listened to the young Irish lad's breathless but shouted description of the reef at the stern, as in front, he watched the small space which existed between *Vandalia* and *Olga* visibly reduce before his eyes. The last estimate on the reef was *"No more than six feet, sir."* There was no longer anywhere to go to escape the collisions of those close ships, or the death trap of the reef, than to get out of the bay, to push through between the vessels and hope they didn't foul. Once made, the decision would need to be acted upon immediately. The gale had been increasing in anger throughout the night and still seemed to be doing so that morning; there would never be a better time to fight it than now.

The officers on *Calliope*'s bridge were desperate in their representations to Kane – the ship must go out now or be lost. Henry Pearson in particular asserted that the decision time was minutes only, and enlisted the aid of the First Lieutenant in urging Kane to make the order. Still, the seaman's concern for his fellow coloured the Irishman's thoughts, knowing an attempt to force past SMS *Olga* or USS *Vandalia* would risk cutting one of those vessels anchors, or of holing a hull with his ram.

But the close proximity of the reef astern, and the closing gap in front of him between *Olga* and *Vandalia*, finally persuaded the Irishman that his officers were right. Running revolutions sufficient only to ease the strain on his anchor cables, Kane was now in agreement that to stay meant wrecking on the reef or by collision, but wanted to wait until the engineers reported that full steam was ready, preferring to keep the anchors in place until the engines had their best chance.

Fortunately, the message came up at that moment, and the awful decision to slip all remaining anchors was then made. The telegraph was now set to *"Full Ahead"* where it would remain fixed for hours to come, the engines hammering at 75 to 80 revolutions per minute. It took a few minutes before it became obvious, but when the slackening chains showed he was progressing, albeit ever so slowly, and waiting for as long as he safely could, the hawsers were slipped at the shackle pins at the last moment they could be. With the death rattle of some monstrous metal snake, they disappeared over the side to the floor of the bay. With them went any option of thinking again: there was now no going back, or changing of mind. Tied to her deck, *Calliope* now had only one small and hopelessly inadequate anchor to hold her off the reef, now she had to rely solely on her engines. If they failed, or were simply not good enough, she would be lost. *Calliope* would hardly be able to steam up to the mooring buoys and collect the chain to reattach to the hawsers. If the phrase *"burning one's boats"* is intended to signify an irrevocable decision to use even lifeboats to feed a furnace and provide motive power, then *"slipping one's anchors"* is a surely exact equivalent when fighting a hurricane. One would not do either without having exhausted all other means to achieve the end, which for both cases, was survival. To give the order to slip an anchor, to knock out the shackle pin and break the chain link and watch one of the most powerful and reliable means of holding position in a storm disappear over the side of the ship, must be an awesome decision for any captain to make. Fritze in *Adler* had made it almost in resignation; Kane was doing it to fight.

Calliope gradually eased her way forward, and making revolutions that would have taken her comfortably beyond 14 knots in a calm sea, she struggled to make a half. Go for a gentle walk in the country and consider you would have outpaced *Calliope* that morning. To people watching on shore, it was a considerable time before they grasped the notion that the closing gap between her and *Vandalia* was due only partly to the American dragging backwards, and suddenly everyone watching caught their breath as the amazing realisation was shouted around the edge of the bay: "*Calliope is trying to go out!*"

Most people on the shore, fully aware that it was a decision that could not be rescinded, thought it the final desperate act of a doomed captain and crew. J.P. Dunning would declare it to be: "*This manoeuvre of the gallant British ship is regarded as one of the most daring in naval annals.*" And unable to see those human beings hidden by spray and wave, the ship itself came to be the thing alive. A huge wounded animal, surrounded by snarling snapping predators, hemmed in by helpless and injured fellows, pushing itself against the pack in an attempt to force a way past to safety. Already, two warships had gone, and another had been beached. It had seemed only time before the remaining large occupants of the bay followed in one way or another. But now here was a ship that wasn't going to sit back and await its fate, or trust itself to the gods of the gale. The realisation was both magnificent and awful, the spectators of a miserable disaster were now the powerless and horrified audience to a titanic struggle to not just survive, but to take on and defeat a most dominant and determined enemy.

The observers could see how close *Calliope* was to the reef, indeed, many thought she had already been in collision with it. To go out was to gamble everything on one throw of a painfully capricious die. At first, it was wondered amongst her audience if she was trying to beach alongside *Nipsic*, but the larger *Calliope* would surely ground further out and be smashed to pieces by the waves. Some thought she might try and do what *Adler* had done, and get herself thrown on top of the reef, but again, her size would mean she would never be able to achieve that, she had almost three times more tonnage than the German flagship gunboat. No, there was only one interpretation, the British captain had decided to take the storm on the chin, battle it face-to-face, and make for the open sea. To all the people clustered despondently around that tiny bay, be they sailors or traders or marines or natives, they will all have known what the attempt meant, what it risked, and the desperation that had conceived it. And they will all have known the force of will needed by the captain who dared to try it.

I have included in the account that follows Engineer Bourke's statement, as an extract from that reported by the Sydney Argus on 5th April 1889 as it is of this particular time he was speaking:

"Mr. H. G. Bourke, the Staff-Engineer, states that when he got the steam up in the first instance he did so in four boilers, and subsequently in the other two, making steam in six boilers. When full steam was got up they were hanging to one anchor. They went ahead at full speed, using every available means to generate steam. The power developed by the machinery was equal to propelling the ship at 15 knots in smooth water, and yet in the hurricane they could only make from half to three-quarters of a knot, just enough to give her steering way. Every man stuck to his post, and did his work manfully in the engine-room. There was not a sound amongst them save in the direction of firing up, and not a single man ventured to ask the question as to danger or otherwise. They all put implicit faith in Captain Kane, and knew that if it were possible he would take her out of danger's way. No man attempted to move from his post, and they were all on duty for 16 hours in the engine-room. Forced draughts were used to exert the greatest power obtainable. He [Bourke] attributed much of the success in maintaining and generating steam to the Westport coal which they were using, this being in his opinion the very best colonial coal. There was not a single hitch in the machinery from beginning to end. The water entered the ship so rapidly at times that there were 18 inches in the wardroom at one period."

That *Calliope* had made some headway against the waves gradually became apparent, but that she would need a number of hours to clear the bay was equally obvious, and now that she was relying on her engines only, every second in the bay was pure, unremitting, danger. To fight the wind and wave needed every ounce of pressure from the boilers. The propeller would need to side-step every encumbrance, the hull to cleave every wave and the engines to not miss a beat, for hour after hour.

The first thing was to avoid *Olga* lying to starboard and gradually falling half a ship length behind, but to do so whilst still trying not to run down *Vandalia*, swinging wildly side to side and just ahead and slightly to port of *Calliope*, was impossible. It was, and still is, the duty of any captain, foremost of all, to do everything he could to save his ship, but the unwritten addendum to that rule was to try not to run down another in doing so, thus destroying that other fellow's chances. At one point, the British cruiser became entrapped between these other two vessels, American on the left, German on the right, and disaster loomed, but the power generated by the engines somehow managed to push the other ships aside and still counter the weather, and *Calliope* gradually inched her way past. It seemed astonishing to her officers that they were not, even now, in the water and the attempt at escape had only just begun.

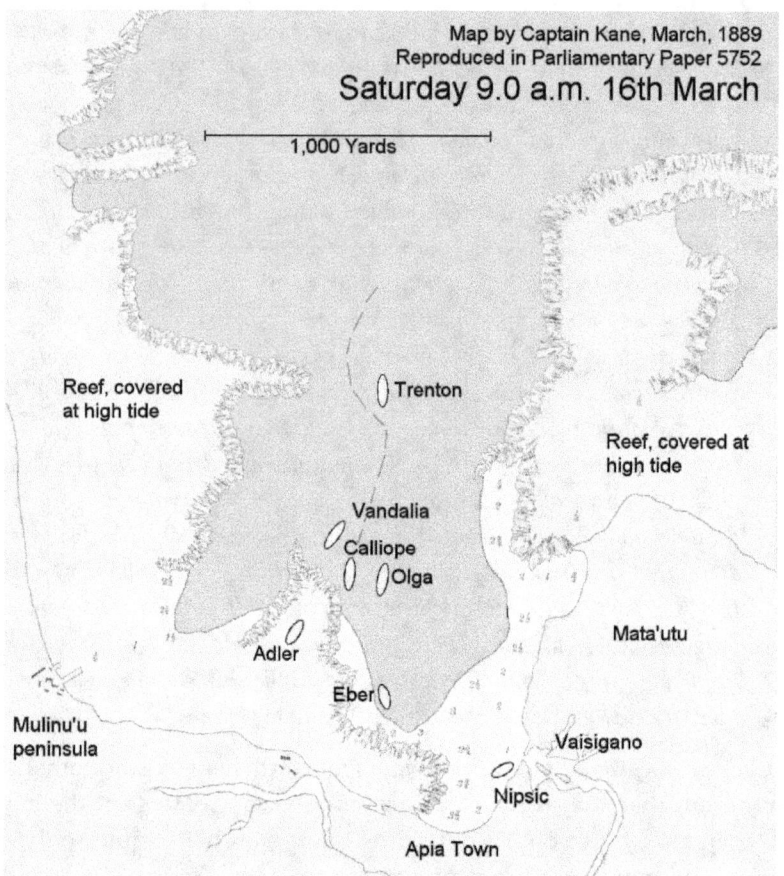

Apia Bay showing the positions the various warships had dragged to by 9.0 a.m. on the morning of 16th March 1889. The layout of the reef is taken from the chart produced by Captain Kane in his report, as reproduced in Parliamentary Paper 5752. These are the positions at the time at which HMS Calliope made her attempt to get out of the harbour. The dashed line shows her approximate track in doing so. The positions of SMS Adler and Eber and USS Nipsic are slightly different to those recorded by Captain Kane, as a result of interpretation of the photographic record.

       Calliope finally staggered past *Vandalia*, and left *Olga* behind, but there was no time for celebration, now she had to find her way out of the bay. Ahead, in the spray and rain, visibility was limited to virtually the length of the ship in front of her prow, but Kane knew well that somewhere in his path was a bottleneck of reef and a little further out, USS *Trenton*. As the rain squalls came and went with vicious monotony, those on shore occasionally had far better visibility of the positions of the ships than had those on the vessels, facing into the lashing spray, dodging the tons of water cascading over them as each wave was pierced.

A big vessel like *Trenton* would not have simply disappeared under the waves, so Kane knew she must still be afloat, but since all the other ships had dragged he had no real idea of where she might be. Kane turned *Calliope*'s head for the centre of the narrowing neck between inner basin and outer as best as he could judge it, using his shuddering compass as the capricious guide in the absence of any visual cues from the bay.

At this point, instinct became the Captain's pilot to direct his ship and her crew. Occasional glimpses of the bay between the squalls showed tantalising snapshots of landmarks and headlands and behind him, those few remaining other vessels, from which Kane must gauge his progress and adjust his course accordingly, before they disappeared in the murk. He was at this time most frightfully busy. The elements of data entering his head, each to be weighed and assessed, were what guided his decisions to the men on the wheel and the engine-room telegraph. What direction was the wind, and how were the waves and currents acting in the part of the bay where he believed himself to be? Where was the reef, and where were the other ships? In a lull of wind the ship raced forward, changing his calculations rapidly and enormously; in a fierce squall she almost lost headway completely and tried to turn broadside: the wheel had to be thrown first one way then the other to keep her straight to the wind and to hopefully survive the assault.

Surely Kane would have had in the back of his mind concerns about his machinery. Pearson recalled that all the officers were simply waiting for something to break. Any ship in *Calliope*'s position would have had a captain worried for his rudder. It had a large surface area to be effective, but this meant turning it into extreme currents and waves was not only difficult but risky, the forces on the wooden material and its post were enormous and should it break, there would then be no way of steering the ship and the game would be up. Even the ropes which connected the huge double wheel to the rudder were at risk as the massive forces needed to turn it against the waves put a strain on them which threatened to snap them like cotton, and the relieving tackles manned to reduce that strain would be of no use if the rudder post snapped.

But it was the engines: how much could Kane rely on them? I suppose the question was academic; his life, his ship, and his entire crew were already relying on rudder and tackles, on engine and screw. Should a piston rod gland fail now, under conditions more extreme and prolonged than had ever been experienced in those English Channel trials, should a bolt snap or strip its thread, well, there would be nothing the crew could do about it. So yes, those concerns may have been in his head, but to give

them more than passing room would deflect his concentration from the
things he must think about; react to; and cater for.

As visibility wavered between poor and nothing, there, central in
the opening, effectively blocking it, the worst possible position in which
she could have been found, lay the enormous hull of the American
flagship, half as big again as *Calliope*. A glimpse of the signals lashing
themselves to shreds on the stays confirmed what Kane had already
guessed as likely: her rudder was gone, and her fires were out. She was no
longer under the control of man; he would get no help from *Trenton*.

Whilst Kane could have had little idea of *Trenton*'s position when
he set off, he had loosed his anchors, and couldn't now change his mind.
He would have to drive past *Trenton* or be destroyed; those were his only
options. He could look for no assistance from that vessel's own crew, who
were now miserably awaiting their fate. Bravely the Americans held
themselves in the rigging, wrapping forearms and legs around lines and
stays, fully exposed to the snatching, grabbing, punching fist of the gale
and icy fingers of spray and rain as hard as hailstones, trying to use even
their own bodies to act as a human storm sail, trying to somehow prolong
the life of the ship and, perhaps thereby, their own.

As with the other warships, she was not only bucking and rearing
along her hull axis, but was swinging wildly side to side, closing the gap
between herself and the reef then opening it up again, whipping her masts
to and fro and threatening each time to snap them like a corn stalk, to pitch
them and their human sails into the whirlpool of the bay. And stretching
out ahead of her, pulled over to her starboard by her dragging, were her
anchor cables. Whatever he did, Kane must not run into *Trenton*, which
would destroy them both, nor run down and cut her cables: to do that
would be to condemn her 400 crew to death, even if it would be only
bringing that fate to them slightly earlier than nature appeared to be doing.
So the starboard side of *Trenton* was closed to *Calliope*.

Between the port side of *Trenton* and the reef were not much more
than a couple of breadths of *Calliope*. It might have been more than that in
reality, but Kane had no way of knowing, the force of the seas smashing
back into the bay from the reef was causing the waves to break before they
reached it and concealed its true position; his ship must avoid such a
swirling mass of whirlpools and currents and debris or the control which
was precarious at best would be completely lost. With both vessel's yard-
arms stretched outboard at main deck level, the real clearance available to
the British ship was negligible. Any attempt to pass so close to a stationary
ship in a dead calm by gentle engine power would be considered

foolhardy and worthy of court-martial. To achieve it in the conditions generated by such a storm seemed utterly impossible.

Admiral Kimberly would later record his view of the manoeuvre in his memoirs reference [10] in the Bibliography, and the passion of the words from someone who was there, and had experienced the thrill and the danger, cannot be improved upon:

> "...one might...on looking astern into the thick curtain of misty haze, have seen the large black hull of a ship looming forth in the dim distance. It was slowly, very slowly advancing right for us. Now up high in the crest of some sea, and then down so low that only her tops could be seen. It was Calliope taking her chances of being sunk by collisions at her anchors, or running the gauntlet of the reefs for the open sea...

> "...To me, it was one of the grandest and most exciting sights I ever beheld. There was just room between Trenton and the reef for Calliope to pass. To collide with Trenton or to strike the reef, meant destruction. In the first instance to both ships, in the second, to herself, and as the great plunging, rolling ship staggered through the boiling surf abreast-us, a man on our lower yard arm could have clasped hands with one of hers. A swerve, a yaw of the helpless Trenton at this moment would have been annihilation, but good fortune attended Calliope on that day for she gained the open sea.

> "It was when her yards lapped ours amidst the war of the elements, that all our long and deep anxiety was turned into admiration for the daring and plucky deed that was passing before our eyes, that then our pent up feelings burst forth into cheers. I will candidly confess, that my extreme anxiety at this supreme moment, made me feel as rigid and as cold as a harp string. As her stern slowly passed our bow, I was so extremely anxious for her safety and success, that I felt by a concentration of mere will, I was helping her seaward.

> "It was one of the grandest sights a seaman or anyone else ever saw. The lives of 250 souls depended on the hazardous venture. All was staked on this grand endeavor, and they won. It was a victory of mind over matter."

The London Telegraph would later tell its readers:

> "We do not know in all Naval records any sound which makes a finer music upon the ear than the cheer of Trenton's men. It was distressed manhood greeting triumph and manhood. The doomed saluting the saved. It was pluckier and more human than any cry ever raised upon the deck of a victorious line of battle-ship. It never can be forgotten, and never

must be forgotten by Englishmen speaking of Americans."

A later editorial in the New York Times, quoting the above paragraph rather dismissively as a kind thought by the old country, tried to suggest the cheers of *Trenton*'s crew came not from admiration but rather from relief mixed equally with anger that such a foolhardy enterprise had been undertaken, having put both ships in such dreadful peril. It poured scorn on the interpretation that *Trenton*'s cheers were anything more noble than simply a misheard expression of fear and resentment that the British were taking such a dreadful chance of snaring them both and dragging them all to destruction. I just cannot see how such a suggestion could be justified. Undoubtedly, the relief at *Calliope* passing without fouling would have been tremendous and would have added weight to the cheers. But they must have expected ships to try and leave the bay, and would have done so them-selves had they still had the power to try it. They must have known that no ship would have been able to see *Trenton*'s precarious position before beginning such a manoeuvre, and that a ship able to try to save itself must needs ignore the fate of another ship disabled and unable to do the same. My great-grandfather was one of the few men on earth to actually hear the cheers, as did all those of *Calliope's* crew and officers who were above decks, cheers that out-sung the howling gale, and he was in no doubt at all that the impulse behind them was kind and magnificent. Kane too, was in an absolutely similar mind, and all the *Calliope*s gave a resounding return as they left behind those brave men who had *wished them well*. No, however much we might wonder at the spirit that could think so magnificently at such a time, the cheers came as the ships *cleared*, not as the British vessel *approached*, and it was, in my mind, unquestionably a genuinely noble gesture, made by *Trenton*'s crew in spontaneous and generous hope that someone might survive when they had apparently lost that hope for themselves.

As they passed, *Calliope*'s damaged fore-yard, even truncated as it was at the starboard side, still passed *over* the port quarter of *Trenton*, so close that it was a miracle the two ships were not disastrously enmeshed. Kane's view expressed afterwards was *"I...went so close to Trenton as to put the fore-yard-arm over her deck, and as Calliope lifted up she rolled to port, and the foreyard over Trenton just cleared her. It was as pretty a thing and as lucky an escape as could well be imagined. I just managed to clear the outside reef by some 60 yards"*. Even with *Calliope* clear, she was still sailing into the teeth of a terrific hurricane, and on *Trenton*, one of the American officers turned to another, and said: *"I wouldn't give a penny for the Calliope and all on board at this moment."*

Whilst very brief and somewhat matter-of-fact, WIT's own views of the situation the ships faced are also worth repeating here using his own, gently naïve words, also recording that fortuitous roll:

"Then the order was passed along to be ready to slip at any moment. I cannot give you time of all that happened. The Captain was preparing to try and save his ship, so he directed all orders and they were carried out directly. Then the order was given to the Chief Engineer to give her every pound of steam he could, and when the captain found the ship going ahead, he gave the order to slip which was done at once.

"After we slipped our anchor, which was two Bowers and one Sheet, this left us with only one anchor in case anything was to happen to our engines, but no, thank God, they never failed us and every man lifted a prayer that day for our safety in this storm.

"Well, our dear old ship still held her own, and was forging ahead, but we had a very serious obstacle in our way, for the other American Flagship, the Trenton, was right across the channel, and you could see her four cables out straight. Well, the only thing the Captain could do, was to pass under the stern of the American and then the order was to double man the relieving tackles, that a purchase put on the Tiller to help the Steering Wheel, and then the great moment arrived for we were getting very close now and we had but a very little distance in between the stern of the Trenton and that yawning Coral Reef just off our Port Side. The time came and the orders was carried out, and so we passed her stern and was coming up on her portside. Then we could see the open sea. As we rolled, so the Trenton rolled, and that saved us getting foul of one another. If such had of happened, we should not of been able to clear, but it did not happen. We cleared her, and their American Admiral called for the Captain and the Britishers, and our Ship's Company responded right heartily, I can tell you, for we had now only about a mile to go before we got to the open sea, and at last we did get out."

Calliope's escape was surely miraculous. It cannot be adequately described just how frightening to the crews the close proximity of the warships would have been. Even in calm seas, the two vessels would have been at great risk of entanglement with their yards and rigging, an event which would have been destructive of wood and rope; on the fierce seas of the hurricane, it would have meant catastrophe for both vessels.

These ships were the two biggest in the bay; the largest was unable to manoeuvre to man's desire and was subject to the whims of the weather, the other was struggling with limited control to thread the tiniest and most dangerous needle. 400 men on *Trenton*, and 250 on *Calliope*, were at that moment in the most awful peril. The manoeuvre had to work first time, there could be no second go at it.

On board *Calliope*, there was no time for relaxation. The engines still thundered hard as Kane had no way of knowing where he was being driven; visibility was restricted to just a few yards around the ship and the whole island of Upolu was surrounded by the reef which had so nearly claimed the ship in Apia. Kane did take a chance and slightly reduced her engines to between 60 and 70 revolutions per minute, to reduce the risks of a failure, safe now, at least, from collisions with the other ships that had been so close. Just as bad as was the lack of knowledge on the position of the reef, the fury of the storm was still increasing. Virtually all the boats had been carried away by the collisions with *Vandalia* and *Olga* and the incessant pounding of the heavy seas. Storm sails were set which gave an immediate calming effect to the ship, but they were repeatedly carried away in shreds by the tempest, which continuously strengthened from the north. During her commissioning trials in the Solent, the engines had been beset by those niggling problems with gland seals; should one have failed at any time that day, the ship would have been lost. But thanks to the excellent maintenance they had received since commissioning, the engines had performed magnificently for 12 hours non-stop since midnight.

As *Calliope*'s stern disappeared into the spray and rain ahead, *Trenton*'s crew could only look back again into the bay, and wait for whatever might be their fate in the misty opacity. The fires in her furnaces had been put out as a result of that previously mentioned design flaw which had been known and derided for years, but which had never been satisfactorily corrected. Her hawse pipes, steel lined holes in the hull either side of the prow through which passed the anchor chains, were located low on the main deck, and in a heavy sea often shipped masses of water. The crew had fashioned wooden bungs which could be pushed into the hole allowing the anchor chain to still pass through a central slot, but a wildly swinging chain regularly dislodged the matting and canvas stacked against the back of them. Violent seas would regularly stove in the protection, and brave men had to try and push it all back against the pressure of tons of cold sea water. With every wave that hit her, *Trenton* was shipping vast quantities of water via these hawse pipes; this water was already on the gun deck, and cascaded down into the bowels of the ship.

Cold water on "red-hot" furnaces was a dreadful danger in a ship; steam generated by such contact burned and scalded men to a horrible death, or might easily rend the boiler apart by an explosion violent enough to split the hull. As the waters got closer in the engine room, there had been no alternative but to douse her fires before the seas did so, avoiding the risk of the explosion but finally depriving the ship of her steam power and her one last real chance of survival. The men who threw water into her furnaces were performing a duty every bit as terrifying as slipping an anchor, but with none of the hope. *Calliope*'s crew had relied on her steam for survival; *Trenton*'s were left with only her anchors. *Calliope* would fight the storm and win or lose; *Trenton* could only endure it or not.

Vandalia's officers, whilst relieved that *Calliope* was no longer running into their stern, knew the relief to be negligible, again only delaying their inevitable destruction rather than allowing them to avoid it. Following that miraculous escape of HMS *Calliope*, the storm if anything, gained force, such that had Captain Kane left his decision to leave any longer, it is extremely doubtful if he would have succeeded. USS *Vandalia* and SMS *Olga* endured a number of collisions, each ship suffering more and more damage, though *Olga* was still the most securely placed vessel. USS *Trenton* continued to drag further into the inner basin of the little bay. By early afternoon, these three warships were the sole remaining vessels afloat at Apia.

Vandalia was effectively under the command of Lieutenant J. W. Carlin, as Captain Schoonmaker had been severely injured in his cabin in one of the many violent swings the ship had been thrown onto. Carlin's cool and calm demeanour throughout the storm would warrant praise and admiration from his entire crew, keeping men at their work and somehow controlling the inevitable feelings of panic that were showing.

Eventually, *Vandalia*'s anchors could hold her no more, and as they parted, an unusual current caused by the vast volumes of freshwater poured by the rivers into the bay from the torrential rain on land pulled the vessel south-eastwards along the side of the western reef, behind *Olga* whose officers by great skill managed to avoid further collision with the rudder-less American vessel. Skirting the edge of the reef, and as a result of heroic efforts of her crew, *Vandalia* appeared for a moment to be approaching the relative safety of the sandy beach, but at 11 a.m. that morning, eventually her stern hit the reef turning her port side to the waves, and she foundered to her main deck, and broke her back.

Samoans, shore-based marines, traders in Apia of every nationality, all watched helplessly as one-by-one, the efforts of the crew of *Vandalia* to get a line ashore failed from less than 100 yards distance - it might just have been a mile. The first attempt was made by sailor F. M. Hammet (possibly Hammar), who volunteered to try and swim to shore with a line attached. Plunging into the seething water, full of debris, he was thrown violently against the side of the ship and knocked senseless, dragged out to the bay and this very brave man sadly drowned. Each boat launched into the huge seas was immediately swamped and its crew dragged straight to the middle of the bay where they too succumbed.

The Samoan native Teoteo, helped by Toga, made a most courageous attempt to reach USS *Vandalia* with a line whilst the gale was at its height, and though regarded as a strong swimmer even amongst his fellow natives, the attempt failed and he only just escaped with his life.

Finally the attempts were called off, and Captain Schoonmaker ordered his crew to the rigging as the ship settled deeper, there to wait whatever would be their fate.

During the afternoon of the 16th March 1889, only two vessels remained afloat in Apia Harbour, which only the previous day had busily hosted a score. The largest vessels of the antagonistic American and German fleets were all that remained, fighting against fate instead of each other.

It was around this time that some more amazingly dangerous efforts to reach *Vandalia* with a line were made from the shore. Firstly, three officers from USS *Nipsic*, Shearman, Purcell and Jones, tried to reach the ship by swimming in the surf with a line attached; all were beaten back to the shore exhausted and unsuccessful. Then, three unnamed natives volunteered to attempt it, and though excellent swimmers themselves, again failed at great risk to their own lives. They had started their attempt a quarter of a mile north of the spot where *Vandalia* lay, but never got within a hundred yards, so fierce was the current and waves. Further attempts were made, but all were unsuccessful and the people on shore had no other recourse than to stand and watch, and wait for whatever would befall the warships.

Suddenly, the massive waves showering over *Vandalia* swept some men from her deck. They attempted to swim to USS *Nipsic* to grab some ropes hanging over the side; some were successful and saved themselves. As previously stated, *Nipsic* was, at that time, broad on to the bay. One man, Chief Engineer A.S. Greene, unable to hold onto the line, was fortuitously seen by natives, who formed a human chain out into the waves and were able to grab hold of him and pull him ashore. Another man, H. A. Wiley, a young naval cadet, was further out, but more Samoans joined the chain and he too was miraculously rescued.

It was not long after these rescues that the captain of USS *Vandalia*,

Captain Schoonmaker himself, exhausted and injured, was washed from the deck with three other officers and drowned in full view of those of his men clasping to the ship. The Captain had been too weak to follow Lieutenant Carlin's begging to enter the rigging, and was bending down when the massive wave hit, dislodging a machine gun which hit the Captain and maybe killed him outright, before he was washed overboard. Lieutenant Frank E. Sutton, Paymaster Frank H. Ames and Pay Clerk John Roache (or Roach, or Roche) were washed off the deck with their captain and all four men perished together.

By 3 p.m., the ship was resting her broken length on the rocky bottom of the bay, with no man left other than those in the rigging. Over the ensuing hours, exhausted *Vandalia* men were regularly washed from that rigging, most to fall to the deck and perish in the waters in full view of those horrified and numbed countrymen on shore. USS *Nipsic* was swung by the waves from her position parallel to the shore to one with her stern pointing out into the bay, and that stern was only some 50 yards from *Vandalia*. Somehow, a small rope was made fast between the foremast of *Vandalia* and the stern of *Nipsic*, and a few *Vandalia* men escaped their vessel by that means before the line parted; further attempts to make a connection failed.

It had soon become obvious, as the storm's power increased, that *Trenton* was losing her battle. Those vital anchors, failing to hold even in the outer bay, were dragging and *Trenton* was being inexorably pushed back into the bay which was now hell's mouth – no burning fires of Hades this but a swirling heaving mass of cold water clutching at ships and sailors to pull them down to the dark and frightening depths of oblivion. As different as it could be to Dante's vision, but a hell even so. Men hung onto the rigging, officers grasped anything they could hang onto on the deck, and everyone waited. Would the storm ease first, or would the ship give in?

Earlier, at 10 a.m. on that terrible day, *Trenton's* rudder and propeller had been carried away. She was no longer controllable. Her anchors still held and she hoisted signals into the rigging indicating her disabled status. Water still continued to deluge through her hawse pipes, despite gallant efforts of people such as Lieutenant W. H. Allen and his men to lessen it. From that time until 6 p.m. in the evening, those anchors, though dragging further into the bay, managed to hold the vessel to some degree with her head to the seas. It was around the middle of the afternoon when she was forced out of her position in the outer bay, and ran close to the eastern reef. Touching it here would have been destruction, but

Lieutenant Brown saved the ship by ordering all the men into the port rigging, and the compact mass of bodies used as a storm sail as already noted.

The gale responded by increasing, one of *Trenton*'s precious anchor lifelines parted, then another, and the question was finally answered: the ship was lost. Everyone on board knew it, everyone knew their chances of getting ashore would be very problematical when eventually *Trenton* was cast against the reef, the end was now tangibly in sight. Those around the bay saw the chains disappear, and prepared to watch the destruction. On the ship, a suggestion was made to hoist her flag, and Admiral Kimberly immediately replied: *"Yes; let the flag go up!"* To shore based onlookers, it seemed the last noble act of a ship from a proud nation about to be lost.

On *Olga*, the approaching massive American flagship was viewed with outright horror by the officers, as through the squalls and spray they caught intermittent glimpses of a sinister black hulk getting ever closer, faster now as the Germans realised the American's anchors had at last parted. Korvettenkapitän Erhardt had seen by the dawn light the space beside them where the previous evening had lain *Eber*; he had watched *Nipsic* ahead of them survive the collisions and beach in the tumultuous surf to an unknown fate; somehow he had avoided *Vandalia* as she dragged past the German's stern and disappeared under the smashing breaking waves forcing her against the reef. With *Calliope* now gone out, Erhardt might just have allowed himself to hope he had survived the gale. Now no longer menaced by surrounding ships, *Olga*'s anchors were sound and holding firm, she was fortunately placed in the best part of the bay, her steam was good and fires safe, and her position was now the safest of any in Apia. As long as the storm didn't worsen dramatically, and it could hardly do that, *Olga* seemed to be likely to be the one ship which would ride out the storm at her moorings. Severely damaged at the prow by the collisions with *Nipsic*, and down her port side by the collisions with *Calliope*, her hull was nevertheless reasonably sound, and the water being shipped at the prow was manageable. Her position was still perilous, and her crew no doubt would have traded many year's pay to be somewhere else, but could they just begin to hope? To imagine a tomorrow with the storm abating and their ship still riding out the waves? It seemed the only bar to that hope might be the American flagship.

Trenton was the largest, heaviest ship at Apia, a massive 3,900 tons of wood and steel. As the final cable broke, no longer able to take on its own that enormous dead weight, the ship was dragged further into the bay with her stern aimed for the reef which had scraped *Calliope*'s own stern a few hours earlier.

The vessel continued to be pushed back into the bay, across to where *Vandalia* had been that morning, to menace *Olga* once again. This time, the large and uncontrollable American ship could not be avoided despite extremely skilful manoeuvring by the German officers controlling *Olga's* rudder and screw, and violent collisions occurred, severing two of the German's anchors which had hitherto withstood the force of the gale. Several boats were smashed from *Trenton* and the American Flag, the 38-Star Navy Ensign so recently hoisted in pride, was torn from the gaff and landed on SMS *Olga's* deck. It was returned after the storm.

It should be clear to appreciate that had *Calliope* not escaped the bay earlier that morning, then she and *Trenton* would have almost certainly collided at this point in the afternoon. This would have caused the destruction of the two vessels with a dreadful loss of life from them both.

Erhardt immediately realised that although he had come so very close to weathering the storm at his mooring, it now counted for nothing, and the fates had conspired against him - two anchors would not hold him off the reef. It seems Erhardt had greeted a recovering Mr. Douglas from *Lily* with *"We have saved your life, now you must save my ship by pointing out the softest spot on the beach"* which the pilot managed to do. Knowing his engines to be less powerful than *Calliope's*, making escape from the bay not an option, Erhardt slipped his remaining cables and was somehow able to steam to the far eastern shore and, just a hundred metres or so north of *Nipsic*, beach the severely damaged *Olga*, where she withstood the rest of the storm in comparative safety - the only vessel, along with *Calliope*, not to lose any life.

For *Trenton* with no rudder and her fires out, such self-determining luxury was denied; the current took her as it had earlier taken *Vandalia* along the southern edge and toward the settling wreck of the other American vessel. Once again, to prove just how capricious nature could be, the forces of the hurricane relented for a short while; as the ships closed on each other, something kept them apart for just sufficient time for *Vandalia's* crew to scramble from the rigging of their sunken vessel to that of the flagship. Just as the last man crossed over, the storm re-took control and smashed the vessels together, throwing *Vandalia's* masts just now emptied of men into the raging surf. Like *Vandalia*, *Trenton* broke her back as she settled to the floor of the bay alongside that other of her fleet. Being so much larger than *Vandalia*, her main deck stayed above water except when flooded by the waves. Only one man on *Trenton* would lose his life, Landsman J. Hewlett who was struck by a flailing rope block. To be quite honest, it was pure luck that both American ships had not been thrown directly onto the reef like SMS *Eber*, and broken up in the heavy seas with catastrophic loss of life.

And so for the few remaining hours of that fateful day, men huddled on the ships and waited. On SMS *Adler*, the wait was in appalling conditions, the upturned hull constantly battered by enormous waves for more than 24 hours before they could be got off - some it is said, demented from the experience. On *Olga* by contrast, the sturdy vessel, despite taking severe damage from the earlier collisions, was fairly safe. The crew of USS *Nipsic* had eventually struggled to shore with the help of natives, though seven brave men had lost their lives in the initial attempts to get the line ashore. The remaining crew of *Vandalia*, though missing 43 of their colleagues, spent the rest of the day and night on *Trenton*. The latter's band was reported to have played the future national song *"The Star Spangled Banner"* through the long night, and raised cheers for the men of *Vandalia*, It was later that survivors from *Trenton* contemptuously dismissed the idea. It was difficult enough to hold onto something robust on the vessel, and a musical instrument did not fit that bill. Those who were still present on shore were moved by the shouts and cries, which were getting gradually weaker as exhaustion and lack of sleep and food took their toll. At around 10 p.m., weariness drove the shore people back to their homes, at least hopeful that no more harm could come to the ships and their men. The shore was soon deserted except for Dunning and the three *Nipsic* officers. These men patrolled the shore all night looking for possible survivors, and found Ensign Ripley who had been washed ashore and unconscious some time earlier. No other survivors were found.

Sunday, 17th March 1889 saw the storm finally begin to abate, though the seas continued mountainous for some time into the day. Natives braving the waves finally reached *Adler* and brought ashore her surviving crew, many mentally broken by the long hours of peril. Again, it was natives, led by the Samoan chief Seumanu, who succeeded in reaching *Vandalia* with lines, and eventually *Trenton* and *Vandalia* survivors made their way in boats those few yards to the shore, now littered with debris from ships and - it must be said - men, and joined the *Nipsic* crew. Even now, the journey ashore was fraught with danger for the natives and crews alike. Stevenson claims *Trenton's* band now played *"Hail, Columbia"* in celebration, one of the new nation's unofficial national anthems.

Of *Eber*, just pitiful smashed fragments remained. German shore marines posted themselves at *Olga*, still imagining possible Samoan attacks even as those same natives recovered bodies from the reef, still threatening with rifle and bayonet any natives who approached the vessel. The American consul made handsome reward for sailors saved, the German's offer was less valuable but this may have been due to the fact it came from his own pocket. Often, it was refused. One Samoan native, who days earlier had been preparing to defend his home and family from the German forces, declined the offer of 3 dollars for each of his rescues, saying *"...I have saved three German lives today; I make you a present of them..."* Most of the extraordinarily valuable flotsam from the wrecked ships was returned without pilfering, when at the time it was normally considered legitimate booty. Even the natives, who had been violated by these men's superior forces, seemed to have been awed by the way nature had shown them to be as fragile as a native canoe.

Kimberly sadly reviewed his Pacific fleet. *Trenton* and *Vandalia* were lost, both had broken backs and *Vandalia* was under water, both would be donated to the Samoan natives and broken up where they lay. Fifty-one American sailors, marines and officers in total had perished. At first sight, *Nipsic* looked to be in the same plight, but soon hopes were entertained of getting her off the sand, since it seemed her bottom was sound whilst the major damage caused from the huge battering her stern had received was confined to the sheathing on the hull, and to the rudder and propeller. Kimberly estimated that even at high tide she would need to be dragged back some 500 feet to re-float her, such was the power of the seas which had driven her ashore. A *"jury-rig"* rudder was fashioned, and sail used to eventually take her back to Hawaii with the assistance of USS *Alert*, though that would be months away.

Lieutenant Carlin in closing his own report stated about his fellow crew from USS *Vandalia* with the moving words:

> *"This does not complete the list of gallant acts and brave men, danger and suffering have effaced from the memory many deeds of valor and it is claimed for the men in general that their conduct before, during and after the gale, will bear the closest inspection, and now that the lips of their gallant Commander are closed forever, the Executive Officer raises his voice in their behalf, and with the earnest hope that, as they have left a clean wake, they may have a fair wind in all time to come, and that they may encounter only the waves of prosperity in their course."*

Fritze, too, though badly injured, had some serious contemplation to make about the German Pacific Squadron. SMS *Adler* would never sail again, but paradoxically she would in a sad way outlast most of the other ships with which she had shared this experience; the timber rotted rapidly, helped by being scavenged by natives, yet the skeletal iron hull remained on the reef for more than 50 years, decaying slowly before the final few remaining rusty and unidentifiable beams were eventually covered by the New Government Building when that part of the reef was reclaimed in the 1970s. The Samoa Museum at Apia has some few relics from the ship, which can be viewed on their web-site.

Eber was gone, along with her Kapitänlieutenant Wallis who had earlier bitterly criticised his own commanding officer's decision to remain in the bay. A New Zealand diver named Keith Gordon has made dives on part of the wreck of *Eber* in Apia harbour, and recovered a few artefacts including utensils, food containers and uniform buttons. He wasn't the first to reconnoitre the site. Soon after the storm, natives succeeded in reaching the wreck and located the vessel's safe. A charge of dynamite intended to dislodge it blew in the side, ropes were attached, and the object was brought up. On shore, about $15,000 in gold was recovered, taken to the house of a local German resident and guarded by a complement of Marines. Natives continued to try and salvage the guns from the wreck.

SMS *Olga* was firmly beached, missing her bowsprit, and with some large holes in her hull, but seemingly sound in bottom. She would be the only German vessel to be refloated and repaired. Although *Olga* lost no life, 93 German sailors, marines and officers from the other vessels were not so fortunate.

I have been unable to ascertain for sure whether any Samoan natives lost their lives, either due to the storm itself or in rescue attempts, but in one reference work *"Glory for the Squadron"* reference [23], it mentioned the Samoan Tui as having perished when, during rescue attempts on SMS *Adler*, a gun broke loose and crushed him. The source for this data may be Stevenson, who records the incident but not the native's name.

Having extricated itself from Apia, *Calliope* was now totally alone. Not even glimpses of reef or coastline were afforded the vessel, and with no sun visible, her position relative to the northern edge of Upolu was quite unfathomable. Kane could not risk reducing speed until he was sure he was well away from Upolu, so kept the vessel pointed at the northerly waves and the nearly full steam was maintained on those engines for many nerve-wracking hours.

The barometer had been fairly steady all forenoon, and at noon was 29.25 inches, the wind was steady but the seas remained tumultuous.

Later in the afternoon, a fleeting sight of the sun amongst the clouds confirmed *Calliope* to be well to the north of the islands, and the speed of the engines was finally reduced to a more safe level. Men started to clean the ship, water had found its way to the main deck, the only time it was ever to happen in the service life of the vessel. It was bailed up and tossed overboard, and fires were lit to help dry the ship. The many numerous but thankfully on the whole, minor injuries could be tended.

At 6 p.m. the wind changed direction, veering to a direction from the north-north-west and two hours later, the barometer had risen to 29.55, all encouraging signs that the hurricane had perhaps done its worst, and the speed of the ship was again slightly eased.

On Sunday the 17th, in much calmer weather and strong sunshine, sailors hung their clothes and hammocks from the rigging to dry. Hot meals were produced and a service of thanksgiving held. Carpenters attempted to make repairs, and the blacksmith forged reinforcing bands to splice her strained and snapped spars together until the ship could reach a dockyard. *Calliope*'s jib-boom had been almost carried away in the collision with *Vandalia*, though the fore-stays keeping the fore-mast upright fortunately remained taut and sound.

On Monday evening 18th March, *Calliope* nervously returned to the mouth of the bay like a puppy returning to the scene of a scolding. A sweep with the glass showed no sail afloat and just a few anonymous masts clustered at the back of the bay. Kane, expecting the port to be dangerously encumbered with wrecks, had no intention of risking entry in the dusk so stood well off for the night. Next morning at 9 a.m. he entered Apia Bay to be confronted with the desolation he had expected, but which was none the less shocking for a seaman to view. Whatever political or national differences might exist between them, at times like these sailors faced a common foe together; survival was applauded; death was mourned.

Kane had hoped to find his anchors, but extricating any from the floor of the bay where literally dozens were intertwined and tangled was impossible - even the mooring buoys to which he had left his chains attached, and that had survived years of Pacific storms, had been washed away to no-one knew where. He had left onboard only one small anchor, and had used most of his coal, so was in no mood to stay in the death-trap which was now Apia; should another blow come on, even a moderate gale would most likely finish him off.

Kane fired his gun for the pilot, and Apia welcomed back the only survivor of the seven warships, eleven schooners and merchantmen and the many island traders that had crowded the port those few days earlier.

Within all this tale of woe, a light-hearted thing perhaps: Kimberly, in his official report, notes *Calliope*'s return with the comment: "*...showing signs of having experienced heavy weather...*" - a masterly understatement if ever there was one!

Captain Kane took the opportunity to address the entire crew of *Calliope* as follows, reproduced from "*The First Commission of HMS Calliope*" by Captain E.W. Swan [13]:

> "*I take the earliest opportunity of thanking you all for the manner in which you behaved in the trying times through which we just passed, thank God, with the safety of our lives and ship. The promptitude with which all orders were obeyed proved yourselves men, Englishmen. And now, although I know you are wearied out with your late exertions, you will, I know, do your best once more, in coaling ship, a job which will take night and day.*
>
> "*The weather has not settled yet, and I shall not feel safe, having as you know only one anchor, until we are out of this harbour once more pointing our way to Sydney. Although I should be perfectly justified in 'piping down' for the remainder of the time that we are here I think you will agree with me that the sooner we are out of this place, the better.*
>
> "*And now for a few words for those men who so nobly did their duty down below in the engine room. I am sure a grateful country will not forget the manner in which they saved the ship. Although I gave the order for everyone to go below I could not expect it to be so cheerfully obeyed, for human nature is human nature; and seeing, as they must, the fearful peril in which the ship was that to go below meant certain death to them if the ship struck; yet every man went down, and did his duty, nobly, grandly, and well.*
>
> "*To them, great praise is due. To Mr. Bourke, Chief Engineer, Mr. Milton and Mr. Roffey, Engineers, our engine-room artificers and stokers. Although it will be harder for them on the way back than for those on deck, they will not be forgotten. Their conduct will be brought prominently before the notice of our fellow-countrymen. The last thing I have to say is that we ought all to thank the Almighty God for His mercy in saving us.*"

At the conclusion of this speech, the Captain seemed to be so moved that he was unable to continue, and no more was said.

Apia Town too had suffered at the hands of the hurricane. The beach road was for a long while impassable with remnants of yard, mast, and hull planking, of uprooted palms and smashed buildings piled across it, buried under tons of displaced sand and debris. Shops and houses directly on the front were mostly destroyed. McArthur's, the British trader who had been trading in Apia for so many years, was present no longer; their pier and wharf with its stockpile of coal had simply vanished.

Snakes and tentacles of anonymous ropes and lines twisted themselves over the small sections of the sandy beach. Uprooted inland trees and smashed bridge debris joined the sad broken bodies of those men not sent out into the Pacific to simply disappear. Some sailor's bodies were found many miles down the coast, including Captain Schoonmaker, all stripped naked by the waves, the rocks and the currents and their bodies horribly lacerated by the coral. Due to their awful condition, bodies washed ashore along the coast were buried, often anonymously, near to where they were found, rather than brought back to Apia.

Captain Kane would speak of the incident when *Trenton's* sailors cheered *Calliope* out as:

> *"Those ringing cheers of the American flagship pierced deep into my heart, and I will ever remember that mighty outburst of fellow-feeling which, I felt, came from the bottom of the hearts of the gallant Admiral and his men. Every man on board the Calliope felt as I did; it made us work to win. I can only say, 'God bless America and her noble sailors!'"*

Admiral Kimberly replied to the letter from Kane which thanked the Americans for the cheers:

> *"MY DEAR CAPTAIN, -- Your kind note received. You went out splendidly, and we all felt from our hearts for you, and our cheers came with sincerity and admiration for the able manner in which you handled your ship. It was a gallant thing, and you did it so well it could not have been done better. We could not have been gladder than if it had been one of our ships, for in a time like that I can say truly with our old Admiral Josiah Tattnall, 'That blood is thicker than water.'*

> *"I thank you many times for your kind offer, but nothing can be done for us under the circumstances. We are trying to get a schooner off tomorrow to meet the steamer for Tutuila and Auckland, to send despatches for our Government and friends at home.*

> *"We have three anchors out in the harbour, and if they would be of any use to you, you are welcome to take them for your use if you can find the buoys. In regard to the boats we will let you have four, all we have left excepting our launch, so if you will man them they are at your service. I*

advise you to get away as soon as possible, as this harbour now is only a
trap.

"With congratulations for your happy escape.
Believe me,
Sincerely your friend,
(Signed) J. A. KIMBERLY, Rear-Admiral, U.S.N."

The letter might also be a reply to a visit Captain Kane made, recorded in his report, number "No. 26". Kimberly's letter is undated but is likely to be around 19th March 1889. It finally closes the loop regarding Josiah Tattnall opened in chapter 2 and continued in chapter 5. The Admiralty in London would add their appreciation of Admiral Kimberly's words to Captain Kane in a letter to Admiral Fairfax in June reproduced in Parliamentary Paper 5756.

The first part of Captain Kane's report is repeated below, and was written after *Calliope* had left Apia and arrived at Sydney:

"H.M.S. "CALLIOPE,"

At Sydney, N.S.W.,
4th April 1889.
No. 26.

"SIR,
"On my return to Apia, on the 19th March after the hurricane, finding that Messrs. McArthur and Co. could not supply us with any coal, their pier, all their lighters, and most of the coal in their store having been swept away, I contracted with the German firm for 150 tons at £4 6s. 0d. a ton.
"The price was very high, especially as the coal has proved to be of very inferior quality, but I had no choice in the matter. Being favoured by fine weather, and working all night, we were able to get it all in by midnight on the 20th.
"2. I called on Captain Fritze, who was still very ill, and on Captain Von Erhardt, of the "Olga", and asked what I could do for them. Captain Von Erhardt asked me to take one of his Lieutenants to Sydney to communicate with his Government, and if approved and found necessary to hire a steamer to assist the "Olga". I very willingly received Lieutenant Emsmann, I.G.N., as a passenger, and have brought him to Sydney.

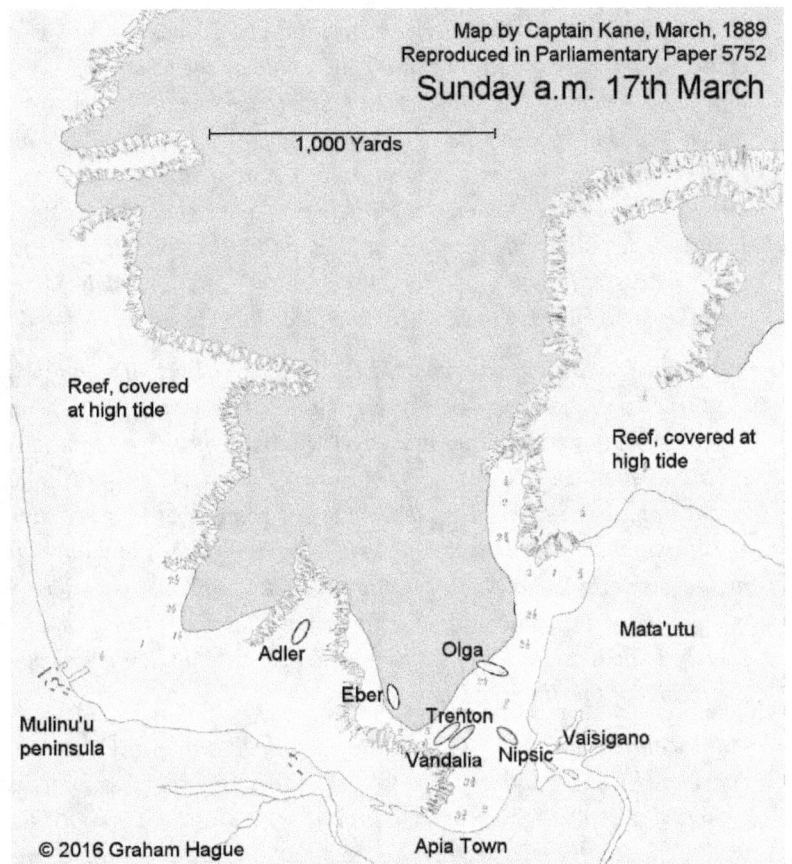

Map by Captain Kane, March, 1889
Reproduced in Parliamentary Paper 5752

Sunday a.m. 17th March

1,000 Yards

Reef, covered
at high tide

Reef, covered at
high tide

Mata'utu

Adler   Olga

Eber

Mulinu'u   Trenton
peninsula   Vaisigano
                      Vandalia   Nipsic

© 2016 Graham Hague   Apia Town

*Apia Bay showing the final positions the warships reached on the morning of
Sunday, 17th March 1889. The layout of the reef is taken from the chart produced
by Captain Kane in his report, as reproduced in Parliamentary Paper 5752. The
ship positions show them either sunk like SMS Eber, USS Trenton and USS
Vandalia, or beached like SMS Adler and Olga, and USS Nipsic. The positions of
the six warships are not quite as those recorded by Captain Kane, but have been
slightly modified following analysis of the photographic record.*

-Continuation of Kane's Report:

"3. The "Olga" appears not to be damaged to any extent under water. She
is just afloat astern, and three feet out of water forward. The engines are
hard on one point, as if something was a little out of line, but that is
expected to get right when waterborne again. If they can find the anchors,
get them in astern and hove taut every tide, while the ship is at the same
time being lightened, I see no reason why she should not come off.

"4. I then called on the American Admiral at his quarters on shore, and offered my services to him in any way, while at the same time I thanked him on the part of our Officers and Ship's Company for the sympathy which was shown us by the "Trenton's" when we were steaming out. He was exceedingly kind and congratulatory, and said they felt as proud of our success as if it had been one of their own ships. The only thing he had to ask for was that our divers should examine the "Nipsic's" bottom, to see if it was still sound. As for the "Trenton" and "Vandalia", nothing could be done for them but to strip and clear them as much as possible.

"5. I sent our divers, who reported the "Nipsic's" bottom sound as far as they could see. The next day, I received a note (Enclosure No. 1*) from the Admiral saying I would do him a great favour by letting him have our diving gear on payment or otherwise. I at once replied that under the circumstances I esteemed myself happy in being able to serve him, and that I would send him our whole apparatus complete, one pump and two dresses, leaving the question of payment, if any, to be settled afterwards. I felt sure that my action in so doing would meet with your approval. I shortly after received an official letter (Enclosure No. 2*) acknowledging the receipt of the diving gear.

"6. I communicated to Colonel de Coertlogon, H.M. Consul, that I considered it right to leave at once for Sydney. He said that, much as he regretted our absence on private grounds, he saw the necessity for that course under the circumstances, and that he did not think anything would be likely to occur for some time which would require the presence of a man-of-war. At the same time he hoped to see one when the fine season began.

"7. The mail schooner sailed for Tutuila on the 20th to meet the steamer from San Francisco to Auckland. I sent my letter, No. 19, of the 20th March by that route, as also a letter (Enclosure No. 3†) to the postmaster at Auckland asking him to telegraph to you the main facts of the hurricane, and if you were at sea, or not in telegraphic communication, then to send direct to the Admiralty a few words to show that we were safe, in the possible event of alarmist rumours getting about in England through errors in press telegrams.

"8. Admiral Kimberly sent Lieut. Wilson, one of his officers, down to Auckland by the mail, with despatches, and orders to charter a steamer to take their people back to San Francisco. There are at present some 500 American sailors on shore at Apia, and it is very difficult to feed them or to keep them under control.

[The second part of this report has been omitted.]

"I have the honour to be,
Sir,
Your obedient Servant,
H.C. KANE
(To)   REAR-ADMIRAL *HENRY FAIRFAX, C. B.,*
Commander-in-Chief H. M. S. "Orlando."

Fritze's injury was a serious scalp wound, suffered as *Adler* toppled onto the reef, but he would recover from it. As stated, Kane handed over his diving outfit to Kimberly for use in salvaging what could be found on both *Vandalia* and *Trenton* and for the inspection of *Nipsic*'s hull. In return, Kimberly gave Kane nearly all the boats he had to replace *Calliope*'s smashed by the seas. Kane made ready, got that coal from the German supplier - who despite suddenly having few customers to buy it still saw the opportunity to charge an exorbitant price for it – but it was slow work with no sizeable vessel available to carry the poor quality material out to the British ship, and Kane was desperate to leave hurricane latitudes altogether.

Calliope had suffered badly in collisions and was in need of urgent dockyard repair, and every moment in Apia was now dangerous. In the generous and warm-hearted letter to the British Captain reproduced above, Kimberly too described the harbour as a death trap and added his own urgings to leave. Whilst agreeing that the military need was now much reduced, de Coetlogon still wished Kane to persuade the British Admiral that a British warship was needed at Apia.

Admiral Kimberly sat down on the 19th March and wrote out his report into the events for the Secretary of the Navy, including the names of those who had died. On 20th March Kane wrote his 19th report for Admiral Fairfax, and this was the first which was not commenting on the lamentable state of politics in Samoa, but instead concentrated on the events of the storm. This letter is referred to in a later report, and was sent via a mail steamer to intercept the San Francisco to Auckland steamer at Tutuila.

Much later on the 16th April, Kimberly wrote a special report to the Secretary of the Navy detailing the heroic efforts of the American sailors, the Samoan natives, and various Apia residents to try and save lives during the storm. These names, perhaps mostly forgotten now, deserve to be remembered, and the report is included here in its entirety.

"Special Report of Rear-Admiral L.A. Kimberly - Conduct of Officers and Men.

"APIA, SAMOA, April 16, 1889.

"SIR: I take pleasure in calling the attention of the Department to the efficient and indefatigable services rendered by the following officers, who were on shore or who reached shore during the recent hurricane at Apia, which was so destructive of life and property:

> *Ensign John L. Purcell, U.S. Navy.*
> *Lieut. John A. Shearman, U.S. Navy.*
> *Ensign H.P. Jones, U.S. Navy.*
> *Ensign H.A. Field, U.S. Navy.*

"These officers worked incessantly, doing all that it was possible to do in saving the Nipsic, in efforts to launch boats and get lines to the Vandalia, and in patrolling the beach and saving life. They all worked until overcome by physical exhaustion. Ensign Field was in ill health when he left the ship and worked until 4 p.m., when he succumbed. He has since been on the sick-list and nigh unto death. Ensign Purcell and Lieutenant Shearman did not yield until after midnight and were promptly at hand early the following morning. Ensign Jones, in addition to his services on the shore, is highly commended by his commanding officer in a letter to me of March 26, of which the following is an extract:

"I beg to call your attention particularly to the valuable services of Ensign H.P. Jones, jr., who was officer of the deck of the morning watch and who superintended the steering of this ship properly and carefully for two long hours to prevent the Olga from cutting us down. He stood bravely at his post by my side on the poop through all the storm, rain, and volumes of smoke, when at times we could see but a few feet ahead, as the blinding smoke and heat were simply terrible. Mr. Jones is a young officer of great promise, and bids fair to be of value to the service and to his country.

"Ensign C.S. Ripley and Pay Clerk S.T. Browne are worth of notice for their active efforts and the valuable assistance they rendered. Teoteo, a Samoan of Apia, made a desperate attempt to swim off to the Vandalia with a line while the gale was at its height. The heavy surf, the jagged reef strewn with wreckage and swept by strong currents, through and over which he attempted to pass, made this effort one of exceeding danger, and in the futile attempt he nearly lost his life. I have learned of no greater risk of life for others being accepted by any one on this occasion, and I commend him to the favorable consideration of the Department, trusting

that his bravery will be recognized in so enduring a manner that his example will be kept in memory and the spirit that animated him fostered and developed wherever acts of courage and sacrifice are cherished. In his intrepid effort Teoteo was assisted in the management of the line by Toga, a native of Samoa, whose father was a Tongan. Charles Fruen, sr., a native of Apia, saved the life of Surgeon E.Z. Derr, of the Nipsic, and in doing so risked his own.

"*Seumanutafa, chief of Apia, and Selu Leauanae did excellent service in saving life, and took the lead in directing the work of the natives. They organized boats' crews and carried out the suggestions of the officers. Seumanutafa took charge of and steered the boat which was the first to carry lines to the wreck in the early morning of the 17th, while it was yet dark, and the passage across the reef and approach to the Trenton was beset with difficulty and danger.*

All the Samoans were faithful, alert, and diligent in their efforts to save life and assist the unfortunate people. Conspicuous among them were the following:

Tatopan.	*Sofa.*
Paniola.	*Tualagi.*
Sigito	*Papalii.*
Fanala.	*Muniaiiuaga.*
Folau.	*William Hunkin.*
Charles Freun, jr.	*Neamea*

"*Of the foreign residents of Apia, the United States vice-consul, Mr. W. Blacklock, was pre-eminently conspicuous for his energy and good services, not only in saving life, but in caring for the immediate and pressing wants of the survivors of the Vandalia, the most of whom were taken to the consulate. Too much cannot be said in justice to his exertions and hospitality on this occasion.*

"*Mr. J.P. Dunning, correspondent of the Associated Press, and Messrs. H.J. Moore, Albert Vicking, Peter Paul, and J.S. Pike, of Apia, were conspicuous in the work of saving life and property, and deserve particular mention in this regard for most praiseworthy services*

"*From a letter by Commander Mullin, of the Nipsic, dated April 26, I quote as follows:*

"*Among my own crew those who rendered services and set examples were John Callahan (quartermaster), who had the mid-watch on the night of March 16, and who was stationed on the quarter to watch the movements of the Eber, which vessel was close under our stern, and to report her approach to the officer of the deck, who was watching the Olga, close on our port beam; Also Quartermaster R.H. Taylor, who was at the conn from 4 a.m. to the time the vessel was beached, never leaving it once, but conning the vessel amid the volumes of smoke and soot which were sweeping aft after the smoke-pipe had been carried away. We were steaming ahead through the night watches. James Lane and Henry Pontseel, seamen, were at the wheel from 1 a.m. till the vessel struck and during the collisions with the Olga, and remained there without flinching. I regret to say that Potseel was drowned. Chief Boatswain's Mate John Bradley and Boatswain's Mate William Cosgrove were very conspicuous during the night in doing all possible. Bradley has been a most valuable man to the Nipsic, and on more than one occasion has he shown himself a thorough seaman. I would be pleased to see him get a boatswain's warrant, for which I now recommend him. He is our leading spirit in times of danger. Brooks Cason, quartermaster gunner, acted as my messenger during a good part of the night and assisted me greatly. He is a brave lad and always at the proper place in time of need. I would recommend the above-named men for medals of honor.*

"Sergeant Grupp and Private William Campbell, U.S. Marine Corps, were conspicuous in worthy and earnest efforts along the beach, aiding the officers and assisting in every undertaking to save life and property. I commend to the notice of the Navy Department, Lieut. John M. Hawley, the executive officer of the Nipsic, for his zeal and energy in getting the Nipsic afloat after she was beached. He had the entire charge of this work, and to his efforts in a large measure is due the fact that the Nipsic is now afloat without more serious injury, and with the possibility of future service to the Government.

"Naval Cadets J. A. Le Jeune, L.A. Stafford, and H.A. Wiley, serving on the Vandalia, are commended as follows, by Lieutenant Carlin, commanding the survivors:

"The gale was terrific and the danger extreme, the ship being on the brink of destruction for fifteen hours. These young officers did their duty in the most commendable manner, distinguishing themselves for coolness, zeal, and pluck."

"I have in previous letters to the Department called its attention to the important services rendered me by Malietoa Mata'afa, and to the exceeding kindness of Captain Kane of H.B.M.S. Calliope. These services are fully described in my report dated March 19, Nos. 21 and 25; March

20, No. 22; and March 21, No. 23; but the subject-matter of the present letter would be fatally deficient without a marked reference to them. I have endeavored in the foregoing to make a just statement of the worthy efforts made by the persons mentioned, my chief sources of information being the written reports of eye-witnesses; and I now respectfully refer the matter to the Department with the statement of my conviction that prompt recognition and reward, commensurate with the character of the services rendered, will be but a simple act of justice, and in the cases of our own men will operate to the great advantage of the service.

Very respectfully, your obedient servant, "L.A. KIMBERLY
Rear-Admiral U.S. Navy,
Commanding U.S. Naval Force on Pacific Station.
[to] The SECRETARY OF THE NAVY."

You should note I have not attempted to correct any spelling errors, whether real or not, particularly in the names, in this report, which is here repeated verbatim.

Kane would wait no longer, and at 7.30 a.m. on the 21st March left for Australia, carrying the German officer to report to the consulate and make arrangements for getting the survivors home, and after an uneventful voyage under greatly reduced sail, she arrived at Sydney on 4th April to a tumultuous welcome. An American Officer, Lieutenant Wilson of USS *Vandalia*, had left Apia the day before *Calliope* in a small schooner *Utumapu*, rescued from the beach and intended to intercept the mail boat to spread the sad news to the world.

On the Samoa beaches, the crews of American and German wrecks were a serious concern for their commanders. Difficult to feed, impossible to house them, sentries were posted to keep the belligerent factions apart, with orders to shoot to kill any miscreants. The mostly German tavern keepers were warned not to serve alcohol to Americans; their taverns and stocks would be destroyed if the order was disobeyed. Vice-Consul Blacklock's proclamation was abrupt and to the point, and read:

"Apia Samoa – March 17th 1889 – To the hotelkeepers at Apia – You are hereby ordered not to sell or give away or allow any liquor to be furnished on your premises to any sailor from any American men-o-war. If this order is not strictly obeyed, your saloon will be broken into, and all your liquor emptied out. Signed, W. Blacklock, U.S. Vice-Consul."

It is suggested that some German saloon keepers did still take the risk.

Peace reigned, but not happily, until the various crews were eventually brought home. In the meantime, *Trenton* survivors erected tents from salvaged sail in the centre of Apia Town whilst other survivors did the same in the grounds of the American Consulate. It would cost the American Government $50,000 to repatriate the men.

In the Roman Catholic Church at Apia, a Requiem Mass was held on 22nd March for the German crew members who had died, conducted by the Reverend Father Remy. The Reverend Father Boltz gave an address in German, and the service was attended by Kimberly, de Coetlogon, Blacklock, Knappe, and others from the ships and the town.

Some idea of the scale of the waves during the hurricane was evident by the sudden presence in the bay of a crescent of shingle bank across the mouth of the Vaisigano, forming a lagoon at its mouth.

USS *Nipsic* was refloated soon on 20th March and SMS *Olga* on the 29th.

On 1st May 1889, the United States Steamship *Rockton* left Samoa with approximately 470 officers and men, leaving just Admiral Kimberly and some 85 crew members at Apia. Sadly, having miraculously survived the terrible storm, two *Trenton* men would lose their lives in accidents before the final batch were taken off. Some 300 to 400 natives, and the crews of USS *Nipsic* and HMS *Rapid*, cheered the men on their way, supported by the band of USS *Trenton* also on board. It had taken Lieutenant Wilson a lot of work to charter and fit out (with accommodation for 450 men) the *Rockton* in Sydney, Australia, all previous efforts to charter a steamer in Auckland, New Zealand having failed.

USS *Rockton* arrived at the Mare Island Navy Yard in San Francisco on 20th May 1889 at 2.0 p.m. She and her passengers were heartily cheered by US Ships *Independence*, *Pinta*, *Hassler* and *Adams* which were in the harbour.

Admiral Kimberly and his remaining staff left Samoa for San Francisco in September 1889 on the mail boat, probably from Tutuila, carrying a number of gifts from Mata'afa in recognition of the services to Samoa rendered by the Americans. Kimberly had presented Mata'afa with a fine boat and monetary gifts as his appreciation of the help given during the storm.

Samoa, after the storm, recovered to some extent. The war that had seemed likely had been terminated before it had started, though tensions between the consuls were still strained. The German consul Doctor Knappe received considerable criticism from a number of quarters concerning his conduct preceding the storm, as reported in the Te Aroha News, Volume VI, Issue 354, 27th March 1889:

> *"Germany and Samoa - Dr. Knappe's Conduct Condemned - Berlin March 23 – Prince Bismarck, in a despatch to Herr Steuble, the recently appointed Consul at Samoa, vice Dr. Knappe, recalled, declares that Dr. Knappe's conduct towards foreigners and the natives of Samoa lacked coolness, that Dr. Knappe had no authority to declare war, proclaim martial law, or attempt to secure the annexation of Samoa to Germany".*

Knappe's subsequent activities as a politician are, perhaps not surprisingly, fairly unknown, although apparently by threat, he persuaded some Samoans to admit that they had started the shooting in the action that had led to the death of the 17 marines in the bombardment of 18th December 1888, presumably to try and offset some of the criticism.

De Coetlogon remained as British Vice-Consul to Samoa until May 1890, when he was replaced by Sir Thomas Berry Cusack-Smith, K.C.M.G. Again, not many of his subsequent activities appear to have reached the internet. There is more about him in the Apia Residents section. There are also more details about Dr. Knappe and about William Blacklock, the United States Vice-Consul in that same section.

Eventually, the Washington conference on Samoa of 1887 was reconvened at Herbert von Bismarck's request and formed the basis for the Treaty of Berlin, 1889, held with British and American delegations in April delayed till May and signed on 14th June of the same year. The treaty launched the *"Political Territory"* of Samoa between the United States, Great Britain and Germany. It guaranteed some treaties made with Samoa in 1878 and 1879, the independence and neutrality of Samoa was recognised, and the Samoan king restored. The agreement ended for the Samoans, when in 1899, Samoa was split into two parts, one controlled by Germany (German Samoa) and the other (American Samoa) by the United States. Great Britain surrendered all rights in Samoa getting in exchange all the German rights in Tonga, the North Solomon Islands and some territories in West Africa.

It is sad to record that the native fighting that started in 1898, known as the second Samoan Civil War, the first being the one encompassing the storm i.e. 1886 to 1894, involved British and American ships shelling Apia on virtually the tenth anniversary of the hurricane, 15th March 1899. The *"Siege of Apia"* was initially a defeat for the Samoans, but Mata'afa's rebels recovered at the Battle of Vailele on 1st April 1899 and defeated the combined British and American forces, which event soon led to the 1899 Treaty of Berlin, and Mata'afa becoming the high chief of Samoa. In 1919, under the Treaty of Versailles, Germany relinquished its claims to the islands and New Zealand administered the former German Samoa as the Western Samoa Trust Territory until independence.

It was 1962 before Western Samoa eventually gained independence from colonial masters, and was renamed The Independent State of Samoa (Malotuto'atasi o Samoa), not without some objections from American Samoa.

So, in total, 51 American sailors and Marines (43 from *Vandalia*, 7 from *Nipsic* and one from *Trenton*), 93 German sailors and Marines (73 from *Eber* and 20 from *Adler*), two civilians and probably one Samoan native lost their lives in the hurricane and its aftermath. Two more American sailors died later in accidents. A great many ships, large and small, were wrecked; the four warships, eleven named smaller vessels and others whose names were never recorded. It is possible, however, that the *Utumapu, Upolu, Nukutiono* and *Vaitele* were, in fact, beached damaged, and were subsequently repaired and refloated, though it seems that the repairs in most cases took a considerable time. The hurricane remains to this day as one of the worst storms to have assaulted the islands in a long history of such storms; certainly the loss of 147 lives would alone have made it so. Thankfully, more recent storms, including the occasional hurricane, have been on the whole much less destructive. Only approximately one-third of those lost in 1889 were recovered for burial, the remainder were washed out to sea forever or left encased in the hull of SMS *Eber*. Amongst the various reference sources, and on the internet, the actual number of sailors of both nations who perished varies. In my text, I have used the number of names on the two memorials, German and American, as being the most likely to be accurate.

I have stated that the contemporary newspaper accounts should be treated with a certain amount of circumspection, but I felt I couldn't end this chapter without an extract from the account which appeared in the *Sydney Daily Telegraph* of Monday, 1st April 1889:

"TERRIBLE HURRICANE AT SAMOA

WRECK OF SIX WARSHIPS
SAFETY OF H.M.S. *Calliope*

"The 16th day of March will long be remembered by those that 'go down to the sea in ships' as the date one of the most terrible shipping disasters of modern times. It was a day of terror, indeed, but also of golden deeds, of staunch courage and good seamanship in the face of appalling storms,

and of heroic rescue by a noble race of (so-called) savages. As we read the cablegram account in which 'horrors accumulate on horror's head,' these deeds of steadfast courage and self-sacrifice, little more than suggested in the brief narrative, mingle feelings of admiration and even affection with the poignant grief and dismay which at first oppresses the heart...

"...And amidst all the horrors of that day, as ship after ship broke from her moorings and drifted upon the reef, shines out the golden deed that places Mata'afa, and his warriors, high amongst the Christian and chivalrous nations of the civilised world. Mata'afa, whom most of his own countrymen regard as the true King of Samoa, came to the beach with 300 of his warriors, and all day, plunging in and out of the surf, saved German and American sailors alike, without any distinction of race. Brothers, then. Forgetful of the recent conflict between himself and the Germans, he saw only his brothers struggling in the surf, the strong swimmer in his agony and the drowning men that were stretching out their hands imploring help. Nobly done, Mata'afa, thou and thy 300."

On the following pages are photographs of the ships in the bay after the storm had abated. They were probably taken around 22nd March 1889. The photographer is not known, but may well have been an Apia resident. They are all in the public domain.

SMS Adler beached on the reef, approximately 2 days after the storm. Note her back is broken as shown by the misalignment of the keel, and also her rudder and propeller have been ripped off when she broached on the face of the reef. (Public domain download from the American Naval History and Heritage Command).

Another view of SMS Adler lying on the western reef. The gun on the poop deck is just visible towards the stern of the vessel; German Marines would soon cover the gun to protect it from the elements. (Public domain download from the American Naval History and Heritage Command).

USS Trenton broadside to the shore and sunk to her gun deck, with USS Vandalia sunk to her main deck alongside and nearer the camera. At the stern of Trenton, lying in a pocket in the reef is a small schooner, with SMS Adler's upturned hull on the western reef behind it in the left back ground. In the far right background, and re-floated, is USS Nipsic, behind Trenton. In the left foreground are the purported remains of SMS Eber. (Public domain, a download from the American Naval History and Heritage Command)

According to Rear-Admiral Kimberly, the prow of SMS Eber, the only major piece of the vessel to be seen after the storm. Trenton and Vandalia are in the right background, and the hull of Adler on the reef in the centre background. Gardiner in "Conway's All the World's Fighting Ships" describes SMS Eber as clearly embodying a ram prow, which does not seem to comply with this photograph. I therefore believe the wreck to be most likely a smaller island schooner or trading vessel and not part of SMS Eber. (Public domain, a download from the American Naval History and Heritage Command)

Ships very soon after the Storm. Trenton and Vandalia on the left, Nipsic on the right and Olga in the background. Note Vandalia's tilted funnel. Beside the stern of Trenton is a capsized merchant schooner. (Public domain, a download from the American Naval History and Heritage Command).

SMS Olga, with a "bow-on" view of US Ships Vandalia and Trenton behind her in the left background. The hole in her bow is temporarily patched with sail cloth. Much of her port side was damaged in the collisions with HMS Calliope. All the ships still have their top masts and yards down.

In this view of SMS Olga, her sailors are drying their clothes in the rigging. Olga fortunately managed to beach on a relatively sandy part of the bay, just to the south of the reef. (Both photos public domain downloads from the American Naval History and Heritage Command).

USS Nipsic. Initially, the vessel was laying broadside to the shore, with her starboard side facing it; seven men died trying to reach the shore from that position. As the storm progressed, Nipsic swung her stern out into the bay as shown in the photograph, making escape via the bowsprit possible. Behind her are Vandalia and Trenton. (Public domain, a download from the American Naval History and Heritage Command).

USS Vandalia as seen from the main deck of USS Trenton. The smoke stack from Vandalia has been removed to be fitted to USS Nipsic. The photograph was probably taken a few days after the storm, as Nipsic and SMS Olga do not appear in the background. (Public domain, a download from the American Naval History and Heritage Command).

USS Nipsic in dry dock at Honolulu. The damage to the propeller is clear to see. The tube of canvas on the left is to permit sailors working inside the hull to use the "head". The propeller was salvaged and remains to this day in the Mare Island Navy Yard at San Francisco. (Public domain, a download from the American Naval History and Heritage Command).

SMS Adler skeletal frame on the reef c. 1930s. The hull had partially righted due to the wave action in the many storms of the years since the hurricane.

The memorial plaque in the chapel of the Mare Island Navy Yard at San Francisco. (Both images public domain download from the American Naval History and Heritage Command).

Whilst at Honolulu, USN Engineers inspected the Nipsic and reported as follows:

U.S.S. NIPSIC (THIRD RATE)

Honolulu, Hawaiian Islands, August 10, 1889

SIR: In obedience to your order of this date, we have held a strict and careful survey on the U. S. S. Nipsic, and we report as follows:

The Nipsic being upon the marine railway, we find her keel is torn off from stem to stern post.

Form the fore-foot to the region of the foremast it is torn off clear up to the garboard.

From this point to the region of the after quarter-deck gun-port there is about 6 inches of keel remaining, and from this point to the stern-post, gradually sloping upwards, it is torn off, including the garboards, the deadwood, and the stern-post up to the lower edge of the stern bearing casting.

The shoe rudder-post and rudder are torn off.

The casting under the counter, to which the rudder-post was attached, remains in place and is in good condition. That portion of the keel remaining in place is rough and ragged throughout.

The fastening bolts are bent over against the bottom planking. The bottom planking is roughened. The sheathing metal is damaged in spots.

Part of port main chains and plates are carried away.

The apron of the stem is carried away.

This damage was done at Apia, Samoa, March 15, during a hurricane.

We recommend a temporary keel, a shoe, a rudder, an apron to the stem, the main chains repaired, and the bottom painted.

Respectfully, your obedient servants,

A. J. KIERSTED,
Chief Engineer, U. S. Navy.
R. E. CARMODY,
Lieutenant, U. S. Navy.
JOHN M. HAWLEY,
Lieutenant, U. S. Navy.

Bizarrely, no mention is made of the propeller!

Shortly after the storm, Captain Mullan was unable to check the *Nipsic's* bottom, but made his own statement as to her general condition:

STATEMENT OF THE PRESENT CONDITION OF THE U. S. S. NIPSIC (3D RATE).

The damages done to this vessel during the hurricane of the 16th day of March, 1889, may so far as known, be summed up as follows: Forefoot gone; both bower anchors gone; jib-boom sprung; starboard foretop-sail sheet bitt gone; mainmast broken at second band from spar-deck; port hammock rail carried away from bridge to gang-way; port main chains carried away; four shrouds of port main rigging carried away; port mizzen chains carried away; mainmast-head sprung; steam-launch, second cutter, whale-boat and dinghy all gone; sailing-launch badly damaged; deck seams opened on quarter-deck; stern-post and rudder gone; main yard gone; upper section of smoke-stack carried away and lower section badly damaged; both after-ventilators gone. In the ordnance department many articles, such as priming wires, cartridge boxes, belts, lock strings, etc., were either damaged by salt water or washed overboard. In the navigation department such articles as deck lamps, log-lines and leads, were swept overboard; the three working chronometers and comparing watch have been rendered useless by being filled with salt water, the seas coming down the wardroom hatch. In examining the magazine 4 inches of water were found therein, but it is now comparatively dry. More or less water was found in the storerooms of the paymaster, containing provisions and clothing. In the engineer's department boilers Nos. 5 and 6 have spread about 3 inches, bending the tie rods and lugs attached to after side. The forward cylinder of the main engine appears to be raised about 2½ inches. The after bunker, starboard side, is carried away along the lower edge.

There is now every indication that between the turn of the bilge, starboard side, and keel from about boiler No. 3 to center line of main engine it has raised from 3 to 4 inches.

The engines cannot be jacked a full revolution, showing that they are considerably out of line. From an examination of the propeller two blades are still left, one of which is badly bent. The rudder and rudder post are gone and the shoe is bent upward.

Very respectfully, your obedient servant, etc

About the Hurricane

It may have occurred to some readers that the storm at Apia should be named not as a "hurricane", but as a "cyclone". Since all those unfortunates who endured the miseries of the storm at Apia, Samoa used "hurricane", and the nick-name given to HMS *Calliope* was "*The Hurricane Jumper*" which I thought made for a good title to this book, I have, consequently, used that epithet throughout.

In today's meteorological world, the formal name of the storm is "tropical cyclone", defined by Wikipedia as "*...a rapidly rotating storm system characterized by a low-pressure center, a closed low-level atmospheric circulation, strong winds, and a spiral arrangement of thunderstorms that produce heavy rain or squalls.*" So the generic name of the storm would be "tropical cyclone", but the phrase "*The Tropical Cyclone Jumpers*" does not fall easily on my ear!

We then come to the more localised names used for a "tropical cyclone". The term "hurricane" is generally used for storms that occur in the North-Eastern Pacific Ocean, and the North Atlantic Ocean. A "typhoon" occurs in the North-Western Pacific Ocean; in the Southern Pacific and Indian Oceans, they are known as "tropical cyclones" or "severe cyclonic storms". Due to a wide range of factors, such storms very rarely form between the 5°N and 5°S latitudes. They are virtually unknown in the South Atlantic Ocean, and will only form over a wide expanse of warm water before beginning to migrate. In the northern hemisphere, the winds in the rotating storm do so clockwise, and anti-clockwise in the southern, for the same reason the water in your bath rotates those same ways as it runs out. Thus the preponderance of such storms originating in the tropics to the east of the Caribbean and which then set off to menace those islands, and the United States mainlands of Texas, Florida and further north are termed "hurricanes". The power which they develop is caused by evaporation of the sea water under the low pressure system, which vapour rises and cools, condensing to clouds and rain. As the cloud system enlarges, so more surface area allows more evaporation, strengthening the clouds and the rain near the centre. As a result, such storms rapidly lose their power over land.

So with the island of Upolu, Samoa lying in the Southern Pacific Ocean, it would today be called a "tropical cyclone" or perhaps just a "cyclone"; but I like "hurricane" and am going to stick with it. I'm not alone in disliking "tropical cyclone": Mr Hoyt in his book on the storm in reference [17] entitled his book:"*The Typhoon that Stopped A War*".

Today, storms such as these have a wide range of elements which are used to "classify" them, usually into category 1 through category 5 (the most powerful). Many of these elements rely on readings taken from equipment that did not exist in Samoa in 1889; satellite images are the greatest source of such data today. All the Navigating Officers of the three nationalities had at their disposal the pressure reading from their barometer; an estimate of the height of the seas in the bay; the direction the wind was blowing from; and the colour of the sky above and around them; all very local, which would perhaps most accurately tell them what was coming once it had arrived.

But a further imponderable is what I have already referred to as "gut instinct". There is no doubt at all that experienced seamen were very good at interpreting their feelings into a weather prediction. The various navy captains (probably accompanied by those Navigating Officers) all visited the elderly and highly experienced and respected ex-seamen ashore to ask their opinion of what the coming weather would be. This had two advantages: not only were they experienced sailors giving their views from what they had encountered at sea, they had also spent many years sitting in a sea front inn and watching the Apia weather. Similar signs at that very local point may well suggest a very similar weather condition to come. It's as good a prediction method against most other things.

I obviously do not have intimate access to what was going through the minds of any of those at Apia in 1889. On the minus side, or factors suggesting a big storm was coming, can be set out the following: Historically, March and April saw the stormy season end usually with a violent finale; all in the bay had recently experienced two or three very bad storms which had wrecked three ships anchored there; Apia was a known trap, only seven years before, a hurricane had wrecked every one of the many vessels in the port; and most insistently, the barometer was falling, and falling rapidly. Any sailor would know that a falling barometer pressure indicated, obviously, the approach of a low pressure weather system. As the centre of that system, which may yet be beyond the horizon, came nearer the pressure indicated would continue to fall. If it rose, one could possibly assume the low pressure system was moving away. And all sailors knew that low pressure meant bad weather: rain, wind, high seas, difficult ship control, and everything ensuing from that.

It does seem that the shore-based captains were in agreement: the weather they were seeing in their bay usually presaged rain, but nothing much in the way of wind; in other words, assuredly *not* a hurricane. English readers of this book may recall the October 1987 storm I have already mentioned in passing. With regards to which, the day before it struck, a BBC weatherperson (I will not name him) laughed away the fears of someone who had written in to the studio expressing her worries about the "hurricane" that was coming. I don't think he ever lived it down, but he was interpreting data from a vast array of elements that the Apia officers didn't have, and he still got it wrong! So we should not point our fingers in 1889 either.

The only barometric data I have are from HMS *Calliope's* Log Book. I have extracted the data for the following dates and compiled a simple graph. I start with the day of the waning of the last major storm, i.e. Monday March 11th, and end with the point at which *Calliope's* barometer was disturbed by the weather on Sunday March 17th, and no further readings were taken. If log books exist of the other vessels, there may well be similar data in them. *Calliope* readings were taken every four hours from midnight, and at roughly two-hourly intervals from midnight on the 15th.

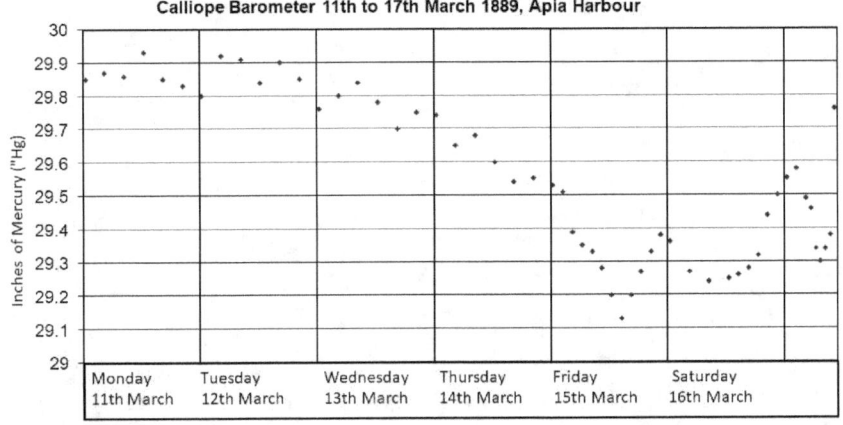

Record of HMS Calliope barometer reading during the storm. [Author's collection.]

The highest reading in this range was 29.93 "Hg at 12 noon on the 11th March, and the lowest was 29.115 "Hg at 1.0 p.m. on the afternoon of the 15th March. Modern "Low Pressure Systems" generally exhibit a pressure of around 29.54 "Hg, which seems very close to the lowest reading at Samoa. The lowest pressure ever recorded was 25.69 inches of mercury (870 millibars) in the eye of Typhoon Tip, in the tropical western Pacific Ocean, on October 12, 1979. This is staggeringly less than that at Samoa. Clearly, pressure alone is not the sole contributor to the destructive capabilities of a storm.

Chapter 8: Going Home.

Only a few miles out of Apia, *Calliope* came across the small schooner *Utumapu*, rescued from the beach, which had been hastily repaired and despatched making heavy work against light winds and a gentle sea, so took her in tow for the remaining 50 miles (80 km) to reach Tutuila in time for the American Officer, Lieutenant Wilson of USS *Vandalia*, to intercept the mail boat with Kane's and Kimberly's various mails. On Friday, 22nd March 1889 the San Francisco to Auckland mail steamer stopped beside the battered little vessel and the wider world first began to learn of the disaster to have befallen the fleets at Samoa.

It had been in 1866, just 2 years after the end of the American Civil War, that the multi-millionaire American entrepreneur Cyrus Field had, at his second attempt and from out of the bowels of the vast hold of Isambard Kingdom Brunel's massive SS *Great Eastern*, successfully laid 3,000 miles of gutta-percha sheathed copper cable onto the North Atlantic under-sea plateau and begun to operate a telegraph service between Ireland and Newfoundland at the rate of $10 per word, thereby finally connecting the extensive land network of the United States with the old-world powers of Europe. Similar connections around the Pacific were still some way off, but by 1889 and 1890, London was connected to Australia via a line which ran from Cornwall down the Bay of Biscay, through the Mediterranean Sea, the Suez Canal, Red Sea, and across the Indian Ocean to Bombay, where it served the Indian sub-continent. From there, other lines snaked out to the Malay Peninsula, and thence Australia, where yet another pair of lines could finally terminate at New Zealand. So whilst messages were still not directly routed, they could nevertheless reach their destination on the other side of the world in a matter of hours.

Sir William Preece would soon (in 1892) be able to transmit the first wireless telegraphic message over a very short land distance in England, but it would not be until the end of 1901 when Guglielmo Marconi would achieve the incredible feat of doing so over the 2,100 miles between Cornwall and Newfoundland. Even then, mobile stations on ships would not become evident until around 1909, and so the news of the 1889 storm at Apia and its devastating consequences would need to use more traditional means to reach its wider audience.

Despite her head start from Tutuila, *Calliope* was soon overtaken by the faster mail boat making its way first to Auckland, New Zealand and then Australia. It would be the mail boat on its arrival in New Zealand to first break the news of the catastrophe via Kane's letter. There was a cable running from Auckland to Sydney at the time, and this was meant as a means for Kane to inform his Admiral in Sydney of the events. In case the Admiral was incommunicado (which it happened that he was) Kane included a request for the Auckland postmaster to briefly inform the Admiralty in London, which it appears he did. Due to the speed at which the dreadful news reached Washington, it is probable that Kimberly made a similar request, though in more detail. It is reported that Kimberly's cablegram covering his initial report cost around $800.

Calliope was a bruised and battered gladiator showing her scars, and whilst not exactly limping back to Sydney she had at least to take care, to use her canvas sparingly on damaged and hastily repaired yards. With little coal available for steam but it still being needed to save the canvas as much as possible, it was always going to be a slow and careful passage. The voyage was mercifully quiet, benevolent nature now taking pity on the vessel that had refused to be beaten by its earlier fury. Lieutenant Emsmann was treated to much goodwill in the wardroom, and much excellent seamanship on the deck, since despite the damage that had been inflicted, drills and evolutions were still practised daily.

As *Calliope* approached Sydney, her crew could not know that the first news of the disaster to reach the New South Wales capital via the New Zealand telegraph cable had mistakenly included the British ship in the storm's apparent total destruction of the fleets, sad and harrowing information for the many in the port who had formed friendships with the crew; the only recently corrected information had filled the people of Sydney with considerable relief and pleasure. The sighting of the corvette one day out by a schooner quickly brought its crew rushing back with the exciting news that *Calliope* was nearing port, and the Australians set about preparing a suitable reception in a style they continue to excel at today.

As HMS *Calliope* passed the South Head she was met by a tumultuous welcome, the Permanent Artillery at the fort turned out en-masse, and their resounding cheers somehow swept across the water to find its way to the deck crew. A ferry leaving the port was lined on the one side with its cheering and waving passengers, as the officers went through the decks with the news: *"There's the Calliope!"*; no further explanation was necessary, no-one bothered any more about schedules, being far more concerned to snatch a glimpse of the suddenly famous warship.

Though much had been done on the voyage to effect repairs, there could be no hiding the fact that she had seen some pretty ugly weather. And for people whose own livelihoods included braving the sea, or whose continued existence on land and source of goods, news from home, and nearly every part of their day-to-day life was subject to the caprice of the oceans, the escape of any ship from a dreadful storm was not some obscure and secret thing – they knew exactly what the vessel and her crew had endured and how perilous had been their survival.

Steam whistles and horns shook the air, and anything that might flutter was waved in the breeze. A host of other small ships joined *Calliope*, escorting her into the magnificent bay in a flotilla remarkably similar to that reserved today for round-the-world yachtsmen and women. Contemporary reports suggest Lord Carrington, Governor of Sydney, despite only one day's notice of her impending arrival, had cancelled all his engagements, issued instructions for the town to be decked out in bunting, and on the day of arrival took himself off in his steam launch, positioning himself in Farm Cove where he could be sure of being the first visitor, and made an impassioned speech of welcome and thanksgiving for the safety of the ship and her crew. The ship's log does not bear out this anecdote which is included in Evans' account and a newspaper article dated that day, though undoubtedly the Governor will have ensured his pleasure was known by the *Calliope*s. Swarms of reporters desperate for first hand news will have made their way out to the ship – woe betide any newspaper that tried to sell tomorrow without a front page emblazoned with the story!

To the crew, the welcome was astonishing, and somewhat unnerving. Unlike today, when the seemingly unending big harbour comings and goings of largely anonymous cargo ships and container freighters makes an interesting though short-lived diversion to someone on the shore who happens to notice them, the arrival of any vessel in any port at that time would never pass unnoticed, even a busy place such as Sydney. The crew were always keenly aware that they must handle their ship well in front of those witnesses who were more than able to note a ship handled poorly, but never had their efforts been under such widespread and popular scrutiny as on that 4th April 1889. They must try to ignore the celebrations and crowds as best they could and perform their evolution, and eventually *Calliope* tied to her mooring in Farm Cove, where only HMS *Egeria* was present from the Australian Station. There was just 69 tons of coal left in her bunkers.

Lieutenant Emsmann remembered his duty and disembarked to make his report to his embassy, and to find a silversmith. The German was so moved by his experiences on that trip that one of his first tasks ashore was to commission from his own pocket the purchase of a claret jug, a crystal glass body and silver spout, on which lay a plaque engraved: "*Der Offizier Messe I.M.S. Calliope H Emsmann Lieutenant zur See 21/3 - 4/4 1889*". The jug was presented to the officers on *Calliope*, and was a very well received gift. Being a personal gift to the officers rather than an official one to the ship, when *Calliope*'s commissioning cruise eventually ended, the jug was raffled between them and was won by Staff Engineer Bourke; it remains in his family to this day, who kindly supplied the author with some images and the history of it.

On the day of arrival, Captain Kane sat down and penned a very detailed report which was numbered "21", dated 24th March. It formed the main article in Parliamentary Paper 5756. For any student of the storm, it is probably the most valuable source of data, and includes some maps showing the various positions of the ships before the storm, and where they ended up.

Visitors to *Calliope* never stopped that day and indeed for the next few days the ship was never quiet, her crew being asked again and again to recount the story of the storm at Apia. Eventually, the ship quietened down and the crew could go ashore, only to be pointed at as their cap-tallies were recognised, their hands shaken, and left with expressions of "*well done*" ringing in their ears. Friends and family on shore were visited, and more celebrations made, this time on an individual basis, and more personal. The day after arrival, the severely injured carpenter's mate Thomas D. John was transferred to hospital with a fractured skull and facial bones. In a letter Navigating Lieutenant Henry Pearson was writing to a friend Mr. J. O. Burgess, the injuries were described somewhat unfeelingly as "*...the wheel...took charge and knocked one young fellow's teeth down his throat...*" Though John survived his extremely serious injuries, 6 months of painful interment in the hospital was followed by passage home, where he was finally invalided out of the service.

The ship, though, was still a British naval vessel, part of a station needed to maintain British interests, and she was in something of a mess. During the return voyage, snapped spars had been spliced and strapped with iron hoops forged by the blacksmith, but it was fortunate these makeshift repairs had not been tested in a strong wind or heavy sea. The ship went to the dockyard where a host of new parts were fabricated and fitted. Her damaged bowsprit was repaired and realigned much like the poor carpenter's broken nose, new yards were manufactured and replacement boats commissioned. Australian craftsmen spent a great deal of effort on the starboard side of the hull repairing the extensive though mostly superficial damage caused to the planking by the collisions with *Olga*.

On the 11th April, HMS *Opal* arrived from Auckland and *Swinger* from Hobart, with *Royalist* the next day also from Auckland. All these ship's crews were anxious to see their squadron's sister ship and to hear first-hand from their colleagues the incredible story of her escape from the hurricane. Two days later, the mail steamer *Lubeck* arrived, with welcome mail from England. The same tide brought a sad and sorry SMS *Olga* to go straight to Mort's Dock for a thorough refit and overhaul, and considerable repairs to the holes in her hull. She had left Apia 9 days earlier. After spending a good deal of the German legation's funds, the ship was soon as seaworthy as she had ever been, but the crew were given the happy news that she was going home. She left Sydney on the 17th June for what was to become an eventful trip back to Kiel. During passage through the Suez Canal, she managed to come into collision with a British merchant vessel, which cost her damage to the sailing rig, and the loss of two boats, one, sadly, the only remaining salvaged part of SMS *Eber*. SMS *Olga* arrived back in Germany on the 9th September 1889, eventually becoming a sail-training ship for young German sailors, before being sold in March 1906 and scrapped two years later.

On Monday the 15th April, HM Ships *Orlando*, *Raven* and *Lizard* arrived in Sydney, the flagship mooring to number one buoy. The Admiral immediately made the order "*Cheer the Ship*" and *Calliope* received three resounding cheers from *Orlando*'s crew. Later in the month, Lady Carrington arranged a picnic for the ship's company in the National Park, to which some 180 or so crew were able to attend, whilst those men forced by duty to remain on the ship were provided with the gift of an excellent quality knife or pipe as their memento. Early in June, Kane and his officers, who by now may have been starting to tire of their notoriety, were invited to witness the opening of the new railway bridge over the Hawkesbury

River, a technological marvel of its time.

It was perhaps not unwelcome then, that on the 10th May, orders were given to sail the now fully repaired ship in company with *Orlando* for Adelaide, but the relief was only temporary. The arrival at Larg's Bay five days later, tying up at the Semaphore Station, was the signal for a new round of picnics and parties, a day of entertainment at the university, and an evening reception and ball for the officers at Government House. On the 25th, the ships sailed for Melbourne, the early afternoon arrival at Port Phillip three days later after encountering heavy head winds was welcome, but heavy fog delayed mooring at Hobson's Bay till late in the evening.

On their way back from playing exhibition matches in England, the New Zealand Maori football team was persuaded to field a side to take on a combined side from *Orlando* and *Calliope*, and soundly thrashed the British in a game of good humour that attracted a large and enthusiastic crowd.

Calliope sailed for trials and firing practice and returned to Sydney on the 9th June. Coxswain of the steam pinnace William Rolfe, who had been injured in a fall at Larg's Bay, and whose condition had been deteriorating steadily in the sick bay cabin, was transferred to St Vincent's Hospital ashore, but sadly died the next day, the second *Calliope* death of the voyage. He was buried in the naval section of the cemetery at Rookwood the day after, a band of marines from *Orlando* providing a fitting and highly appreciated tribute.

Later that month, *Orlando* set off for Norfolk Island with part of her brief being to look out for HMS *Dart*, out from Auckland and overdue at Sydney; everyone fearing the worst after news that a long boat carrying her name had been found washed up on the north New Zealand coast. This time, the story had a happy ending, the ship limping into Sydney on the 30th with her exhausted but relieved crew having suffered a nightmare passage every bit as frightening as *Calliope*'s hurricane at Apia. The 25 stormy June days had included losing the boats off North Cape in a dreadful gale, and later being forced to lie-to for a harrowing seven days and nights in another. Two men had been washed overboard, though thankfully both had been rescued. HMS *Dart*'s ship's log for that period rarely shows the wind to have dropped below force 3 or 4 and often significantly higher, and that voyage will have stayed in the minds of her crew for the rest of their lives.

On the 9th July, *Calliope* sailed for Noumea, arriving one week later (*Lizard* had arrived a few hours earlier on the 16th) and here the crew found themselves in a completely different atmosphere to the good wishes universally encountered to date. A salute to the French flag and men-of-war *Thetis* and *Saone* with 21 guns failed to quell the indignation and anger felt by all in the port, whipped up to hysteria by the next morning's newspapers, that by arriving late, the British ships had deliberately slighted the 100th anniversary celebrations for Bastille Day (14th July) which had only just ended. The feelings were strong, and an official reception on the 23rd given for the British by the French Governor, Monsieur Pardon, was a cold and strange affair, no entertainment provided and no ladies invited, Madame Pardon the only female present to share the talking and smoking which was the only fare on offer to the officers. One can just imagine the stiffness and awkwardness of that evening.

An invitation to certain of the people of Sydney, Australia to visit the vessel on Friday, 5th July 1889.

Over the next few weeks, *Calliope* made the round of British outposts and missionary stations in the surrounding islands of New Caledonia, to ensure that there were no problems which Victoria's representative must needs resolve. Most areas were quiet, but it was felt necessary to visit the islands of Ranu and Walu in August where natives had been aggressive and threatening to locals and the Christian leaders, all resolved without the need for punitive action, the exhortations of the missionaries Messrs. Morton and Gillan seemingly enough to calm the situation.

Whilst in Port Sandwich, a steamer arrived with news of a

distressed Australian vessel in Havannah Harbour, and *Calliope* immediately left to offer assistance. Kane found the three-mast schooner *George Noble* of Sydney with a cargo of copra from the Gilbert Group. Her captain and three of the crew had already perished, apparently from some form of poisoning, and though the remainder of the crew had also suffered greatly, most were on the mend, to be immeasurably helped by medicines provided by *Calliope*'s surgeon, Valentine Duke.

On the 15th August, *Calliope* again reached Noumea and found mails dating back to 3rd June waiting for her crew. A fortnight later, an evening dinner and dance for the French was hosted by Kane and his officers; it attracted some 80 visitors and was hugely enjoyed by all. To finally seal the reconciliation after the previous month's unpleasantness, a cricket match organised between *Calliope* and a Noumea eleven was won by the island team, and when on the 4th September, the newly arrived mail-boat carried the news that *Calliope* was to return to England, the French inhabitants were courteous and genuinely delighted for the crew of the ship which had forged friendship out of anger. When she left the bay the next day, those new friends now cheered the ship homeward where they had earlier cursed her arrival, and the French vessels in the port wished them well by signals and shouts from their crews. Whatever the political affiliations or tenseness between nations, a sailor on any ship would well know what going home meant to another.

Though they were to return to their families, the course was not yet for England. They would need to return to their Australian fleet and take their leave properly. Admiral Fairfax too was going home, though not on *Calliope*; he had been promoted to Second Sea Lord of the Admiralty, one of the few such to be elevated to the position from a sea-going officer.

For the first two days out of Noumea, head winds and heavy seas seemed to be trying to thwart *Calliope*'s release, but on the 9th a strong northerly breeze sent her dashing on her way. Perhaps to show that she was as pleased as the men, on the 10th *Calliope* made 294 miles in one day under sail alone, all canvas set, the studding sails billowing their huge areas as their extended lower yards grazed the wave-tops, the bulbous prow smashing its way through the blue ocean in what was by far the best day's run of the whole voyage.

The day after *Calliope* arrived back at Farm Cove, Rear-Admiral Fairfax gave up his command of the Australia Station. He and his lady, in a tradition dating back hundreds of years and still sometimes performed today, were rowed from Sydney's Admiralty House across the water in a boat crewed by six Lieutenants from the fleet's ships, to "*Man-Of-War Steps*" from where they left to board the evening train for Melbourne. To many *Calliope*'s, their Admiral's departure was almost like confirmation of their own return, the news received at Noumea which had been so looked for and welcome could perhaps finally be believed.

The people of Auckland, New Zealand, had taken Admiral Fairfax to their hearts, and a few months later would send their congratulations to him on his appointment to the Admiralty. Fairfax replied with the following letter received by the town on 9th January 1890:

> *"Sir, — I beg you will convey to His Worship the Mayor, the Councillors, and citizens of Auckland my high appreciation of their expression of regard and very kind congratulations contained in the address which I have had the honour to receive. Mrs Fairfax and I will ever look back with pleasure on our stay in your beautiful town, and remember the cordial hospitality and kindnesses shown to us by the whole community. With every good wish for the prosperity of Auckland. — I remain, sir, yours truly, (signed) W. Fairfax, Rear-Admiral."*

The last two men I know to have deserted HMS *Calliope* left the ship during its time at Sydney. Perhaps friendships made in the town were just too strong to be broken, even to go home, or maybe home held little to entice the adventurers back when compared to the goldfields from which people were, as always in the telling, picking nuggets off the ground. The Chinese steward Ah Fook, accompanied by 19-year-old Ordinary Seaman Richard Curtis, left the ship and I have uncovered no record of their eventual fate. Them being deserters does not overly concern me; I hope they lived happy lives and started families that with any luck live in Australia still.

The few days before departure were spent provisioning and coaling the ship, and the officers were invited to a celebration and farewell meal on the flagship *Orlando*. Lord Carrington too, still well remembering the vessel and her exploits, arranged that the traditional sending-off ceremonies for a vessel bound for home would be very special indeed for *Calliope*. The captain and officers of the ship had found great friendship among the members of the Australian Naval Officer's Club in Sydney, which still today continues to display memorabilia of the ship, including a painting by HF Gregory presented to the club by *Calliope*'s officers as a mark of thanks for the kindness and hospitality received.

It is perhaps hard for us today, when the other side of the world is just two days of comfortable flight away – the residents only a telephone call - to understand the feelings of the people at that time who were preparing to say goodbye to friends for perhaps years, maybe even forever. Even those in Australia, who now firmly thought of them-selves Australian, were still proud of the old country, and still reminisced about it. The people of Australia and New Zealand, and indeed, all the small islands with their dependencies and missions scattered around the globe, fully appreciated the efforts of sailors who spent months on the trip out to the station, and years of their lives on it, offering assistance, protection and support; sailors who risked their lives in battle or storm; sailors who were far from their own family and home and loved ones. Inhabitants of Sydney and Auckland, Adelaide and Wellington, and all those far-away corners of the Empire, always took these men to their hearts and tried to give them a little of the family closeness they had left behind in the old country. And whilst the friendships forged were strong in both directions, the Australians could well understand the mixed feelings of those husbands and fathers and sons who could now return to the relatives they had not seen for years.

An unknown British sailor put it thus:

"Like all our people out here in the southern hemisphere, they seem to think they can never do enough for a blue-jacket. They will feed you, lodge you, walk you out, and show you all the places of interest, continually saying 'You don't see this in the old country,' or 'What do you think they would say to that in the old country?' The 'old country' lingers in all their ideas and thoughts. Of course, I don't mean the real bred and born colonial; yet even the 'coming nation' like to have the idea that they are imitating the 'old country's' ways, and all would like to visit that lump of mud situated somewhere under their feet, of which they have heard so much from their fathers and mothers."

Knowing that *Calliope* would still need to spend many weeks at sea, would encounter new storms and hazards, and face new adventures before home was reached was one thing; the knowledge that the friendships made would soon be separated by years before there was any likelihood at all of them being renewed in person was another. In those days, a naval ship leaving the Australia Station for home, might not be expected to return for a decade, if at all. Much could happen in between, and in many ways, the passing could be thought permanent – the sadness of a parting countered by the joy for the crew's reunions to come. *Calliope* would, indeed, never see the Southern Continent again.

Wednesday, 2nd October 1889, dawned bright, heralding the new spring to come for the inhabitants of Sydney. Even on that last morning, visitors to *Calliope* still came aboard, as they had done for the last few days, to wish the crew *bon voyage* and safe journey home. Bunting again bedecked the town, and street parties were held, bands played naval music and the usual patriotic songs and ballads. Lord Carrington and a number of dignitaries congregated on the lawns of Government House for an excellent view as at around 4 p.m. that afternoon, *Calliope* finally detached her anchor chain from the mooring buoy and lifted her holding gear from the Farm Cove mud it would never again embrace. Under gentle steam, she sailed around the bay, giving and receiving salutations from every ship in the port, before slowly proceeding down the majestic harbour and passing the lines of warships and steamers to a spectacular send off, her long *Homeward Bound Pennant* gaily displayed from the main mast truck.

Although this is the phrase used by Evans in his record of the voyage, and the American Navy today, the *Homeward Bound* is perhaps more usually known in the Royal Navy as the *Paying Off Pennant*. The tradition appears to have begun in the early nineteenth-century, the ship's crew using every small bit of bunting and cloth they could find to tie into a long streamer sometimes hundreds of feet long, and traditionally equivalent to the length of the ship plus a foot for each year she had been away from home. It was flown from the main truck (i.e. main masthead) in place of the usual masthead. The practice seems to have originated from the idea that by tying up all the rags in this way, the crew were showing to the world that the cleaning cloths were no longer needed.

Going home they were, but not without duties to perform on the way. On board the ship were 25 invalids and time-expired men being repatriated to England, seven new men for HMS *Dart* to be transferred at Lizard Island, and seven prisoners. On the deck were jammed stores for both *Dart* and HMS *Rapid*, and a new whaler boat to replace the temporary one used by HMS *Dart* to take the place of those lost during her stormy passage in June. Very slow progress was the order of the first few days and they were soon passed by *Orlando* set for Moreton Bay. After three days of steaming against a strong current, the heavy use of the coals made Kane also put into Moreton Bay, finding *Orlando* still there, and acquaintances were renewed far sooner than had been expected. No leave was given, coaling was completed and early on the 9th the ship weighed anchor; this time finding kind weather, good progress being made averaging 180 miles a day. On the 14th, the rendezvous with HMS *Raven* at Cooktown allowed her stores to be transferred, and the next day at Lizard Island, HMS *Dart* was able to offload her own provisions and the spanking new whaler, a welcome sight. Her crew bade farewell to *Calliope*, which then turned north and headed for the Great Barrier Reef; she was now truly on her way home.

Wisely not daring to try to navigate the reef at night, *Calliope* anchored off "*No. VI*" island in the Howick Group, north of what is now Cairns. Similar precautions continued each night up the coast until on the 18th, Cape York bore due south and the Torres Straits beckoned. The fine sailing avoided the need to coal at Thursday Island, and nearly a week after saying goodbye to the most northerly part of Queensland, some small islands between Timour Laut and Timour were at last sighted. The passage had been hot but calm, and the ship's scuttles opened allowing a draught of air to pass through the ship.

The equator had been crossed for the fourth time on the cruise, and *Calliope* was now in the northern hemisphere, another beacon lighting the way home, another waypoint passed. The crew would have been most surprised, and not a little horrified, had they been told then they had not yet finished with the zero latitude meridian!

On the 29th, the volcano Tamborah was sighted, the scene of a massive eruption in April 1815 costing around 92,000 lives that scientists today estimate ejected between 40 and 90 cubic kilometres of magma into the air, up to 100 times the volume of the 1980 Mt. St. Helens eruption, and that had sent dust 1,500 miles east-west and 900 miles north-south. The subsequent global effects had supposedly led to snow in Boston in July and a famine across wide parts of Europe (1816 was known as the year of the missing summer in Europe as a direct result of this eruption) and it is suggested that an equivalent number of people died worldwide from those effects. Volcanologists today rate eruptions by the Volcanic Index, and give the Mount Vesuvius destruction of Pompeii equal footing with Krakatoa as 6. Recent research appears to be re-evaluating Vesuvius to a 7, which would make it on par with the 7 rating for Tamborah.

On the 6th November, *Calliope* again anchored in Singapore but just too late for one of her invalid passengers, AB William Gill who had died the previous day from his illness, not helped by the excessive heat and humidity. He was buried the next day, but the funeral party had little time to complete the morning ceremony in the little cemetery some four miles north of the coaling wharf at Tanjong Pagar before being required to assist in coaling ship which carried on from 1 p.m. to midnight under lights. The next day, the refuelling was resumed and a total of 370 tons taken in. On the 9th, Singapore and its annual 2.6 million tons of shipping, a staggering amount for the day, were left behind once more.

On 12th November 1889, *Calliope* passed an aged and dilapidated

Turkish warship, the log records as the *Erzegroul*. This vessel had already experienced, and would continue to endure, a chequered voyage of its own, and is, I believe, worthy of another of my digressions.

Sometime in the April or May of 1890, the London correspondent of the Manchester Guardian would write in one of its weekly issues under the rather laconic heading *"The Troubles of a Turkish War-ship"* the following article:

> *"A curious story comes to me from the East of the voyage of a Turkish war-ship from Constantinople to Japan, conveying to the Mikado a decoration from the Sultan. It is now over nine months since the Erzegroul, as the vessel is called, left the Bosphorus. She had broken down three or four times - once in the Suez Canal - and she has been delayed in every port she entered by the want of funds. She was delayed at Aden for weeks, and at Colombo for three months. At last she got as far as Singapore, but the voyage so far having been unexpectedly long, her ammunition had given out, and she was unable to fire the usual salute to the port. Accordingly the Governor gave orders that, an explanation having been given of this discourtesy, she was not to be treated as a man-of-war, and the port dues were demanded; but the captain had no money for the purpose, and was equally unable to purchase the necessary coals to enable the vessel to proceed to Japan. He had when the last mail left been some months in Singapore waiting for remittances from Constantinople, which either never came or did not come in sufficient time. I believe the ship is still at Singapore."*

The story didn't end there, and in fact, as might almost be expected from the troubles to date, the cruise did not have a happy ending at all. On Sunday 14th July 1889, the *Ertugrul* (as I believe the correct spelling of the name of the ship to be), with a crew of about six hundred men and carrying many gifts for the Japanese emperor, including a jewelled Order of Merit, had sailed from Istanbul with a ceremonial send-off. After the difficult passage described above lasting nearly a year, the ship finally anchored in Yokohama Harbour on 7th June 1890 and her captain, Osman Pasha, presented two letters from the Sultan Abdülhamid II and the gifts he had sent. Official ceremonies and banquets were held in honour of the Turkish delegation, and on 15th September 1890, the steam frigate left Yokohama. Three days later the vessel was struck by a violent hurricane and wrecked off the island of Oshima, near the Cape Kashinozaki Lighthouse. Reports vary, but somewhere between 540 and 589 people drowned, only around 69 being rescued by luck and the heroic efforts of local Japanese. Whilst the ill-fated *Ertugrul* was destroyed, very cordial relations between Turkey and Japan were forged out of the disaster and last to this day; a magnificent tomb and memorial to the lost crew imposingly resides on Cape Kashinozaki Hill.

The 6th December 1889 saw *Calliope* reach Aden, and join HM Ships *Ranger* and *Pigeon* as mute surveyors of the sad masts and funnel of a French steamer that had sunk in the mouth of the bay, though fortunately not completely blocking it. The next day, Brigadier-General Hogg visited the celebrated British corvette, and was saluted with 13 guns as he left. On the 8th, *Calliope* sailed north, passing the Perrim and Daedalus Lights and the Brothers Rocks before reaching Suez on the 16th.

The next stage would be passage through the Suez Canal, but before that a party was got up to visit Cairo, during which the remains of the fortifications at Tel-El-Kebir were also visited, perhaps Kane sharing with his comrades his exploits that handful of years earlier.

Early morning on the 17th December saw *Calliope* enter the narrow canal, "*gareing up*" for the night in the basin at Ismailia. Another early start, another stop at the passing station just 15 miles short of Port Said, and at 11 a.m. on the 19th, *Calliope* moored up at the Mediterranean end of the canal having finally completed her passage through it. This navigation of the waterway was another milestone on her journey home; another stage of this last part of the voyage had been completed.

But almost before the slack on the mooring cables could be taken up, Kane was visited by dispatchers with new orders; *Calliope* was to return immediately back through the canal to Aden! This news, as unwelcome as any might have been for a ship's crew who thought they were going home, was due to difficulties which had developed between the British and Portuguese governments, brewing up since the middle of the year. Of a sudden, it appeared that *Calliope*'s return to England might well be delayed for several more months and another potential war!

Chapter 9: Zanzibar.

The area of Africa known at the time by Britain as the Shire Highlands had been first visited by a European explorer when sometime in 1859, Dr. David Livingstone camped for a short period at the side of a large and beautiful lake, which, since the locals said the name for it was nyasa, became known as *Lake Nyasa*, slightly amusing since *"nyasa"* was, in fact, one of a number of local words for *"lake"*. In surface area, it is larger than all but the four largest United Kingdom counties. Lake Malawi, as it is now known, is some 560 km in length by 75 km at its widest, and is the most southerly of the series of lakes occupying the geological feature described further north as the Great Rift Valley.

In the 1880s, commercial interests found the area worthy of exploitation by plantation and mining, and the Portuguese, laying an historical claim to the area, had objected to the presence of British businesses in the lands.

On 19th August 1889, the acting British consul on what had become known as Nyasaland, Mr. John Buchanan, issued an ultimatum to Portugal to give up pretensions in the disputed lands, and recorded his concerns that a supposedly scientific expedition led by the celebrated explorer Alexandre Alberto de la Rocha Serpa Pinto (1846-1900) was accompanied by considerably more military might than was needed simply for protection from hostile natives. And it had been news received on 18th December that year that Pinto's *"scientific expedition"* in Makololo country had engaged in some very non-scientific military activities hardly commensurate with a simple defence against hostile local natives, that had led Great Britain to decide that some retaliatory sabre rattling was needed.

Kane immediately commenced to coal his ship, whilst his officers went ashore to arrange for the disembarkation of the invalids, who were rather hurriedly transferred to HMS *Melita* to continue their passage to England. If *Calliope* was needed for battle, she didn't want to start it with a full sick bay.

At 9 a.m. on the 20th December, *Calliope* entered the canal again, and passed a merchant steamer heading north which just happened to share her name, so at least one *Calliope* was still heading for England! It gave the naval ship's crew little comfort. On the 21st, HMS *Calliope* provisioned at Port Suez and then headed for Aden, spending Christmas Day 1889 in the Red Sea. The day started damp but soon became fine and calm and the lower decks were given permission to sing their shanty songs and Christmas Carols throughout the afternoon. In the evening, Kane and his officers dined in the wardroom with the men.

The orders awaiting the ship at Aden were short and explicit, *Calliope* was to proceed at once to Zanzibar on the eastern coast of Africa, and join the British East Indies Squadron under Rear-Admiral, Sir E.R. Freemantle, KCB, CMG. Zanzibar was hardly a popular station for those on the ship who had already endured its miseries; the oppressive heat, sickly climate, and lack of interesting shore leave being the *highlights* that the posting offered.

But to underline that such concerns might be the least of the crew's worries, *Calliope*'s deck was loaded with a magnificent 37-foot steam pinnace and a number of machine guns and ordnance, and coaling took the place of the normal Sunday routine. Forced to wait until the next day for the mail steamer to bring the charts of the East African coast that *Calliope's* Navigating Officer must have, Kane steamed her out of the harbour on the last afternoon of 1889 and headed her south yet again.

On the 4th January 1890, *Calliope* made 300 miles in one day in favourable winds and sea on a voyage that averaged 9 knots under sail and steam, and soon crossed the line for the fifth time on the voyage.

On 10th January, another ultimatum from Petre, the British Minister in Lisbon, to the Portuguese Minister for Foreign Affairs Senor Gomes, could now be supported, as seems usual for the time, with the threat posed by a considerable amount of military force. The Atlantic Squadron had been commanded to approach Portuguese interests and had appeared off Las Palmas on 29th December. Four days later, the Mediterranean Squadron had arrived in Gibraltar as further indication of Britain's determination, and *Calliope* was hurrying to join the East Indies Squadron to be the group to threaten to invade Portuguese colonies and possessions in and near the disputed areas.

Zanzibar is an island off the east coast of Africa and lying in about 6° southern latitude. At the time of the dispute with Great Britain, it was notionally an independent country, though throughout its history, it had usually been under the *protection* of some more powerful nation or another. Today, it is a semi-autonomous region of Tanzania and faces that country's Indian Ocean coastline.

The island had been subject to rule by Omani Sultans who had made staggering sums from the slave trade. Britain had spent a number of years trying to abolish the trade, which had only officially ended in 1873, but had been left with blockade as the only practical method to try and control those still illegally engaging in it. In 1886, a treaty between Germany and Britain had shared out the territory of the Sultanate of Zanzibar on the African continent, leaving only the island of Zanzibar itself, along with the slightly smaller island of Pemba, as independent. The main town on the island, also called Zanzibar, lies approximately mid way on its west coast, facing the mainland of Africa. Arriving early afternoon on 13th January, *Calliope* found the East Indies fleet comprising *Boadicea* (flagship of Rear-Admiral Freemantle), *Reindeer, Algerine, Pigeon, Stork* and *Calliope*'s old friend from China, HMS *Satellite*. Proving that Europe was always pushing and shoving in this region as much as in any other, also present were the German gunboats *Sperber* and *Schwalbe*, and the French gunboat *Bouvet*. Later, HMS *Turquoise* joined the group. *Calliope* unloaded the steam pinnace and transferred the deck cargo to the ships in the squadron and the next day, received the traditional visit from the Admiral.

On the 9th February, the news that the elderly Dowager-Empress Augusta of Germany had passed away in Berlin two days earlier was marked by "*half-masting*" the ensign and the firing of minute-guns in respect. Her death is possibly one of many attributed to the dreadful influenza epidemic of 1889 and 1890 that decimated large parts of Russia, Europe and Great Britain. The Empress' eldest son Frederick had married Victoria, the first-born child of Britain's Queen Victoria and Prince Albert; Frederick and Victoria's eldest son Wilhelm would later become the hated "Kaiser Bill" of the First World War - hated by the British that is. During that Sunday, coaling was made to replace the fuel used in the hasty rush from Aden, but not surprisingly, the natives made very slow work of it in the oppressive heat.

Seven crewmembers from *Calliope* were selected to man the large steam pinnace, helped by two "*seedies*", local natives, all under the command of a warrant officer. The pinnace was despatched on the 11th to steam to the island of Pemba, some 30 odd miles (50 km) north of Zanzibar.

Her orders were to search out and stop dhows suspected of engaging in the slave trade. At the same time, the British fleet sailed south for an undisclosed destination, but with all crews told to prepare for action. As the ships proceeded, crews were formed into landing parties ready to go ashore wherever the destination might be.

The negotiations with Portugal had been continued and the tensions between the governments were ultimately resolved to the public satisfaction of both, with outright hostilities having been averted. This might well be a rather diplomatic way of saying that Britain got what it had wanted, and the areas around the Nyasaland Districts were agreed to be under British control. It seems likely that both sides felt genuinely justified in their original positions, but that Britain had simply bullied her former ally into submission. The Berlin Conference of 1884/1885 had defined the approximate limits of rival claims by Germany, Britain, France, Belgium and Portugal in the areas, with a proviso that no claim would be valid unless "*effective occupation*" could be demonstrated – supported by a rather tenuous definition. Portugal clearly felt they had met the required criteria, Britain fearing the risk of missing out on something worthwhile, did not. Serpa Pinto's "*scientific*" expedition having gained a military success in Makololo could hardly be ignored by Britain whose government had repeatedly warned against such an action, and the scene had been set for dispute. Once again, any claims by the indigenous natives seem to have received little attention anywhere.

The British fleet sailed on, heading for Pomba Bay in order to meet up with the Cape Squadron which had also been despatched to the area, and in extended sailing order late on the afternoon of the 13th, the two fleets came in sight of each other and both turned north for Zanzibar. HM Ships *Raleigh*, *Curacoa*, *Brisk* and *Kingfisher* had now enhanced the group, though Admiral Wells had stayed behind at the Cape and was not in the fleet. The opportunity was taken to indulge in the usual drills and fleet steam tactics, before Zanzibar was reached early on the 17th.

With the arrival the next day of another *Comus* class corvette HMS *Conquest* from the China station after a long voyage, the East Indies squadron could now muster 14 ships, with no war to fight. Instead a sailing regatta was held on the 24th, which gave no success to the crew of HMS *Calliope*, but in the rowing competitions the next day, *Calliope*'s fine new Sydney built cutter and whaler, replacing those boats smashed to pieces at Apia, proved to have been beautifully designed and crafted. *Calliope* crews finished first as follows: cutters manned by bluejackets; cutters by marines; whalers by bluejacket; whalers by stokers and idlers;

whalers by officers; and dinghies. For her boat recognition, *Calliope's* crew had chosen an identification flag comprised of the four stars of the southern cross on a blue background to mark their great friendship with the people of Australia, and to further make the point about the worth of the Sydney boat designers, following each win the boat's crew hoisted a large white banner on which was painted a kangaroo and the phrase "*Advance Australia*", the motto of New South Wales. I know the song "*Advance Australia Fair*" composed by the Scot Peter Dodds McCormick was first performed in 1878, and became the Australian National Anthem in 1984, but I have been unable to find out anything about its earlier use as a motto for New South Wales. My apologies to any Australians encountering this who might think me a poor researcher.

For the next few days, sailing around the area in company with much of the fleet was the order of the day, touching Mombasa and Malindi, the northernmost point on the East coast of Africa reached by da Gama in his cruise at the end of the fifteenth-century. And it was here that *Calliope* and *Satellite* received the news they had been waiting for: they could both resume their interrupted journeys home to England. On the 10th February, the 1,430 ton corvette *Satellite* and her crew of nearly 200 left Manda Bay at Lamu to the ringing cheers of the fleet, and half an hour later, *Calliope* streamed her own Paying Off Pennant yet again and took her leave of the third squadron with which she had served on her eventful commissioning voyage.

With seven of her crew steaming a pinnace around Zanzibar and Pemba Islands, *Calliope* needed to find them before going very far, but it was *Conquest* who located the vessel and put a relief crew on board while *Calliope* coaled ship. To the intense embarrassment of the *Conquest* captain, his officers managed at the same time to put their ship aground on a sand bar, and as the steam pinnace pulled up alongside *Calliope* to disembark crew members full of the news of this event, Kane wondered if he might need to go to the assistance of this one of his similar *Comus* class cruisers – in the end it was unnecessary and after a few hours, *Conquest* floated off on the tide none-the-worse for the adventure.

Even then, *Calliope's* homeward bound trip must still be delayed, as shortly after midday came the astonishing news from the shore that the Sultan Sayed Khalifah had died suddenly just a year or two after his succession. Normally the signal for riots and mayhem until the new order established itself, the ships present were brought close in shore and their rifles prominently levelled at the town, and landing parties again prepared to go ashore to protect the Consulate and British-owned interests.

Though the atmosphere was tense, there was no overnight trouble, and *Calliope* was able to discharge her seedies and embark a new batch of time-expired men and invalids, ready to take them home. Early on the 15th February, the Consul General inspected the ship, wished the crew well, and at 9:15 a.m. *Calliope* sailed around these latest comrades before taking the 10 a.m. tide north. She was heading home again, but this time the crew were more wary, wondering if anything else might yet happen to interrupt the trip, especially as the seas and wind combined to hold her back. Captain Kane was unaware that the day after her departure, his father, Sir Robert John Kane, died in Dublin, Ireland. Had he not had to divert to Zanzibar those few weeks earlier, Kane might well have been able to pay his last respects to his celebrated parent in person.

For *Calliope*, progress was exceptionally slow for a few days with strong head winds and heavy seas, but on the 19th the line was crossed for the sixth and final time during the voyage, or so the crew hoped, and on the 26th she moored once more in Aden. Here there was worrying news, not of more action but this time of old friends. The faster HMS *Satellite*, which had left Malindi before *Calliope*'s latest adventures at Zanzibar and therefore had almost a week's head start, had not yet arrived in Aden. Such matters always caused concern, the memories of the fruitless search for HMS *Wasp* near Singapore those years ago never far from the crew's thoughts.

On the 27th in fair winds and calm seas, *Calliope* sailed north and again approached Port Suez at the southern end of the canal. On the 9th March, *Calliope* left Port Suez and some 3 months after she had first entered it on her way home, once more entered the canal only to be forced to lie-to in "*Guillaume Dock*" some 10 miles north of Suez. A dhow laden with stones had sunk in the canal near Chalouf following a collision with the Messageries Maritimes Company's steamer *Australien*. It was midday on the 10th before *Calliope* could resume the run, finding it clear to Ismailia and anchoring in the basin for the night. Despite an early start next day, she was forced to "*gare-up*" at the first station, but during the afternoon she was once again moored in Port Said.

This time, no unwelcome order changes interrupted the routine of coaling ship and on the 12th the run to Malta commenced, arriving one week later to find present in Valletta Harbour most of the Mediterranean Fleet under Vice-Admiral, Sir Anthony Hiley Hoskins, KCB, one of which was yet another *Comus* class screw-corvette, HMS *Carysfort*. Again the ship was coaled and on the 22nd, the crew's worries about HMS *Satellite* were dispelled when that vessel joined the posse of ships in that wonderful natural harbour. Had Kane waited a day longer in Aden, his crew would have had the satisfaction of seeing *Satellite* sail serenely into the bay, having been forced to use her steam to fight against a heavy sea and strong head winds which had decimated her coal supply, a prudent diversion to the Seychelles to replenish being the reason for her tardiness.

Leaving Malta on the 24th, a week's run saw *Calliope* reach Gibraltar, arriving in thick fog, but the crew were still able to receive mails and provision the ship. At 5.30 p.m. on the 31st, *Calliope*'s anchor lifted from the mud a mile off the rock, the next it would bite its tangs into would be English. A strong northerly all the way to the Bay of Biscay presaged problems, and this time the bay of storms handed *Calliope* a *buffeting* (WIT's description) in contrast to the relative calmness of the outward passage three years earlier. Now the old salts in the crew declared they could smell England, and early on the 7th April, some even swore they could see the glow if not the actual lights of the Lizard. All the crew shared in the excitement.

Heavy rain and fog shrouded the channel and the fearsome Eddystone, until *Calliope* was within 1½ miles of that terrible rock which had for hundreds of years cruelly claimed so many sailors' lives when they were just 14 miles from Plymouth and safety. The men could see on the rock for the first time the newly completed Douglass Lighthouse, its monstrous 160 feet and powerful beacon dwarfing the stumpy Smeaton's Tower which had withstood the fury of the English Channel for 130 years, and whose lower section and foundations are still visible on the rocks today. The author can claim to have paid his few pence and clambered up the many steps of Smeaton's salvaged and re-erected tower on the Hoe whilst on a business trip to Plymouth, and seen amidst the horizon's evening twilight the 26,000 candela flash of the current light, which in 1982 was the first Trinity House Lighthouse ever to be automated 100 years to the day after the then Duke of Edinburgh had laid the tower's final stone. Today, the lighthouse is solar-powered.

At 9.30 a.m. on the 7th, *Calliope* made fast to a buoy in Plymouth Sound, and discharged her invalids and time-expired men, sailing later that evening for Portsmouth. For the crew, the arrival in their homeland was almost an anti-climax. Early on the 9th, *Calliope* arrived at Spithead. A steam trial on the 10th was completed satisfactory, and the Commander-In-Chief, Admiral Sir John E. Commerell GCB, VC., inspected the ship, and heartily commended the company on their successful voyage and especially the escape at Apia. At 5 p.m. that evening, she was lashed to the Pitch House jetty: *Calliope* was home at last.

But she wouldn't have much rest. The very next day, stripping the ship of her canvas, rope and other gear commenced. On 30th April, her crew were paid off, and the voyage, the extraordinary commissioning voyage of HMS *Calliope*, had finally ended.

Chapter 10: *Calliope* Crew.

The circumstances of *Calliope's* escape from Samoa became public knowledge in Britain via that New Zealand and Australia cable whilst the ship was still struggling to reach Sydney on the other side of the world.

At question time on the 1st April 1889, Sir C. Palmer (Jarrow) first raised the matter as recorded in HC Deb (House of Commons Debates) 01 April 1889 volume 334 cc 1250-1:

> *"I wish to ask the First Lord of the Admiralty whether he can give any information as to the escape of Her Majesty's ship Calliope, in the hurricane off Samoa, which proved so disastrous to the squadrons of other Powers; what class of ship she was; and whether she owed her safety to her greater steaming power, or to the superior seamanship of the crew? Any information the First Lord can give would be specially interesting, in view of the debate upon which the House is about to enter."*

> *"Lord George Hamilton replied: I have had no information since Saturday morning of the sad catastrophe that has occurred to the German and American Squadrons at Samoa. Early on Saturday morning I received a telegram from the Naval Commander-in-Chief in New Zealand waters, stating that a hurricane, which suddenly broke over Samoa, had totally destroyed the German and American Squadrons, but that the Calliope had escaped and got out to sea; and he adds that she was uninjured as regards her engines and her hull, from which I infer that she suffered some minor injuries. The Calliope is a vessel of the "C" class, and we have no particulars at all as to how she effected her escape. Perhaps I may be permitted, as representing the English Board of Admiralty, to express here publicly our deep regret and sympathy at the terrible calamity which has befallen the Squadrons of two friendly Powers."*

MR. O. V. Morgan (Battersea):

"Can the First Lord of the Treasury give the House the names of the officers of the Calliope?"

MR. W. H. Smith:

"They are in the Navy List, and can be seen by any hon. Gentleman who goes into the Library."

The debate which was to follow these questions was a discussion regarding the Report on Naval Resolutions and other questions regarding Naval Defence.

The Officers of HMS Calliope c.1890. Seated far left is Chaplain Evans, seated centre is Captain Kane, and seated far left on the deck is Midshipman Frank Brandt. I would assume one of the gentlemen second and third from right at the back may be Lieutenant Marchant, on the basis of it appearing to be a different uniform. Unfortunately, I have been unable to identify any of the other officers. (From "The First Commission of HMS Calliope"; Swan).

The front page of the 27th April 1889 edition of the Illustrated London News. HMS Calliope actually passed to USS Trenton's port side, and a lot closer than even the artist dared depict. (Author's collection).

Hansard continues to record in HC Deb 2nd April 1889 volume 334 c 1384:

> *"Sir George Baden-Powell (Liverpool, Kirkdale) asked the First Lord of the Admiralty whether he could give the House any information as to the acts of seamanship by which Her Majesty's Ship Calliope escaped disaster during the hurricane which visited the Samoa Islands last month; and whether orders had been given for any of Her Majesty's ships to visit those islands for the protection or aid of those who may have suffered by the hurricane?"*

> *"Mr. Forwood: No detailed Report has yet been received as to the circumstances under which the Calliope effected her escape from Samoa; but so far as can be gathered she must have returned thereafter the hurricane was over and conveyed the news to Auckland, from which place it was sent to England by cable. Full details will, no doubt, be reported by the Commander-in-Chief in the next mail. The Commander-in-Chief on the Australian Station has ordered Her Majesty's ship Rapid to leave Auckland to-morrow for Samoa, calling at Fiji."*

Captain Henry Coey Kane and his crew received plaudits from many fronts in the old country. A parliamentary discussion was inaugurated when certain Irish members of the house demanded official recognition of the skills and bravery shown. The request was refused on the grounds that the crew were simply *"doing their duty"*, though it was freely acknowledged that they had performed it very well indeed. Saving a ship whilst under enemy fire might well be rewarded, but saving a ship from the weather was simply expected. A Parliamentary question, reported in The Morning Post of 4th June 1889 recorded the gist of the debate:

> *"Mr. W. Corbet (Wicklow East) asked the First Lord of the Admiralty whether any official reward or honour would be bestowed on Captain Kane for his splendid handling of his vessel in the teeth of a hurricane which destroyed all the vessels which remained at the anchorage he left, as stated in the letter of the Lords of the Admiralty of May 21st, or whether the following cold official record, contained in the paper just laid upon the table, was intended to be the only recognition of the distinguished bravery and seamanship of a gallant Irishman under circumstances that have no parallel in the Naval history of England: 'My Lords are of opinion that great credit is due to the officer commanding for the example he set and the confidence he instilled into those under his orders'."*

> *"Lord G. Hamilton in reply said that it had never been the custom in the Naval Service to use sensational language in praise of officers who had*

well performed their duties. The high approval by the Admiralty of the conduct of Captain Kane and his officers and men had been publicly conveyed to them in terms which they would understand, and which were in accordance with the feelings and traditions of the Naval Service. (Hear, hear). To confer a special reward or other honour upon an officer for successfully navigating his vessel through a storm would be to reverse the established practice of the Navy under which every commanding officer was personally responsible for the safety of his ship, and would be tried by court-martial if he failed in his duty. (Ministerial cheers.)"

The matter was not permitted to rest, since more than a year later and with the ship and her crew back in Britain, the same publication dated 19th July 1890 reported further discussion in the august house, though it failed to elicit much of a different response. Like its predecessor, it is not recorded in Hansard:

"Mr. T. Healy (Longford North): I beg to ask the First Lord of the Admiralty whether any and what reward, promotion, or recognition had been given to the Captain, Engineers, Officers and crew of H.M.S. Calliope for their gallant conduct in the hurricane at Samoa last year."

"Lord G. Hamilton: No general reward has been given to the officers and crew of the Calliope for the successful navigation of the vessel during the hurricane at Samoa last year, as it is contrary to the traditions of the Naval Service that services of this nature, however gallant, performed in the ordinary course of duty afloat, should be regarded as deserving of special and immediate recognition. The position of the late officers of the Calliope is, however, as follows — The Captain is now in command of the Inflexible, one of the largest ironclads in the Navy; the first Lieutenant has since been made a commander; and the chief engineer has been advanced to the rank of staff engineer. The remaining officers have received appointments to important ships. The gunner's mate, who specially distinguished himself, will be promoted to gunner as soon as he qualifies. The Admiralty have formally expressed their high approval of the seamanship displayed on the occasion, and this will have due weight in considering the services of the officers for promotion or future employment."

These responses presumably failed to completely appease those tabling the questions, but the existence of the debate implies how strongly the magnificence of the escape was viewed by the British public and their representatives in the House – after all, politicians usually only get publicly excited about things which they think will be exciting the minds of their voters. I always try to take political rhetoric with a ton or two of salt, and Mr. Corbet's phrase *"...under circumstances that have no parallel in the Naval history of England..."* being voiced in the same century as Trafalgar seems even for a politician just a little over the top, but there is no doubt at all that *Calliope*'s escape was seen by most as bordering on the miraculous; a masterly demonstration of British spunk. The enthusiasm should also be tempered by the fact that Irish nationalism was very powerful at the time, and many Irish MPs in the house used Kane's Irish ancestry, and the apparent lack of recognition of an Irishman's abilities, as fodder for their own political ends.

Another comment as follows:

"UNITED PRESS ASSOCIATION. London, 23rd May. Mr. Goschen, speaking at Sheffield, referred in glowing language to the splendid achievement of Captain Kane, the officers, and the men of H.M.S. Calliope, in bringing that vessel safely out of the dangers of the recent hurricane at Samoa. The incident, said the Chancellor of the Exchequer, was a monument to the splendid seamanship, nerve, and perfection which was characteristic of the British Navy."

In January 1893, the Lord Bishop of Ripon in lighter vein, apparently responding to the answer to Mr. Corbet's original question, was moved to pen a poem, published in The Strand Magazine volume V issue 25, and referring to the court martial of officers who failed their duty:

"What shall be done for Kane?
Who brought his vessel safe through wave
With skilful hand and heart as brave:
What shall be done for Kane?

"What shall he have? "We solve the knot,"
Cries the First Lord, impartial;
"If Kane had failed, he would have got
Our pickle rod -- court-martial."

"Then talk no more of praise or gain,
Our English principle is plain:
When storm winds rise to hurricane,
If Kane escape he 'scapes the cane!"

Even 10 years after the events, Mr. Gibson Bowles would record his own, equally jingoistic views during another debate in the House of Lords (Parliamentary debates during 13th March 1899: Navy Estimates):

"It will be in the memory of honourable Members how Her Majesty's ship 'Calliope' was the only vessel which escaped from foundering in a

hurricane off Samoa. She was not a better ship, nor were her crew and engines superior to those of the German vessel which foundered, but her escape was undoubtedly due to the traditions of the British Navy."

Soon after news of the hurricane became public in England, a flamboyant and eccentric émigré French aristocrat of, it seems, doubtful pedigree, was so moved by the heroic actions of the ship and men of his adopted country that he determined to remedy the perceived omission of British tribute from his own pocket, commissioning Messrs. Henry Lewis & Co., of 172, New Bond Street, London, to strike a fine medal commemorating the event, a gold version for Captain Kane with a bronze or pewter version intended for each crew member. The obverse carries the inscription:

"BRITISH SEAMANSHIP AND CAPTAIN H.C. KANE OF HMS CALLIOPE, FROM AN ADMIRER, THE MARQUIS DE LEUVILLE"

The so-called "Calliope Medal" shown larger than actual size. Calliope's crew were each given a copy of this counter in bronze or pewter at the end of the voyage. Captain Kane's was in gold. Author's Collection.

A coat of arms, presumably de Leuville's, adorns the reverse. These counters are difficult (and expensive) to find nowadays, but the National Maritime Museum has a few examples. I felt rather annoyed with them when I discovered this. OK, get one, maybe two examples, but leave the rest for collectors such as family descendants. I am convinced they were bidding against me when I purchased my copy, and they had superior purchasing power. The image in this book is that of my own example, won on an on-line auction since my ancestor unfortunately left the ship at the end of the voyage and never received his copy.

Not satisfied with even that generous gesture, the celebrated author of *"Entre-Nous"* sat down and penned a noble epistle, which commences with these three verses:

"Wild off Samoa through the rocks and shoals;
Rolled the hurricane's heedless roar;
And half a fleet full of human souls;
Was wrecked in sight of the shore."

One Captain alone had the courage and dash
To gallantly put out to sea;
The deed must be quick as the thought - a flash,
Or the port is - Eternity!

And crash o'er the ship went the cyclone's blast,
O God, all on deck it must whelm:
But a British Flag flew high on the mast,
With a British hand at the helm.

…a song set to music by one Michael Watson. The Marquis' entire ditty is as effusive and unreserved in its adoration of Captain Kane as was Mr. Corbet in the House, and I would love to know what that pragmatic Irishman really thought of it all – I rather feel he might have viewed the attention as well-intentioned but embarrassing nonsense. The British Library has a copy of the original poem print which can be viewed on-line.

De Leuville appears to have been another character worthy of further research. He was born in England in 1841 or 1843 and was a very well-travelled man, though there were regular hints concerning his reputedly dubious noble ancestry. He composed a vast number of songs and poems, and was (in his own eyes at least) an accomplished artist. He was, most assuredly, an infamous rake and was notorious on both sides of the Atlantic for his love of being in the limelight. He came to the ribald attention of the popular press for engaging in a dramatic and highly public jealous confrontation in London's Hyde Park with Prince Eristoff, a romantic rival for the heavily-bejewelled hand of the wealthy American widow Mrs. Frank Leslie (born Miriam Florence Folline), which ended in the severance of their two-year engagement by the acutely embarrassed lady, and ignominy and eventual bankruptcy for the unfortunate Marquis. This all happened a few years before his generosity to the crew of HMS *Calliope*, so it appears he may have come-about somewhat; his character seems to have been ebullient and unlikely to be held in check for long. In 1891, Miriam Leslie married her fourth husband Willie Wilde, a brother of Oscar Wilde, so neither of the Hyde Park combatants claimed her hand (and fortune). In fact, as *Calliope* sheltered in Apia a month or two before the hurricane, the Russian Prince was arrested for Grand Larceny in New York, by pawning a sealskin coat he hadn't paid for.

An unknown London Correspondent writing to *The Star* newspaper in Christchurch, New Zealand in May 1889 was most condemnatory in his view of the real reasons for the medal and the song, and began his article with:

> *"The grotesque fat man who calls himself (though unknown to the Almanach de Gotha) the 'Marquis De Leuville,' whose craving for notoriety seems utterly insatiable, has recently been trying to advertise himself through the odd medium of the Samoa hurricane. It seems this mountebank has had a medal struck, bearing, of course, his own name, and what, I presume, is his family crest, as its most conspicuous ornaments, and this he purports to have presented to Captain Kane as a mark of his (De Leuville's) flattering opinion of British seamanship generally and Captain Kane in particular.*
>
> *"Not content with this, the Marquis has written and had printed a copy of some doggerel verses, surmounted by a pictorial representation of his medal, and this effusion he is sending by post to officers of the British navy, accompanied by a four-column notice and a picture of himself from a publication called The Elocutionist."*

The text seems to suggest the presentation to have already been made, which was impossible in 1889 with Kane in Australia. I think it is the style of the time and can be read as *to be* presented. Things got little better throughout the article, which finished with this masterly, if exceedingly disparaging, assessment of the Marquis:

> *"De Leuville is a familiar figure at a number of third-rate clubs, and occasionally finds his way, I regret to say, into the St. George's. His personal appearance is as remarkable as his achievements, suggesting a happy blend between Oscar Wilde at his worst and a frowsy French cook. Oil seems to exude from every pore of the man's complacent countenance, whilst in dress and manner he affects the ducal Bohemian. Stories about the Marquis are almost as numerous as the hairs of his superb moustache, but as he set most of them afloat himself, they lack authenticity."*

This chap's full handle is (supposedly) the resplendent William Redivivus Oliver de Lorncourt, Marquis de Leuville. I have read the first poem in his work *Entre-Nous*, entitled *"To Florence"* and just managed to avoid being physically sick; I haven't had the stomach to go any further yet. An account of his life is available on Amazon as a Kindle e-Book.

<u>Captain Henry Coey Kane, RN.</u>

Henry Coey Kane had been born in the Booterstown area of Dublin on 15th December 1843 into one of the most influential Catholic families in Ireland. His father was the celebrated Research Scientist, Sir Robert Kane (1809-1890), a Fellow of the Royal Society and a strongly minded Irishman who had served on the Irish Relief Commissioners board set up in the 1850s to investigate and recommend the best way to minimise the disastrous effects of the Irish potato blight that was to decimate so many families on the island. Sir Robert, the only Catholic member, never attended a single meeting of the body which has since been criticised for its ineffectiveness, though those members of the commission who did attend seem to me to have tried hard to alleviate the want caused by the disease, in what was effectively an unwinnable situation.

Kane's father (knighted in 1856) had, in that same year which saw his son's birth, written a book which is still considered one of the most influential in the history of Irish independence: "*The Industrial Resources of Ireland*". Kane's mother Katharine (*nee* Bailey) was a noted botanist and writer in her own right, having produced amongst her various titles the well received "*Irish Fauna*", a book on botany used as a class-book in Trinity College. It was said that a misdirected proof of one of her works had been despatched by the printer to Sir Robert in error, and that it was his returning the manuscript to her personally which made their initial introduction.

The name *Kane*, along with *O'Kane*, is an anglicised version of the Gaelic *Ó Catháin* which seems to derive from a powerful family in the twelfth-century who took in battle a large area of what is now known as Co. Derry in Ulster.

As a child, Henry Coey Kane shared the house in Gloucester Street, Dublin, with no less than eight siblings, many of whom achieved prominence in their various chosen careers.

Educated at the prestigious Castleknock College located just a few miles west of Dublin city centre and still in existence today, it was on the 6th March 1858 that fourteen-year-old Henry first joined HMS *Illustrious* as a naval cadet. Within a few months he transferred to HMS *Brunswick* and was soon made Midshipman. A spell on HMS *Melpomene* was followed by him joining HMS *Defence* on 21st March 1863 with promotion to Sub-Lieutenant coming in July that same year and full Lieutenant the year following, and transfer to HMS *Victoria and Albert*. Time was then spent on HM Ships *Excellent, Hector, Excellent* again (as third Lieutenant) and

Caledonia before he joined HMS *Lord Warden* on 26th November 1870.

During his time on this vessel, Kane was the author of the reports which first appear to have brought him to the specific attention of their Lordships; those august gentlemen expressing their satisfaction at a "*... clear and able report on fortification of Cadiz...*" and later in February 1874 the "*Report on Fortifications of Carthagena.*"

A short spell on HMS *Duke of Wellington* was followed by HMS *Volage* in July 1874 and in January 1877, Kane was promoted to Commander. In August 1879, Kane was one of the Committee Members for the Gunnery Manual re-write, something which would later be noted for his "*...care, accuracy and great ability shown...*"

Later that year, Kane was transferred to HMS *Northumberland*, the sixth of eight to carry this illustrious name, and in December 1880 he was "*...strongly recommended for promotion by Captain [???] who gives high testament to his abilities and zeal...*"; unfortunately, the Captain's name on a fold in the record is quite unreadable to me, but may be Captain George Stanley Bosanquet. Kane's excellence in French and Italian, and fair abilities in German and Spanish, led to him being marked out as "*... a very good officer in every way...*" by his C-in-C. It was probably after being described even more fulsomely as "*...in every way well acquainted with his duties which are well performed: an officer of very considerable attainment in the theory as well as practice of his profession...*" and "*...strongly recommended for advancement, an officer of great ability & judgement, zealous and able...*" that led to Kane being involved in some exciting adventures in Egypt.

In the autumn of 1882, Kane joined HMS *Alexandra*, missing the bombardment of the town of Alexandria by that vessel and that WIT had experienced whilst on HMS *Sultan* on 11th July of that year, but nevertheless being engaged in some important land actions with the Naval Brigade in the latter part of 1882 as part of the British attempts to secure and retain control of the Suez Canal. By coincidence, the Captain of HMS *Alexandra* was Charles Hotham, WIT's old captain from HMS *Charybdis* those years before.

On the 20th August 1882, Kane was in command of the British party that attacked and seized Lock Weir at Ismailia. He was wounded in this action; I have been unable to ascertain precisely how, and I can only assume it to have been reasonably minor, as within a week, he and his forces captured the railway station at a nearby town. These exploits earned him praise from Captain Robert Fitzroy, the Captain of HMS *Orion* and the commander of the Naval Brigade in the area.

After an attack on 28th August by forces under Arabi Pasha (also Ahmed 'Urabi) on the small village of Kassassin (and its important Canal Lock) about 22 miles west of Ismailia had been repulsed by the British forces stationed there, Kane was sent as part of the reinforcements, and distinguished himself in the successful defence against the second, more determined attack on the 9th & 10th of September. This battle was particularly fierce, intended by 'Urabi as an attempt to regain control of at least part of the canal, and significant British forces were lost, though they were ultimately successful in driving off the Egyptian "rebels", mainly due to some very fortunate last minute reinforcement.

Within just a couple of days, General Garnet Wolseley commanding the British forces decided to attack Ahmed 'Urabi at the town of Tel-El-Kebir (roughly: *"The Great Mound"*) and the last remaining defence for the rebels before Cairo. The town protected the north side of the Sweetwater Canal and the railway that linked Ismailia with Cairo, so was a critical part of the rebel plans. Personal reconnaissance by Wolseley allowed him to identify weaknesses in the defence, and the attack launched early on the 12th September was a resounding success, though some small sections of the Egyptians showed dogged and brave resistance before being overwhelmed. Kane was part of this assault, and British forces were later able to enter Cairo with no opposition. The assault on the position at Tel-El-Kebir, led bravely by men of the Black Watch as part of the Highland Brigade, began at 4.55 a.m.; by 6.30 a.m. the railway station and many trains had been captured, only the engines escaping down the track, and by 7 a.m. the weary troops were partaking of an uninterrupted victory breakfast, surrounded by thousands of camels and vast amounts of the rebel army's stores. A great victory that effectively ended the rebel opposition, though not achieved without heavy cost to the British forces.

'Urabi had fled the rout at Tel-El-Kebir, but realising he had failed in his rebellion, gave himself up to British Cavalry, and was eventually exiled to Ceylon (now Sri Lanka). A few days later, Kane was involved with the attack on forces still dug in at Zagazig 15 miles to the east of Tel-El-Kebir, another town on the branch of the canal near Ismailia. Captain Fitzroy would repeat and reinforce his praise and thanks for this officer's efforts in a letter to the naval command dated 17th September 1882 and recorded in Kane's service record.

On the 30th September, the Naval Brigade was singularly honoured for its work in this campaign, as being the first to receive the cheers at the magnificent Cairo victory parade in front of the newly reinstated Khedive, Tawfik Pasha.

After 19 years of exile, 'Urabi was permitted to return to Egypt from Ceylon on 1 October 1901, and remained in his birth-country until his death on 21 September 1911.

In November 1882, Kane joined HMS *Euphrates*, and was promoted to Captain in recognition of his services in the operations in Egypt. At the start of 1883, he was made Naval Attaché.

The British influence in Egypt so gained was to last until Gamel Abdel Nasser and the crisis in 1956 that again revolved around the Suez Canal. And like most of my other asides, the Egyptian campaign, even the battle at Tel-El-Kebir itself, are the subjects of a great many books that go into far greater detail than I could possibly match within these pages.

On 23rd January 1885, Kane's appointment as Naval attaché was extended for 1 year from the 8th, and again for another year from 1886. In February of that year, his mother died in Dublin. On 1st February 1887, their Lordships approval was expressed of the zeal and energy displayed as Naval Attaché, and stated he had performed his duties in a thoroughly able manner. The diplomacy gained, learned, perhaps just enhanced by his time in this position would soon come in very useful. Their Lordships appreciation of the valuable information contained in his reports, for example, was conveyed to him regularly, but Kane wanted command of a ship, and by then their Lordships had found one for him.

Kane also made a reputation for himself as a straight talker. He was an outspoken critic of the education system for British Naval officers, regularly attesting to his belief that officers in other nation's navies out-performed those in the British navy, particularly in the languages and sciences. It was reported in a parliamentary debate (House of Commons Debate 17th March 1887 volume 312 cc642) that he had stated:

> *"In certain of the Foreign Navies, the officers from 20 to 30 — that is, the sub-lieutenants and the lieutenants — are better educated, and, I think, are better officers, taking them all round, than ours are."*

Captain Henry Coey Kane left *Calliope* at the end of the commissioning voyage on 1st May 1890 and after a few weeks on half pay, for a short while became, as Lord Hamilton stated in the House, the commanding officer of Barnaby's HMS *Inflexible*. In 1891, he was gazetted a CB (Military Division of Third Class) followed by a highly prestigious move that reflected how well Kane was regarded in Naval circles: on the 20th March 1892, he was appointed Captain of HMS *Victory* at Portsmouth, a post he retained until 19th April 1894 joining an illustrious group of officers in that commission. Kane's Service Record gives the dates for this commission as

29th December 1891 to 19th February 1894. He was also Flag Captain to the Commander in Chief for the re-commission of HMS *Duke of Wellington*, one of the most magnificent wooden naval vessels ever constructed. A period of temporary service at the Admiralty followed, as Director of Naval Ordnance and Torpedoes on a remuneration of £150 per year, a post he held for three years until his successor was eventually appointed.

Kane was made Rear-Admiral on Boxing Day 1897, and was placed on the Navy's Retired List at his own request on the 25th August 1899, receiving retired pay of £650 per year, and having served slightly more than one year as junior and almost exactly 35 years as senior, committee, and whilst on half pay. In May 1903, he was made Vice-Admiral, and full Admiral in February 1907. He seems to have spent his declining years at St John Stoke, Guildford, England. He was made Knight Commander of the Bath in 1911 and died on 30th January 1917. His unmarried sister, Florence Elise Kane, was the sole executrix of his will, which amounted to the princely gross value of £3,172 9s 11d.

I have found no record of Kane ever marrying, but like the archaeologists, I must be careful not to confuse *"absence of evidence"* with *"evidence of absence"*. Just because I can find no record does not mean it didn't happen, though the balance of probability is that Kane remained a life-long bachelor. Kane's will is held at the National Probate Office.

Lieutenant Robert Kyle McAlpine

Of Kane's officers at Samoa, the First Lieutenant, Robert Kyle McAlpine, whom Kane described as "...*a zealous and hard-working officer with an admirable temper...*", joined HMS *Immortalité* in July 1890 and was promoted to Captain at the end of 1896, and Rear-Admiral in November 1906. He died in Hove, Sussex, of multiple sclerosis and complications on 22nd September 1923 aged 72 years.

Staff Engineer Henry George Bourke

Staff Engineer Henry George Bourke had been born 24th October 1844 in Devonport, the only child of Michael Bourke, an Irish seaman, and Mary Ann Odgers of Plymouth. Henry married Amelia Campbell, daughter of an Irish coastguard who had several postings in England. Fleet Engineer Bourke's career included joining, on 2nd March 1882, HMS *Sultan*, the battleship on which WIT was also serving at the time. On 16th August 1886, Bourke joined HMS *Calliope* for her commissioning voyage during which time he was promoted to Staff Engineer (16th October 1887), then Fleet Engineer 28th May 1889. After *Calliope*'s return to England, he left the ship and after various duties on a number of ships, on 1st January

1896, he joined HMS *Victory* based at Portsmouth. Fleet Engineer Bourke died on 5th March 1898 in the Royal Naval Hospital Haslar of pneumonia.

Lieutenant Henry Pearson (1852?-1936)

Lieutenant (later Captain) Henry Pearson was born around 1852 at Darjeeling, West Bengal, his father being a member of the Bengal Civil Service. Pearson was invalided from the Royal Navy in 1897 due to poor eyesight, and moved with his wife and daughter to St. James's Lane, Winchester, Hampshire, England. He became an active member of the cathedral's congregation, and died as noted below. A memorial in Winchester Cathedral, Hampshire reads:

> *"In memory of Henry Pearson Captain RN of this city who died 17 August 1936 aged 84. He was navigating officer when HMS Calliope (Capt. H C Kane) was brought out of Apia Harbour in Samoa in the hurricane of 16th March 1889."*

So even nearly 50 years afterwards, the event was still considered worthy of remembrance. The author's parents lived for many years in Winchester, but they do not seem to have known of the memorial.

Lieutenant Pearson, along with Lieutenant McAlpine, were most vociferous in urging Captain Kane to get full steam up, slip the anchors and force his way out of the bay before it was too late.

Lieutenant (later General) Alfred E. Marchant (1863-1924)

Lieutenant Alfred E. Marchant, Royal Marine Light Infantry commanding *Calliope's* marines, distinguished himself during the Boer War when as Captain he took command of the Naval Brigade whilst under intense enemy fire during the famous battle at Graspan Heights (1900), following which he was promoted Major. In October 1914, he was Senior Brigade Officer with the rank of Colonel of the Naval Brigade, and later that same year was an attendee at the funerals of some of the sailors from HMS *Bulwark*, representing the Royal Marines in that sad duty.

HMS *Bulwark* mysteriously blew up on the morning of the 26th November 1914 whilst moored at Sheerness, it was assumed the result of an accidental magazine detonation. But being so soon after the declaration of war with Germany, speculation that sabotage was the cause was rife at the time, and continues in some minds to this day.

Colonel Alfred Edmund Marchant was appointed one of two Marine Aides-de-Camp to His Majesty, King George V on 12th October, 1910.

Marchant's obituary from London Times Weekly, 31st January 1924 states:

"We regret to announce that Major-General Marchant, CBRMLI (retired) died of pneumonia at Ospedaleti, Ligure, Italy on Jan. 21st at the age of sixty-nine. The son of Mr William Lavington Marchant of Adelaide, South Australia, where he was born on Feb. 26th 1863, he entered the Royal Marines as a probationary lieutenant in September 1881, and was posted to the RMLI. He was promoted to Captain in August 1890, Major in Nov. 1899, brevet Lt. Col. in Dec 1907, brevet Colonel June 1910, and Colonel and Commandant in Jan.1911. In the Great War he served with the R M Brigade during the defence of Antwerp in October 1914. In April 1915, he was appointed to command the Chatham Division RMLI with the temporary rank of Brigadier-General and held the appointment until April 1918. In the following August he was placed on the retired list with the honorary rank of Major-General. General Marchant served with the Royal Marine Battalion at Suakin from July 1884 to April 1885 and was present at the actions of Hasheen and Tofrek, and was wounded in the attack on McNeills zariba, receiving the Egyptian Medal with two clasps and the Khedive Bronze Star. As a lieutenant he commanded the Royal Marine detachment of HMS Calliope and was serving in her when she made her wonderful escape from the hurricane in the harbour of Apia, Samoa, under the command of Captain H C Kane, RN. In the South African War {Anglo-Boer War}, he served throughout with the Naval Brigade. After the action of Graspan he brought the Naval Brigade out of action and was promoted to Major. He was present at the actions of Belmont, Modder River, Magersfontein, PaardEberg, Osfontein, the capture of Bloemfontein, the

entry into Pretoria, and the actions at Diamond Hill and Bergendal, being three times mentioned in despatches and awarded the CB and the Queen's Medal with seven clasps. From 1904 to 1906 he served again in Australia and was ADC to the King from 1910 to 1918. General Marchant married in 1890 Mary C Homersham, and secondly in 1897 Edith Mary Turner, who survives him with two daughters."

Actually he was aged 60 when he died, not 69 as stated.

Boatswain William Marshfield

Calliope's Boatswain, William Marshfield, was not finished with the navy after Samoa, nor was he finished with excitement and danger. He joined HMS *Victoria* in the same capacity, and was on board the navy's newest and most powerful battleship when she carried the flag of Vice-Admiral Sir George Tryon, Commander-in-Chief of the Mediterranean Fleet. During manoeuvres on 22nd June 1893 off Tripoli, two parallel lines of dreadnoughts, headed on the right by *Victoria* and on the left by HMS *Camperdown* carrying the flag of the famous polar explorer, Rear-Admiral Sir Albert Hastings Markham (1841 – 1918), were heading slightly north of east separated by some 1,200 yards of sea (6 cables). Intending to reverse the steaming direction of the fleet, the ships were inexplicably ordered by Tryon to execute a change of course that would likely result in the sinking of every vessel in the fleet! Both lines of the squadron were ordered to make a 180° change of direction by each making an *inward* turn towards each other, but with clearly insufficient room for the manoeuvre to work. Of all the ships in the fleet, *Camperdown* was the only one to repeat the order at the dip, the accepted manner by which a captain of a vessel could advise his commanding officer that the order had been read, but not understood.

Whilst composing his own message to explain his concerns, Markham was dismayed and embarrassed by Tryon hoisting a new signal: *"What are we waiting for?"* – a somewhat public rebuke from a Commander-in-Chief to an Admiral under his command. Waiting no longer, the original message was hoisted as a return, and at a little after 3.30 p.m. Tryon signalled the order to be executed, despite his own officers urgently telling the Admiral of the danger. Inexorably the lead ships made their turn towards each other. After completing some 120° of turn only, the inevitable occurred, and *Camperdown* buried its bow and underwater ram deep into the starboard forward side of the flagship; the two vessel's speed then pivoted the ships around each other and the gaping hole was enlarged to a chasm. Even then, with an immediate list to port surely signalling the end of his command, Tryon seemed unaware of the reality of the disaster, rejecting offers of boats from other ships, preferring to direct his vessel to try and beach on some land about four and a half miles away. The distance was far too great for the mortally damaged vessel, and just a few minutes later, HMS *Victoria* capsized, and an internal explosion burst the hull as it proceeded to dive to the bottom of the Mediterranean, taking Tryon and any possible explanation of his actions with her, along with hundreds of her crew.

Some analysts believe the antagonism already evident between the two men had led Tryon to engineer a situation to embarrass or confuse Markham, supported by the existence of a letter written by Tryon only days earlier, the gist of which stated that officers have a duty to ignore a peacetime order that would clearly place their vessel in extreme risk. So was it a simple test, and should Markham have disobeyed this clearly dangerous order? Or should he have observed the universal rule of the Royal Navy not to cut across a superior officer, and to make his turn at a wider radius to pass outside the Commanding Officer, again in contradiction to his orders? Should he have ignored Tryon's abrupt final signal, and defended himself against any possible future recrimination by completing his signal to the Vice-Admiral that in his opinion, the order was extremely dangerous?

Perhaps the ingrained centuries of naval training to unquestionably obey a superior officer's orders, come what may, was just too much for Markham. Whatever might have been the reasons, more than 350 men and the best and most modern British warship in the Mediterranean theatre were gone in moments. Markham did not escape criticism in the subsequent enquiry, for blindly following a clearly dangerous order, but the majority of the blame was placed on Sir George Tryon, though no real explanation of his conduct was established.

William Marshfield's *Calliope* luck did not desert him on HMS *Victoria*, and he fortunately survived the disaster.

Recent dives on the enormous wreck show her to be buried bow down in the mud like an arrow, with her stern pointing vertically up to the surface of the sea. Images of the wreck can be found on the internet.

Lieutenant (Later Rear-Admiral) Arthur William Carter.

Arthur William Carter 1856-1931 was a son of Rev. Thomas Garden Carter, Vicar at Linton in Kent, and his wife Louisa, *nee* Turner. An extract from *"The Linton Estate: the property of Messrs Carter Bros."* in The Pastoral Review, Sydney, c. 1909 reads:"[He] *joined the Navy on the 15th January 1870 and was promoted sub-Lieutenant on 20th June 1875, Lieutenant 13th December*

1879, Commander 1st January 1894, Captain 30th June 1899, retiring with the rank of Captain on 28th January 1905. He was appointed Rear-Admiral on the retired list on 5th November 1908. He served with the Naval Brigade in the Soudan with the Nile Expedition for the relief of General Gordon 1884-5, and received the Egyptian medal with Nile clasp and Khedive's Grand Star. He was Lieutenant on the 'Calliope' on the occasion of the great hurricane at Apia in 1889, when that vessel, by a splendid piece of seamanship on the part of her crew, escaped the fate of most of the other warships then in the harbour. The Admiralty expressed admiration at the officers' behaviour on that occasion, and specially referred to Lieutenant Carter. He retired from the Navy in order that he might assist his brother in the management of their joint property [in northern New South Wales]."

In 1911, Carter and his wife Monica returned to Bournemouth, England where they both died in 1931.

The Midshipmen.

By the end of his life, Captain Kane will have had the satisfaction – and occasionally, the sadness – of seeing virtually all the young midshipmen with whom he had shared the Samoan adventure and on whom his calmness and daring will have had the most profound effect, progress through the navy ranks with remarkable and spectacular success, and inevitably in some cases: tragedy.

Kane had eight midshipmen with him at Apia, four of his own and four loaned from Admiral Fairfax's flagship, HMS *Orlando*; Fairfax presumably seeing the possibility of action in Apia as providing these young officers with a rare opportunity for some real-life training. Of these eight teenagers, no less than five would equal their captain's ultimate status and achieve Admiral rank, another two Captain and the other Commander. At the outbreak of the First World War, Kane and his officers had long been retired from the navy, so it was left to those midshipmen at Samoa, many of whom were already commanding vessels of their own, to shoulder arms in their country's defence.

<u>Midshipman Cecil Henry Fox.</u>

On loan from HMS *Orlando*, a stocky and robust fifteen-year-old Cecil Henry Fox was, it seems, the youngest officer on *Calliope* at Samoa, and was, like his captain, an Irishman, having been born in Monkstown on 27th May 1873. The connection made the respect the youngster had for his commanding officer almost reverence, something he would still acknowledge when writing of the events at Samoa more than 60 years later. The reader will recall it was Fox who repeatedly staggered from *Calliope's* wheelhouse to the stern and back to Kane with a breathless description of how close the ship was to the reef behind. His violent and dramatic welcome to shipboard life aboard *Calliope* at Samoa will surely have helped Fox when he later collaborated in the extensive re-writing of the *"Seamanship Manual for Boys"* whilst a Lieutenant on HMS *Impregnable*.

Shortly before the outbreak of the First World War, the now Captain Cecil Fox had been placed in command of the light cruiser HMS *Amphion* and the Third Flotilla, East Destroyer Squadron. Just hours after the declaration, the vessel left Harwich on 5th August 1914 for the first British Naval wartime patrol in the North Sea; in doing so she would become part of the first naval action of the war to exact losses on the Germans, and within a day of that success, would herself become the first British Naval casualty with considerable loss of life. It would be as dramatic an initiation into war as her crew could ever have anticipated.

The Third Destroyer Flotilla led by *Amphion* and accompanied by the destroyers *Lance* and *Landrail* had left Harwich port in the early hours of that first day of war and just before lunchtime spotted a German ferry, the *Konigin Luise* under Commander Biermann, laying mines, having been already converted by the Germans in anticipation of the expected declaration. The German vessel was sunk at about 12.22 p.m. on that first day of war by gunfire from either *Amphion*, or more likely *Lance* (actually credited with firing the first naval shell of the war from her forward gun which has since been lodged in the Imperial War Museum in London). First blood was thus to the Royal Navy, but would soon be avenged by the Germans.

Another similar vessel was sighted, the *St. Petersburg* but rather than laying mines, she was conveying the German Ambassador out of England. Engagement between the vessels commenced, but Fox, recognising the diplomatic status of the German ship and unable to attract the attention of the excited signallers on the other British vessels, took *Amphion* between those others of his group and the German, so fouling the range to prevent any further exchange of fire, and the German Ambassador continued home without any further interference. The British would not be so fortunate.

Returning to England, *Amphion* ran into one of the mines which had been laid just hours earlier by *Konigin Luise*; her engines were immediately stopped but she drifted on about a mile and a half to the north-west to run into another mine in the line. This second blow was almost immediately mortal, and she sank very rapidly by the head with the loss of nearly 150 men. Ironically, some of the casualties were the rescued German sailors from the minelayer itself, presumably confined below and therefore unable to escape; as they had watched the things disappear into the grey sea off the stern of their ship only a few hours earlier, could they have imagined that the next day some of those same devices would be the direct cause of their own deaths?

The disaster caused widespread consternation in the British Admiralty. At first, the response was to say nothing, a terse and blunt instruction being the subject of an internal telegram from the censor D. Browning to the Seaman's Enquiry Office on the 6th:

> *"I have received strict instructions that the incident you saw me about is NOT to get out to the press - I look to you to see that it does not get out through your office."*

The underlines are Mr. Browning's, though I have not corroborated that the *"incident"* he was so concerned about was indeed the actual sinking and not something associated with it. Obviously it could not be hidden for long, and it was certainly a sobering event for a nation embarking on its first full naval war in more than one hundred years to lose a major vessel and so many lives on just the second day.

A detailed and exhaustive investigation was made in the subsequent enquiry as to whether the explosions were a result of the mine or the ignition of leaking internal oil fuel. It was concluded the first explosion was the mine which severely damaged the fore part of the ship having exploded under the bridge, and the second was also a mine which almost immediately detonated one of the ship's magazines, and caused the vessel to sink within seconds. It was decided the leaking oil had not been heated sufficiently to cause or contribute to the second conflagration.

Fox survived the disaster though was badly burned, spending some time in hospital at Shotley. Despite his injuries, just a couple of months later, he was in command of HMS *Undaunted*, and in company with destroyers *Lance*, *Loyal*, *Legion* and *Lennox*, sank four German mine-laying torpedo boats on 17th October 1914 in an action in the Thames Estuary which was considered "*...most creditable...*" Fox's Naval Service record suggests these were destroyers, but I rather think they were indeed torpedo boats. On 29th March 1916, he married Eleanora Isabella Somerville in London, and was invested with his CB at Buckingham Palace on 26th June 1918; he eventually achieved the rank of Rear-Admiral, and retired in May 1922. Throughout his naval career, he received excellent commendations from his superiors, especially for his physical abilities and judgement capability. He was regularly assessed as "*...an officer of marked ability...*" and collaborated on a dramatised play about *Calliope*'s escape at Samoa, broadcast by the BBC on its Home Radio service in December 1950 and repeated in April 1951. He died in 1963 aged 90, easily the longest surviving officer from *Calliope*'s Samoan adventure.

Midshipman Wilmot Stuart Nicholson

Born 18th May 1872 in Rochester, Kent the eldest son of an Army Major, Wilmot Stuart Nicholson had been promoted to Captain in 1909 and at the outbreak of war was Flag Captain to the Vice-Admiral Commanding the 4th Battle Squadron. His career was punctuated by mostly good but some bad reports, including causing a (minor) collision which resulted in him being "*...warned to be more careful in the future...*", and "*...attention called to large number of punishments by warrant in HMS Attentive which cannot be considered satisfactory...*".

Admiral Wilmot S. Nicholson standing 2nd from right. Location believed to be HMS Curacoa c. 1929. [Public Domain]

As hostilities began, he commanded HMS *Hogue*, a venerable armoured cruiser that formed (with HMS *Euryalus*) part of the Royal Navy's Cruiser Force "C". He was mentioned in despatches for towing the heavily damaged HMS *Arethusa* out of action off the Heligoland Bight on 28th August 1914. The following month, in company with HM Ships *Aboukir* and *Cressy*, HMS *Hogue* entered the North Sea on patrol, heading for the area known as the "*Broad Fourteens*". Heavy weather had prevented the attendance of a protective destroyer screen, and this fact, coupled with an unwise but deliberate policy of ignoring the command to zigzag in submarine waters, would condemn a great many British sailors to a cold and unmarked grave.

On the 22nd September and in much improved weather, submarine *U9*, approaching from slightly west of north and commanded by Otto Weddigen, saw the three almost identical ships proceeding abreast of each other at a sedate 10 knots heading approximately north-east and couldn't believe his luck. HMS *Aboukir* in the centre, with *Cressy* on her port and *Hogue* to starboard. A well-aimed torpedo launched at 06.25 a.m. struck the *Aboukir* on her port side and stopped her dead in the water, the ship immediately beginning to list heavily and commencing to sink. Initially assuming the detonation to have been caused by a mine, Captain J. Drummond on the stricken vessel and senior officer of the group requested both the other ships to turn towards *Aboukir*, and prepare to stop and take off survivors. What happened next would generate a formal order from the British Admiralty to all capital ships whilst on patrol in potentially submarine infested waters, not to stop for any reason, not even the rescue of comrades.

U9 manoeuvred in front of the squadron and to the east, to the other side of the stricken *Aboukir* where Captain Nicholson in *Hogue*, whilst not so certain about it being a mine, may at least have felt that if it had been a torpedo, he would be protected by the fast settling wreck. *Hogue* had manoeuvred to within less than a nautical mile from *Aboukir*, when two torpedoes loosed at 300 yards range at 06.55 a.m. proved him disastrously wrong, and with one of them finding the magazine, a massive detonation mortally damaged *Hogue*. *U9* broke surface during this attack to confirm its presence should any on the British ships have still been in doubt, and was fired on by brave gunners from the sinking HMS *Hogue*, but with no discernible effect. *Hogue* disappeared under the waves within a quarter of an hour.

Despite having had the true nature of the danger confirmed, *Cressy* (Captain Johnson) continued to manoeuvre towards *Aboukir* and that third British cruiser was hit by another torpedo from *U9* at around 07.20 a.m., though it was a superficial wound only. A quarter of an hour later, Weddigen turned his submarine once more to the scene, and at close range despatched his last remaining torpedo; the German was rewarded with another heavy detonation in the remaining cruiser that would end with the sinking of that third and final member of the squadron. With many of her boats still in the water around the settling *Aboukir*, the loss of life from *Cressy* was particularly horrendous. More than 1,450 British seamen in total from the three ships paid the penalty of that disastrous patrol. Whilst many at the time thought a pack of submarines must have been responsible, and that the British had even sunk some of the attackers, there seems no real evidence for that belief. One German submarine had destroyed three British cruisers in just a few minutes.

The reasons for the patrol to be in that area were hidden underneath a mask of military secrecy, but the area was close to a known enemy submarine base, and although the earlier heavy seas would have certainly kept these threats away, the weather had recently improved; it must have been expected that the U-boats would be leaving the base for patrol and that some would surely encounter the ships. Why the cruisers had not turned back to meet up with their destroyer screen, was another question asked at the enquiry but with no satisfactory answer forthcoming.

A few hundred survivors were picked up by merchant ships and trawlers in the area, among them Captain Nicholson. Whilst his immediate superior officers were criticised, some such as Rear-Admiral Christian in command of the force in the absence of Rear-Admiral Campbell, quite severely, Nicholson seems to have been absolved of any major responsibility for the debacle. At the enquiry, Campbell surprised the board by stating he was not aware of what purpose his command was intended to serve! The main criticisms levelled at Nicholson were the failure to ensure the engine room watertight doors on HMS *Hogue* were kept closed – the fact they were partially open certainly contributed to the ship's rapid sinking; and that he stopped for survivors (albeit having been ordered to) when he must surely have suspected a possible submarine attack.

Later in the war, Nicholson would become Captain of HMS *Aurora*, in action on the Doggerbank in January 1915, and in March of that year was again mentioned in despatches concerning the efforts to tow HMS *Landrail* and *Undaunted* back to port following their collision:

> "... *their Lordships appreciation expressed of the good seamanship which enabled the two damaged ships to be brought safely into harbour under very trying conditions...*"

On several occasions, he carried out successful operations with units of the Harwich force, which culminated in him being invested with the C.B. by the King at Buckingham Palace in June 1917.

In 1920, Nicholson was made Rear-Admiral, becoming Chief of the Submarine Service between 1923 and 1925, and promoted to Vice-Admiral at the end of that service. He retired from the navy in 1927, and was made Admiral in 1930, an Officer of the Legion of Honour.

Whilst Nicholson's career up to retirement had been, with the exception of the fairly minor criticism regarding HM Ships *Attentive* and *Hogue*, almost blemish-free, he must be one of the few Admirals to receive a memorandum from the Naval Intelligence Department, recording their Lordships "...*severe displeasure...*" This memorandum – which I cannot trace for what may become obvious reasons – was written in 1941, and most likely concerns the actions of Nicholson's second wife.

In October 1899, Nicholson had married one Muriel Ellis, but they were divorced some years later, itself something that in those times the Admiralty would not have approved of. In November 1934, Nicholson married Christobel Sybil Caroline Eyre, MD. Nicholson's service record swaps some of these names around, the order quoted in this text is taken from *The Peerage*. A member of Britain's wealthy upper-middle class, she was obviously a woman of strong beliefs, though how well thought out they were, is now difficult to tell. Both the Nicholsons seem to have been beguiled into the common belief of the 1930s that National Socialism was a force for national good. In this, they were not too different to many European communities; between the wars fascism was seen as a reasonable alternative to the growing perceived curse of communism. In 1936, the year of the abdication of Edward VIII in England, the Nicholsons travelled to Berlin as guests of the German government, and were introduced to Herr Hitler, who clearly made a very favourable impression on the Admiral's wife, at least. This admiration is easy to castigate today with our hindsight of the true reality of Nazism, but at the time Hitler was indeed viewed by many as Germany's saviour, and a good model for similar saviours around Europe; Mussolini in Italy, and Moseley in the UK being prominent among them.

Christobel, or Caroline Nicholson was an ardent supporter of Prime Minister Chamberlain, and viewed the *"Peace In Our Time"* deal at Munich in 1938 as a triumph for British politics and German innate honesty and goodness. By early 1940, the phoney war with Germany was leading many to suppose that Germany too would rather desire Great Britain to have remained neutral.

At the outbreak of the Second World War, the Nicholsons were already under investigation by Britain's Secret Service, MI6. Perhaps the Berlin visit was one reason; another was the subscription by Caroline to the *"New Germany"*, a Nazi publication in the late thirties. It had also become clear that the Nicholsons were associates of a well-known fascist sympathiser in the UK, the Conservative politician Captain Ramsay. A member of the *"Right Club"* which effectively described its political leaning as well as being seen as an amusing pun, he seems to have introduced the Admiral and his wife to membership, something vehemently denied by the Nicholsons. Much was later made by MI6 of the purchase by Caroline of a uniform intended for the female members of the club; her rather tame explanation was that she thought it was a cocktail dress that her husband had admired when worn by the female members of the club during friendly visits, and that she had wanted one for herself only to please him.

Also a member of the Right Club was one Anna Workoff, a distant relative by marriage to Nicholson himself. She was a far more active fascist, and the one to cause the real trouble. In early 1940, she, and an American Embassy worker called Tyler Kent, somehow obtained some sensitive information from the Embassy. Bizarrely, Anna showed the documents to Mrs. Nicholson.

Even the files recently released after 60 years of closure are cagey on the content, but it seems to be two main (though utterly separate) items. Firstly, and the thing guaranteed to set Caroline's fervour ablaze, was information regarding Churchill (then First Lord of the Admiralty) and Roosevelt, the American President. The data from early 1939 appeared to describe the leasing of destroyers for the coming war, and made it clear that both men believed that American participation in a war not yet started was inevitable, even perhaps, desirable. Mrs. Nicholson saw in this a denigration of Mr. Chamberlain, and perhaps even an attempt by Churchill to force war on the country against the best efforts of Chamberlain to prevent it. There was also much made at the time of Churchill being strongly influenced by his Jewish American mother.

Caroline's reaction was that such perfidy on the part of Churchill must be brought out in the open so that punishment could be instigated. It was vital to her that Mr. Chamberlain, or even the King, should be informed. As a first step, she copied the documents in her own hand.

The other document was the military thinking behind the Norwegian Expeditionary Force, which would undoubtedly have given the enemy much very useful information. It was this realization that seems finally to have jolted Mrs. Nicholson into an understanding of her risky position, and scared her into confiding to her husband what had occurred. It is reported a most heated quarrel between the couple ensued, culminating in the Admiral demanding the documents be destroyed. If he was so angry, why did he not simply take them and put them on the fire himself? As it happened, Mrs. Nicholson took the extraordinary step of placing her copies in an envelope and passing them to their housekeeper to take home for safe keeping, instructing her that if she was asked, then all she knew was that the envelope contained Admiral Nicholson's will! Turning up a few minutes late the next day for work, the housekeeper was asked by an edgy Mrs. Nicholson whether the police had been after her for the documents, and told her to bury the envelope in the garden! The housekeeper, understandably becoming alarmed at such ridiculous instructions from her highly nervous employer, that night opened the packet, was herself scared by what she found, and decided to take the contents to the police the next day.

Initially, the authorities could not, of course, verify if the data was a hoax or real, being a handwritten copy. But fairly soon, MI6 and the Americans confirmed the content to be substantially correct, a warrant to search the Nicholson's flat at 8 Ashburn Gardens, SW7 was sworn out, and following the discovery of a lot of apparently pro-German material, the lady was formally arrested under section 18(b) of the Defence Regulations. The charge sheet sworn out on 22nd April in The King v. Christobel Sybil Caroline Nicholson lists 4 counts of obtaining or recording information which might be directly or indirectly useful to an enemy, contrary to Section 1 (1) (c) of the Official Secrets Act 1911, and Regulation 3 of the Defence (General) Regulations 1939.

Police and MI6 records clearly show that the British authorities were totally convinced that the Admiral had always been fully aware of his wife's actions, but seem to have been unable to prove it.

At her trial, and since she was so patently guilty, her defence made no effort to refute the evidence and only offered the character of someone easily led, and despite her qualifications, someone fairly stupid in the ways of the world: take note of her ridiculous attempts to hide the documents with her housekeeper! So it was a surprise to all when the jury, confused by some unclear direction from the judge, found her *Not Guilty*! The security services were having none of that, and immediately re-arrested her as she left the court. She spent many months in Holloway awaiting further trial, or even charge, until she was reluctantly released in the later months of the war when her danger to Britain was felt to be low. Even in prison, she devoted herself to supporting the generally hopeless causes of a number of women languishing with her in Pentonville, but eventually she was worn down by the relentless regime and her health suffered badly.

The couple spent the rest of their lives in the condition of having to obtain approval for any change of address, and to report to the local police stations on a regular basis. It is no wonder, perhaps, that their Lordships had found it necessary to express their displeasure at the situation!

In January 1946, Nicholson was one of a number of founder subscribing members of "The Forces Pension Society Limited" intended to promote and improve the pensions of retired forces personnel. He died 9th June 1947. His widow continued to exchange correspondence with members of the many fascist organisations that still flourished in Britain, even seemingly becoming more open about it now that she was no longer under the restraining influence of her husband, and continued to be under the watchful eye of the security service for the rest of her life.

For what it is worth, my belief is that Caroline Nicholson was a vocal supporter of the fascists, and certainly anti-Semitic, who felt that the American-Jew Churchill had forced the nation into a war with a country who should have been good friends with Britain in the fight against Communism. But in truth, I think she was rather a weak person, who liked the idea of her politics far more than the reality. Membership of the Right Club was a thrill for her, especially when she could cite a personal meeting with Herr Hitler to the sort of society it attracted. Why did Anna Workoff show her the documents? It wasn't part of the plot, since they had been shown already to an MI5 agent within the Right Club, Joan Miller, and had also been passed to Duco del Monte, the Assistant Naval Attaché at the Italian Embassy who had them transmitted to Wilhelm Canaris in Berlin. Perhaps Anna was simply exciting her glamorous friend, and Caroline perhaps did hope to embarrass Churchill at some future point. Whilst the affair has been investigated thoroughly and a number of hefty books written on the subject, Caroline's role has always been documented as trivial and I think in reality that is exactly what it was. Her ludicrous attempts at hiding the documents with her housekeeper suggest a person exceedingly naive in the ways of espionage.

For a very interesting read about the fascinating Joan Miller and her espionage exploits, search out her autobiography *"One Girl's War: Personal Exploits in MI5's Most Secret Station"*, published in Ireland in 1986. You'll wonder how MI5 found out, or kept, anything secret! Joan Miller died in 1984.

Midshipman Sidney Robert Drury-Lowe

Sidney Robert Drury-Lowe (born 19th October 1871) was part of an immensely powerful family on both his parent's sides. His father was Colonel Robert Henry Curzon Drury-Lowe and his mother, the Colonel's first wife, Ellen Senhouse. Sidney and his elder sister Florence spent much of their early childhood in great splendour at the Senhouse ancestral home Nether Hall near Maryland in Cumberland. He had a rather topsy-turvy naval career, though not as unusual as Nicholson's had been. Mentioned in despatches for his services in the Somaliland Expedition 1903-4 and graded as "...*very efficient*..." during the Inspection of HMS *Hyacinth* in 1905, he also received the unfavourable comment:

> "...*as second-in-command of the Barracks* [at Portsmouth] *has failed in the performance of his duties as Executive Officer and will be superseded...*"

One has to wonder if personality clashes sometimes made their appearance in these reports, and the rather damning comment doesn't seem to have put any blight on his command career. In 1908, Drury Lowe was Commander on the 14,900 ton HMS *Magnificent* under Captain E. F. B. Charlton., and a 1909 recommendation by Rear-Admiral Pearse, for example, strongly urged promotion.

At the declaration, Drury-Lowe was the Captain of HMS *Chatham*, a 5,400-ton fast light cruiser. The British were keen to locate a German light cruiser, the 3,400-ton, 23½ knot SMS *Königsberg*, launched in December 1905. Her speed and powerful armament of ten 10.5 cm (4¼ inch) and eight 5.2 cm (2 inch) guns, and two 18 inch torpedo tubes, made her a significant threat to the shipping routes in the East Asia theatre and Australian waters where she was thought to be based.

The true whereabouts of SMS *Königsberg* were eventually revealed by her attack on and eventual sinking of the British light *Pelorus* class cruiser HMS *Pegasus* on 19th/20th September 1914 in Zanzibar harbour near what was then German East Africa, where the German vessel was station ship at Dar-es-Salaam. Trapped in the port, the British ship was cleaning her boilers and her engines were in the process of being overhauled, so with no way of getting under way or manoeuvre lasted not very long in the engagement. To my mind, German spies in Zanzibar had alerted their masters to the fact that the British cruiser was undergoing the servicing and would therefore be virtually defenceless.

In response, the British Admiralty arranged a concentration of fast cruisers to conduct a thorough and prolonged search which on 30th October resulted in *Königsberg* being discovered by HMS *Chatham*, the German hiding in shoal water about six miles up the Rufigi River Delta, opposite Mafia Island. Owing to her greater draught, *Chatham* could not reach the German, which was probably aground herself excepting at high water.

Part of the crew of *Königsberg* had clearly been landed ashore and was well-established on the banks of the river. Both the entrenchment and the German cruiser were bombarded next day by *Chatham*, but owing to the dense palm groves amid which the German ship lay, it was not possible to estimate whether any damage might have been caused. It was certainly close enough to encourage the German cruiser to move even further up river on the 1st November, where it was well out-of-range of *Chatham*'s six-inch breech loaders. The German vessel remained blockaded in the river and was eventually scuttled by her crew in July 1915 having been effectively neutralised and severely damaged by gunfire from HMS *Severn* a few days earlier.

A 1976 film starring Roger Moore and Lee Marvin entitled "*Shout at the Devil*" dramatising the Wilbur Smith novel of the same name, appears to me to have been based (somewhat loosely) on these events, but that might simply be coincidence.

Just prior to this engagement, which was considered a well conceived action, *Chatham* had grounded at Mombasa early in the morning of 2nd October 1914, the ship needing to have all its ammunition, fuel and as much else that could be taken off, before HMS *Banffshire's* pull and the *Chatham*'s engines at full astern finally managed to get her off the Leven Reef at the high tide the next day. Fortunately, diver inspection over the next few days proved her hull to have suffered no damage. Drury-Lowe was reprimanded gently, and told to "...*exercise greater care in future...*" Whilst in command of HMS *Zealandia* in February 1917, a collision between that ship and HMS *Commonwealth* in what Drury-Lowe admitted was "...*an error of judgement...*" meant he was again "...*cautioned to be more careful in the future...*"

Drury-Lowe had married Clare Susan Charteris in November 1909. He was made a Companion of the Order of Saint Michael and Saint George in June 1916 for his services to the War effort. He stood as an Independent candidate for the Westminster Abbey constituency in the General Election of November 1922 but failed to dent the traditional Conservative majority, who were known at the time as the "Unionist Party". He died on 24th January 1945 as Vice-Admiral.

Midshipman Frank Brandt

Frank Brandt was born on 2nd October 1871 the son of Francis Brandt, of the Indian Civil Service (a Judge in the High Court, Madras), and Lucy Sophia (nee Dobson) in Cheltenham. He seems to have been raised by a maiden Aunt, Miss E.C. Brandt in Torquay. His service record suggests the abode of this Aunt was in Saint Rocque, Jersey, Channel Islands, but his great-granddaughter assures me that Saint Rocque was in fact the name of the house in Torquay, England.

His early naval career record was exemplary: "...*very zealous officer...*", "...*thoroughly recommended for promotion...*", "...*very clever, attentive, capable and zealous...*", "...*excellent zeal and judgement...*" He seems to have invented an improved gyroscope for which he received much appreciation and recognition. His management of the Torpedo Flotilla "... *deserved great credit ...*" a phrase repeated on more than one occasion as he progressed through the officer ranks. In October 1910, his application to retire was refused, it being deemed inadvisable for him to take his considerable experience and fine skills out of the service. His only career blemish, and one in which we have already seen he was not alone, was the grounding of HMS *Maidstone* in 1912 for which he was "...*admonished...*"

In July 1914, Brandt was placed in command of HMS *Monmouth*, 9,800 tons; another slow, ageing, under-armed vessel of a bygone era (launched in 1901), which formed part of the West Indies Squadron under the flag of Rear-Admiral, Sir Christopher Cradock. The fleet included the 14,150 ton HMS *Good Hope* (the flagship, launched a few months earlier than *Monmouth*) and the more modern HMS *Glasgow*, 4,900 tons launched 1910 and commanded by Captain John Luce. Both the main capital ships were crewed in the main by inexperienced raw sailors and boys, and were so badly designed that much of their weaponry was unusable in any sort of sea except a dead calm; such conditions are rarely to be found in the southern oceans of the world. The ships were old-fashioned examples of poor design and were typical of the worst sort of vessel the Royal Navy had equipped itself with during all those years of peace since 1815. *Monmouth* in particular was crewed almost exclusively by ex-Scottish fishermen and reservists, including at least one former *Calliope* crewmember, Able Seaman James Spiller of Sedbury, Devon. He had first joined the Navy at age 16 and was loaned to *Calliope* from HMS *Orlando* for Samoa. He left the Navy in May 1900 for the coastguard service, but re-enlisted at the outbreak of the First World War; like nearly all his shipmates, *Monmouth* was his first posting.

The British fleet was sailing in the southern Pacific, searching out the German East Asiatic Squadron, a task force comprised of the armoured cruisers *Scharnhorst* and *Gneisenau* both 11,420 tons and launched in 1907/8, and the light cruisers *Dresden*, *Leipzig*, and *Nürnberg* all around 3,500 tons and launched between 1906 and 1908. The latter vessel was a sister ship of SMS *Königsberg* that we have already encountered. The German squadron under Vice-Admiral Maximilian Johannes Maria Hubertus von Spee had moved from Asia when Japan entered the war on the allied side, and had headed for South America to operate against British shipping in that area.

In an interesting coincidence, during its voyage across the Pacific, the German squadron approached Apia Harbour on Upolu in October 1914 hoping to find the battleship HMAS *Australia* present, and if not that, exact revenge for the annexation of the island by New Zealand at the start of the war. Von Spee was very concerned that the battleship alone might constitute an equal match to his entire squadron. *Scharnhorst* and *Gneisenau* approached the tiny bay to find it empty, and instead a garrison of soldiers from the New Zealand Wellington Regiment gallantly lining up on the dock, prepared to trade their rifle bullets with the ship's shells. It seems that only the presence of German owned buildings behind the soldiers prevented the regiment from being destroyed, and von Spee eventually took his ships back out to sea after a tense couple of hours of stand-off. Though von Spee missed her by a week, we'll encounter the Australian ship a little later on.

At the outbreak of the war, German Samoa was, as implied, *"owned"* by Germany and the trading stores were almost universally owned by German nationals, but the New Zealand Naval Forces had quickly despatched troops and the first warship of the naval group, HMS *Philomel*, to take the islands, meeting with no resistance. They would stay for many years until Samoa was granted independence in June 1962; the first Pacific island group to achieve this.

As did their officers, the untried crews of Cradock's ships knew in their hearts that they would be in for a difficult time should they eventually find their quarry, and at around 5 p.m. on a blustery 1st November 1914 just 35 miles or so to the west off the coast of Chile near Coronel, the fleet was heading just east of north when at last they encountered that powerful and far more modern German fleet coming towards them from the north. The ensuing battle, the first fleet action for the Royal Navy for a hundred years, was a disaster for the British.

Von Spee too knew that Cradock's squadron was significantly weaker than his own. Whilst in the hostile, though supposedly neutral port of Coronel Bay, Luce on HMS *Glasgow* had picked up strong radio transmissions with the same call sign – that of SMS *Leipzig*. Returning to the fleet with the telegrams and messages, he shared this intelligence with his Admiral, and Cradock saw a rare chance of picking off at least one enemy ship, since weakening the German fleet one ship at a time seemed to be his best chance of success. In chasing down the *Leipzig*, Cradock was successfully lured into the path of von Spee's entire squadron.

Although Cradock had conceived a plan where he was going to trap *Leipzig* on her own, it seems the German Admiral had set a carefully laid trap of his own with *Glasgow* the intended victim. Neither side apparently expected to encounter each other's fleets.

Cradock was faced with a stark choice: fight or run. He reversed the course of the British fleet so that both antagonists were sailing almost due south, but the faster German vessels *Scharnhorst, Gneisenau* and *Leipzig* were closing down the British over the following hour and a half, until Cradock made his fateful decision to turn and fight.

The British vessels spread out into line abreast while the German ships to the north-east approached, intending to engage the British fleet with the latter outlined against the setting sun. Cradock brought his ships together and turned south, following which he made a number of attempts to close the range to the German vessels, but von Spee maintained a distance of some 18,000 yards between the fleets. Eventually, the sun set at around 6.50 p.m. that evening, and von Spee finally closed on the British fleet and opened fire.

The British vessels were silhouetted against the twilight of the Southern Hemisphere's summer evening sky making the fleet easy to target and range for the well-trained and experienced German gunners who quickly scored hits, whilst the untested crews on the ageing British cruisers could scarcely see their foe in the oncoming grey twilight dusk and the rain squalls. Cradock managed to close the range to some 6,000 yards, but rather than helping his own gunners, it made the British easier targets for the German.

The British could only use the enemy's gun flashes to estimate distance – a difficult thing for even an experienced crew in good light – and with no chance of seeing the splashes they had no means of telling how accurate their own fire was. As if that were not enough, the Germans were soon to be aided by the many fires that had quickly broken out on the two British capital ships, making them easy prey. By around 7.30 p.m. on that stormy evening, even the German gunners could not find the range and had, temporarily at least, ceased firing, but already the two largest British ships had each fired their last shell in battle.

Good Hope had been quickly disabled and was heavily on fire, and at around 7.50 p.m. that evening, flames started by a shell from *Scharnhorst* eventually reached the magazine and she blew herself to pieces with all hands lost, including Rear-Admiral Cradock. Captain Luce on HMS *Glasgow* saw the immense explosion, and described the flames to have reached 200 feet or more. A heavy rain squall hid the dreadful cataclysm from the view of the Germans. Most of *Good Hope*'s crew and superstructure simply disappeared in the blast, and the hull, reputedly glowing dull red from the heat of the fires within, settled some 10 minutes later, boiling the bitter cold sea around it to hissing and spitting malevolence. One of the war's many human tragedies was that twin brothers, Edward and Harry Turner died together in *Good Hope* on that day, leaving two widows and eight orphans in Cheltenham, their home town.

Frank Brandt's *Monmouth* had already been mauled by fire from *Gneisenau* and was no longer firing her guns. She was listing heavily to port and down at the bow, her forward turret shattered and burning. Von Spee ordered his light cruisers to make a torpedo attack, but as the range was closed and whilst *Monmouth* obstinately refused to strike her colours, she was pounded by shell-fire without mercy. *Glasgow* had broken off the engagement around 8.10 p.m. and had attempted to withdraw with *Monmouth* to the west, but lost sight of her at around 8.50 p.m. bearing approximately due east; there would thus be no British witnesses to recount *Monmouth*'s ultimate end.

Monmouth attempted to escape north-west, perhaps the intention also being to draw the German's fire away from *Glasgow*, but by doing so she ran into range of the light cruiser *Nürnberg*, rushing down from the north. It seems the officers on *Nürnberg* realised *Monmouth* was finished, and directed their searchlight onto the British ship's ensign that was still flying - a clear invitation for the British officers to surrender. There was no response from the British ship, and according to von Spee's report, at approximately 9 p.m., the German cruiser finished HMS *Monmouth* off with many dozens of shells delivered at almost point-blank range with no reply, and just as with *Good Hope*, *Monmouth* went to the distant bottom taking her entire complement with her, including Brandt and Spiller, and still flying her colours; most probably, there had long been no-one on deck left alive to strike them.

Damaged and burning, HMS *Glasgow* escaped from the disastrous Battle of Coronel, along with HMS *Otranto*. Unaware of her sinking already, the Germans were still looking for *Good Hope* and made no attempt at rescue of British sailors that, in the heavy seas and oncoming darkness, would have been nigh on impossible anyway. Those few men from either ship who might have been able to leave their vessel would have quickly perished in the cold, dark and choppy seas. The part played by the slow and under-armed merchant cruiser *Otranto* appears to have been understandably negligible.

Cradock has been subsequently criticised by some militarists for not waiting for support from another of his fleet, the equally elderly and slow battleship HMS *Canopus* and her 12-inch guns, and he could probably have avoided the action should he have wished by turning away to the south-west. But to run when his orders were to find the enemy and engage him clearly never entered the Admiral's mind. It is even suggested that a memorandum written by Cradock just a short while before the battle, that he must make sure not to suffer the same fate as "*poor Troubridge*", signalled his intention to engage the enemy at all costs.

Rear-Admiral Ernest Troubridge, second in command of the British Mediterranean Fleet under Admiral Sir Archibald Milne, had been court-martialled for failing to chase down in HMS *Gloucester* the German cruiser SMS *Goeben* in the Adriatic at the outbreak of the war. He was subsequently acquitted of the charge.

The then First Sea Lord, Winston Spencer Churchill, was accused by Lord Zetland of appointing Cradock to the command of an inadequate squadron for the needs of the American Station (and thereby at least being partially responsible for the calamity); a charge vehemently rebutted by the future Prime Minister, but which does seem to have some merit.

Shortly after the Coronel battle, the Admiralty directed all surviving vessels to proceed to Abrolhos Rocks on Brazil's coast, some two and a half thousand miles to the north-east of the Falkland Islands, there to await more ships from other areas including the battlecruisers *Invincible* and *Inflexible* from the North Sea Grand Fleet. The British were implacably dedicated to destroying von Spee's fleet and intended to do so with a much more powerful fleet than the German - there would be no mercy after Coronel.

The pleasure and satisfaction of Cradock's adversary, Admiral von Spee, was short-lived. Despite being flushed with victory, he was privately doubtful that his success would to any degree impair the Royal Navy's capacity to wage naval war. Visiting Valparaiso harbour on the Chilean coast some two days after the battle, he declined to accept a bouquet of flowers from the German residents with the comment that "*...they would do well for my grave*". Nevertheless, he decided on a bold move, to round Cape Horn and attack the British dependencies at the Falklands and South

Georgia, precisely the move that had concerned Cradock. The British response to the dreadful news of Coronel had been the formation of that large force as a prelude to finding and destroying the Germans, and this force under Admiral Doveton Sturdee happened to be in Port Stanley as the German fleet arrived just a few weeks after Coronel.

Hardly before the bold Gothic headline type had dried on the German newspapers back home celebrating their victory, it was the turn of von Spee's squadron to face destruction by a more powerful enemy fleet.

The German fleet comprising the five ships *Scharnhorst, Dresden, Gneisenau, Nürnberg* and *Leipzig* approached the islands on their eastern side towards the entrance to Port Stanley. The two fleets then sailed almost due east with the British Fleet of *Invincible, Carnavon, Inflexible, Cornwall, Macedonia, Glasgow, Bristol* and *Kent* to the northern side.

von Spee had missed a golden opportunity to attack the British whilst they re-coaled at anchor. After a fascinating chase with the British ships slowly wearing down the Germans, von Spee's two heavy cruisers *Scharnhorst* and *Gneisenau* finally allowed the fleets to close to about 6 miles separation to confront their pursuers in a valiant attempt to give the faster and lighter cruisers the chance to escape to the south-east – the sacrifice was ultimately unsuccessful. *Glasgow* and *Cornwall* stopped *Leipzig* whose officers surrendered, but the damaged vessel would soon sink; HMS *Kent* sank *Nürnberg* and von Spee himself was one of the many human casualties when *Scharnhorst* settled to the bottom of the South Atlantic, sunk along with *Gneisenau* by *Invincible's* and *Inflexible's* combined shelling. His two sons, one in *Gneisenau* and the other in *Nürnberg*, both joined their father in death. von Spee's forebodings in Valparaiso those few weeks before had been all too real.

It is interesting to note that HMS *Canopus*, which had failed to join Cradock's squadron at Coronel, had been beached on the Falklands as a sort of guard ship, and it was her shells (some of which were dummy practice shells) which had added to von Spee's concern about what he might find in Port Stanley, and had helped prevent what could have been an absolute disaster for the British. The unmanoeuvrable fleet would have stood no chance if the German Admiral had engaged immediately.

Another slightly bizarre tale is that of a Falkland Islands resident, Mrs Muriel Felton. The lady, wife of a sheep station manager, was telephoned by authorities in Port Stanley to look out for the German Fleet. She and her maids took turns to ride up to a nearby hilltop and spend the day watching the ocean, with the movements of the German vessels being relayed back to the Port Stanley naval officers, who were thus able to position certain of their vessels in the best place to intercept. The Admiralty later demonstrated their thanks by presenting each of the three ladies with a silver platter, and Mrs. Felton was awarded the OBE for her efforts.

Finally, it seems very likely that Naval Intelligence played a part in this battle as at Coronel; a false signal sent in a cracked German code apparently helped lure von Spee to the islands where Sturdee was waiting for him.

Two German ships escaped from the Battle of the Falklands: the auxiliary collier *Seydlitz* and the cruiser *Dresden*, but the latter vessel's destruction was simply postponed. After a desperate game of cat and mouse among the islands at the southern tip of South America, she sought refuge in Cumberland Bay (Bahia Cumberland), on the north coast of Mas a Tierra Island (also known as Robinson Crusoe Island, part of the Juan Fernández Island Group) off the western coast of South America, indeed not far from Coronel. Again, she may have been misled by a fake signal in that same cracked German code. On Sunday 14th March 1915, she was finally cornered in the bay by British ships led by *Glasgow*, and Captain Luce (under the circumstances, perhaps understandably ignoring the politics of Chilean neutrality) exacted the final revenge for *Monmouth* and *Good Hope*. HMS *Kent* is also credited with sinking *Dresden* in some sources. German historians maintain the vessel was scuttled, which seems the most likely and matches the entry in *Glasgow*'s log, which records a German Officer visiting Luce on *Glasgow* whilst his ship flew a white flag, it was during the interview that the *Dresden*'s fore-magazine blew up and the ship sank, most likely from a scuttling charge than damage from battle. So perished the last remnant of the German East Asian Squadron; all that now remained of the Kaiser's fleet of ships in the Pacific were a few commerce raiders.

One of *Dresden*'s officers to survive was Wilhelm Canaris, later to become the Third Reich's spy-master, a conspirator in the plot against Hitler in July 1944 and who was brutally executed for his complicity by the Nazis less than a month before the Second World War ended in Europe. von Spee would, of course, be immortalised by the Kriegsmarine of the Third Reich when it named the first of the new Germany's *"pocket battleships"* after the famous Admiral, the vessel being chased down by HM Ships *Ajax*, *Exeter* and *Achilles* before being scuttled in the mouth of Montevideo's River Plate off Uruguay soon after the start of the Second World War. The author used to work with an Inspector who had been a chief stoker on HMS *Ajax* during that battle, a most colourful character forever known as *Chiefy* Barton.

1,660 British seamen lost their lives at Coronel, with none from the German ships. In contrast, 10 British sailors died at the Falklands along with 1,871 from the Kriegsmarine. I have mentioned it elsewhere; a ship need only fear another of greater armament and might; these two battles certainly demonstrate the truth in that old saying.

Brandt's name is honoured on the Plymouth Naval Memorial, Devon, England and he left a widow Beryl Pennington, whom he had married in September 1900 and four pre-teenage children. Given his career up to his death that in many ways was more successful than others we have touched on, I am certain that had he survived Coronel he would have followed his colleagues to flag rank.

The Battle of Coronel was the first fleet defeat for the British in a hundred years, and Cradock's the first death in action of a serving Admiral since Nelson; the second such death would involve another *Calliope* midshipman, but that story is to come.

Midshipman John Collings Taswell Glossop

John Glossop was born 23rd October 1871 at Newland House, Twickenham, the son of George Goodwin Pownall Glossop, vicar of Twickenham, and his wife Eliza Maria Trollope. He had become commanding officer of a number of ships including coincidentally (as will become clear later) the 3rd HMS *Hood*, before taking command of HMAS *Sydney* in June 1913. Soon after the start of hostilities, he was pitch-forked into battle against the German cruiser SMS *Emden*.

It is worth recording that during time of war and at that time in the history of the nation, the still fledgling Australian Navy came under the direct control of the British Admiralty, and RN officers filled most of the senior positions on the vessels. So Glossop was in fact still Royal Navy even whilst commanding an Australian Navy warship.

In early August 1914, the German raider SMS *Emden* had detached from von Spee's squadron already mentioned and embarked on a series of attacks on allied shipping and resources which had earned her a reputation perhaps somewhat more elevated than was really deserved. Her victims were mostly unarmed merchant vessels, and whilst she did sink a French *Arquebuse* class destroyer *Mousquet*, she had not baulked at shelling some oil storage tanks at Madras on her way out to the Pacific.

What had perhaps captured the public's imagination, mostly in

Britain, was that she quickly earned herself the reputation of waging a *"gentlemanly war"*. None from the 23 merchant crews known to have encountered her were killed in her attacks, her captain preferring to bring his victim to a stop by signals and the implicit threat of her guns, take the crew off, and sink the vessel by scuttling charges; the crew would be extremely well treated and released at the earliest opportunity. The official list of Allied ships sunk by the *Emden* is: *Indus, Lovat, Killin, Diplomat, Trabboch, Clan Matheson, King Lud, Timeric, Ribera, Foyle, Clan Grant, Benmohr, Ponrabbel, Troilus, Chilkana* and *Ayesha*. Those captured and subsequently released by *Emden* were: *Kabinga, Gryferale, St. Egbert, Glenturret* and *Newburn*. She also captured *Exford*, but this was later recaptured by the British, and the collier *Buresk*.

Just eight days after his Admiral's striking victory at Coronel, on the 9th November 1914, Captain Karl von Müller, intending to land a party of marines on the Cocos Islands with the aim of cutting the important telegraph cable at the wireless station there, finally ran out of luck. Despite a disguise which ingeniously included a false additional funnel for his ship, she was recognised from the shore as she approached the station. In response to frantic signals for assistance, HMAS *Sydney* was detached from nearby convoy duty to intercept, and was the first to reach the scene. As the battle erupted, *Emden* scored first with some very long range hits which killed four of the crew on *Sydney*, but soon the fast and more powerfully armed Australian light cruiser was causing mortal damage to the German, which was eventually beached, on fire and utterly disabled.

Glossop took *Sydney* off after the *Buresk* which had been trying to ram the Australian, but to prevent its recapture she was scuttled by her German crew (the Admiralty records maintain the *Buresk* was sunk by HMAS *Sydney*) so he returned to *Emden*. He would later say in an interview with the Australian poet "Banjo" Paterson:

"Then we went back to the Emden lying in the shallow water and

signalled her 'do you surrender.' She answered by flag-wagging in Morse
'we have no signal book and do not understand your signal.' I asked
several times but could get no answer and her flag was still flying, so I
fired two salvos into her and then they hauled their flag down. I was
sorry afterwards that I gave her those two salvos, but what was I to do? If
they were able to flag-wag in Morse, they were surely able to haul a flag
down. We understood there was another German warship about and I
couldn't have the Emden firing at me from the beach while I was fighting
her mate."

Even during the First World War, the act of *"striking the colours"*, i.e.
lowering one's flag, was a universally accepted sign of surrendering the
ship, and it would then be in honour bound to take no further military
action in battle, howsoever the circumstances around it might change,
unless it could be recaptured by a force friendly to it. Such gallantry had
long disappeared by the Second World War.

The excerpt above was recorded in *"Happy Dispatches...Recollections*
of World Famous People", Chapter 12 by Andrew Barton Paterson (1864-
1941), originally published as a collection of Paterson's journalistic
interviews and articles by Angus & Robertson, Sydney, 1934. *Banjo* was the
author of many wonderful poems, including *"Waltzing Matilda"*, and more
pertinently for our story: *"The Ballad of the Calliope"*, which opens:

"By the far Samoan shore, where the league-long rollers pour;
all the wash of the Pacific on the coral-guarded bay;
Riding lightly, at their ease; In the calm of tropic seas,
The three great nations' warships at their anchors proudly lay.

"Riding lightly, head to wind; With the coral reefs behind;
Three German and three Yankee ships were mirrored in the blue.
And on one ship unfurled; Was the flag that rules the world-
For on the old Calliope the flag of England flew."

At the time of writing this narrative (2010), an image of *Banjo* currently
adorns the front of the $10 Australian banknote.

Whether or not there was any real thought of it, those last shells
broke all further resistance, and with the lowering of her flag, SMS *Emden*
finally surrendered, her crew having been dreadfully injured and
hundreds killed during the battle. Those who had struggled ashore had
spent just one day in the heat and flies, and their wounds were already
horribly infected, their sole doctor with no medicine to fight disease.

Glossop had requested the German Captain's surrender in a letter that would today seem astonishing for enemies at war with each other:

> "*Sir,*
>
> "*I have the honour to request that in the name of humanity you now surrender your ship to me. In order to show how much I appreciate your gallantry, I will recapitulate the position.*
> "*You are ashore, 3 funnels and 1 mast down and most guns disabled.*
> "*You cannot leave this island, and my ship is intact.*
> "*In the event of your surrendering in which I venture to remind you is no disgrace but rather your misfortune I will endeavour to do all I can for your sick and wounded and take them to a hospital.*
> "*I have the honour to be, Sir, Your obedient servant, John CT Glossop Captain.*"

I don't know how the letter was conveyed from *Sydney* to *Emden*, but its contents were acknowledged somehow. Glossop took the wounded on board his ship, charged his four doctors with their care, and headed north-west for Colombo (capital of Ceylon, now Sri Lanka, and then a British Dependency) at his best speed. The interview with Paterson was conducted just a week after the battle, and soon after *Sydney* had arrived with her cabins packed with those desperately injured prisoners, and the awful stench of their diseased wounds permeating every corner of the ship. Paterson's text hints that Glossop was genuinely upset by his decision to fire those last salvos – quite proper in the passion of battle perhaps, but a dreadful memory in the cold indifference of a lonely bar on a quiet evening, thousands of miles from home.

It so happens that not all of *Emden's* crew were captured; a party sent ashore on Direction Island evaded capture and commenced a thrilling and amazing six-month journey back to the Fatherland. They captured a schooner, the *Ayesha* and sailed across the Indian Ocean in it, landed on the Red Sea coastline and walked across the desert before being rescued by Ottoman troops who took them to Istanbul in May 1915. From there they returned to Germany to a, quite justifiable, hero's welcome.

Thus ended Australia's first naval battle action of the First World War – a remarkable success in an official report; a horrific and abiding memory of the dreadful waste of war for those actually involved. Kapitan von Müller survived the battle, but died in 1923 aged just 50. During the search of the wreck of *Emden*, *Sydney's* crew salvaged a large number of Mexican silver dollar coins. A long and involved correspondence soon began between Australia and the Admiralty which eventually culminated in a number of these coins being mounted and given to various Australian bodies; the rest sold as souvenirs. Some 100 found their way to the UK where various persons in the Admiralty were presented with them; two were given to the King and a few others to various museums and institutions. Copies made into named medals fetch very high prices these days.

Further writings on this particular episode in World War One naval warfare can be found by author Edwin P. Hoyt, one of the Samoa Hurricane chroniclers.

Commodore Glossop also presided over the courts-martial of the mutineers from HMAS *Australia*, the vessel von Spee and his German East Asiatic Squadron had been looking to surprise at anchor at Apia in the first months of the war. This mutiny, of little interest now but which at the time generated considerable attention and curiosity, had been precipitated when that vessel, after a relatively quiet and unremarkable war record in Europe and the Pacific, arrived back in Fremantle on Wednesday, 28th May 1919 with most Australian sailors seeing home for the first time in four years. The crew were immediately given four days of leave and enjoyed every moment in the town that welcomed them with open arms and real pleasure. The celebrations were typically Australian: exuberant, good humoured and full blast. All had a grand time, the relaxation especially welcome after the drab years of war spent so far from home.

But within the ship seethed resentment, built up from such diverse causes as the lack of reasonable leave for the Australians in Britain; confusion over pay; and discord between the British and Australian crew members, the latter believing themselves to have been unfairly subjected to an unnecessarily harsh regime of discipline.

It appears that at some point, certain members of the crew believed that they would be given the opportunity to return the hospitality provided by the town, by being permitted to invite family and friends on board the ship for a day of celebration on the following Sunday, although in fact, June 1st had always been intended as the sailing date for Sydney. On that day, a somewhat belligerent request by a deputation on the quarterdeck of nearly 100 sailors dressed in their finery, to extend the stay in the port and allow the party to take place, was summarily refused by Captain Cumberlege (also spelt in some sources Cumerlege) who felt himself obliged to object to being, as he felt, dictated to. A number of sailors then took the matter into their own hands by "*sabotaging the vessel*", though they could hardly have honestly intended it as an alternative method of prolonging the time in the port. The classic case of small issues spiralling out of control as they bounced back and forth between people of utterly dissimilar views.

The word *"sabotage"* seems severe, conjuring up visions of damage and destruction, whilst in fact the duty stokers simply abandoned their posts leaving the vessel unable to raise steam until the Petty Officers and alternate watch undertook the duties, and the ship left port no more than a few hours behind schedule. A small thing in reality, wrong of course and without any doubt a mutinous act, but not, one must say, Fletcher Christian stuff. On the other hand, the perpetrators would have well known they were committing an act for which they must receive punishment. It hardly needs to be noted that the question over the extended stay was simply the final straw in a haystack of resentment and mistrust which had been building over a number of years, rather than it was the single cause of the dispute.

Some sources maintain that the stokers were pressurised into their actions by other, unknown masked sailors. After the ship left Fremantle, they voluntarily returned to their duties.

Most of the mutineers were dealt with by the Captain, and received periods in the cells of up to 90 days, but the five ringleaders (as believed by the captain but never formally accused as such) were arraigned by court martial on 20th June 1919; each pleaded guilty to the charge of *"mutiny without violence"* and were sentenced to various periods of up to 2 years imprisonment, some with hard labour, and all to be followed with ignominious dismissal from the service. The Australian political opposition's dismay over the severity of the punishment was appeased by a remittal of the sentences, directly leading to the consequent resignation of a number of senior naval officers who felt let down by the leniency being shown. Commodore Dumaresq, Commanding His Majesty's Australian Fleet, submitted his resignation on 19th December 1919, some 5 days after Rear-Admiral, Sir Percy Grant, RN, First Naval Member of the Australian Naval Board.

One of the five accused Australians had earlier been nominated (by ballot) for a Victoria Cross following the raid on Zeebrugge on 23rd April 1918. Leading Seaman Dalmorton Rudd was not awarded that honour, but did receive the Distinguished Service Medal. His younger brother Leonard was another of the five mutineers. It is my opinion that the punishments handed out were, as the Australian Government contended, unnecessarily harsh and hardly warranted.

All five sailors eventually served precisely six months in prison and were released the day after Dumaresq's resignation – just in time for

Christmas. It is easy to feel some sympathy for the men, but in fact, they could well have been charged with a far more serious crime (as ringleaders, incitement to mutiny) an offence that at the time, carried the death penalty as its maximum sentence. Although the war had been over for six months, until the peace treaty was actually signed (on 28th June 1919 a week or so after the court martial sat), the crew were subject to Royal Navy war-time regulations and discipline, and the sentences had been handed down by the Admiralty in London rather than Commodore Glossop. Part of the anger displayed by the senior officers present in Australia was that they felt the men had already been too leniently dealt with in respect of the relatively minor charges laid against them.

Ruffled feathers were smoothed at least on the surface, and the high-ranking naval resignations were withdrawn on 13th February the following year, but the ill-feeling generated took quite a while to settle down, and probably never did completely. I suppose to the British subalterns, unfairness was a way of life and might just as well be endured without complaint; to the Australians, the ideas seemed stupid, demeaning and unnecessary, and why should they put up with them? The opposing sentiments needed sensitive handling at officer level: this seems to have been unforthcoming, and strife was inevitable; perhaps the surprise might really be the relative mildness of its eventual eruption.

Glossop married Ethel Alison McPhillamy in All Saints' Cathedral, Bathurst, New South Wales, Australia in January 1918 and returned to the British Royal Navy in 1921 retiring later that same year as Rear-Admiral. He earned the Japanese Order of the Rising Sun and the French Légion d'Honneur, as well as having been Mentioned in Despatches and appointed Commander of the Bath for the action against SMS *Emden*. He died of septicaemia on 23rd December 1934, and his life is commemorated by a memorial in Holy Trinity Old Church, Bothenhampton, Dorset, England which reads: *"Retired Officer de Légion d'Honneur. Churchwarden of his parish 1922-34"*. A portrait of Glossop by the Australian painter James Quinn is in the Australian War Memorial.

What was surely the greatest tragedy to hit the Royal Australian Navy in the Second World War was the sinking of HMAS *Sydney* II by SMA *Kormoran* off the West Australian coast on 19th November, 1941, with the loss of 645 lives.

Midshipman, the Honourable H.L.A. Hood

Born in October 1870, the Honourable Horace Lambert Alexander Hood had entered the Royal Navy in 1883, and during his training he took all the great naval prizes — Beaufort Testimonial, Goodenough Medal, Ryder Memorial Prize — before joining the ships *Temeraire* and then *Calliope* as midshipman. At his examination for the rank of Lieutenant, he gained five firsts, being comfortably the top of his year, and thereby achieving a record unsurpassed at the time of his death and for many years after. He became Post Captain in January 1903, and Rear Admiral in May 1913. In attaining that rank, he matched that of his great-great-grandfather, Admiral Samuel Hood, 1st Viscount Hood.

Captain Hood was employed in the gunboats service on the Nile and was present at the battles of Atbara and Khartoum, where he received a mention in despatches. Promoted to commander, he was awarded the fourth class of Mejidie. When captain of HMS *Hyacinth* he landed in command of a naval brigade for the capture of the Mullah's stronghold of Illig, 21st April 1904 and was again mentioned in despatches, awarded the Distinguished Service Order (DSO), the general East African medal (Somaliland, 1902-1904), and in 1906 was appointed a Member of the Royal Victorian Order (MVO), an award originally directly issued by the sovereign herself as an order of chivalry.

In 1910 he was in command of the Royal Naval College, Osborne; in January of that same year he had married a young widow, Ellen Floyd Touzalin Nickerson, in her home town of Burlington, Des Moines, Iowa. He was naval secretary to the First Lord (Winston Churchill), and shortly after the beginning of the war was given command of the Dover Patrol, the miscellaneous collection of vessels of all ages and sizes which greatly helped to stop the German rush to Calais by breaking up the enemy's right flank among the Belgian sand dunes, and which afterwards protected the Belgian army's front with long-range guns. As the war continued, Rear-Admiral Hood was given command of cruiser force "E" with his flag in HMS *Juno*, followed quickly in May 1915 by command of the Third Battle-Cruiser Squadron with his flag in HMS *Invincible*.

Much has been written about the Battle of Jutland, or as the Germans call it, the *Skagerrakschlacht*. It was the first major home waters fleet battle of the war; there has never been the like since, and given the size of today's navies, it is unlikely that such an event could occur again – thank God. Each side claimed victory: the British made the best of what they would later describe as a "...*tactical loss but strategic gain...*" whilst the Germans were in no doubt of the success of their modern warships and trumpeted their vanquishing of the so-called most powerful maritime navy in the world. Kaiser Wilhelm hailed the battle as heralding the end of the illustrious days of Trafalgar. Both viewpoints have merit.

In the cold light of day, the outcome favoured the British more than the Germans, but that doesn't mean the British won the battle. In terms of numbers of ships sunk and men lost, the Germans were clearly the victors, but since Great Britain had huge naval resources in the Grand Fleet that could sustain those losses far better than could the smaller German High Seas Fleet, it was in truth a hollow victory for the Kaiser. The Imperial German Navy knew perfectly well that they had been extremely lucky to have survived at all; they had left good ships behind in the cold North Sea and taken heavily damaged ones back to port. If the British had failed to take the opportunity to totally wipe out the German Fleet, it made little real difference – the survivors would never take on the might of the British again, and for their further contribution to the war effort, they might just as well have been sunk.

All the claims and counter-claims on both sides of course take no account of the terrible human cost; so many families in the homelands of Britain and Germany would have taken little comfort from the posturing of politicians trying to see a way of making a dreadful situation look good. Every man who drowned in the cold muddy sea or who was blown to dust in the immense destruction of exploding magazines had families who would miss them; and had their hopes of starting their own or watch them grow destroyed as horribly as the ships that had been their home.

The bare facts are that the casualties amounted to the loss of three battle cruisers, three armoured cruisers, eight destroyers and more than 6,000 men from the British Grand Fleet, countered by one battle cruiser, one pre-dreadnought, four cruisers, five destroyers and some 2,500 men from the German High Seas Fleet.

I have visited the British Jutland web-site on the internet and viewed the page upon page of names of those who perished. It is really sobering to do it, and puts the number 6,000 into reality. Some of those who died were crew of the, at the time, current HMS *Calliope* that had taken the name in 1914 and was part of the engagement.

The whole story is one which deserves far more than part of a chapter in this book to do it true justice, and trying to précis the events to a simple broad outline is difficult. Equally, there is so much written about the battle, it would take a lifetime to read it all, I think. So please take the trouble to hunt out some of the excellent factual documents that have been published if my particular analysis is found wanting.

Basically, there was a desire on both sides to precipitate a fleet battle but under very precise conditions that were, of course, more favourable to each side in their turn. To the British, the war's stalemate in the muddy fields of France and Belgium needed to be broken somehow, and one possible way of forcing the Kaiser to the negotiating table might be the destruction of his High Seas Fleet followed by an unbreakable blockade of his home ports. The British were convinced that if they could engineer such a confrontation, the vastly superior might and numbers of the British Grand Fleet would surely win the day.

To the Germans, the presence and implied threat of that Grand Fleet in Scotland had already effectively blockaded that route into Germany, and with the channel ports and squadrons doing much the same in the south, they faced great problems in maintaining a supply of war materials to continue the conflict, or to make their own influence the greater. They needed to break the barrier somehow, to lessen the might of the British naval forces. The Germans were fully aware of the immense power and size of the British Fleet, and equally certain that the outcome of any direct sea battle between the fleets would be the annihilation of their own. If they indeed took it on *en-masse*, they would need to destroy British ships at an impossible rate to come out on top, and a one-for-one attrition would soon leave the British utterly victorious.

So whilst each side would have had no objection to a confrontation, indeed both sides actively desired it, the Germans especially needed to find a tactical advantage to exploit.

The British commander of the Grand Fleet was Admiral Lord Jellicoe, one of the survivors of the sinking of HMS *Victoria* in 1895 that we have already encountered, and a man who had been an officer on one of WIT's many ships. A popular man likened by the British public in the years of peace to Nelson himself, he was in fact, quite the opposite of "Britain's Hero" in the time of this war.

At Trafalgar in 1805, Nelson's 27 ships of the line took on the combination of 15 Spanish and 18 French equal vessels and seven other

French frigates and brigs under Admiral Villeneuve, having enticed them out of Cádiz, and managed to destroy most of them, only six seaworthy vessels returning to the safety of the port. No British vessel was lost, though some were badly damaged. The stunning victory was made that much more dramatic and poignant by the Admiral's own death so early in the battle.

Jellicoe had no such risky intentions these hundred and some years later, and was perfectly able to ignore the clamouring of a British press, the mouthpiece of a public still assured in their minds of the superiority of the Royal Navy in all matters and desperate for a naval success with which to counter the depressingly consistent lack of such from the troops on the continent. To Jellicoe, bottling up the German fleet and controlling the supply sea-ways was a slow but effective means of helping to achieve the ultimate victory, there was no need for any showy or dangerous battle tactics.

In May 1916, the Kaiser appointed Admiral Speer as the commander of the German Home Fleet, and in doing so found a man much more in the mould of Nelson. Speer concluded that his only chance of defeating the British Grand Fleet lay in breaking it up into smaller units, and dealing with each in their turn. Sporadic and random German naval shelling of Britain's east-coast towns had Speer's desired result of arousing public wrath, and he knew the only way for Jellicoe to counter the assaults would be to spread his force along the entire coast-line, perhaps giving the Germans the chance of taking on a part of the British forces rather than the whole.

But Jellicoe was easily able to ignore the armchair Admirals, and take the safer, longer view. He kept his fleets intact and ready, and was able to intercept German naval signals. Whilst allowing his enemy to think he had succeeded in separating a force of British ships upon which Speer could unleash his entire High Seas Fleet, Jellicoe prepared his own trap with the rest of the British Grand Fleet in readiness to spring an unpleasant surprise. Speer fell for it, and the scene was set.

The plans and machinations of both sides inexorably drew to a terrifying climax at the end of that month of May. It all came to a head on the 31st, as the cold day waned to a colder evening.

Having enticed the Germans by the offer of easy pickings, Jellicoe's fleet had intended to tie up with Beatty's battle cruisers, but the swashbuckling Beatty, like a naval General Custer, had pushed ahead alone and encountered the German Admiral Hipper and his ships. Beatty was luckier than the American Army hero, and was able to retire, but left two of his most powerful ships behind, and Jellicoe's trap was already compromised.

The first of Beatty's force to go was the battle cruiser HMS *Indefatigable*, Captain C.A. Selby. Hit by a number of shells, fires raged in the front turret which quickly spread to the magazines. A deafening explosion shattered the vessel into pieces and glazed the damp sea air with a shock wave as physically powerful as the mental one for the onlookers. Worse was to come, and quickly. HMS *Queen Mary*, Captain C.I. Prowse, a modern fast battle cruiser, pride of the fleet, much vaunted to the public as proof of Britain's continuing superiority afloat, disappeared in an identical mushroom cloud of acrid, yellow, hellish smoke, which rose over two thousand feet into the grey evening air. One of the crew lost was Able Seaman William Thomas Hague of Stockport, Cheshire.

It seems quite possible that the British capital ships, and perhaps even some of the heavy cruisers (HMS *Defence*, Captain S.V. Ellis, HMS *Warrior* Captain V.B. Molteno, and HMS *Black Prince* Captain T.P. Bonham) which were also lost on that day, had succumbed to internal explosions triggered by incorrectly stored cordite stacks. As *Queen Mary* was destroyed by a massive detonation of extraordinary ferocity right in front of him, Vice-Admiral Sir David Beatty was said to have commented to his flag captain A.E.M. Chatfield on the flagship battle cruiser HMS *Lion*: *"There seems to be something wrong with our bloody ships today."* That apparent laconic statement to mark the sudden and violent deaths of some 1,500 men on that vessel alone seems cold and unfeeling now, but at the time was probably simply indicative of the shock and disbelief all the British commanders were feeling on that evening, and whilst he was correct in his belief, the reasons for the catastrophe were deep and complicated and partially perhaps, could be laid at his own door.

The blame for the practice of storing large amounts of cordite under battle conditions beside the magazines, in direct contravention of all the naval regulations regarding it, has been ascribed to a number of reasons, but the most likely (that I have encountered) is the one which places the responsibility directly on a dearth of good test-firing facilities at the Rosyth base. The guns were so powerful to achieve their 12 mile range that to unleash a broadside anywhere near habitation risked breaking everyone's windows with the shock. This meant British crews were inaccurate due to lack of practice, and to make up for the failing, were encouraged to maintain a high rate of fire; it was the support to *this* requirement which necessitated the pre-storage of the cordite outside the protection of the magazine walls, and the leaving open of blast doors to speed up the supply of ordnance from magazine to weapon. There are even suggestions that Beatty had himself flouted the regulations and *ordered* the practice. It is also worth recording that earlier in the day, and but for the heroic efforts of HMS *Lion's* magazine crew, who, despite being dreadfully injured and unable to escape, flooded a burning magazine with sea-water, Beatty himself would probably not have been around to make the comment.

Rear-Admiral Hood and his Third Battle-Cruiser Squadron had also pushed ahead of Jellicoe's fleet in an attempt to tie up with Beatty's battle squadron, but instead came in sight of the main German fleet at around 6.30 p.m. on the evening of that 31st May. Captain Arthur L. Cay on *Invincible* succeeded in inflicting some hits on *Lutzow* which would ultimately contribute to the German ship's sinking, but before that happened, the generally poor visibility on the day suddenly cleared for a few minutes catching *Invincible* in the open as it were, and a combined salvo from *Lutzow* and *Derfflinger* easily penetrated the British vessel's armour and, presumably, once more found unprotected cordite charges stacked near the magazines. *Invincible's* four magazines exploded almost simultaneously to take Hood and all but six of the crew of more than 1,000 men to their deaths. Hood was only the second Admiral of the British Royal Navy to lose his life in the First World War conflict, the first, as we have already mentioned, being Cradock at Coronel.

The photographic image of the two widely separated halves of *Invincible,* her shattered fractures resting on the shallow muddy floor of the North Sea and the prow and stern ends protruding starkly vertical against the choppy sea, is an enduring and wretched icon of the battle. Recently, scuba dives on this and many other Jutland wrecks have been made, but whilst those earlier dives seem to have preserved the respect to be accorded a war grave of such sad humanity, recent indications are that unauthorised and illegal salvage attempts have been made in an effort to get the valuable materials out of the sea's clutches. To commemorate the 90th anniversary of the action, in 2006 the 14 British wrecks had been designated as *"protected places"* under the terms of the Protection Of Military Remains Act of 1986; something of no interest to the uncaring scavengers who see any grave's content as potential monetary gain. There seems little to see as a recognisable wreck of *Queen Mary* - just scattered piles of buckled steel beams and deformed shells, of amputated gun muzzles and twisted armour plates scattered between the larger chunks of hull. It seems inconceivable that any of her crew had been rescued from the sea.

When details of the battle and the losses became publicly known, the death of Rear-Admiral Hood was felt keenly in the Admiralty, and equally so by the British public. Beatty himself described Hood's death as a *"...national misfortune..."* Hood had been born in London's Mayfair district as the fourth child (third son) of the 4th Viscount Hood (Francis Wheler Hood) and Viscountess Hood, (Edith Lydia Drummond Ward, daughter of Arthur Ward Esquire). He and his wife the Honourable Lady Hood lived at East Sheen Lodge, Sheen, Surrey and his death left two young children fatherless. His name is honoured on the Portsmouth Naval Memorial, Hampshire.

A final irony surrounds the modern battle cruiser (for its time) launched two years after his death by Hood's widow, the fourth of five British warships to bear the name: HMS *Hood*. Commissioned too late to serve in the Great War, the pride of the Royal Navy would become a venerable and out-of-date anachronism, destined to meet a similar fate to *Invincible*, this time from the modern guns of *Bismarck* on 24th May 1941. The shock felt by the British public to the loss of this vessel was very similar to that felt at the loss of the Admiral almost 25 years earlier.

So five Admirals and a Captain survived the Samoan Hurricane with Kane, and played their part in the Great War that perhaps the German military position in Samoa had presaged. What might have been Brandt's future is pure speculation, but I have little doubt he too would have made Admiral had he not so sadly perished at Coronel. In my view, the loss of Brandt at Coronel in 1914 and Hood at Jutland in 1916 deprived the Royal Navy of two of Great Britain's most charismatic, intelligent and powerful naval figures and would undoubtedly have seriously reduced the capability of the service. We have no way of knowing whether their possible survival would have shortened the war and saved thousands of lives, but I do rather think it likely.

Midshipman Edmund James Prendergast

Of the other two midshipmen, Edmund James Prendergast was born 10th February 1872 in London's Grosvenor Gardens, Middlesex, England. His father, Lennox Prendergast, was a Lieutenant-Colonel in the Royal Scots Greys and in 1881 an active Member of Parliament. Edmund's grand-father, Guy Lennox Prendergast, was a very influential person in the nineteenth-century. Edmund had a bad report from Captain Kane, who recorded depriving him of a month's time for leaving *Calliope* without permission in July 1889. He was made Lieutenant in December 1893 and retired in 1912 at his own request with the rank of Commander, having married Violet Pratt-Barlow in January 1907. He seems to have spent the war years on HMS *Vernon* for Wireless Telegraphy service, for which in October 1919 he was awarded the OBE, and reverted to the retired list in 1921; he died on 25th January 1936.

Midshipman Hugh Fitzroy Hopkinson

Hugh Fitzroy Hopkinson (his service record records this as two separate names: "Fitz Roy") was yet another *Calliope* midshipman to be born in October this time on the 11th, 1871, to banker and Army Agent George Henry Hopkinson and Blanche Isabella Somerset; the eldest son in a considerable family at St George Hanover Square, Middlesex. Hopkinson was the 28th great-grandson of Dutchman Wolfger van Amstel who was born in Amstellan, Netherlands around 1075, to start an extremely long and influential line of Dutchmen.

On his return to England after Samoa, Hopkinson continued his studies at the Royal Naval College Greenwich, and in 1894 was promoted to Lieutenant whilst on HMS *Pygmy*. He seems to have had recurring problems with debts and lifestyle – their Lordships noting in August 1894 a dishonoured cheque drawn by this officer, something in those days considered a serious lapse in that social class. One year later, he reported his debts to have been cleared, but during 1896 their Lordships were obliged to express their serious displeasure at Hopkinson being convicted by Portsmouth Magistrates of disorderly conduct whilst drunk. Around this time, two applications to commute part of his forthcoming retired pay to lump sums were declined by the board, suggesting his financial circumstances to be still rather strained.

Ordered to the naval hospital at Haslar for survey, he was initially found unfit, but eventually he continued his service only to be severely censured again in 1902:

> "...their Lordships dissatisfaction expressed, and informed that he cannot be excused for the insufficient care that has been taken in maintaining the Gunnery efficiency of Melampus."

This ship was an *Apollo* Class protected cruiser, built 1890 and scrapped in 1910. In 1905 he requested retirement but this request was withdrawn a few weeks later, and after five years in the Ballycastle Coast Guard, Co Antrim, Hopkinson finally retired in June 1910, with the rank of Commander being granted the following year. He was apparently still in need of immediate funds, and commuted £60 of his £295 retired pay for the sum of £794 11s 6d in December 1911 followed by a further £30 for £392 11s

0d in July 1913.

Whilst this midshipman's career seems to have been rather muted when compared to his contemporaries, Hopkinson was to surprise everyone who knew him (and perhaps himself) by rising to the occasion during the first World War when he arranged the transport of the Portuguese Army from Lisbon to Brest, even receiving in 1917 an expression of their Lordships appreciation for the service as partial counter to those earlier censures. He was granted the Portuguese Order of Avis (Second Class) in 1918, followed by the Portuguese Order of Christ the year following, and was promoted to the rank of Captain (Retired) in recognition of his wartime services. This seemingly colourful character died in June 1922 apparently never having married. Sources variously state his year of death as 1921, 1922 and at age 48 (which would be 1919/20).

Crew

A crew list was published in one of the fiftieth anniversary celebrations of the hurricane event, *"The First Commission of HMS Calliope"* [13] . My own research suggests it is slightly inaccurate in terms of some of the names and their spelling. I have reproduced the list herein at the end of the book, embodying those corrections and additions I have managed to glean from contact with a very few other families of crew members. I apologise to any reader with a family member who notices a mistake, and there does appear to be quite a few variations of surname, based on the fact that records of the time were hand-written and the script often confusing. "I"s and "J"s are frequently misread; there are many other similar slips.

Of the enlisted men, little of course is available in the public records. Enlisted crew at that time were not encouraged to keep diaries or journals, and had they wished to do so, the materials they needed would have been purchased out of their own meagre wages, and even finding the time to maintain them would be difficult. Nearly all history regarding the seamen is therefore family anecdote, and the only sensible way to collate such data that I could think of was a request for information via an internet site: "http://www.grahamhague.com/". The response has been just a handful of contacts, but I guess that is not too surprising, and those who have answered usually have interesting family stories to tell about the people if not the event, but even so detailed histories of the men are sparse. In fact, it seems I might have been extremely lucky to have had an ancestor who was blessed with a wonderful memory and the inclination to set his recollections down on paper. I know I am extremely lucky the old notebooks actually survived the years, including two occasions when my grandparent's Reigate homes were "bombed out" during the Second World

War blitz. And in 2007 I was fortunate indeed to be able to exchange e-mails with a *son* of one of *Calliope*'s crewmen: James Cresswell Moore.

The stories in this section of the chapter may, I freely admit, have limited interest for the casual reader. They are the few snippets of information I have been able to glean from the Internet or family members of the ordinary sailors aboard *Calliope* at Samoa. Sailor's experiences were usually not thought to be significant or worthy of recording for posterity, so little exists in the public domain. But family members do occasionally research their history, and some of them found my website and noticed my call for any stories about the crew that they might like to share. The stories that follow are often simply a list of ships served on, and dates of birth and death, but occasionally a little more is known. Hopefully, those family members who contributed to this section will enjoy seeing their memories or knowledge of their ancestors in print, and will be able to show it to future family members when the time comes.

As closely as I can, I have listed the names in this section in alphabetical order and given them their rank at the time of Samoa (i.e. March 1889). On occasion in these lists, I have found it necessary to depart from the alphabetical order to avoid images over-running pages or leaving great white spaces at the foot of the page. Apologies for that - I am an amateur editor as well as author!

Whilst it will not be possible to regularly update the lists in this book with any new data, my website is still active and should any new surfer find it and wish to add their own ancestor's story to the Crew List and Crew Stories pages, the website includes a contact e-mail address which will find me, and I'll be pleased to add the details to the web page. On occasion, and usually when I have noticed yet another typo, I will submit a revised text to the publishing group, which will include any such additional information I have obtained since the previous amendment.

If anyone has internet access and would like to find out about a seaman ancestor who served in the nineteenth- or early twentieth-century Royal Navy, then the National Archives at Kew holds records covering the intake period 1853 to 1924 and although you cannot *view* your ancestor's record on-line, you can search for it and order a copy to be downloaded as an image file, or travel to Kew and view it for free. The way I found to access the records (as of January 2016) is as follows:

Go to the site...

"http://www.nationalarchives.gov.uk"

...and at the top, click the down arrow and choose *"Search our records"* from the drop down list. Now type in the search box *ADM188* (no spaces!) and click the search button. You will get some 500,000 hits, but the one you want should be at the top, entitled *"Admiralty: Royal Navy Registers of Seaman's Services"*. This is a hyperlink, clicking it will take you to a new search page where you can type in your ancestor's name and also his year of enlistment if you know it (use a good range if you don't) and then click *"search"*. With any luck, your ancestor's record will be the only one listed, with sufficient information to allow you to identify the correct one if there are multiples, and again clicking its hyperlink title will take you to the page where you can order a download of the document. For officers, use *"ADM196"* instead of *"ADM188"* and follow much the same procedure.

When I tried this procedure in 2020, I discovered that if you have an account with the National Archives (which is free to set up) and you sign in, then some of these records can be downloaded as a PDF file *for free*. If you have a seaman ancestor who served in the Royal Navy prior to the Second World War, it would surely be worth trying out this procedure to see what you can find at nil cost! This option may not, of course, be permanently available!

Stoker William Burton Alsford

William was born in 1870 and died around 1949. He ended his service in the Royal Navy as a Leading Stoker in 1904 while serving in HMS *Narcissus* following which he married & settled down in Lancaster Road in Southsea, moving later to Lovedean, a small village just outside Portsmouth & finally to Durham Street in Portsmouth. After leaving the Navy he worked in the Dockyard until he retired.

Ordinary Seaman Joseph Attwell

Born 14th April 1870 at Fareham, Hampshire, Joseph enlisted in 1888 at the age of 18 for 12 years. He had probably served as a "boy" before that date. He joined the Royal Fleet Reserve at Portsmouth in 1901 after completion of his first enlistment period. He served on many ships including *Royal Oak* and *Excellent*. It appears that he then re-enlisted for two more 5-year stints which took him through World War I. Some of his WW I time may have been on the so-called "concrete" ships.

Ordinary Seaman Joseph James Barber

This gentleman came from Poole in Dorset. He is possibly listed in error as James Baker in the *Calliope* crew list. He joined *Calliope* from *Orlando* - probably on temporary loan. He had joined the Navy in 1886 and served in HMS *Orlando* transferring to *Calliope* on 20th January 1889. He was transferred to HMS *Egeria* on the 23rd April 1889.

Sick Bay Steward Second Class Sidney Barend

Sidney Barend was born in Hackney, Middlesex circa 1861. He joined the Royal Navy as a domestic 3rd class in June 1879 aged 18, again probably after a period as a "boy". He was 5'6" tall with dark brown hair, brown eyes and a dark complexion. His trade was given as "Clerk". The main vessels he served on were: *Rifleman* 1881-84 as Assistant SBA (Sick Bay Attendant); *Amethyst* 1884-85 SBA/SBS 2nd Class; *Clyde* 1885-87 SBS 2nd Class; *Calliope* 1887-90 SBS 2nd Class; *Rodney* 1890-93 SBS; *Hood* 1893-96 SBS; *President* 1897-01 SBS (Shore pensioned); *Pembroke* 1 1914-17 SBS *Thalia* (Aberdeen) 1917-18 SBS; *Nairn* 1918-19 SBS. He was then demobilised. Barend's service record shows he was recommended for his Long Service & Good Conduct medal whilst aboard *Calliope* ("Traced Medal 18.11.89") but the same note was also made 8 months later on 24th July 1890 when he was serving on HMS *Pembroke* and it was to this latter ship that his LSGC medal was named (naming "S. BAREND 2ND SK B:STEWD: H.M.S. *PEMBROKE*."). It is unclear why two "traced medals" notes are on his service record. The Times reported his Long Service award in September 1890.

Pensioned off from the Navy in 1901, Barend rejoined in August 1914 after the outbreak of World War 1. He served on *Pembroke* 1 (Chatham shore based establishment) for three years before joining HMS *Thalia* (depot ship Aberdeen). He ended his war service aboard HMS *Nairn* (an armed steam yacht used as a local patrol boat). For his World War 1 service he was later awarded the British War Medal named to "108779 S BAREND. S.B.S. R.N." Sidney Barend married Minnie in Scotland in 1886 - they had a daughter Edith (born in Scotland in 1899). They were living In South Leyton, Essex at the time of the 1901 census but had moved back to Scotland by the time of the 1911 survey. After the war Sidney seems to have remained in Scotland - dying in 1942 at the age of about 82.

Able Seaman (General Service) Willie Bennet

He was born in 1870 in Portsea, Portsmouth and served until 1899. It seems his main occupation was as "*shop boy*" before joining up. One of Willie Bennett's forebears was a Peter Bennett who was supposed to have sailed with Captain Cook on his 2nd and 3rd Voyages of discovery on the *Resolution*, but I have not been able to independently verify that. The surname could well be different, anyway.

Able Seaman Ernest Jesse Denyer

Ernest was born in Selsey, Chichester, Sussex. He seems to have joined the navy for 12 years on his 18th birthday, 18th April 1889 but like many crew that is usually the date of his actual service, most seamen having joined earlier as boys, possibly in his case on 2nd February 1886. He initially served on HMS *Impregnable*, followed by a long list of ships including HMS *Calliope* for the Samoa hurricane. His last ship seems to have been HMS *Victory* which he left in April 1911.

Ordinary Seaman William Harding

William was born in Handley, Hampshire in 1868 and enlisted in the Royal Navy as a Boy Seaman in 1885, Service Number 133768. He served in *Calliope* as an Ordinary Seaman, his first sea-going appointment. At the end of her commission in 1890 he went on to serve in *Wallaroo* (1891), *Rapid*, a composite screw corvette (1891 to 1895) and *Australia* (1895-96). In 1896 he transferred to HM Coastguard and served in different stations on the south coast of England, e.g. Ventnor, Stokes Bay and Fishbourne. He was mobilised in 1914 and served at sea in the armed boarding steamer *Stephen Furness*, patrolling the northern Irish coast (1915-16) and the armed merchant cruiser *Kildonan Castle*, deployed in the Northern Patrol on the blockade of Germany (1916-18). He was demobilised in February 1919 with the rank of Petty Officer 1st Class. He was awarded the 1914-15 Star, British War Medal, Victory Medal and RN Long Service and Good Conduct Medal. He also had the unofficial medal produced and presented by the Marquis of Leuville for the officers and crew of HMS *Calliope*. [Author's Note: a Henry B Harding was a stoker on *Calliope*, and may well have been a relative of William's.]

Carpenters Mate Thomas D. John

Thomas was severely injured during the storm, suffering a fractured skull. On *Calliope*'s return to Sydney, he was transferred to St. Vincent's Hospital, Sydney where after some months of treatment, he was able to take passage back to England and was eventually invalided out of the service.

Leading Stoker Mark King

Born 22nd November 1861 on Hayling Island, Hampshire. His previous occupation seems to have been as a Groom. He joined the Navy on 2nd October 1882 as a Stoker 2nd Class and was discharged dead on 3rd June 1910.

Cooper David Francis Mahoney

See record for David O'Mahoney.

Lieutenant Henry G. Monckton

In 1894, Monckton, with the rank of Lieutenant, was commanding HMS *Sunflower*, a sailing ship.

Skilled Carpenter's Mate Julius W. Newberry

Also recorded as Newbury. This gentleman may at some time have served on HMS *Superb* as "Shipwright". He was born on the island of Guernsey, date unknown. Commissioned around 1890, he retired from the Navy around 1913 but was recalled for War service and died in 1918.

Leading Seaman James Cresswell Moore

James Cresswell Moore was born in September 1865 at Basford, Nottingham, and joined his first ship, HMS *Northumberland* as a Boy on Jan 1st, 1883. He subsequently served on HM Ships *Invincible*, *Duke of Wellington*, *Alexandra*, *Dart*, *Pembroke*, *Wildfire*, *Howe* and then *Calliope* for the period January 1887 to October 1889. His son (who provided these details to the author in 2007) remembers him saying that he was one of the men assigned to the wheel to help steer *Calliope* out of the bay. After an honourable discharge from the Navy he joined the Sherwood Foresters as a Sapper and saw service in India and France during the First World War. He married in 1902 and died in 1948 aged 84.

Carpenter Michael O'Brien

Michael William O'Brien was born on 6th October 1861 in Jersey, Channel Islands. He was the son of Michael O'Brian and Mary Ann O'Moore. His father passed away while Michael was still young and he grew up in Jersey with his mother and elder sister.

On his birthday in 1879, at the age of eighteen, Michael began his formal service as a rating in the Royal Navy for a ten year period. He is described as being 5'3" height, brown hair, brown eyes and a fair complexion.

A second entry, which is not dated, modifies his height to 5'6" with the trade of carpenter and the addition of a tattoo on his left arm reading "*sailor*" and "*true love*".

Michael left the navy on the 15th April 1890; HMS *Calliope* was his last ship. He moved to Bristol where in 1891 he is recorded as the landlord of the Bird in Hand pub. Living with him was his mother Mary Ann and his brother-in-law James Giles.

Cooper David Francis O'Mahoney

David was born in 1855 in Cork City, Ireland, and died on the 1st November 1939 in Cardiff, South Wales. Married to Annie Swanton of Cork, he was living in Kent when a member of *Calliope's* crew at Apia. After retirement he worked at Gravesend Dockyard. On the death of his wife, he moved his three children Frances, Kathleen and Robert to Cardiff. Appears on occasion to have been identified in navy service records as "David Mahoney".

Able Seaman (General Service) Frederick Rex

This gentleman was born at Portsea Island, Hampshire on 2nd December 1867. His father and grandfather were both Stonemasons. It was said that he ran away to sea at the age of thirteen. Although he appears in the *Calliope* crew list as an Able Seaman, to family knowledge he was, or became, a Signalman. He married Anne Marie Wood from Chartham in Kent (circa 1895). He left the navy probably in 1897. At that time he joined the Coastguard Service and was stationed at Rye Harbour. In about 1910 he left the service and retired with his family to his wife's home village of Chartham near Canterbury where he died on 27th February 1934.

Chief ERA James Richards

On Sunday, 3rd February 1889, the day after *Calliope*'s arrival at Apia, Kane discharged forty-two year old Chief ERA (Engine Room Artificer) James Richards accompanied by an AB seaman and a blacksmith to HMS *Royalist* for transport back to Sydney. Richards had been taken ill shortly after the ship left New Zealand and his condition had been deteriorating steadily in *Calliope*'s sick bay. Unfortunately, he died a few days after *Royalist* departed Tonga for the run to Auckland and later in the evening of that same Wednesday 13th February, his body was committed to the deep.

James Friend Richards was born 24th January 1847 in the East Stonehouse district of Plymouth in Devon. He was the eldest son of a professional Royal Navy sailor who had travelled the world. He married Elizabeth Marks on 19th July 1868 and joined the Royal Navy on 12th April 1871, when he was described as being 5'11 in height, with black hair, black eyes and dark complexion and as being a fitter by trade. He died 14th February 1889 at 4 a.m. from hepatitis and an abscess of the liver in the sickbay of HMS *Royalist*. By the time of his death, he had accrued three Good Conduct badges and had therefore been awarded the Royal Navy Long Service and Good Conduct Medal.

This gentleman's eldest son, James Marks Richards would subsequently become the Chief Carpenter on HMS *Warrior* and would be killed at the Battle of Jutland - apart from Petty Officers, the only officer on board the ship to perish. *Warrior* had been heavily damaged by fire from the German battlecruiser SMS *Derfflinger* and four other High Seas Fleet battleships, which caused large fires and heavy flooding in the British cruiser. The engine room crew - of whom only three survived - kept the engines running for long enough to allow her to withdraw to the west. She was taken in tow by the seaplane tender HMS *Engadine* which also took off her surviving crew. She was abandoned in a rising sea at 8:25 a.m. on 1 June when her upper deck was only 4 feet (1.2 m) above the water, and HMS *Warrior* foundered shortly afterwards. The wreck lies upside down on the sea-bed, at a depth of about 80 metres and, so far at least, seems to have escaped the attentions of the illegal metal salvage scavengers that have plundered many other Jutland wrecks, in total indifference to their "War Grave" status.

Assistant Engineer James Robert Roffey

James was born in 1862 in Woolwich Kent, the second of seven children. He was the eldest of the two sons of James Roffey (later Sir James Roffey of Havant, Hampshire) and his wife Emma Roffey. Sir James was also in the Royal Navy and became Chief Inspector of Machinery. James Robert married Fanny Munro Petman in 1897 and they had at least one child, a son called Bernard Wilson Roffey, possibly there were others. James Robert Roffey died on 17th July 1914 aged 51. He is buried in Havant Cemetery in an adjacent plot to his parents Sir James Roffey (died 1st May 1912 aged 79) and Dame Emma Roffey (died 28th November 1914 aged 76) and his wife Fanny Munro Roffey (died 15th October 1936 aged 71).

Able Seaman Joseph Potter

Joseph came from Dover and was born 13th April 1864. After his naval service he served in the Coastguard at Sheerness and died in 1911 aged just 47 years.

Coxswain second class William Rolfe

Died in St. Vincent's Hospital at Sydney on 10th June 1889 following an accidental fall at Larg's Bay a few days earlier.

Ordinary Seaman James Spiller

James Spiller was born in Sedbury, Devon on 5th November 1870 and joined the Navy on the 1st November 1886 as a Boy *second class*. After 20 months on the training ship *Boscawen* he joined HMS *Orlando* and on the 5th November 1888, having engaged to serve for 12 years, he was rated as an Ordinary Seaman. Spiller served on *Orlando* from 5th June 1888 to 28th July 1891, except for the period between 20th January 1889 to 12th September 1889 when he served on HMS *Calliope*, presumably on loan. Spiller was rated as an Able Seaman on 1st May 1891 and on leaving *Orlando* he served mainly aboard the Battleships *Alexandra*, *Resolution*, *Revenge* and *Hibernia* until in May 1900 when he joined the Coast Guard Service being awarded the Long Service Good Conduct Medal in 1910. At the outbreak of World War 1 he was a Leading Boatman in the Coast Guard but on the 1st August 1914, he returned to the Navy as an Able Seaman and died on 1st November 1914 when HMS *Monmouth* was sunk at the battle of Coronel, Captain Frank Brandt (also in this section).

Leading Seaman William Isaac Thorndale

Like so many sailors, WIT joined the navy as a boy, in his case, aged 15 years. He served in HMS *Sultan* during the bombardment of Alexandria in 1882. WIT left *Calliope* at the end of the commissioning voyage to join the Coastguard service at Ballycroneen, (now) Southern Ireland. In 1884, he married Jane Dowling, daughter of Anne Dowling. He had one son Harry (1892) who died after just a few hours and two daughters, Winifred Sarah (1893) and Evelyn Baverstock (1895). Continued coastguard service at Studland in Dorset 1910 and retired to Reigate in 1919, his service extended by the war years. Naval Service : 1876 : HMS *Fisguard*, HMS *Implacable*; 1877 : HMS *Trudeyant*[?], HMS *Liberty*; 1878 : HMS *Lion* (these were all training ships); 1878 : HMS *Iron Duke*; 1879: HMS *Lapwing*, HMS *Charybdis*; 1881 : HMS *Duncan*; 1882 : HMS *Duke of Wellington*; 1884: HMS *Sultan*; 1885 : HMS *Excellent*, HMS *Minotaur*; 1887 : HMS *Calliope*; 1890 : HMS *Excellent* for paying off.

Crew Members known to have "left the ship" without permission:

In this section, I include details of some of HMS *Calliope's* crew that I have been able to identify from a specific source [38]. The vehicle for obtaining sufficient data allowing me to select the appropriate person from Kew's National Archives of Seaman's Service Records, is a publication which lists the newspaper classifieds requesting information on a Royal Navy deserter. I am uncertain exactly how reliable the data is; I am relaxed that the reference work accurately repeats the newspaper ads, but not that the original advertisements told the whole story at the time. The reader will see what I mean from the various entries.

The text in italics is the content of the newspaper classified advertisements recording a deserter, preceded by the date when the advert was posted

James William Cooper, Ordinary Seaman.

3rd September, 1888. Born at Chichester, 20 years of age, 5ft 5in. High, brown eyes, dark-brown hair, dark complexion. £3 Reward if apprehended within two years. Plus £5 Colonial Governments.

This young man, born 19th December 1869, had a very eventful and varied navy career. His gradings by his superior officers included many "Good" and "Very Good", but were interspersed with "Indifferent", "Refused to do duty" and "Insubordination" in addition to having "Run" from HMS *Calliope!* He spent time on a large number of ships including a second spell on HMS *Calliope,* and in quite a few gaol cells. After discharge, he then re-enrolled in the Navy for two additional five-year periods extending into the First World War!

Richard Cossentine Curtis, Boy.

1st October, 1889. Born at Lankylas, Cornwall, 19 years of age, 5ft 6½in. high, brown eyes, dark-brown hair, fresh complexion, moles on the right side of face, woman tatooed on right forearm, bracelet on wrist. £3 reward if apprehended within two years. Plus £5 NSW.

Actually born Lanteglos on 8th June 1870, he spent 7 days in the cells for his escapade from HMS *Calliope,* but went on to serve on many ships with consistent "Very Good" character references.

John Doel, Stoker.

13th July, 1888. Born at Gosport, Hants, 27 years of age, 5ft. 7in. High, brown eyes, light-brown hair, sallow complexion. £3 reward if apprehended within two years. Plus £5 NSW.

Born 4th November 1861, he received almost universal "Very Good" character references, and his apparent "desertion" from HMS *Calliope* is not recorded in his Service Record, which may suggest that his absence from *Calliope* was never intended to be permanent.

John Arthur Edwards, Able Seaman.

5th July, 1889. Born at St. George's, Middlesex, 25 years of age, 5ft 6in. High, hazel eyes, brown hair, fresh complexion. £3 reward if apprehended within two years. Plus £5 NSW.

Born 10th June, 1864, this young man had mostly "Fair" and "Good" reviews, but also seems to have spent some eight separate spells in Gaol or the Cells! The entry "RQ" meaning "Run, Query" suggests it was not certain that he had deserted *Calliope*, and the entry was subsequently struck from his Service Record.

William Ellis, Ordinary Seaman.

9th December, 1887. Born at Lambeth, London, 19 years of age, 5ft. 4¾in. high, light-blue eyes, light brown hair, fair complexion. £3 Reward if apprehended within two years. Plus £5 NSW.

Voluntarily returned to the ship. The information in the advertisement did not categorically identify this gentleman's service record from among a large number with that name in Kew's National Archives.

Ah Fook, Wardroom Cook.

1st October, 1889. Born in China, (not described). £3 reward if apprehended within two years. Plus £5 NSW.

Left the ship with Richard Curtis, see above entry. There is no seaman's record for this gentleman at Kew's National Archives. I have no information at all about him, neither prior to his service on HMS *Calliope*, nor after he deserted.

William Ernest Gibbs, Cook's Mate, Second Class.

7th November, 1888. orn at Gosport, Hants, 23 years of age, 5ft 8in. High, grey eyes, light-brown hair, fair complexion. £3 reward if apprehended within two years. Plus £5 NSW. Arrested by Wollongong police.

Born 17th April, 1865, William received mostly "Good" or "Very Good" character assessments. His punishment for leaving the ship was in "Lewes Gaol" in February 1890. As "Cooks Mate", William was part of the crew of HMS *Camperdown* when she collided with HMS *Victoria* as described in the section on Boatswain William Marshfield in chapter 10, and fortunately survived.

Montgomery Hamilton, "D 3rd Class"

10th April, 1889. Born at London, England, 20 years of age, 5ft 5in. High, hazel eyes, dark hair, sallow complextion. £3 reward if apprehended within two years. Plus £5 NSW.

Born 7th July 1869, this gentleman has the shortest Service Record I have yet encountered, but there may be a page missing. It records he joined

HMS *Calliope* on 12th January 1889, so that will have been on the Australian Squadron, so I presume he had served on other vessels and was transferred, probably from HMS *Orlando*. He seems to have deserted *Calliope* on the same day she returned to Sydney after the storm, 4th April 1889. He then appears to have returned to HMS *Royalist* on 9th May to be incarcerated in Brisbane Gaol for 90 days, followed by dismissal from HM Naval service.

His rating on his service record is "D3C", I can only guess that it may be "Diver, 3rd Class".

<u>George Jarvis, Senior Cook.</u>

19th November, 1887. Born at Wickham, Hants, 33 years of age, 5ft 7½. High, grey eyes, brown hair, fair complexion. £3 reward if apprehended within two years. Plus £5 Colonial Governments.

Born 15th August 1854 at Isleworth in Middlesex, his Service Record shows almost universally "Good" and "Very Good" character assessments, on occasion "Exemplary". The record does not show him to have "Run" from HMS *Calliope*, so perhaps his inclusion in this list is subject to an error in the research for reference [38] somewhere. It does, however, record him having "Run" from HMS *Immortalité* whilst in Portsmouth sometime in 1891, and spending 21 days in Canterbury Gaol. He later spent 8 days in Gaol after a number of warrants for his arrest were issued whilst on HMS *Crocodile*.

<u>Arthur Lee, Boy 1st Class.</u>

9th December, 1887. Born at Southgate, Middlesex, 19 years of age, 5ft. 3in. High, blue eyes, red hair, fair complexion. £3 Reward if apprehended within two years. Plus £5 NSW.

Voluntarily returned to the ship, so the escapade does not appear on his service record.

Promoted to Ordinary Seaman.

10th August, 1888. Born at Southgate, Middlesex, 19 years of age, 5ft 4in. High, blue eyes, auburn hair, fair complexion. £3 Reward if apprehended within two years. Plus £5 Colonial Governments.

This desertion does appear on Arthur's service record, but there is nothing further on it about him, so it appears he successfully started a new life in Australia.

John H Sharman

20 July, 1888. Born at Woolwich, 22 years of age, 5ft 5in. High, grey eyes, brown hair, freckled complexion. £3 reward if apprehended within two years. Plus £5 NSW.

I have not been able to categorically identify this gentleman's service record from among the large number with that name in Kew's National Archives.

Alexander Spencer Stone, Able Seaman.

20th July, 1888. Born at St. Heliers, Jersey, 24 years of age, 5ft. 7in. High, grey eyes, brown hair, fair complexion. £3 reward if apprehended within two years. Plus £5 NSW.

Arrested by Woter police. He spent 7 days in *Calliope's* cells as a result of leaving the ship. His service period expired 27th February, 1892.

The descriptions are as printed in the local newspapers of the time. The source is reference [38] in the bibliography list, supplemented by the person's Seaman's Service Record held at the National Archives, Kew, London.

Please note that the above content is not intended to be a source for criticism of these men, nor is it included as a list of shame. Conditions on nineteenth-century warships of any nation were not particularly pleasant, the rules were strict and the pay meagre. I am only including these names because their actions had the strangely *fortuitous* result of some details of these people being published, and I think they do deserve to be remembered. These desertions are those that occurred in Sydney Australia, as that seems to be the only place the events were recorded, or at least, that survive today. I genuinely hope those men who never returned to the ship had successful and happy lives, however things may have turned out for them. I also think some were incorrectly accused of desertion.

Of the 12 men listed, Arthur Lee, John Sharman, James Cooper and William Gibbs do not appear in Swan's crew list record for Samoa, but all were part of the crew of HMS *Calliope* when she left on her commissioning voyage from England in March 1887, so presumably their omission from Swan's list is an inadvertent error on his part.

Chapter 11: Epilogue for HMS *Calliope*.

Facts and figures are often dull and meaningless even when related to the most exciting of stories, but in this case, the mathematical details of *Calliope*'s voyage do perhaps try to tell a story of their own. Between her departure from Plymouth, Britain on 1st March 1887 until she moored up in Plymouth on 7th April 1890, that amazing cruise had lasted 1,133 days, shared almost equally between being at sea and moored in a port. From her commissioning date (25th January 1887) to paying off (1st May 1890) the cruise had lasted 1,192 days. During that time she travelled nearly 77,000 nautical miles, approximately half of that distance under sail alone or sailing with the assistance of steam.

Voyage Statistics as published by Chaplain Evans:

Duration: 25th January 1887 (commissioning date) to 30th April 1890. (Rev. Evan's interpretation of the paying-off date and official end of the voyage), a total of 1,191 days.

Distance run under steam alone: 38,647.5 nautical miles.

Distance run under steam and sail: 27,294.3 nautical miles.

Distance run under sail alone: 10,872.6 nautical miles.

Total distance run: 76,814 nautical miles.

Number of days at sea: 528.

Number of days in port: 663.

Water distilled: 3,528 tons.

Coal consumed: 8,479.6 tons.

Courts Martial: One person, a domestic.

Desertions: 12 persons on the Australian Station, one person (Arthur Lee) actually did it twice. Data for elsewhere seems not to be available. 12 is considered an exceptionally low total for the time and place. Most were recaptured, or voluntarily returned to the ship when they found that life away from the ship was not as easy as they thought it would be.

Please note that the number of days "at sea" and "in port" are those calculated by Reverend Evans, and total 1,191. Her "at sea" passage of 76,814 nautical miles in 528 days suggests an average speed of 145 nm per day, or 6 knots.

Calliope had become universally well regarded at every port she visited, a powerful salute to Captain Kane's genuine diplomacy. The number of misdemeanours and punishments recorded seems near enough the average for the time; Chaplain Evans seems to feel it was much better. The escape from the storm at Apia had brought great credit to the ship and her men, her captain, and to the Australian Fleet. Thankfully, she had never been called on to fire her big guns in anger, and her crew had never needed to board another ship under fire nor land on a hostile beach, but even so the voyage can surely only be described as a great success.

But those approximately equal steam and sailing figures obfuscate a story which foretells the death of sail; her performance when analysed dispassionately adds another voice to the hubbub that steam was the only way forward for warships (excuse me for that) and that sail was fast becoming history, something only for training ships semi-permanently moored to a wharf. Whilst glorious windjammers and clippers would continue to ply the oceans on a fragile commercial basis for many years, even up to the outbreak of the Second World War, the technology was pretty much out-of-date for a warship well before the end of the nineteenth-century.

The vast majority of *Calliope*'s sail alone mileage, some 80% of the 10,873 total, was made during the first few months of her first year of voyage, that long run down to the Cape and then across the southern ocean to Singapore. Much of that part of the journey was, in reality, simply prudent planning: training the crew in how to handle the vessel under sail alone, in case the relatively untried engines should prove unreliable in reality.

The maps on the following pages are a very rough approximation of the outward and homeward voyages undertaken by HMS *Calliope* on her commissioning trip. Whilst in the northern and southern Pacific areas, she made many shorter voyages between various ports and islands, which it would be confusing to include here. Both maps compiled by the author.

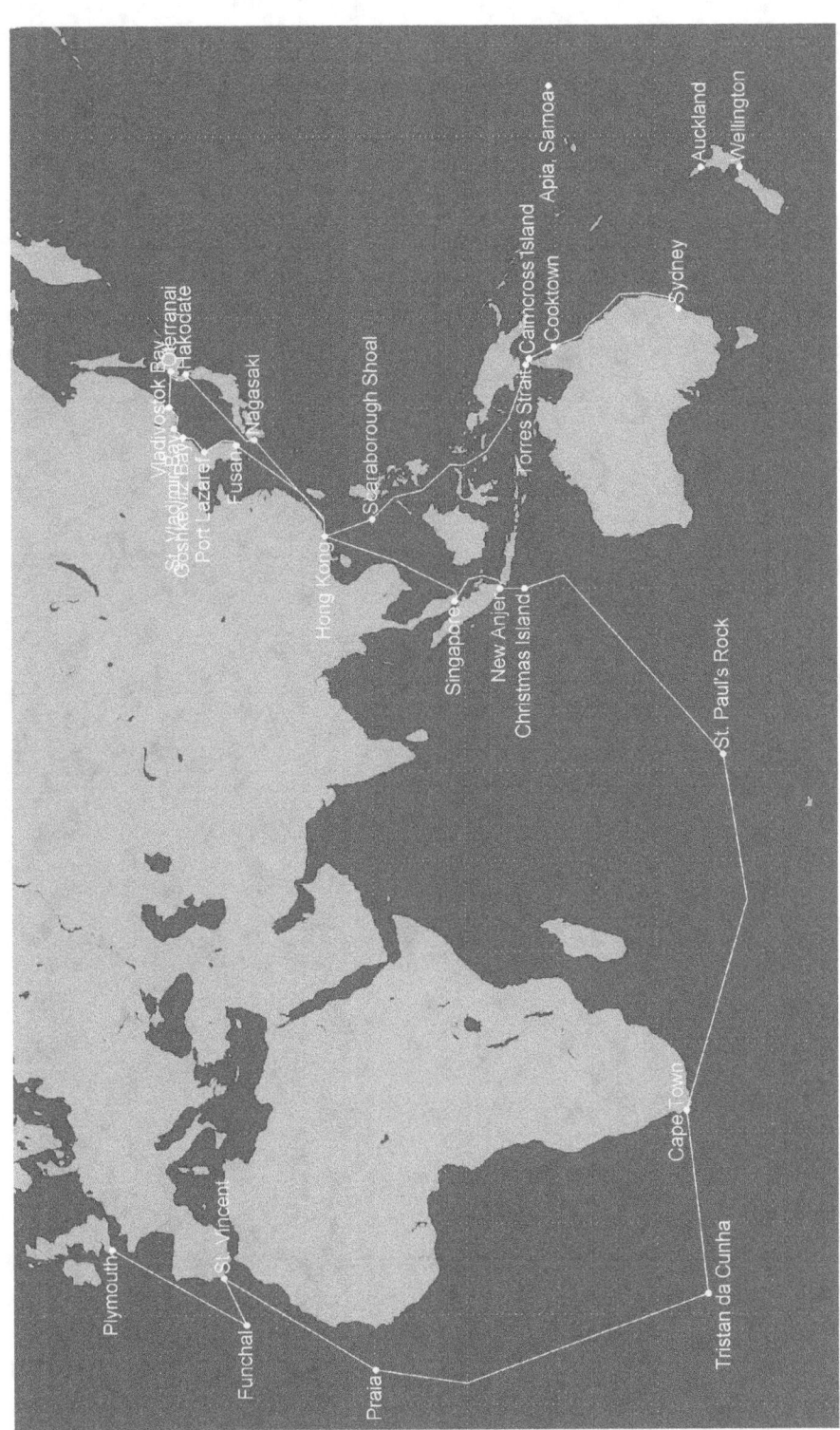

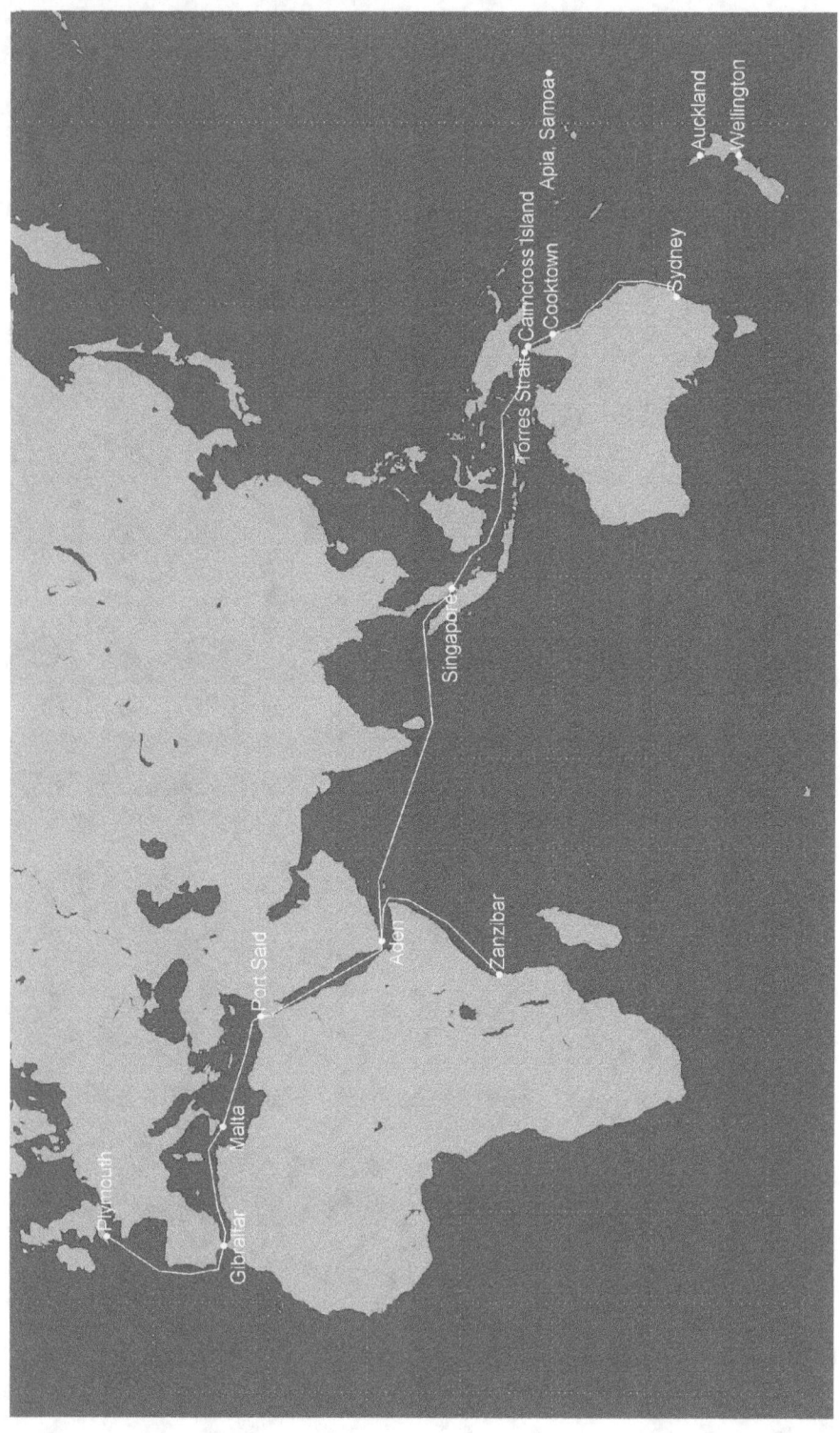

For the rest of that extended commissioning duty, the truth is that she was a steam warship, with her sails to be unfurled only when the wind was good and the circumstances allowed it, and rarely without her furnaces lit and the screw turning in support. That 35 year-old Admiralty Circular advising steam to be the secondary source of motive power was long defunct. Her speed trials showed her steaming characteristics to be good under fine conditions, but badly compromised by any sort of a head sea, and this observation too was not lost on the new breed of naval designers.

Partly as a result of these particulars, she would be the last of the British screw-corvettes, an era was coming to an end and in many ways she had contributed to it, had herself helped to light the way forward with the beacon of her own success. Allied to the good seamanship of her crew and the enterprise of a resourceful Captain prepared to gamble all on a dreadful risk, it had been her powerful engines and steam which had saved her at Apia; her sail equipment had only helped her cover large distances when speed or power had not been important. She was the best of the bunch at Apia, but even then she was a stepping stone only, a way-point on an important journey naval designers were taking, but by no means the final destination. After those two long voyages at the start of the trip, less than 4% of her other mileage had been completed without a boiler hissing its excess steam out the relief valves. In just a few more years, no warship's mast of any maritime nation would any more carry canvas.

These comments are not intended to her discredit. The twentieth-century's modern naval vessels will themselves no doubt be looked on in the twenty-first as amusing and ungainly points on a line which probably never ends, much as today's nuclear submariners must view those diesel predecessors of World War One, for example. But the line is fragile and without a regular "stake-in-the-ground", could never have continued the trend.

American commentators of the storm at Apia in 1889 pronounced *Calliope*'s modern design and her forward-thinking designer's insistence on reliable steam power as the major reasons the ship survived and their own didn't; one year later she returned home out-of-date and superseded by circumstance and technology. Let's not be sad about it, she had her time; she was for a short while a queen of her kind; she survived an adventure which many didn't; so we'll not begrudge her that thoroughly deserved if fleeting moment of glory.

As it seems with all ships whether they have performed wonderful tasks or not, the log of *Calliope*'s first commissioning voyage ends matter-of-factly and without fanfare. The last dated entry is both incorrect and muted: the 30th April 1890 seemingly followed by the 1st of that same month, when it should have read "May", of course. And that last entry on that misidentified day comprised a single, stark sentence on an otherwise sadly empty page: "*Captain Woodward of HMS Duke Of Wellington came on board and paid off the ship.*"

The New York Times of 13th November 1890 reported that *Calliope*'s repair bill would top $75,000, around £15,000 and a not inconsiderable sum in those days. After such a thrilling and internationally recognized adventure, it might be expected that the cost would be worth it, and that the ship would go on to even greater things, but it was not to be. In truth, her career after that commissioning voyage was the opposite in almost every way. Those matter-of-fact statements of storm and sea in her first commissioning log only sharpen in focus the stirring events she had once been part of, whilst in contrast, the records for her next commission are miserable and depressing.

The 1897 to 1905 commission under Captain (later Vice-Admiral) H. P. Routh limited her world to the waters around Great Britain and down to the western Mediterranean, on what were in reality just training voyages. Without intending any slight on the towns, the record of a trip from Aberystwyth to St. Ives seems so banal against the exotic intrigue and excitement of Singapore, Hong Kong and Zanzibar; of Nagasaki, Vladivostok and Sydney. The most glamorous place visited in those later trips was Tangiers, but she spent most of her time at Portsmouth.

The only real excitement came soon after her re-commissioning when a cable separated and divers were employed to locate the lost anchor in 18 fathoms, it being eventually recovered, and a collision in heavy fog on 28th April 1897 with the steamship *Springfield* which resulted in a severe spring to the bowsprit (again!) and the smashing of an anchor, a gun, and some other minor damage. The incident was, of course, investigated by an enquiry but does not appear on Routh's service record, and was clearly deemed to be not his fault; rather the *Springfield* was steaming much too fast and without sounding her fog siren, and in consequence only appeared to the officers on *Calliope*'s bridge when it was far too late to avoid.

There was a report in a couple of Australian newspapers in March 1906 that *Calliope* had been sold to Spain, but this appears to have been erroneous. Nevertheless, in that year, *Calliope* was out of date and virtually useless now as a warship, her raison d'être. There could be no military reason or benefit to be derived from the expense of equipping the ship and sending her once again to the far side of the world. As she had herself helped to prove, steam was the future, but even that was now being developed to power new and amazing machines. That innovative idea of extracting its force by using the steam pressure to blow across the multiple blades of a turbine instead of pushing a huge and heavy lump of metal piston along a cylinder, was an idea strangely opposite to the usual flow, it being an unappreciated American invention developed by the British. It meant her massive reciprocating engines would in just a few more years be little more than a joke - interesting in their time but now just another part of history. Naval designers at the turn of the century may have looked on those designs of just 15 years pedigree just as today's archaeologists might view the Roman's hypocaust method of heating a house - clever for its time but now impractical or superseded by technology.

I should, of course, qualify these musings that the reciprocating engine still had a lot of life in the early part of the twentieth-century, who can forget the images of the monstrous engines of RMS *Titanic*, for example?

So *Calliope*'s remaining active service extended as far as January 1905 with her final duty as tender to HMS *Hawke*, until HMS *St. George* replaced her even in that role. She was de-commissioned, her top masts, yards, rigging, boats, ordnance and any readily removable brass fittings and the like taken off, and the hull left with its forlornly stunted lower masts towed to the Motherbank off Portsmouth, alongside so many other hulks the Navy was hoping to find buyers for; if unsuccessful in that, she would soon go to destruction in the breakers yards or perhaps even just left to rot away in the mud. It is difficult not to imagine the ship as the elderly relative of an unfeeling family, once the young and beautiful darling of the hopeful clan, now pushed into a dingy and unsympathetic retirement home where past glories are of little interest to a new and brashly young world making its own mark.

But fortunately, in April 1907, the newly formed Tyne Division of the Royal Naval Volunteer Reserve in Gateshead needed a training ship and the commanding officer, E.W. Lloyd, Commander, RN retired, looked around for a suitable drill ship, somehow coming to hear of the grand old lady. Her reprieve assured, she was towed by HMS *Seahorse*, another long serving naval vessel, under a navigating party from the Royal Naval Barracks at Portsmouth, and eventually on the 14th December 1907, found the berth on the Tyne kindly provided by Messrs. Armstrong-Whitworth Company, at which she was to remain for the next 45 years.

In 1915, *Calliope* was renamed HMS *Helicon* to act as a recruiting depot for the Royal Naval Division, some 18,000 recruits passing through as the largest number for any such centre in the war. The reason for the name change was because that original name was required for a new *Calliope* (the fourth to bear it), a light cruiser launched in 1915 and the lead ship of her own class of two. She served in World War I and was present at Jutland in that infamous battle at the end of May 1916, described in chapter 10. That fourth *Calliope* was sold in 1931 at which point "our" *Calliope* was able to revert to her original and illustrious name.

In 1952, 68 years after her launch, *Calliope*'s rotting timbers could be patched up no longer and the costs of maintenance had spiralled too high to be justified; the end had finally come for the vessel which had escaped the terrible hurricane at Samoa. The year before, the BBC had broadcast a dramatized radio play about her escape; now the vessel was towed to the breakers and finally destroyed. Many locals, knowing the unique history of the ship, hurried to the yard to salvage what they might. The wardroom oak panelling was rescued by the Reverend Harry Chappell, a former RNVR Navy Chaplain, and used to surround the new organ in the recently re-built war-ravaged Christ Church in North Shields, Tyne and Wear, where it is still an imposing sight.

But the training depot still needed a ship, and the sloop HMS *Falmouth* launched in 1932 was renamed *Calliope* when she replaced the Samoan survivor at Gateshead. In 1968, even that last floating *Calliope* was broken up and the Royal Naval Volunteer Reserve along with the name moved to the brick-built shore-based establishment that it still occupies today, most likely the final HMS *Calliope* of them all.

The mahogany steering wheel from our third *Calliope*, or at least one wheel section from it, inscribed *"Fear God and Honour the King"* was donated to Samoa, and spent much of its time outside one of the official buildings; one part now resides in the New Zealand museum, on loan from the Auckland Museum and can be seen there today, and is most probably the Samoa wheel, as that had been sent to Auckland for repair. The quotation now reads *"HMS Calliope, Samoa 1889"*. The wheel was massive, and its summit stood some six to seven feet above the deck. It is one of the few artefacts from the vessel to exist today outside the shore establishment.

In 1975, Lord Louis Mountbatten was guest of honour at the Annual Dinner at HMS *Calliope*. I am not sure if this was the Samoa Hurricane dinner or another occasion. My great-grandfather was apparently a guest at one of these dinners, possibly the 1939 event in recognition of the 50th anniversary of the storm. Not being one used to such affairs, he acted on the advice given him by a friend, that after every mouthful, he should place his knife and fork on his plate whilst he chewed it; only to be distinctly annoyed when a waiter presumed him to have eaten his fill and removed his plate! For a long time, the family had a copy of the menu, but this now seems to have been lost at some point.

The fourth HMS Calliope, launched 17th December 1914. She was damaged in the Battle of Jutland (see data for Midshipman Hood in Chapter 10). Ten of her crew were lost in that action. In September 1917, she helped sink four German minelayers in that same area of the North Sea.

Yet even recently, HMS *Calliope* has again been under pressure: initially placed in an unedifying backwater on the Tyne amongst warehouses and dilapidated factories, the building is today labelled an ugly monstrosity amongst the new developments which have grown up around it, offices and modern flats which seem to be the trendy future for so many dock-land areas. There are suggestions that the Navy should move the establishment away from the Tyne, now a lucrative business and residential area, to another site without even the grace of water nearby; if it happens, it will be a sad day indeed. Latterly (2016), some significant investment in the facility seems to suggest her future is not now as precarious.

It is a tenuous link, but there was, in fact, another HMS *Calliope* and a story that coincidentally involves another vessel by the name of *Falmouth*. In November 1907, a brand new Milford Haven trawler named *Calliope* and registered "M.214", owned by a local man Mr. David Pettit, began to land her catch on the quayside of this famous and important fishing port. Trawlers were built strong, since the jockeying for position on the rising tide to get over the harbour bar first for the best fishing grounds often resulted in collision; some minor, some more dangerous. In August 1908, the trawler *Calliope* collided with the trawler *Falmouth*; the latter was beached but eventually re-floated, whilst *Calliope* tried to continue to the fishing area, only to be forced to return with a jammed rudder. In April 1911 another minor collision with the Bristol trawler *Lynmouth* resulted in no serious damage to either vessel. It was a case, however, of the third time being unlucky. In 1914, the 240 gross tonnage vessel was requisitioned by the Admiralty for war service under number 367, fitted with a single three-pounder gun, and used for minesweeping duties. Now named "HMS *Calliope* II", in March 1916 a collision off the Butt of Lewis (the northernmost tip of the Isle of Lewis in the Western Isles of Scotland) saw the ship finally lost.

Chapter 12: Epilogue for WIT.

When *Calliope* steamed past the Eddystone Rock on that rainy, misty day in April 1890, twenty-eight-year-old WIT was in poor health. The chest injuries received in the accident in South Africa whilst outward bound were seriously hampering the work of the Petty Officer whose duties were *"Captain of the Fore-Top"*. He was required to go aloft and supervise the management of the topsail; taking charge of a job he had himself performed many times in his career. It took a lot of effort even for a fit man, and in heavy weather was especially difficult for one in whom chest muscles were damaged and tight. Dragging himself up the ratlines in the shrouds became more and more exhausting.

During his return voyage, WIT had worried that he would not be able to pass the coming *"Survey"* before being permitted to continue his active service, and the fear that he might be declared unfit for sea duty left him anxious and apprehensive. Soon after arrival in England, he discovered there was an opening for men with sufficient naval time to join the expanding Coastguard Service. The downside was that WIT would lose his Petty Officer status (and pay) and revert to Leading Seaman, though his time would still count overall to his pension, and he would not need to undergo a medical check. He discussed the situation with his wife Jane who had seen so little of him in those six years following their marriage. His poor health and a not unnatural desire to settle down, perhaps sharpened in focus after the near miss at Samoa, were enough to reconcile him to the wage reduction, and he elected to apply. On hearing his reasons for doing so, his Captain gave him a glowing recommendation and a note that, except for his health, he would have been a very valuable member of any active ship's crew, and he was accepted for H.M. Coastguard. It is interesting to note that nearly every *Calliope* family I have been able to get into contact with records their own seaman ancestor as trading the navy for the coastguard when obliged to leave active service – it seems the brine really did mingle with the blood in their veins.

WIT's first service on land was in the coastguard team at Ballinacourty followed by Ballycroneen and then East Ferry, all villages on the south coast of Ireland, not far from Cork.

WIT with wife Jane and daughters Evelyne on the left and Winifred on the right. Probably taken at Ballycroneen, Ireland c. 1896/7.

The first-born son whose life only lasted a few sad hours, was followed by two healthy daughters and as the years passed and they reached early teens, the political troubles became more of a worry to someone who stood as an emblem of British rule, despite the neutrality of offering protection to everyone on the coast. The late nineteenth-century was no less a turbulent time in Ireland than the centuries which preceded it, nor indeed than the one that would follow. Added to ensuring the safety of local shipping and to prevent smuggling, was a need to patrol and watch for the running of arms to aid the republican cause, and this put the Coastguard in direct conflict with the Republican Men. It was felt prudent to train the teenage girls in how to use the shotgun if such dramatic defence ever became necessary, and whilst thank goodness it didn't, often was the time those isolated families living in the terrace of coastguard cottages were obliged to flee a noisy mob in the street outside; a deliberately constructed interconnecting door between each of the houses permitting the families to filter along to WIT's cottage at the end where they would all wait together for whatever would come. The threats were usually voluble and made when the men were away at work, the only real violence directed at property, but the mental anguish was considerable.

During this period, WIT received a number of promotions, finally to Chief Petty Officer, before his return to England. I cannot ascertain if WIT's move to the UK was at his request and as a result of the troubles. If it was, it was a sensible move. During the early part of the twentieth-century, attacks on Irish coastguard buildings and their occupants had become widespread, well organised, and vicious. Often upwards of 200 men would surround a building or cottage, cut the telephone wires and blockade the streets to prevent any chance of rescue or outside interference. They would then rouse the inhabitants, always meting out a rough handling for the men. If they were lucky, women and children were allowed to dress before then being forced to watch the building, containing all their possessions and whatever wealth they had over the years accumulated put to the torch with the howling mob dancing delightedly around it and humiliating their helpless victims however they could.

WIT's naval service record for this time is extremely difficult to interpret. He appears in the Irish census for 1901 as Coastguard Chief Boatman, this will have been at East Ferry. What does seem clear is that WIT was stationed at Limerick in 1904, and arrived at Studland Bay in Dorset, England, in December 1910; the family is recorded in the 1911 census at that Coastguard Station. Part of the intervening period is quoted as Rye Harbour (a place in West Sussex, England) but also seems to suggest this was still in Ireland, and the family memory is that he went direct from Ireland to Studland Bay. Winifred Sara, the elder daughter, was a teenage schoolteacher in Studland village in 1911 - my lovely Great-Aunt Winnie.

However and whenever he reached Studland, WIT at once fell in love with the wind-swept sandy coastline, then a sanctuary of sea birds and old sailors. Always a devout man, he would have been appalled at the thought of the nudist colony that now controversially occupies much of the beach. He would have probably been pragmatically unable to imagine why anyone should wish to walk around undressed. The incessant coastal erosion will have made a great deal of what he knew no longer visible, and I am certain that if he were put there now, he would have great difficulty in recognizing it as his beloved Studland. Perhaps it is as well he cannot see it today.

WIT was 53 when the First World War broke out. As a result, he overstayed his retirement until 1919, and when he finally left the coastguard on 29th June that year, it was after a total naval career of nigh 44 years. He and the family returned to their home town Reigate, WIT to take up the usual retirement activities of bowls and golf, and that other pleasure which is the universal old-man's delight: to enthral the youngsters of the town with the sort of tale that had perhaps kindled the flame of his own adventures a lifetime before - and, of course, finding the time in 1932 to write down his memories before his death in August 1949 aged 88 years. He even played a game of cricket in Reigate when aged 66, reported in the local newspaper! He was interred in the grave that had been prepared for Jane following her death 10 years previously.

Whilst his memoirs end abruptly with *Calliope*'s return, and suggest there was more which has since been lost, it means the history of the rest of his working life is as much a mystery as are the stories of most of the other men on *Calliope*: his shipmates, the crew who shared with him the comradeship of working up a new vessel; who marvelled as he did at seeing messy, noisy, smelly steam take over as the prime motive force in the beautifully clean "*tall ships*" that they had joined as boy sailors; men who experienced alongside him the terrible nightmare of the storm at Samoa. A perfect storm taken on and survived by men and their ship; all of them to become: *The Hurricane Jumpers*.

HMS *Calliope* CREW LIST at Apia, 16th March 1889.

Sources: "*The First Commission of H.M.S. Calliope. January 25th 1887 - April 30th 1890.*" by Captain E. W. Swan. Some additional data from "*The Cruise of H.M.S. "Calliope" 1887-1890*" by the Reverend Arthur C. Evans, and other additional amendment supplied by family descendants or historical publications. The spelling of a number of the names has been found to be occasionally inaccurate and has been (hopefully) corrected in this list where plausible alternatives were advised to me.

Officers:

Captain	*Henry Coey Kane*
Executive Officer	*Robert Kyle McAlpine*
Navigating Officer	*Henry Pearson*
Lieutenant	*Arthur W. Carter*
Lieutenant	*Henry G. Monckton*
Lieutenant	*Montague G. Cartwright*
Lieutenant R.M.L.I.	*Alfred E. Marchant*
Chaplain	*The Reverend Arthur C. Evans M.A.*
Fleet-Surgeon	*Valentine Duke B.A, M.B.*
Staff-Paymaster	*Beechey Rogers*
Staff-Engineer	*Henry G. Bourke*
Surgeon	*Arthur Cropley*
Assistant Paymaster	*Tom Seaman*

- Officers Continued

Engineer	*William Milton*
Assistant Engineer	*James R. Roffey*
Gunner	*Charles O. Martin*
Boatswain	*William Marshfield*
Carpenter	*George T. Grant*
Midshipman	*The Honourable H. L. A. Hood*
Midshipman	*Frank Brandt*
Midshipman	*Wilmot S. Nicholson*
Midshipman	*Edmund J. Prendergast*

A Guest of the Captain:

4th King's Own Regiment, formerly R.N.	*Major R.H. McCarthy*

Officers Loaned from HMS *Orlando*:

Midshipman	*Sidney R. Drury-Lowe*
Midshipman	*Hugh F. Hopkinson*
Midshipman	*John C.T. Glossop*
Midshipman	*Cecil H. Fox*

Petty Officers First Class:

Quartermaster	*Edward Pratt*	Boatswains Mate	*Thomas E. Saunders*
Quartermaster	*Oscar Clark*	Boatswains Mate	*John R. White*
Quartermaster	*Robert G. Smith*	Boatswains Mate	*John Hamilton*
Captain of the Main-Top	*Thomas Gibbs*	Captain's Coxswain	*James Pudge*
Captain of the Fore-Top	*Robert Newton*	Gunners' Mate	*James Howlett*

- Petty Officers First Class Continued

Captain, Forecastle	William J. Brown	Gunners' Mate	William H. Smith
Captain, Forecastle	Henry B. Sellick	Gunners' Mate	William Elgie
Captain, Quarterdeck	Henry Mullins		

Petty Officers Second Class:

Captain of the Mizzen-Top	Alexander Turner	Second Captain, Fore-Top	Henry T. Morgan
Coxswain second class	William Rolfe	Second Captain, Main-Top	Thomas Carr
Second Captain, Quarterdeck	Henry Parnell		

Signal Staff:

Yeoman of Signals	Patrick J. Dalton	Signalman	William Read
Leading Signalman	Frederick G. Withers	Signal Boy	Henry Prewitt
Leading Signalman	Frederick F. Husband	Signal Boy	Richard Jeffers
Qualified Signalman	Arthur Sutton		

Leading Seamen:

Frederick J. Brown	John Beare	Edmund Godding
William I. Thorndale	William F. White	Ephn. B. Wright

A.B's (Seamen Gunners):

Charles J. Searle	Frederick Ross	Richard Gardiner

- A.B's (Seamen Gunners) Continued

William J. Shepherd	Alexander S. Stone	Samuel Moss
Joseph J. R. Dick	Gustavus Miles	Thomas Healan
Fredrick Fozard	William J. Steer	John Stocks
James Watt	Alfred G. Every	John T. McDaniel
William H. Ransom	Daniel Regan	Henry Deacon
Richard W. Sullaway	James Stapleton	George E. Munday
David Kinnear	Frank Beach	John T. Francis
Harley Horton	Michael Cull	

A.B.s (General Service):

William Rawlinson	Alfred J. Thompson	James Fensham
James Crawford	Charles Ham	Isaac Briscoe
Henry Hamilton	Grge H. Spreadbury	William H. Phillips
William T. Searle	Thomas Carroll	George J. Hammerton
Walter H. Walsh	James R. Baldry	R. H. Durrant
Joseph Potter	Frederick W. Rex	William Miller
William Cole	Thomas Smith	James A. Flower
Patrick Donovan	John Johnson	William Webb
James E. Wright	Henry G. Russell	Henry Woolley
George A. F. Smith	William Faiers	George H. Jefford
William Trimble	James Young	William T. Sweet
Thomas Read	Frank Pulford	William E. Tull
Benjamin Tyldesley	Michael Hall	James H. Pook
James W. Pickels	Thomas P. Jolley	John A. Edwards
Arthur Turner	Charles Burdett	William Nye
William T. Sheppard	Albert E. Smith	Willie Bennett
Louis W. Morgan	Charles G. Reynolds	

Ordinary Seamen:

Henry T. Keene	William G. Jell	Edward G. Sturt
James C. Moore	George E. Lane	Edwin Wedlake
George Munden	William Harding	Ulick Stanton
Joshua Snaith	William Ellis	Ernest J. Denyer
William J. Stratton	John D. Rodgers	Angus Murray
Henry Osmond	Charles Rodgers	George A. Bax
William Hill	George A. Shaver	Charles W. Johnson
Robert Day	Thomas McFarlane	Thomas Bumstead
Alfred A. Sturt	John W. Smith	Cecil F. Gulliver
Thomas Parker	Joseph Attwell	William Wisldon
Richard C. Curtis	George Edwards	George Easter
William Grey	William Langdon	Joseph J. Barber/Barker
Arthur Lee		

Ordinary Seamen (on loan from *Orlando*):

William Rook	Philip Rodd	Philip Rendle
William Toms	James Spiller	Frederick K. Stimpson
William Allen	John Hedges	Willie C. Hunt
Joseph J. Barker/Barber	George Moog	Alfred F. Hood

E.R.A's (Engine Room Artificers):

Edwin Wood	Alfred W. Neville	George G. C. Haines
James Richards		

Leading Stokers:

Henry Aldred	Ernest A. Welling	Mark King
Thomas Clavell	Richard Thorpe	George W. Childs
Thomas Searle		

Stokers:

John Doel	Edwin W. Beale	James Picknell
Henry Knight	John T. Welsh	Frederick C. Bennett
James Osman	Walter Wright	William McWilliams
George E. Peach	John Whitwick	William C. Cole
William Alsford	Henry Treagus	Herbert Thomas
Andrew Shier	John Charlton	Charles H. Terry
Charles Gilbert	Paul Childs	Thomas Buxey
Thomas Chubb	Henry B. Harding	Walter Shering
William Breedon	John Elliot	

Other Members of the Ship's Crew:

Master At Arms	Harry Sebright	Skilled Shipwright	James Gillespie
Ship's Corporal	Thomas C. Dobinson	Skilled Shipwright	Duncan Ferguson
Armourer's Crew	Arthur Thurston	Ropemaker	John McDonald
Captain of the Hold	James Christmas	Sailmaker	Thomas Lucas
Skilled Carpenter's Mate	Julius W. Newbury	Sick Berth Steward, Second Class	Sydney Barend
Carpenter's Mate	Thomas D. John	Plumber's Mate	Richard P. Frost
Carpenter's Crew	Frederick Stephens	Cooper	David O'Mahoney
Carpenter's Crew	Michael O'Brien	Writer, Second Class	Edward N. Luxon
Carpenter's Crew	William H. Marsh	Caulker	Charles W. Down

Other Members (Loaned from HMS *Orlando*):

Armourer	William Ruse

Stewards:

Captain's Steward	Richard May	Wardroom	William C. Costick
Captain's Steward	William Brine	Wardroom	Ah Sam
Assistant Steward	George T. Chapman	Warrant Officers Mess	Henry Ayling
Ship's Steward, Second Class	William G. Crocomb	Gunroom	William Birch
Ship's Steward, Boy	Michael Finnie		

Cooks:

Ship's Cook First Class	George Jarvis	Wardroom Cook Assistant	Montgomery Hamilton
Captain's Cook	George Crawford	Wardroom Cook Assistant	George W. Pavey
Wardroom Cook	Ah Fook	Gunroom Cook	John E. Codd
Cook's Mate, 2nd Class	William Gibbs		

Royal Marine Artillery:

Corporal	George Champ	Gunner	Albert Shearman
Gunner	James Lord	Gunner	Dennis Barnett

Royal Marine Light Infantry (Sergeants):

Robert Searl	Alfred E. Walker

Royal Marine Light Infantry (Privates):

George Graybourne	Edward M. Collett	George Credland
William Wilde	George H. Skidmore	James Woods
William E. Brown	Frank Wright	Charles Cox
Alfred B. Miller	Frederick A. Gray	Robert Scott

- Royal Marine Light Infantry (Privates) Continued

Thomas Jones	Walter Jenkins	Frederick F. Bullers
Robert J. Stamp	John Irvine	William Shawyer
Edward J. Wells	Thomas Boles	James Shealds
William C. Doust	William Shurmer	John W. Carroll
William Delaney	Charles Boxall	Joseph Statham
Arthur Cove	Andrew Bowie	Frederick F. Rigsby
Henry Cort		

Boys:

James Cooper

I think there will have been a number of boys on the ship, but Captain Swan does not record their names. The person above is only known because he deserted the ship whilst still classed a "Boy".

American Crew known to have been present at Apia, 16th March 1889.

Sources: JP Dunning account dated February 1890; Admiral Kimberly's *Special Report* dated 16th April 1889; *Indiana State Sentinel*, 17th April 1889; *Alexandria Gazette*, 19th August 1889; *Indianapolis News*, 31st January 1894; *Los Angeles Herald*, 21st May 1889; the Memorial Plaque on display at St. Peter's Chapel at the Mare Island Navy Yard in San Francisco; Lieutenant R.G. Davenport's personal diary. The lists are not complete; I have not been able to find a source for all the various crews present. Even the United States National Archives Catalogue on-line search results do not seem to have digitised records of crew lists for any of the American ships at Apia.

The American Naval History and Heritage Command web-site has an image which is clearly from the diary of (then) Lieutenant Richard G. Davenport, though they do not attribute it to him - it is reference NH43829. Compare it to the attributed NH43810. It shows the photograph of the wrecked ships at Apia that I have reproduced on page 234, and lists the officers of USS *Vandalia*, but possibly at the time Davenport joined the ship (1st November 1887). Since the diary record was obviously made *after* the storm, they were almost certainly present at the time, and I have included those officer's names as being present at Apia. The only exception is Henry Lyon, who seems to have transferred to USS *Trenton* before the storm.

Also according to that Heritage Command web-site, an Inventory of the Naval Records Collection of the Office of Naval Records and Library in Record Group 45, Appendix L, Sub-Entry 119, records that there are Log and Journal entries for USS *Nipsic* covering the years 1877-1890, but they also don't seem to have been digitised.

There is a lot of confusing information regarding the names of the men who perished on the American, and indeed, the German ships. The names of the 51 Americans who perished are recorded in a number of places: Kimberly's early reports; various newspaper reports; and the memorial plaque. The names are occasionally spelt differently at each reference, and the variations are most likely phonetic, perhaps caused by them being taken down from word-of-mouth. I guess the most reliable ought to be the plaque, presumably taken from official records, but I have found some doubtful spellings even on that; even so I have used that as the source for those who died. Where I have come across an alternate spelling, I have noted the fact in these tables with the other option(s) separated by a slash mark.

The names are listed in alphabetic order, not by rank, but the rank quoted is that pertaining at the time of the storm.

USS *Nipsic*

J. Bradley	Chief Boatswain's Mate	Survived
Brooks Cason	Quartermaster Gunner	Survived
S.T(S?). Browne	Pay Clerk	Survived
J. Callahan	Quartermaster	Survived
G. W. Callan	Apprentice	Drowned
W. Campbell	Private Marines	Survived
W.K(C?). Cole	Naval Cadet	Survived
J. Corrine(?)	Past. Assistant Paymaster	Survived
W. Cosgrove	Boatswain's Mate	Survived
R.G. Davenport	Lieutenant	Survived
Dr. E.Z(C?). Derr	Past. Assistant Surgeon	Survived
C.A. Doyen	Second Lieutenant of Marines	Survived
H.A. Field	Ensign	Survived
T.G. Fillette	Lieutenant of Marines	Survived
H.C. Fisher	First Lieutenant of Marines	Survived
H.E. Frick	Past. Assistant Engineer	Survived
J. Gill	Seaman	Drowned
W.W. Gilmer	Ensign	Survived
Grupp	Sergeant Marines	Survived

- USS Nipsic Continued

G.W. Hall	Chief Engineer	Survived, died on return journey
G.C. Hannus(?)	Lieutenant	Survived
J.M. Hawley	Lieutenant	Survived
J. Heap	Apprentice	Drowned
T. Johnson	Steward	Drowned
H.P. Jones	Ensign	Survived
D. P. Kelleher/Kellcher	Coal Heaver	Drowned
A.J. Kiersted	Chief Engineer	Survived
J. Lane	Seaman	Survived
D.P. McCartney	Chief Engineer	Survived
F. McCurley	Commander	Survived
R.G. Mitchell	Lieutenant	Survived
D.W. Mullan	Captain	Survived
H. Pontseel	Coxswain	Drowned
J.L. Purcell	Ensign	Survived
J.K. Seymour	Ensign	Survived
J.A. Shearman	Lieutenant	Survived
R.H. Taylor	Quartermaster	Survived
J.A. Tobin	Past. Assistant Engineer	Survived
W. Watson	Fireman	Drowned
H. Webster	Past. Assistant Engineer	Survived
W.P. White	Ensign	Survived

Some of the names in the table above have been read by me from the image of Lieutenant Davenport's handwritten diary. Davenport uses the abbreviation "Past." in his diary, or it might be "Post.", but I think it most likely to be shorthand for "Passed". It is simply a progression of rank, for example: "Assistant Engineer", "Passed Assistant Engineer", "Engineer" and "Chief Engineer". There were also levels such as "First", "Second" and "Acting", and the British Royal Navy seems to have had a similar structure of rank.

USS *Trenton*

W.H. Allen	Lieutenant		Survived
G. Bart	Seaman		Leg broken
J.J. Blandin/Blanden	Ensign		Survived
S.H. Boutwell	Sailmaker		Survived
J. Brady	Pay Clerk		Survived
R.M.G. Brown	Lieutenant		Survived
A.J. Clark	Pay Inspector		Survived
B.C. Decker	Naval Cadet	Injured in fall to deck	
N. von F. Farquhar	Captain		Survived
B.C. Fernald	Carpenter		Survived
R.W. Galt	Past Assistant Engineer		Survived
W. Gibson	Coal Heaver		Scalded
S.L. Graham	Lieutenant		Survived
Fugi Hachitaro	Cabin Steward		Survived
E. Hendrickson	Lieutenant		Survived
J. Hewlett	Landsman		Killed
R.W. Huntington	Captain of Marines		Survived
L.A. Kimberly	Rear-Admiral		Survived
H.W. Lyon	Lieutenant Commander		Survived
H. Main	Past Assistant Engineer		Survived
C.H. Matthews	Assistant Engineer		Survived
A.A. McAllister	Chaplain		Survived
J. McLaughlin	Boatswain		Survived
G.A. Merriam	Lieutenant		Survived
J. Nicholls	Marine Corporal	Survived, accidentally killed later	
F. Noefleet	Past Assistant Surgeon		Survived
L.L. Reamy	Lieutenant		Survived
B. Ricklin	Seaman	Survived, accidentally killed later	

- USS Trenton Continued

H.O. Rittenhouse	Lieutenant	Survived
J.E. Rostedt	Ordinary Seaman	Leg broken
B.O. Scott	Lieutenant	Survived
C.H. Stoddard	Machinist	Survived
H.J. Tressett	Acting Gunner	Survived
J. Westfall	Acting Gunner	Survived
Dr. C. A. White	Doctor of the Pacific Station (Medical Inspector)	Survived
S.S. White	Assistant Surgeon (Fleet Surgeon)	Survived

USS *Vandalia*

E. Ambrose	Seaman	Feet terribly cut by ratlines
F.H. Arms	Paymaster	Drowned
H. Baker	Landsman	Drowned
W.E. Bowen	Machinist	Leg probably fractured
C. Boyle	Seaman	Inflammation of hand
W. Brisbane	Cabin Steward	Drowned
W. Brown	First Quartermaster	Drowned
J.W. Carlin	Lieutenant	Survived
Carole	Private Marines	Survived
M. Cashen	Corporal of Marines	Drowned
J. Coleman	Sergeant Marines	Survived
Dr. F.J.B. Cordeiro	Past. Assistant Surgeon	Dislocated knee-cap
M. Craigin	Captain After-Guard	Drowned
A.E. Culver	Lieutenant Junior Grade	Survived
Pen Dang	Landsman	Drowned
B. F. Davis	Yeoman	Drowned
T. G. Downey	Paymaster's Yeoman	Drowned

- USS Vandalia Continued

C. Eggart	Captain of Top	Badly injured right side
M. Erickson	Ordinary Seaman	Drowned
H. C. Gehring	Private of Marines	Drowned
J.H. Gibbons	Ensign	Survived
A. Goldner/Goldne	Private of Marines	Drowned
G. Gorman	Carpenter	Drowned
N. B. Green	Bayman	Drowned
A.S. Greene	Chief Engineer	Survived
J. Griffin	First Class Fireman	Drowned
E. M. Hammar/Hammer/Hammet	Seaman	Drowned
J. Hantchett/Manchett	Sergeant of Marines	Drowned
Dr. J.H. Harvey	Surgeon	Severe nervous prostration
C. H. Hawkins	Steerage Steward	Drowned
H.P. Hawley	Surgeon	Survived
F.R. Heath	Lieutenant Junior Grade	Survived
Yee Hor	Ward-Room Cook	Drowned
W. Howat	Coal Heaver	Drowned
Jensen	Ordinary Seaman	Eyes inflamed by sand
F. Jones	Private of Marines	Drowned
S. G. Jordan	Private of Marines	Drowned
M. H. Joseph	Engineer's Yeoman	Drowned
Ah Keau/Kiau/Kean	Cabin cook	Drowned, or possibly survived
T. Kelly	Second Class Fireman	Drowned
J. Kelly	Ordinary Seaman	Drowned
N. Kinsella	Corporal of Marines	Drowned
C. H. Kraus/Kranz	Private of Marines	Drowned
C. P. Kratzer	Ordinary Seaman	Drowned
H. Krayden	Quarter-Gunner	Foot badly cut

- USS Vandalia Continued

J.A. Le Jeune	Naval Cadet	Survived
T. F. Lissman	Sergeant of Marines	Drowned
Melville	Fireman	Survived
J. Mohl	Seaman	Knee injured
A. Montgomerie	Private of Marines	Drowned
E. Moole Jnr.	Naval Cadet	Survived
G. Murrage	Bayman	Drowned
P. Neilson	Ordinary Seaman	Foot cut
E. O'Neil	Seaman	Cut in arm
Ah Pack	Seaman's Cook	Drowned
T. Riley	Landsman	Drowned
C. S. Ripley	Ensign	Survived
J. Roach/Roche	Pay Clerk	Drowned
C. M. Schoonmaker	Captain	Drowned
J. Sims	Private of Marines	Drowned
L.A. Stafford	Naval Cadet	Survived
H. P. Stalman	Bayman	Drowned
C. E. G. Stanford	Landsman	Drowned
A. Steen	Fireman	Arm badly lacerated
F. E. Sutton	Lieutenant of Marines	Drowned
H. Webster	Past Assistant Engineer	Survived
A. Welch	Captain of Top	Bad wound in right foot
G. H. Wells	Private of Marines	Drowned
H.A. Wiley	Naval Cadet	Survived
J. Willford	Private of Marines	Drowned
G. Williams		Survived
J.C. Wilson	Lieutenant Junior Grade	Survived
H. Wixted	Private of Marines	Drowned

It will be noted from the lists above that at least two American sailors from USS *Trenton* would die in accidents before finally the crews were repatriated, and one (at least) from illness on the journey home. Their stories are recorded below, and are some of the few American Crew stories I have been able to unearth.

The web-site "http://www.history.navy.mil/" used to have comprehensive life stories of the major officers involved at Samoa (Kimberly, Mullan, Farquhar), but today seems to have taken them off the site. At least, I cannot now find them to record the links herein. The web-site owners recently (c.2012) changed their name to the American Naval History and Heritage Command, and the change in records available on-line seems to have originated then.

American officers and residents at the grave of Captain C. M. Schoonmaker of USS Vandalia, shortly after the storm. From left to right: Mr. Hart, News Correspondent; Mr. J.P. Dunning, Associated Press correspondent; unidentified man; Ensign John H. Gibbons, of USS Vandalia; Chief Engineer Albert S. Greene, of USS Vandalia; two unidentified men, the rightmost of which may be Lieutenant Carlin, USS Vandalia; and Captain Norman H. Farquhar, Commanding Officer of USS Trenton. [Naval History and Heritage Command, NH 97918]

The bodies of 19 American servicemen were exhumed and repatriated in June 1891 with most being buried in the Mare Island cemetery at San Francisco. Captain Schoonmaker's remains had already been repatriated, and he is buried at Wiltwyck Cemetery, Kingston, Ulster

County, New York.

<u>Paymaster F.H. Arms, USN (?-1889), USS *Vandalia*.</u>

The *Los Angeles Herald*, Volume 31, Number 178, 31st March 1889 reported:

> *"Paymaster Arms was appointed from Connecticut in 1864, and had been on duty on the Vandalia since May 1887. His family reside at the Crawford House, New London."*

<u>Ensign J. J. Blandin, USN (1862-1898), USS *Trenton*</u>

He was a key person in the rescue of personnel of *Vandalia*, and is mentioned by Kimberly with his name seemingly misspelt. Some 9 years later he was Officer of the Deck and on the poop deck with Captain Charles D. Sigsbee when the USS *Maine* blew up in Havana Harbour, Cuba, on 15th February 1898 just 2 weeks after he was made Lieutenant. He was injured by a flying fragment of debris and died 5 months later from the blow that he received on that occasion. He is recorded in the Naval Historical Centre records as having survived the *Maine* explosion, but the page seems to have been removed. His service record is: Cadet Midshipman, 28th June 1878. Ensign, 1st July 1884. Lieutenant, Junior Grade, 31st July 1894. Lieutenant, 1st February 1898. Blandin died 16th July 1898.

The story of the American-Spanish War that followed the explosion on USS *Maine* is one that cannot be condensed into a simple paragraph in this book.

<u>Lieutenant R.M.G. Brown USN (?-?), USS *Trenton*.</u>

Captain Farquhar in his report dated 19th March 1889 states:

> *"Lieutenant R.M.G. Brown, the Navigator, was by my side the whole time, and to his excellent judgment, one time at least, the ship was cleared of a reef. Had we struck it I fear few of the 450 people onboard of Trenton would be alive today."*

I have not been able to find a full copy of this report.

Lieutenant of Marines James W. Carlin (1844-1900), USS *Vandalia.*

James W. Carlin was born in 1844 in a log cabin in Carthage, Illinois. In 1862, he enlisted in the 118th Regiment and fought in the Civil War. In 1864, he received an appointment to the U.S. Naval Academy at Annapolis, graduating in 1868. Commander Carlin served for over 30 years in the navy and died of typhoid fever on 13th December 1900.

Naval Cadet W.C. Cole, (1868-1935), USS *Nipsic.*

William Carey Cole was born in Chicago, Illinois on 23rd August 1868 and was appointed a naval cadet on 5th September 1885. He graduated from the Naval Academy on 7th June 1889 after the storm, returning then to USS *Nipsic*. In 1907, as Lieutenant Commander, he became navigator of the newly commissioned USS *Kansas*. In 1919, he served as Assistant Attaché at the United States embassy in London, and later Assistant Chief of Naval Operations in Washington. He retired with flag rank on 1st September 1932 and died at the Naval Hospital, Mare Island Navy Yard, Vallejo, California, on 28th May 1935.

<u>Lieutenant Richard G. Davenport (1849-1926) USS *Nipsic*.</u>

He was born in Washington D.C. on 11th January 1849 and started naval service on 13th June 1865 with a practice cruise on USS *Macedonian*, followed by a number of other practice ships. His first navy ship appears to have been USS *Sabine* in 1869. He joined USS *Nipsic* on 10th October 1887 as navigator, although his own diary record shows 1st November 1887 and left 26th July 1890. The records of his naval service finish with USS *Castine* on 8th December 1896, but as he was later Commander and then possibly Rear-Admiral there seems to be later data missing. In May 1898, he seems to have been Lieutenant Commander in Key West, Florida, possibly on USS *Suwanee*, immediately prior to the Spanish-American War.

He was a prolific recorder of his service time, a search of the Heritage Command web-site for his name results in a large number of pages from his handwritten diary, most with images of the ship he was stationed on. His whole life story would be very interesting, I think. But his life wasn't all smooth sailing.

The Indianapolis News reported on 31st January 1894 that Lieutenant Davenport had asked for a *"Court of Honor"* to pass verdict on his conduct whilst Navigating Officer of *Nipsic*. It seems Davenport, as third officer on the ship, was heavily criticised in some quarters (primarily Lieutenant Purcell, an Ensign on *Nipsic* at the time of the storm) for his decision to leave the beached vessel, thereby setting a bad example to the men by stripping off his clothes and swimming to shore. Purcell seems only to have mentioned this criticism a number of years later when Davenport attempted to join the New York Yacht Club and was refused entry because of Purcell's voiced objections. The court was careful to find no criticism of Davenport's conduct during the storm, but the verdict of the court was *"...conduct was unbecoming an officer..."*, but with *"...mitigating circumstances..."* This sounds somewhat ominous, but seems to me to be grossly unfair, the only imputation being the *"...time and manner when Lieutenant Davenport left the ship..."* when it was grudgingly acknowledged *"...that the order to abandon the ship had been given, and that the Captain testified that officers and men were free to leave the ship in any manner they saw fit..."* How he was condemned for doing just that I don't know. Nevertheless, the court was emphatic in its findings.

Strangely, Lieutenant Purcell was also censured by a court, for not, despite his claims to the contrary, bringing the matter to the attention of his superior officers at the time of the alleged actions if he had felt them to be cowardly, and only doing so years later to a civilian organisation, not the proper thing to have done. He was accordingly censured quite heavily in his turn. It was thought he had acted out of malice for a superior, though brother, officer.

The reports on both officers can be found on the internet and make interesting reading. It does look as if Purcell had harboured a grudge against Davenport, possibly over something that had happened during their time together on *Nipsic*.

The event cannot have had much impact on what seems to have been a very commendable continuing career in the navy for Davenport. He died 30th May 1926 in Washington.

Seaman B.F. Davis, USN (?-1889), USS *Vandalia*.

The *Los Angeles Herald*, Volume 31, Number 178, 31st March 1889 reported:

> *"One of the lost, Ben Davis, is understood to be a relative of a wealthy family somewhere in the East, but was disowned for marrying a girl his inferior in social position. When his wife died Davis came on to San Francisco, and only a few weeks ago signed as a seaman on board the Vandalia."*

A sad story lies hidden there, I think.

Captain Norman von H Farquhar, USN (1840-1907), USS *Trenton*

Norman von Heidreich Farquhar was born in Pottsville, Pennsylvania, on 11th April 1840 and attended the U.S. Naval Academy during 1854-59. He retired from active duty in April 1902 upon reaching the statutory service age limit of 62. Rear-Admiral Farquhar died at Jamestown, Rhode Island, on 3rd July 1907 and was buried in Section 1 of Arlington National Cemetery. His wife, Addie Whelan Pope Farquhar is interred with him.

Assistant Surgeon Ezra Zacharias Derr (1851-1935), USS *Nipsic*

Derr was born in Frederick County. Maryland on 12th January 1851. He was appointed Assistant Surgeon 3rd March 1873 and promoted to Passed Assistant Surgeon in 1877 on the training ship *Minnesota*. This man left USS *Nipsic* in a boat with a few sailors, and was saved from drowning by a shore based resident of Apia, as described in chapter 7. He died 24th August 1935 near the same place that he was born. At some point, he attained the rank of Captain.

Chief Engineer Albert S. Greene (?-1896), USS *Nipsic*

His birth date is unknown, but his first naval appointment was his commission as a Third Assistant Engineer from New York on 17th February 1860. His details on the American Naval History and Heritage Command web-site (Heritage Command reference NH 72209) were contributed presumably by a relative, but strangely do not mention his time on USS *Nipsic*. He died 8th March 1896.

Seaman G. Gorman, USN (?-1889), USS *Vandalia*.

The *Los Angeles Herald*, Volume 31, Number 178, 31st March 1889 reported:

> *"George Gorman, one of the crew of the Vandalia, was well known among Pacific Coast seafaring men. He has a family living, it is thought, either in Vallejo or Benicia."*

Boatswain's Mate Gray USN (?-?), USS *Trenton*.

This man attempted to assist Gunner Westfall to cover the ventilator holes which were open on the spar deck with the water pouring down them. It seems the attempt was unsuccessful, but Gray does not appear on the memorial plaque so is assumed to have survived the effort.

Cabin Steward Fugi Hachitaro USN (?-?), USS *Trenton*.

This man performed an extraordinary act of heroism in saving the life of Lieutenant John S. Wilson from USS *Vandalia* at great risk to his own. Wilson had attempted to cross from *Vandalia* to *Trenton* when the two vessels were close together and settled on the floor of the bay, but had fallen into the tempestuous water on the deck of his ship. He was clutching the so-called Jacob's Ladder on *Vandalia's* main-mast with only his head above the waves, but was clearly exhausted and in imminent danger of being swept away to be drowned. The Japanese steward on *Trenton* saw the plight of the officer, and immediately climbed over the stern of his own ship and down to the water, climbing onto the main-yard of *Vandalia* lying precariously on the wreck. Hand over hand, he made his way along the yard to where the semi-conscious Wilson was gradually losing his grip. Hachitaro stayed with Wilson in the surging waves, supporting the officer, at risk from the vessels being slung together to crush them both or for the mast to be broken from *Vandalia* and cast into the waters. Comrades on *Trenton* threw a line to the men; Hachitaro attached it to Wilson's unresponsive body, for him to be hauled aboard *Trenton* to the ministration of others and eventual safety, before the line was again passed down to the steward, who was just able to attach it to himself before exhaustion overtook him - he too was then hauled aboard *Trenton*. Just a few minutes later, *Vandalia's* main-mast to which the men had been clinging was carried away by the waves and disappeared in the surf. Hachitaro was quite rightfully awarded a gold Life Saving Medal for this daring act of bravery which undoubtedly saved Wilson's life. [40]

Ensign H.P. Jones, USN (1863-1938)

Hilary Pollard Jones served the United States Navy in both the Spanish-American War, and the First World War. In 1912, he commanded the battleship USS *Rhode Island*. During the First World War he commanded patrol units and later a division of the Transport Force, receiving the Distinguished Service Medal for his outstanding service. Admiral Jones retired in 1927 but served as naval advisor at the Geneva Disarmament Conference and the London Naval Conference of 1930. A prominent member of the Society of the Cincinnati, Admiral Jones died 1st January 1938. He is interred at Arlington National Cemetery.

Chief Engineer G.W. Hall USN (?-1889) USS *Nipsic*

He died at Leone on Tuituila Island, on his way home from Apia on 10th July 1889 from dysentery and gastric fever. His family resided at Syracuse, New York and he had been in the service for a number of years.

Seaman E.M. Hammet/Hammar, (?-1889), USS *Vandalia.*

As reported in my text chapter 7, this very brave man attempted to swim ashore from his ship with a line, and drowned in the attempt. His name does not appear on the memorial, but the name Hammar does appear, and may be a misspelling on the memorial itself, or in the source references.

Seaman J. Hanchett/Manchett, USN (?-1889), USS *Vandalia.*

The *Los Angeles Herald*, Volume 31, Number 178, 31st March 1889 reported:

> *"John Manchett was recently employed on one of the ferryboats running across San Francisco bay, and signed as a recruit of the Vandalia."*

The memorial apparently names this man as John Hantchett.

Apprentice First Class J Heap, (1870-1889), USS *Nipsic.*

As were a number of the crew members of the American vessels, Joshua Heap was British, born in Wallasey, England, on 15th December 1870 the fifth of nine children. His mother was Elizabeth (formerly Ambler, nee Robinson) and Samuel Heap (a local Police Sergeant) was his father. He enlisted in the United States Navy in November 1885 aged just 14 years, and was described as having a florid complexion.

Landsman James Hewlett (?-1889), USS *Trenton*

One of the African American sailors standing near the starboard *"bridle port"* when it was stove in by a massive sea and was killed instantly by the force of the blow at around 8 a.m. on the 16th March. Different sources record different ways in which this unfortunate gentleman lost his life.

Captain of Marines R.W. Huntington USNM (1840-1917), USS *Trenton.*

Robert Watkinson Huntington was born on 2nd December 1840 in that part of Hartford, Connecticut which today is known as West Hartford. He entered Trinity College in the autumn of 1860 but left the college at the outset of the Civil War in order to enlist, on 23rd April 1861. On Saturday, 17th November 1917, Colonel Huntington died at his residence at Charlottesville (University, Virginia) and was interred at the Wayland family cemetery, Heards, Virginia. His second wife, Elizabeth Sherburne (Whipple) Huntington died on 13th March 1922 and was interred beside her husband.

Cook Ah Keau, USN (?-1889?), USS *Vandalia.*

Although his name is recorded on the American memorial plaque, intriguingly, it is possible that Ah Keau from USS *Vandalia* actually survived the storm. I have been in contact with a Samoa family, whose tradition has it that an ancestor, whom they knew as Ah Kiau, swam to shore from USS *Vandalia* when she foundered, liked what he found on the island, and decided to stay and start a new life. I guess he may have realised the American Navy would not take a very tolerant view of that idea, and to allow himself to be presumed drowned shows great presence of mind to me!

Seamen J. & T. Kelly, USN (?-1889), USS *Vandalia.*

The *Los Angeles Herald*, Volume 31, Number 178, 31st March 1889 reported:

> *"John and Thomas Kelly were employed in the navy some time before going to Samoa. It is believed that their relatives reside in this city."*

I have combined this paragraph for the two men, as the article implies they were related, and were possibly brothers.

Chief Engineer Kiersted, USN (?-?), USS *Nipsic.*

In his memoirs, Kimberly notes that Fleet Engineer Kiersted volunteered to make the passage in the repaired USS *Nipsic* and rendered the most valuable services both professionally and by example. He also took charge of many of her repairs on reaching Honolulu.

Seaman C. Kraus/Kranz, USN (?-1889), USS *Vandalia.*

The *Los Angeles Herald*, Volume 31, Number 178, 31st March 1889 reported:

> *"Charles Kranz was also known here, and previous to entering the navy it is believed that he worked as a deck hand on one of the steamers plying between San Francisco and Yaquina."*

I haven't been able to find the name *Kranz* on the memorial, and I have assumed it actually refers to C.H. Kraus, but this might be an incorrect assumption on my part and may be a misspelling on the memorial itself.

Rear-Admiral Lewis A. Kimberly, USN (1830-1902), USS *Trenton*

Lewis Ashfield Kimberly was born in Troy, New York on 2nd April 1830. He was appointed a Midshipman in the U.S. Navy in December 1846 and served off Africa in the sloop Jamestown in 1847-50. After duty as President of the Board of Inspection and Survey, Rear-Admiral Kimberly retired in April 1892.

He died at West Newton, Massachusetts, on 28th January 1902.

Naval Cadet J. A. LeJeune, USMC (1867-1942), USS *Vandalia.*

Naval Cadet John Archer LeJeune was born at Pointe Coupee, Louisiana, on 10th January 1867. He was specifically mentioned by Kimberly in his report. He became a Marine Corps officer and was later the 13th Commandant of the Marine Corps, 1920-1929. Today, Camp Lejeune, North Carolina, bears his name. Lieutenant General LeJeune died 20th November 1942 at the Union Memorial Hospital, Baltimore, Maryland, and was interred in the Arlington National Cemetery with full military honours.

Lieutenant Commander Henry W Lyon, USN (?-?), USS *Trenton.*

He was mentioned by Kimberly in his memoirs, as being Executive Officer of USS *Trenton*, whilst Davenport's diary shows him to have been on USS *Nipsic* in 1887. I presume he had changed ship prior to the storm.

He took command of USS *Nipsic* when she returned to Hawaii after the temporary repairs effected at Apia. He later commanded USS *Dolphin* during the Spanish-American war, and by 1906 he was Rear-Admiral. There is a commendation certificate to this officer dated 11th November 1920, made when he was commander of USS *Westerner*.

Commander Dennis W. Mullan, USN (184?-1928), USS *Nipsic*.

Dennis Walbach Mullan was born in Maryland, probably in the early 1840s. He was appointed to the U.S. Naval Academy from Kentucky in September 1860 and graduated in 1863, receiving the rank of Ensign in October 1863.

On 18th September 1890, he was presented by Governor Jackson of Annapolis, Maryland, with a gold watch and chain for his services during the storm at Apia.

On 30th June 1897, he was confirmed following court martial to be discharged from the service on account of two charges of drunkenness, but this was later commuted to be reduced in rank and to be suspended from rank and duty for a period of five years. After his retirement in July 1901, Commander Mullan seems to have overcome his problems to spend a contented life and died at Annapolis, Maryland, on 17th December 1928.

Despite criticism in some quarters, I believe this man performed his duties in the time leading up to the storm in an exemplary manner, and nothing seems to suggest he fell from that level during the hurricane. It appears that he did decline to command the repaired USS *Nipsic* back to Honolulu, having aborted the first attempt to do so, and those decisions seem to have earned him disfavour in Rear-Admiral Kimberly's eyes. I think he was a good officer of an old ship and difficult crew, he acted with creditable diplomacy in a difficult political situation, and does not warrant any negative comment.

Corporal John Nicholls, USMC (?-1889), USS Trenton.

On 4th May 1889, the remaining sailors, after USS *Rockton* had taken off the majority, were ordered to relocate to a timber shed on McArthur and Company's land. Whilst fixing his hammock screw to a timber beam, the beam gave way and a load of timber stored on top of it fell and crushed the unfortunate Nicholls who died immediately. He was buried within two hours.

Ensign John L. Purcell USN (?-?), USS Nipsic.

Purcell with two other officers tried to reach the settled USS *Vandalia* with lines from the shore; this was a very brave undertaking, but was unsuccessful, all three fortunate to return to shore alive. His actions were warmly recorded by Admiral Kimberly in his "Special Report" dated 16th April 1889.

This officer was in 1894 involved in a dispute with Lieutenant Davenport, as detailed previously in the entry for the latter person. I have not been able to find out anything else about Lieutenant Purcell.

Seaman Bernhardt Ricklin USN (?-1889) USS Trenton

This very unfortunate gentleman was shot and killed on 10th June 1889 in an Apia tavern run by a German Herr Voigt, who did the shooting. The story is that an intoxicated Voigt went behind the bar to collect a revolver, intending to scare away some native boys making a noise in the street outside. Whilst picking it up, the gun discharged and the bullet hit the American sailor in the heart; Ricklin staggered outside and died almost immediately. It is reported in some sources that Voigt was putting the gun away and uncocking the trigger when the incident occurred. Some of the dead man's crewmates who had been outside the inn became very threatening to the German, believing it not to have been an accident, but order was eventually restored by a group of American marines. Voigt was taken into custody, but the eventual outcome was that the shooting was deemed accidental and the Tavern-keeper was released without charge.

Paymaster's Clerk J. Roche/Roach USN, (1861?-1889), USS Vandalia.

The *Los Angeles Herald*, Volume 31, Number 178, 31st March 1889 reported:

> *"Paymaster's Clerk John Roche was appointed from Ilion, N. Y. He was 28 years of age and a man of athletic build. His nearest relative is J. Jeffrey Roche, who is a poet and assistant editor of the Boston Pilot."*

The memorial names this man as "Roach", which is probably incorrect since Kimberly also records him as "Roche".

Captain C. M. Schoonmaker, USN (1839-1889), USS *Vandalia*

Cornelius Marius Schoonmaker was born on 2nd February 1839. He was appointed to the U.S. Naval Academy in September 1854 and, following graduation in June 1859, he served for about two years off the African west coast. He became Commanding Officer of the steam sloop *Vandalia,* on the Pacific Station, in 1888

Schoonmaker had been made Acting Midshipman on 28th September, 1854 and Midshipman on 9th June, 1859. He was promoted Lieutenant on 31st August 1861; Lieutenant Commander 24th December, 1865; Commander 14th February 1873; and Captain 7th October, 1886.

The Schoonmaker family was politically very important and influential in the United States. The Captain's great-grandfather was Corneilius Corneliusen Schoonmaker, holding office in the 2nd United States Congress between 1791 and 1793, and other family ancestors held similar positions in the eighteenth- and nineteenth-centuries. I cannot verify a connection, but a number of naval men in the twentieth-century shared the surname Schoonmaker.

Bayman H.P. Stalman, USN, (1865-1889), USS *Vandalia.*

Henry Percy Stalman was born in Clerkenwell, London and was just 23 years old when he died in the Samoa Hurricane. His father, also Henry Percy, emigrated from England in 1871, and was a painter and sign-writer. Our Henry's grandfather Edmund was a theatre manager. The name Stalman suggests that they might be of German descent but the family have been able to trace their ancestors back to the north of England in around 1200 when the name appears as *Stalmyn.*

The American branch of the family seem to have been very unlucky after reaching California: Henry Percy Senior died about 4 years after arriving, aged 34, leaving a wife, Bertha, and a young family.

Machinist C.H. Stoddard, USN, (?-1891), USS _Trenton_.

Charles Herbert Stoddard (known to his family and mates as "Charley") survived the storm, but seems to have been very badly affected by it. In a letter written to his mother by his uncle, it states that Charley had been suffering for some time. An obituary in the local newspaper stated: _"His death was due to hardships he endured on the occasion of the hurricane hitting U.S.S. steamship Trenton at Samoa March 15-16, 1889."._ Charles is buried in Thomaston, Maine, USA beside his father, who was a shipbuilder.

Lieutenant F.E. Sutton, USMC, (?-1889), USS _Vandalia_.

The _Los Angeles Herald_, Volume 31, Number 178, 31st March 1889 reported:

> _"Lieutenant of Marines Francis E. Sutton (whose name was erroneously given as Hilton) was appointed to the Naval Academy from New York in 1877. He graduated sixth in the class of 1870, and, after his course, returned to the academy for examination for promotion and passed second. On his application he was appointed Second Lieutenant of Marines, being the first graduate of Annapolis to enter the marine force. He was promoted to be First Lieutenant, March 9, 1888, and been stationed at Mare's Island. He had just been detailed to command the Marine Guard of the Mohican, but the Vandalia sailing suddenly for Samoa before the arrival of her commanding marine officer, Lieutenant Sutton took his place expecting to fall in with the Mohican on the cruise. His father is a resident of Rome, N. Y. At the Navy Department Lieutenant Sutton was regarded as having been one of the brightest and most intelligent officers of the Marine Corps, and his loss is greatly deplored."_

Quartermaster R.H. Taylor USN, (1870-1956), USS _Nipsic_

Born 8th September 1870 in Staunton, Virginia and died 24th March 1956, Taylor is buried in Evergreen Cemetery, Brighton, Massachusetts. Whilst Admiral Kimberly in his Special Report nominated a number of sailors for the Medal of Honor, I have carefully scanned the on-line records and have only confirmed Richard Taylor as having actually been awarded the honour for his heroic efforts during the hurricane.

Gunner Westfall USN (?-?), USS *Trenton*.

With Boatswain's mate Gray, he attempted to cover the ventilator holes which were open on the spar deck with the water pouring down them. Gunner Westfall later reported (reproduced in and transcribed from Kimberly's memoirs "*Samoan Hurricane*"):

> "*We went aft on the gundeck and up on the spar deck and crawled along till we got to our destination and went to work. About one minute afterward we were both struck by a sea, and in five seconds were hurled one hundred feet aft. When I recovered my senses, two men were dragging me out from under a mass of wreckage near the main mast. I tried to stand, no use; the last sea had been too much. I was half drowned and my right foot was hurt.*"

Both Gray and Westfall appear to have survived this dangerous attempt.

Naval Cadet H.A. Wiley, USN (1867-1943), USS *Vandalia*.

Henry Aristo Wiley was born in Pike County, Alabama, 31st January 1867 and graduated from the Naval Academy in 1888. He died 20th May 1943 at Palm Beach, Florida. As a cadet at Samoa, he was saved by the extremely courageous combined efforts of Samoans, other American sailors, and the American Consul Blacklock. He would later (as Vice-Admiral) re-live his experiences, such as he could recall them, to a reporter for the *Northern Advocate*, 21st August 1925 in Sydney, Australia.

German Crew known to have been present at Apia, 16th March 1889.

Sources: *The Maitland Mercury*, Tuesday 2nd April 1889; the German memorial at Apia, Samoa; *The Samoa Times*; Lieutenant Gaedeke's *Report to Kommander Fritze*; some family descendants; some German web-sites.

The following lists are not a comprehensive list of all the crews of the German ships at Apia; I have been unable to find a source for them. Due to the nature of the tragedy, the crew list for SMS *Eber* is almost complete, but there may have been some crew ashore at the time of her destruction, survivors who are therefore missing from my list. Some names, primarily those from *Olga*, and a few from *Adler*, were published as survivors by an Australian newspaper after the storm. I have used English translations of the rank. The names of the 93 who lost their lives are taken from the German memorial at Apia, consecrated on 4th January 1891.

I have therefore had little independent corroboration regarding most of these names.

SMS *Adler*

Arend von	Captain Lieutenant	Survived
Aviszus Hch.	Ordinary seaman	Drowned
Blaul Bernh.	Ordinary seaman	Drowned
Busch Charl.	Ordinary seaman	Drowned
Dr. Fereszkiewicz		Survived
Fischer Frdr.	Ordinary seaman	Drowned

- SMS Adler Continued

Fischer Pl.	Leading seaman	Drowned
Fritze E.	Commander	Survived
Goetze	Engineer	Survived
Jannusch Frdr.	Ordinary seaman	Drowned
Jungmann Hch.	Stoker	Drowned
Keila Ptr.	Ordinary seaman	Drowned
Lafsen Hns.	Ordinary seaman	Drowned
Lenke Rob.	Ordinary seaman	Drowned
Loser Wilh.	Ordinary seaman	Drowned
Markus Pl.	Ordinary seaman	Drowned
Meisinger Leo	Ordinary seaman	Drowned
Oeloner	Lieutenant	Survived
Paeters Wilh. (Peters)	Ordinary seaman	Drowned
Raschke Frz.	Clerk	Drowned
Remus Alb.	Ordinary seaman	Drowned
Schneegotzki Alb.	Ordinary seaman	Drowned
Souchon	Lieutenant	Survived
Szezodrowski	Paymaster	Survived
Wahrenberg Krl.	Ordinary seaman	Drowned
Wenk Herm.	Leading seaman	Drowned
Wilhelm Hgo.	Leading seaman	Drowned

Fritze's rank is also stated as "Oberkommandierenden Kapitan" in one German source.

The *Samoa Times* of 23rd March 1889 records a Seaman *Lawissen* as having drowned from SMS *Adler*, but his name does not appear on the memorial and I assume the report to be in error, or it may have meant *Lafsen* who is recorded on the memorial. The newspaper report also misspells many of the names, presumably as further errors, and omits Seaman Busch.

SMS *Eber*

Arneman Aug.	Leading stoker	Drowned
Bahr Gust.	Armourer	Drowned
Balke Christ.	Leading seaman	Drowned
Bassendowski	Master's Mate	Survived
Bathke Gust.	Ordinary seaman	Drowned
Boldt	Stoker	Survived
Borgmann Wilhm.	Leading seaman	Drowned
Braasch Grg.	Ordinary seaman	Drowned
Brost	Seaman	Survived
Bunnies Krl.	Acting Paymaster	Drowned
Burmeister Krl.	Ordinary seaman	Drowned
Delp Grg.	Ordinary seaman	Drowned
Dietrich Ad.	Engineer	Drowned
Dormann Johns.	Leading boatswain's mate	Drowned
Eckardt	Sub-Lieutenant	Drowned
Ehlart	Seaman	Survived
Eilart Krl.	Boatswain's mate	Drowned
Engel Aug.	Stoker	Drowned
Ernsthausen von	Sub-Lieutenant	Drowned
Fabricius Hch.	Ordinary seaman	Drowned
Fick II Theod.	Leading stoker	Drowned
Gaedeke F.	Lieutenant	Survived
Gross Johs.	Ordinary seaman	Drowned
Henkels	Leading Stoker	Survived
Hoenemann Oo.	Engineer	Drowned
Jacob Ed.	Leading seaman	Drowned
Jahnke Alb.	Leading seaman	Drowned
Jansen Ad.	Ordinary seaman	Drowned

- SMS Eber Continued

Jeczawitz	Helmsman	Survived
John Grg.	Stoker	Drowned
Jordan Wilhm.	Armourer	Drowned
Jost Hch.	Ordinary seaman	Drowned
Keitel Joh.	Ordinary seaman	Drowned
Keyer Fred.	Ordinary seaman	Drowned
Kiaups Johs.	Ordinary seaman	Drowned
Klee Gerh.	Leading armourer's mate	Drowned
Kluck Herm.	Ordinary seaman	Drowned
Kluge Ed.	Steward	Drowned
Kuhwede Krl.	Stoker	Drowned
Kukowsky Boleslv.	Engineer	Drowned
Kunze,	Subpaymaster of Marines	Drowned
Kusabs Mart.	Ordinary seaman	Drowned
Lammert Oo.	Boatswain's mate	Drowned
Leppke Ech.	Leading seaman	Drowned
Lewandowski Frz.	Ordinary seaman	Drowned
Linke II Herm.	Leading stoker	Drowned
Machenhauer Dr.	Assistant surgeon First Class	Drowned
Maffry Ant.	Sick berth attendant	Drowned
Malachinski Wilh.	Ordinary seaman	Drowned
Manhold Joh.	Ordinary seaman	Drowned
Metzentien Eml.	Leading stoker	Drowned
Michel Bruno	Stoker	Drowned
Mohr Rud.	Ship's musician	Drowned
Moldenhauer Alb.	Artificer's mate	Drowned
Müller Krl.	Supply assistant	Drowned
Müller II Aug.	Leading artisan	Drowned

- SMS Eber Continued

Nagraczus Jul.	Ordinary seaman	Drowned
Noack Hch.	Leading seaman	Drowned
Norck Mart.	Ordinary seaman	Drowned
Oldenburg Aug.	Ordinary seaman	Drowned
Pahlow Ewd.	Stoker	Drowned
Piel	Seaman	Survived
Pulow Aug.	Ordinary seaman	Drowned
Pusch Frz.	Boatswain's mate	Drowned
Rehann Ptr.	Ordinary seaman	Drowned
Rohde Eml.	Leading seaman	Drowned
Sagert Oo.	Clerk	Drowned
Scharf Hnry.	Ordinary seaman	Drowned
Schoodt Ernst	Engineer	Drowned
Sinner Grg.	Leading seaman	Drowned
Stein Hlmth.	Leading seaman	Drowned
Tamm Ad.	Leading seaman	Drowned
Teuber Theod.	Chief engineer	Drowned
Thiele	Leading Stoker	Survived
Uhrhammer Hch.	Artisan	Drowned
Vandrey Wilh.	Ordinary seaman	Drowned
Wallis Eugen,	Captain Lieutenant	Drowned
Wentzien Krl.	Leading stoker	Drowned
Weÿher Dan.	Leading artisan	Drowned
Witt Herm.	Stoker	Drowned
Wolscon Aug.	Ordinary seaman	Drowned

One German web-site source appears to record the names Eckardt and Von Ernsthausen as one person, i.e. *"Eckardt, v. Ernsthausen"*. I have viewed a photograph of the memorial itself, and agree the names are separated by a comma, but I believe this actually means that there are *two* names on the one line, as happens elsewhere on it. Since the *Maitland Mercury* also seems to record the names as two separate people, I have done so in my list, but this may therefore be in error. Another German website records the two different person's names as *Ehrhardt* and *von Ernsthausen* but that first is surely incorrect, being the name of SMS *Olga's* Commander.

SMS *Olga*

Burchard, Otto	Lieutenant	Survived
Ehrlich	Captain Lieutenant	Survived
Dr Elste	Surgeon(?)	Survived
H. Emsmann	Lieutenant	Survived
Baron F. von Erhardt	Corvette Captain	Survived
Grossman	Engineer	Survived
Schenke, Carl	Boatswain's Mate	Survived
Schirmer	Lieutenant	Survived
Thiede	Paymaster	Survived

I have scoured the internet for data about the German officers but have been unsuccessful in unearthing much at all. This includes German language web-sites. An Australian descendent of a German crew member found my web-site, as did a German researcher - I admit that it was always going to be a long shot given the language difference. So, sadly, I have very few crew stories at all about the officers and men of the Kriegsmarine, who were on the German ships at Apia in March 1889. I suspect crew lists at least would be available in some German archive, presuming they survived the Second World War, but there don't appear to be any on-line indexes or lists available to narrow down the search for them.

Otto Friedrich Wilhelm Burchard (1865-1904) Lieutenant SMS *Olga*.

This gentleman was wounded in the action in Samoa on 18th December, 1888 at Fangallii (see page 113).

A German contact has sent me a great deal of information about this gentleman's family, which I am trying my best to translate. Otto was born 6th September 1865 and seems to have been a Lieutenant at Samoa. After his return to Germany in September 1889, on 1st June, 1896 he married one Friederike Wilhelmine Clara Goering, an older half sister of the Third Reich's Hermann Goering from the latter's father's first marriage.

The Burchard family has a significant history in Germany in the nineteenth-century which makes fascinating reading, though obviously it would not be right to include it here.

The couple had four children before Otto died on 10th January, 1904 shortly before his 40th birthday, apparently from those wounds received at Samoa. His eldest child Marie Margarethe, was not yet seven years old.

Bootsmannsmaat Carl Schenke (?-1911), SMS *Olga*.

Possibly born in Cologne Germany, Carl left SMS *Olga* soon after the vessel returned to Kiel, where he was promoted to Boatswain's Mate. He emigrated to Sydney Australia on the passenger ship *Kaiser Wilhelm II*, where he started his family. He became a naturalised Australian in 1904, and passed away in 1911.

The German Memorial at Mulinuu near Apia, Samoa. It carries the names of those officers and marines who perished in the conflict at Fangallii on 18th December 1888, described on page 113, as well as the names of those who died in the hurricane. The separate black memorial in front commemorates one of the two Lieutenants lost in that 1888 conflict, and was possibly placed there because the gentleman's name had been inadvertently omitted from the main memorial. The phrase "Unserem sohn" translates as "Our Son", so it may have been an additional marker laid by the man's family during a visit to Upolu. [Rickard Törnblad / CC BY-SA (https://creativecommons.org/licenses/by-sa/4.0)].

Residents of Apia, 16th March 1889.

A few residents of Apia are named as partaking in rescue attempts during and after the storm. I am sure that many other, unnamed persons gave great help to the sailors, risking their own lives in the process, but have now been sadly forgotten, or were never even recorded at the time. This book is partly in their memory too.

As stated in the text of this book, there are conflicting data about whether any Samoans lost their lives in the rescue attempts. One reference source I found lists a single Samoan native as having perished. Although I have been unable to independently verify this data, I have included his name herein for completeness and because I would rather err on the side of including him than wrongly leaving him out of the story.

Sources: JP Dunning account dated February 1890; Admiral Kimberly's *Special Report* dated 16th April 1889; *"Glory for the Australian Squadron"*, May/July 1996; Kimberly *Letter*, 26th March 1889; many contemporary newspaper accounts.

Samoa Natives

Alo		Survived
Anapu	Son of Seumanu	Survived
Apiti		Survived
Auvaa		Survived
Fanala		Survived

- *Samoa Natives Continued*

Folau		Survived
Fuapopo		Survived
Charles Freun Jnr.(Fruean)		Survived
William Hunkin		Survived
Ionia		Survived
Malietoa Mata'afa	Chief of Samoa	Survived
Manono	Chief	Survived
Mose		Survived
Muniaiiuaga (Muniaiga)	Known as "Jack"	Survived
Neamea		Survived
Paniola		Survived
Papalii		Survived
Pita		Survived
Salu Anae		Survived
Selu Leauanae		Survived
Seumanu Tafa	Chief of Apia	Survived
Sigito		Survived
Sofa		Survived
Taupau		Survived
Tatopan		Survived
Tete		Survived
Teoteo		Survived
Tepu		Survived
Toga		Survived
Tualagi		Survived
Tui		Killed

Foreign Residents

W. Blacklock		U.S. Vice-Consul	Survived
H. de Coetlogon		British Vice-Consul	Survived
Dr. Knappe		German Vice-Consul	Survived
Mr. Douglas		Captain and Owner of *Lily*	Survived
J. P. Dunning	Associated Press Correspondent		Survived
Charles Fruen Snr. (Fruean)			Survived
H. J. Moore (Moors)		Plantation Owner	Survived
Anthony Ormsby		Trader from Tuituila	Drowned
Peter Paul			Survived
J. S. Pike			Survived
Albert Vicking			Survived
Unknown, an "old man"		Hawaiian Mate from *Lily*	Drowned

It may seem strange to put the two "Charles Fruen" in different lists, but this is how they appear in Kimberly's report, senior calling himself an American citizen because his father was one, and junior calling himself a Samoan native presumably because he was born there. The different spelling is also true to Kimberly's report, but I think *both* of them are incorrect, and should be the option shown in brackets.

<u>William Blacklock</u>

There is quite a lot on the internet for people with this name, around this time and even in Samoa. It would be easy to mix different people up. The most likely person was born in Melbourne, Australia, in 1856. His death is given as the same place, in 1960 and so aged 103. If born in Australia, I guess he would have been British, but there is a record of a person with this name, birth date and birth place, as having been naturalized as American on 10th May 1880 recorded on his passport application 40 years later. The image of the application document is very difficult to read accurately.

Our William Blacklock was definitely a Sydney businessman in 1925, and it is equally certain he was appointed U.S. Vice-Consul in Apia 12th September 1888; U.S. Vice-Consul-General in Apia on 25th July 1890; and United States Commissioner-General at Apia 20th October 1890.

Blacklock seems to have retired on 2nd November 1896, but was again appointed as Consul at Samoa on 3rd December 1897 for an unknown period of time; and then possibly Vice-Consul-General at Nuku'alofa in Tonga between 1898-1904. In January 1913, he had been residing in Sydney, Australia for about four years on his doctor's advice, but had a large store in Pago-Pago on Tuituila, It was from Sydney that he made some quite significant claims against the American Government for damages to property he owned incurred during the American and British bombardments of Samoa in 1899. Claim No. 8 was for a total of $2,476.27, of which he seems to have received $800. His Samoan wife Apele Tietie, from whom he was divorced in about 1895, died back in Apia in 1933. He had a number of children born in Apia.

William Blacklock and family at Samoa, 1895.
Source: Andrew, Thomas, 1855-1939. Andrew, Thomas, 1855-1939: [The
American Vice-consul General's house, "Matamoana" (Sea-View), Samoa].
Cusack-Smith, Thomas Berry (Sir), 1859-1929: Photographs of Samoa. Ref: PA1-
o-546-19. Alexander Turnbull Library, Wellington, New Zealand.
http://natlib.govt.nz/records/22649916

The report of the final inquiry into the claims of American citizens was sent to the American Senate and President William H. Taft on 10th January 1913. He authorised the expenditure in settlement, and of claims for $64,677.88, the amount of $14,811.42 was eventually paid. Great Britain had several years earlier reimbursed its own subjects in the sum of £3,645 for similar claims. There had previously been settled claims from the American Government to the German ($40,000), Norwegian ($400), Swedish ($750), Danish ($1,520) and French ($6,782.26) governments.

British Vice-Consul Henry de Coetlogon (or Coertlogon).

Prior to his appointment as Vice-Consul of Samoa, de Coetlogon was in very severe straightened circumstances, and had been forced to earn a living as a lowly labourer in the United Kingdom.

The majority of the data I have located about this man was printed as his obituary in "The Tablet, the International Catholic News Weekly" of 23rd May 1908:

"COLONEL DE COETLOGON.- Henry de Coetlogon, who died at Oxford on April 23, had the melancholy distinction of being the last European officer to see General Gordon alive. Lord Cromer, in his recent work on Egypt, quotes him as one of the military experts who knew that it was hopeless to attempt to hold Khartoum against the onrush of the Isdahdi's hordes. Coetlogon had joined the Egyptian army after having served in the 15th East Yorkshire and other of MM.'s regiments. He accompanied Hicks Pasha in his ill-fated expedition up the White Nile, but was told off to keep up the line of communication, and so escaped the slaughter that befell the rest of the expedition. He was able to reach Khartoum and to hold the place until the arrival of Gordon, occupying the interval by strengthening the fortifications. When Gordon arrived he took an entirely different view of the situation from Coetlogon. He declared Khartoum to be "as safe a place as Kensington Gardens," ordered roadways to be cut through the fortifications Coetlogon had built up, and sent Coetlogon himself down to Assouan in charge of invalids to rest after his " past " anxieties. The sequel is too well known to require repetition. Coetlogon's next service was in the Egyptian gendarmerie. The last fifteen or sixteen years of his life were spent in foreign stations as H.B.M.'s Consul. In that capacity he was at Samoa at the time when two rival princes, one a Catholic and undoubtedly the rightful ruler of the island, were at war. Colonel De Coetlogon belonged by descent to an old Breton family, but his branch had been

settled in this country for some generations, and had conformed to the Established Church. He was himself a convert of that excellent type, the disciplined and loyal soldier of the old school. R.I.P."

I don't have any information about *"Isdahdi"* which may be a different description of the *"Mahdi"* I mentioned in chapter 2. The sad sequel mentioned in the obituary is, of course, Gordon's death at the siege of Khartoum. And I do not know what was meant by *"...MM.'s regiments"*.

I have already touched upon the situation at Khartoum on page 69. It would appear de Coetlogon had been very fortunate indeed to have incurred General Gordon's displeasure to an extent that resulted in him being absent from the city when it was overrun, very similar to his continuing luck in avoiding death in the ill-fated 1883 *Hicks Pasha* expedition (actually the British Colonel William Hicks), who was one of those killed at the battle of El Obeid that de Coetlogon missed.

The Grey River Argus, 18th January 1890 reported a great deal of discontent in Apia against de Coetlogon, though it doesn't mention what the reasons for those feelings were. In fact, it was claims by the German authorities that de Coetlogon had made signals to the Mata'afa natives at the time of the German Bombardment mentioned in Chapter 4, which contributed to the death of a number of German marines. A public meeting held in Apia resolved to petition Sir John Thurston, the High Commissioner in Australia, to replace de Coetlogon. On 7th June 1889, HMS *Rapid* left Samoa in order to convey Sir John back to the islands from Fiji in order to convene a hearing over the charges, arriving on the Sunday. It seems McArthur and Sons also had a grievance against the British Vice-Consul impugning his administration of justice, and some heavy penalties invoked against the trader. This was an action by Mr. Frank Cornwall against the traders dating back to 1882, and which had settled with Mr. Cornwall receiving judgment from de Coetlogon in the restoration of disputed land, and the sum of £41,276 and costs of about £3,000, the total a staggering amount at the time and heading for £6 million in today's money. McArthur's had lodged an appeal against the ruling, and it is this which formed their complaints to Sir John. The accusations were vehemently denied by de Coetlogon, and Thurston found no evidence to substantiate the charges, which were subsequently dismissed. Nevertheless, the British Vice-Consul was replaced in early June of that year, possibly to take up the same post at New Caledonia.

The obituary shows he died back in England in 1908.

John Preston Dunning

This man was the AP (Associated Press) war correspondent, despatched to Apia to cover the growing political tensions between the nations of Germany and America, arriving in February of 1889 some three weeks before the hurricane. His subsequent 30,000 word report completed 30th March which took two weeks to arrive at the AP headquarters as it was sent by mail, was copyrighted to the New York Times and Tribune, and appeared in print on the 13th and 14th April, being considered at the time a milestone in journalistic reporting. He was very instrumental in saving a number of lives on the day of the storm, and stayed up overnight in case any further survivors struggled ashore. He was warmly mentioned in Kimberly's *Special Report* dated 16th April 1889.

During his lifetime, he acted as AP correspondent in Cuba, Puerto Rica and the Philippines. His life was rather eventful, as he had become a very heavy drinker and was fired from the AP office for his drinking and over the possible embezzlement of $4,000 to fund his gambling addiction, though this latter offence does not seem to have been proven in a court of law. The amount is huge by today's standards, and would surely have been very difficult for anyone to actually obtain by fair means *or* foul.

Due to his drinking, he was fired by newspapers soon after being hired by them, but was fortunate to be taken on by AP to cover the Spanish-American war, reconciling with his wife, Mary Elizabeth before leaving for Cuba. She had left him over his extra-marital affairs, and probably the drinking and gambling as well. They had a six-year-old daughter, also named Mary.

In 1898, Dunning was intimately involved with a sensational trial over the murder of his wife. Dunning's ex-lover, Mrs. Cordelia Botkin, was convicted of sending 35-year-old Mrs. Mary E. Dunning a box of arsenic poisoned candy, which the recipient sampled on 9th September 1898. This revengeful act also killed Dunning's wife's sister, a Mrs. Leila Deane. The note that accompanied the box read: *"With love to yourself and baby. Mrs. C."*

Both ladies suffered extreme torment before dying a few days after, of what the doctor finally realised was arsenic poisoning. Elizabeth's father thought the handwriting on the note to be familiar, and compared it to a bundle of insulting letters his daughter had received from Botkin, and decided they matched. The family recalled Dunning who arrived heartbroken, and when shown the note, immediately confirmed it to be in Cordelia's handwriting.

During the December 1898 trial, Dunning was called to the stand, admitted to numerous affairs with women he could not in the most part recall, and refused to name three that he admitted he could. This earned him two nights in the county jail for contempt of court, before the defence withdrew the offending question. The trial was supposedly one of the most famous criminal cases ever tried on the Pacific Coast.

The findings of the first trial were overturned due to a procedural error, but Botkin was eventually found guilty of murder after a number of appeals and the second trial, and was sentenced to life imprisonment. Despite continuing to maintain her innocence for the murders, Botkin died in San Quentin State Prison of *"softening of the brain, due to melancholy"* on 7th March 1910. There is a lot on the internet about this case. Believe it or not, the Internet Movie Data Base IMDB has an "18-minute" short entitled: *"The Mischievous Case of Cordelia Botkin"*, though the clip only ran for a minute for me!

Botkin had initially been incarcerated at the Branch County Jail, and enjoyed privileges which included unescorted days out! One day, the judge who had sentenced her happened to be visiting the grave of his wife and was astonished to see Cordelia riding a street-car quite alone. It seems the lady was trading sexual favours with the guards to be allowed out of jail. Cordelia was soon transferred to San Quentin where her "excursions" abruptly ended.

Dunning was renowned for his writing expertise throughout his sadly short life, but the revelations about his drinking, gambling and love affairs took their toll. He died a couple of years before Cordelia of a brain tumour on 17th April 1907 at the age of 44 years.

The IMDB short is one minute of awful acting, particularly by the Dunning character, but the story could well be good enough for a book, or even a movie - it has the requisite elements of scandal, murder, adventure and sex in abundance!

Charles Fruean Snr.

This man, as we have seen like quite a few residents of Apia, decided to submit a claim in 1899 asking $1,472.50 for damages to plantation property at Papautu, in the outskirts of Apia, and to his house and its furnishings in Apia Town, caused in the Samoan War bombardment the year before. He was asked to provide proof of American citizenship, and when he was unable to do so despite having an American father, his claim was recommended for dismissal. It seems he never received a penny.

His American brother, one Sergeant Fruean, apparently went through the American Civil War unscathed, the family having originated in Boston Massachusetts, and being on the Union side of the conflict. Charles' father had left Boston for Samoa before 1833, before even religion had found the islands.

William Faivae Hunkin.

His father Matthew was born in Cornwall England in 1815 and came to Samoa in around 1842, living in Tuituila. Matthew's fourth son William presumably moved to Apia at some point before 1889. William was a boat builder.

Malietoa Mata'afa

This man was a long-term Samoa Chief. He was at the centre of the German, American and British disputes in the months preceding the storm, and was also heavily involved in the war in 1898/9. There is a tremendous amount of data about him on the internet, and it doesn't seem sensible to simply repeat it here. There are a lot of images of this man, some including his family, on the net.

He participated in the rescue of German and American sailors during and after the hurricane.

One source states he died in Apia on 14th February 1912 aged 84 years, Wikipedia states 6th February, as does Facebook.

Harry Jay Moors

An American merchant born 1854 who had settled on the island in 1879, Moors had three cacao plantations, and a cocoa plantation, on the south side of Savai'i. He had large and at the time, growing trading interests in Samoa and the Ellice Group (now Tuvalu), and other large properties. In 1899, he was summoned by Chief Justice Chambers for a letter published in the Samoa Herald disputing the authority of the Supreme Court, and was let off with a fine. He died in Apia 13th February 1926. He had a son and four daughters.

H.J. Moors wrote the books *"With Stevenson in Samoa"*, and *"Some Recollections of Early Samoa"*.

Doctor Wilhelm Knappe.

Born 20th October 1855, Knappe attended the Universities of Leipzig, Gottingen and Berlin. He graduated in Law and in 1886-7 was Commissioner of the Marshall Islands. After his suspension by Bismarck as a result of his time in Samoa, he was Director of the National Bank in South Africa until his restoration to the Foreign Ministry in 1894 for service in Canton, and later Shanghai, where he stayed until his ill-health in 1905 forced his retirement. He died on 5th February 1910 in Berlin at the age of 54.

Peter Paul

He was a German-born, American-naturalized native resident of Apia. He seems to have had property in the town and the surrounding area. He too, along with William Blacklock and others, made claims against the American Government for reparation for damages sustained in the bombardments of 1899, his claim gradually escalating to $2,773.25 but of which he received only $500. He was married in Apia by Blacklock not long after the storm.

Anthony Ormsby, Trader.

Apia when the storm struck.

As you may have gathered from my text in Chapter 7, this man was a trader with McArthur & Co. and perished when the *Lily* was run down by USS *Nipsic* during the storm. He was a Maori half-caste from Alexandra, Waikato, New Zealand, and had lived on the nearby island of Tutuila for some 5 years. It seems he had married into a Samoan family possibly named *Aumavae* and owned land on the island, and died with a fairly substantial estate. It is presumed he was visiting his friend, fellow trader and English harbour pilot Mr. Douglas, in

Seumanu Tafa

I have only found a little about the family ancestry of Seumanu Tafa.

A gentleman called Alexander A. Willis persuaded his wife to write her story, entitled *"The Story of Laulii, A Daughter of Samoa"* [41]. There is an entry which reads *"Seumanu Tafa (bird-catcher) and his wife, Faatu lia a Upolu (the wind that blows across the island of Upolu)"*. It states that Seumanu Tafa was a convert to Christianity and therefore only had the one wife. He lived in one of the best houses in Samoa. His wife was a very religious person, and though, as chief's wife, she was not permitted to talk to the people, she took an interest in local affairs and spoke through her *Tulafale* "talking women". The term can also be used for men talking for the Chief. She also spoke to schoolchildren regularly via these women. *Faatu lia a Upolu* was well known and well regarded by the inhabitants of the neighbouring island of Savai'i, so her name was derived from the fact that the wind at Savai'i reaches the island after passing over Upolu and therefore contained her breath - a nice idea. I think the subject and author of the book, Laulii, was one of her Tulafale.

Interestingly, the book also mentions Henry Fruean, one of the first white settlers on the islands, and obviously a relative of Charles' mentioned earlier. The book is an absolute gem, and has unique and glorious stories of life on Samoa in the 1880s. Although Laulii and her husband left Upolu for San Francisco in 1886 and so missed the hurricane, I found this book so fascinating that whilst it can be read on the internet, I bought a facsimile reprint on Amazon.

<u>Tui.</u>

This man's name appears in the Journal of the Australian Naval Institute article *"Glory for the Squadron"* as being the only Samoan native to lose his life, being crushed by a gun which came loose on SMS *Adler* during rescue attempts. I have not found the source that the publication used for this data.

The book by Laulii Willis mentioned above talks about a native named Tui as an abbreviation for Tuietufuga who was her brother, but I have no idea if this is the same man who lost his life.

BIBLIOGRAPHY.

The following publications and documents provided much of the supporting background data to the story. Many of the books are reprints of earlier editions, and some have been reprinted more recently than is listed here. Most of the twentieth-century publications will have used nineteenth-century articles as their source. The National Archives at Kew hold the *Calliope Ship's Logs* for the commissioning voyage and were indispensable for the description of the vessel's voyage.

I have read a number of other books and publications to generate background to the story, too many to sensibly list here unless my text refers to a specific incident gleaned from them. There are numerous sources on the internet, some of, in my opinion, dubious reliability, but many seem to make a genuine effort in accuracy. Just enter "Calliope, Samoa" in the search engine and you get a plethora of hits, nearly 75,000 when I last tried it in Google. The internet has therefore provided a lot of data about the events, and for my many digressions.

All these details are correct at the time of compilation and checking of the data, i.e. March 2020, but there is no guarantee that articles and books are still available.

The general format is: *Title*, author, publisher, date, ISBN (where allocated).

[1]   *Admiralty Circulars*: No 177, R Osborne, 26th December 1854; No 263, R. Osborne, 26th August 1856; No 270, Thomas Phinn, 3rd October 1856; No. 30, Robert Hall, 30th April 1873; No. 34, 4th August 1875.

[2]   *A Hundred Years Ago and Long Before*, George Turner, Macmillan, 1884

[3]   *Ships Log*, HMS *Calliope*, March 1887 to April 1890, National Archives reference ADM53/12898 through ADM53/12901.

[4]   *Parliamentary Paper*, number 5756, HMSO, April 1889. I have a photocopy of the document obtained from the British Library.

[5]   *Royal Navy Officer Personal Records*, National Archives microfilm reference ADM196. *Royal Navy Seaman's Personal Records*, National Archives microfilm reference ADM188. Photocopies taken at the Archive, but copies can be purchased over the internet.

[6]   *The Illustrated London News*, Volume 94 (XCIV) number 2610, 27th April 1889.

[7]   *The Cruise of HMS Calliope*, Rev. A. C. Evans, privately published by Griffin and Co., Portsmouth, 1890. There has been a recent (c2010) reprint of this book.

[8]   *The Story of the Great Storm at Samoa (Retold for Young American Folk)*, JP Dunning, St. Nicholas Magazine, *"St. Nicholas, an Illustrated Magazine for Young Folk"*, volume 17, November 1889 to April 1890.

[9]   *A Footnote to History – Eight Years of Trouble in Samoa*, R.L. Stevenson. Cassel & Sons, 1892.

[10]   *Samoa Hurricane*, LA Kimberly, Rear-Admiral USN (retired), c. 1897, reprinted by the Naval Historical Foundation, 1965.

[11]   *The Saving of HMS Calliope*, W. Marshfield, Penny Pictorial, 21st June 1913. I have an incomplete image of this article.

[12]   *Sea Escapes and Adventures*, "Taffrail" (Commander Taprell Dorling, RN), Phillip Allan, 1927.

[13]   *The First Commission of HMS Calliope*, Captain E.W. Swan RN, privately published by Andrew Reid & Co, Newcastle, 1939.

[14]   *Deeds that held the Empire – At Sea*, A. D. Divine, John Murray, 1939.

[15]   *The Escape of HMS Calliope*, Commander A. B. Campbell, published as part of the series *"Great Exploits"*, OUP, 1940.

[16]   *Samoan Adventure*, Rear-Admiral Cecil H Fox, RN (Retired), Radio Times (BBC Publications), April 1951.

[17]   *The Typhoon That Stopped a War*, Edwin P Hoyt, David MacKay, 1968.

[18]   *Great Seamen*, Oliver Warner, G. Bell, 1969.

[19]   *Seamanship*, Lt. G.S. Nares, RN. Facsimile reprint (of the 1862 second edition) by Gresham Books, 1979, ISBN 0905418379.

[20]   *Conway's All The World's Fighting Ships 1860-1905*, Robert Gardiner, Conway Maritime Press, 1979, ISBN 0851771335.

[21]   *Seamanship, Steam and Steel: H.M.S. Calliope at Samoa, 15 - 16 March 1889*, DK Brown and *The Imperial German Navy and the Hurricane at Samoa*, G. Koop, both articles from *Warship*, volume 12, 1988, ISBN 0851775365.

[22]   *The Journal Of Jean-Francois de Galaup de la Perouse 1785 - 1788* volume 2, edited by John Dunmore, The Hakluyt Society, 1995, ISBN 0904180395.

[23]   *Glory for the Australian Squadron: HMS Calliope at Samoa 1889*, Graham Wilson, Journal of the Australian Naval Institute, Vol. 22 No. 2 May/July 1996.

[24   *The British Battle Fleet, Its Inception and Growth through the Centuries*, Fred T. Jane. Conway Maritime Press, 1997, ISBN 0851777236.

[25]   *After the Storm: True Stories of Disaster and Recovery at Sea*, J. Rousmaniere, McGraw-Hill 2002, ISBN: 0071377956.

[26]   *The Sail and Steam Navy List (All the Ships of the Royal Navy 1815-1889)*. Rif Winfield & David Lyon, *Chatham* Publishing, 2004, ISBN: 1861760329.

[27]   *Learning the Ropes: An Apprentice in the Last of the Windjammers*, Eric Newby, published by John Murray, London, 1999. ISBN 0719556368.

[28]   *American Naval History and Heritage Command*. Located at 805 Kidder Breese Street SE, Washington Navy Yard, DC 20374-5060. The web-site of this organisation provided the biographical data of the American Officers as quoted herein, and is heartily recommended for anyone wishing to view images and read more about the Hurricane at Samoa.

[29]   Lieutenant Gaedeke (of SMS *Eber*) report to Kapitan Fritze on the loss of SMS *Eber* dated 20th March 1889.

[30]   *Personal Memoirs of Life in the British Royal Navy 1876 to 1890*. William Isaac Thorndale. 1932. Unpublished.

[31]   Foreign Office records, held at the National Archives, London, in series FO/58/235 through 256. Home Office records, held at National Archives, London, in series HO/144/22478 through 22479 and KV/2/902 through 904.

[32]   *Personal letter from Navigating Officer Henry Pearson to J. O. Burgess*, 9th April 1889. Unpublished.

[33]   *New Zealand Coal* magazine, volume 18 number 1, Summer 1973.

[34]   *New York Times*, 14th April 1889. Carried the Associated Press correspondent AP Dunning's cabled account.

[35]   *History of Ships* magazine, *Samoa Hurricane Part 85*, edited by E. L. Cornwell. New English Library Ltd. 1974.

[36]   *San Francisco Chronicle*, 14th April 1889. Another newspaper article to carry the Associated Press correspondent AP Dunning's cabled account.

[37]   *Claims of American citizens, Apia, in the Samoan Islands*, 10th January 1913, United States Department of State.

[38]   *Ship's Deserters 1852-1900!*, Jim Melton, Library of Australian History, Sydney, 1986.

[39]   *The Elements and Practice of Rigging, Seamanship, and Naval Tactics.* 1794. David Steel. London. Originally published in two volumes.
An original edition copy of this publication is very difficult to find, and unsurprisingly hugely expensive. It has been reprinted in four volumes as a paperback by the Cambridge Library Collection, at a total cost of slightly under £25 per volume. Volume 1: ISBN10 1108026516 and ISBN13 9781108026512. It is also available in its entirety on-line at:
https://maritime.org/doc/steel/index.htm

[40]   *Annual Report of the Operations of the United States Life-Saving Service for the Fiscal Year ending June 30, 1890.* Washington, Government Printing Office, 1892.

[41]   *The Story of Laulii, A Daughter of Samoa,* Laulii Willis, J. Winterburn & Co., San Francisco, 1889.

On-line read:
https://archive.org/details/storyoflauliidau00williala/page/n8/mode/2up

ACKNOWLEDGEMENTS.

I would never have completed this manuscript were it not for my dear wife Dorothy and my aunt Evelyne Holliday (herself a published author) who provided help, support and encouragement, and who both sadly never got to see the manuscript finished. My wife, in particular, put up with hour upon hour of me sitting at the computer, or in London at Kew, or anywhere else my research led me, never once complaining about it.

And I most certainly must not forget my many friends who nagged me to stop fiddling with it and get on with publishing it.

Usually, this section would include the author's thanks to the staff of the publishing group who provided the professional assistance needed to turn a raw manuscript into a structured and grammatically correct text suitable for offering to the public. Since this book is "self-published" I did not have access to any such experts, unless I wished to pay a significant amount to them for their services - which I was unable to consider. So as well as being an amateur historian, researcher and author, I am also an amateur editor and graphic designer (for the cover) and in all probability this status clearly stands out to an experienced reader. All I can do is apologise for any spelling and grammatical errors, and any awkward sentence construction in the text, and hope that my layout and formatting of the content is acceptable. Perhaps it might be seen as "...*a good story badly told*..." and be accepted as such.